The Political Trajectory of
J. T. MURPHY

The Political Trajectory of
J.T. MURPHY

RALPH DARLINGTON

University of Salford

LIVERPOOL UNIVERSITY PRESS

First published 1998 by
LIVERPOOL UNIVERSITY PRESS
Senate House, Abercromby Square
Liverpool, L69 3BX

Copyright © 1998 Ralph Darlington

The right of Ralph Darlington to be identified
as the author of this Work has been asserted by him
in accordance with the Copyright, Design and Patents
Act 1988.

British Library Cataloguing-in-Publication Data
A British Library CIP record is available

ISBN 0–85323–733–6 *cased*
       0–85323–743–3 *paper*

Set in Monotype Plantin by
Wilmaset Limited, Birkenhead, Wirral
Printed and bound in the European Union by
Bell and Bain Limited, Glasgow

Contents

Abbreviations   vi

Chronology   vii

Preface and Acknowledgements   xviii

Photographs   xxvii

Chapter One   **The Early Years in Sheffield, 1888–1917** 1
                    Murphy's early years as a militant
                    engineering shop steward in Sheffield
                    during the First World War

Chapter Two   **The Shop Stewards' Movement,**
                    1917–1919   30
                    Assesment of Murphy's theoretical
                    contribution to the National Shop
                    Stewards' and Workers Committee
                    Movement

Chapter Three   **Towards Bolshevism, 1919–1920**   54
                    Murphy's political evolution from
                    syndicalism to communism and towards
                    the need for a Bolshevik-type
                    revolutionary party

Chapter Four   **The Communist Party and the**
                    Labour Movement, 1920–1926   87
                    Murphy's involvement with the Red
                    International of Labour Unions and his
                    influential role directing the British
                    Communist Party's industrial work and
                    relationship with the Labour Party

Chapter Five   The Comintern and Stalinism,
                1926–1928   133
                Murphy's close links with the Comintern
                in Moscow and the impact of the rise of
                Stalinism inside the USSR on his political
                development

Chapter Six   The 'New Line', 1928–1932   163
                Murphy's role in pushing the CPGB
                towards acceptance of the Comintern's
                ultra-left 'new line'

Chapter Seven   Towards Left Reformism, 1932–1936   201
                The factors underlying Murphy's
                expulsion from the CPGB and his
                subsequent involvement with the Socialist
                League inside the Labour Party

Chapter Eight   Popular Frontism and Re-appraisal,
                1936–1965   234
                Murphy's embrace of Popular Frontism
                during the Second World War and the
                re-evaluation of his political convictions
                made in later life

Conclusion   Drawing together some of the central   261
                themes of the book and the course of
                Murphy's political trajectory

Notes   269

Index   311

Abbreviations

ACM	Amalgamation Committee Movement
AEU	Amalgamated Engineering Union
ASE	Amalgamated Society of Engineers
BSP	British Socialist Party
CCP	Communist Party of China
Comintern	Communist (Third) International
CP	(British) Communist Party
CPGB	Communist Party of Great Britain
CPSU	Communist Party of the Soviet Union
ECCI	Executive Committee of the Communist International
ICC	International Control Commission
IFTU	International Federation of Trade Unions (or 'Amsterdam International')
ILP	Independent Labour Party
NAC	National Administrative Council (of the shop stewards' movement)
NBM	New Britain Movement
NEP	New Economic Policy
NLWM	National Left Wing Movement
NMM	National Minority Movement
NUGMW	National Union of General and Municipal Workers
NUTGW	National Union of Tailors and Garment Workers
PICTU	Provisional International Council of Trade and Industrial Unions
PLP	Parliamentary Labour Party
Politburo	Political Bureau
Profintern	Red International of Labour Unions
RILU	Red International of Labour Unions (Profintern)
SDF	Social Democratic Federation (in 1908 renamed the SDP)
SDP	Social Democratic Party (in 1911 renamed BSP)
SLP	Socialist Labour Party

SPD   Social Democractic Party (of Germany)
SS&WCM Shop Stewards' and Workers' Committee Movement
SWSS   South Wales Socialist Society
TGWU   Transport and General Workers Union
TUC   Trades Union Congress
UCWU   United Clothing Workers' Union
UMS   United Mineworkers of Scotland
USSR   Union of Soviet Socialist Republics (Soviet Union)
WSF   Workers' Socialist Federation
WSPU   Women's Social and Political Union

Chronology

1888

Dec: Birth of Murphy (9th).

1910–1914

'Labour Unrest': strikes of miners, seamen, dockers, transport and railway workers.

1914

Aug: First World War breaks out.

1915

Oct: Clyde Workers Committee formed.

1916

Nov: First National Shop Stewards' Conference.
Sheffield engineers' strike in defence of conscripted workmate Leonard Hargreaves.

1917

Jan: Formation of Sheffield Workers Committee.
Feb: Russian Revolution, Czar overthrown (in the month of March by western calendar).
Mar: Amalgamation Committee Conference in Birmingham at which Murphy opposed plan for breakaway engineering union.
May: English engineers' strike over Trade Card Scheme and dilution.
Second National Shop Stewards' Conference in Manchester (5th–6th).
Aug: Third National Shop Stewards' Conference in Manchester (18th–19th) which elected a National Administrative Council (NAC).
Murphy joins the Socialist Labour Party.
Oct: Russian Bolshevik Revolution (in the month of November by western calendar).
The Workers' Committee pamphlet published.

1918

Jan: Joint national conference of the SSWCM and newly merged Amalgamation Committees (5th–6th).

NAC of shop stewards' movement rejects strike call against the war (25th).

Mar: SSWCM Conference in Sheffield, with representatives of the miners' reform committees and the railwaymen's vigilance committees (9th–10th).

Apr: SSWCM Conference in Manchester (13th–14th).

Sept: Last wartime SSWCM Conference in Birmingham (7th–8th).

Nov: War ends.

German revolution topples the Kaiser.

Dec: Khaki general election with Lloyd George coalition elected into office.

1919

Jan: Forty-hour Clydeside strike.

Special SLP Conference agrees new programme 'Plea for Reconsideration of Socialist Tactics and Organisation' and sets up SLP Unity Committee (11th–12th).

Mar: Founding Comintern Congress (2nd–6th).

Apr: SSWCM Conference in Sheffield, attended by miners and railwaymen.

Sept: New SLP executive dissolves Unity Committee.

1920

Jan: National Shop Stewards' Conference (10th).

Feb: Amsterdam Conference of Sub-Bureau of Comintern (3rd–7th).

May: London dockers refuse to load munitions for Poland on *Jolly George*.

July–
Aug: Communist Party of Great Britain formed at Unity Convention in London (31st July–7th August).

Second Congress of Comintern (17th July–7th August).

Oct: Provisional International Council of Trade and Industrial Unions set up.

Dec: British Bureau of RILU set up.

SSWCM National Administrative Council meeting in Sheffield (9th–10th).

1921

Jan: Shop Stewards' NAC meeting (26th and 27th).
Shop Stewards' National Conference (27th and 28th).
Second Communist Party 'Unity' Congress (29th and 30th) in Leeds.

Feb: Joint meeting of CPGB executive committee and national shop stewards' NAC (21st).

Mar: National Shop Stewards' Conference in Sheffield, with representatives from the miners and dockers which renamed itself the National Workers' Committee Movement.
Introduction of New Economic Policy (NEP) in Russia.

Apr: 'Black Friday' (15th) failure of 'Triple Alliance'.
Third Congress of Communist Party (23rd–24th) in Manchester.

June–
July: Third Congress of Comintern (22nd June–12th July).

July: First Congress of Red International of Labour Unions (RILU) in Moscow (3rd–19th).

Oct: British Bureau of RILU 'Back to the Unions' and 'Stop the Retreat' conference in London (15th).

1922

Feb: First ECCI Plenum (24th February–4th March).

Mar: Fourth CPGB Congress (18th and 19th) in London and appointment of Commission on Organisation headed by Pollitt, Palme Dutt and Inkpin.
Beginning of 14 week engineers' lock-out.

May: EC meeting of the Comintern (19th).

June: British Bureau merged with SS&WCM.
Second ECCI Plenum (7th–11th).

Oct: Fifth Congress of CPGB Congress (7th–9th) in London with adoption of Report of Party Commission on Party Organisation.

Nov: General Election (15th) with Conservatives returned.

Nov–   Fourth Congress of the Comintern (5th November–5th
Dec: December) reaffirms united front policy.
Second Congress of RILU (19 November–2nd December).

1923

June: Third enlarged ECCI Plenum (12th–23rd): virtually entire CPGB leadership invited to a special British commission.

Oct: Failure of German Revolution.
Dec: General Election (6th) with creation of first minority Labour Government led by Ramsay MacDonald.

1924

Jan: Death of Lenin signals burgeoning power struggle inside Bolshevik Party.
May: Sixth Congress of CPGB in Salford (17th–19th).
        Thirteenth Congress of Communist Party of Soviet Union (CPSU) confirms triumvirate of Zinoviev, Kamenev and Stalin in power.
June–   Fifth Congress of Comintern (17th June–8th July) launches
July: assault on 'Trotskyism'.
July: Third Congress of RILU (8th–22nd).
        Fourth ECCI Plenum (12th–13th).
Aug: National Minority Movement launched at conference (23rd and 24th) and British Bureau of RILU absorbed into MM.
Sept: TUC Congress (1st-6th) at Hull addressed by leader of Russian trade unions, Tomsky.
Oct: Labour Party conference votes to exclude CP members as individual members.
        Attempted prosecution of J. T. Campbell for 'incitement to mutiny' and red scare around the forged 'Zinoviev' letter. In the general election that followed (29th) Conservatives returned to power under leadership of Stanley Baldwin.
Dec: ECCI Presidium meeting discusses the 'British Question'.

1925

Mar: Fifth ECCI Plenum of Comintern (21st March–6th April).
April: Anglo-Russian Trade Union Committee set up.
May: Seventh Congress of the CPGB (30th May and 1st June) in Glasgow.
July: 'Red Friday' (31st July) and announcement of nine-month coal subsidy.
Aug: Second National Minority Movement Conference (29th–30th).
Sept: Scarborough TUC Congress (7th–12th).
        Labour Party Conference in Liverpool (29th September–2nd October) reaffirms decision to expel CP members.
Oct: Arrest and imprisonment of 12 CP leaders for sedition.

Dec: Fourteenth Congress of CPSU: Zinoviev and Kamenev defeated.

1926

Feb: Sixth ECCI Plenum (17th February–15th March).

Mar: Special National Minority Movement Conference (21st).

May: General Strike (4th–12th) followed by six-month miners' lockout.

June: ECCI meeting discusses the lessons of the British General Strike.

July: Public condemnation of the British TUC's role in General Strike by Russian trade unions (7th).
United Opposition of Trotsky, Zinoviev and Kamenev formed.

Aug: Third National Minority Movement Conference (28th and 29th).
ECCI Presidium (7th) discusses CPGB's objection to Russian trade unions' criticisms of the British TUC role in General Strike.

Sept: Inaugural conference (18th) of National Left Wing Movement inside the Labour Party.

Oct: Labour Party Conference, Margate (11th–15th).
Eighth Congress of CPGB in Battersea (16th and 17th).
Zinoviev replaced as president of Comintern by Bukharin.

Nov– Seventh ECCI enlarged Plenum (22nd November–16th
Dec: December) with main item of discussion the CPGB's role in the General Strike.

1927

Feb: TUC General Council decision to withdraw official recognition to trades councils affiliated to the National Minority Movement.

Apr: Kuomintang massacre of Chinese Communist Party members in Shanghai.
British government's Trade Disputes and Trade Unions Bill proposed.

May: Eighth ECCI Plenum (18th–30th).
Britain breaks off diplomatic relations with Russia (26th).

Aug: Fourth National Minority Movement Conference (27th–28th).

Sept: Trotsky expelled from the Presidium of Comintern (28th).

TUC Congress Edinburgh (5th–10th) withdraws from Anglo-Russian Committee.
Second National Left Wing Movement Conference (24th–25th).

Oct: Labour Party Conference, Blackpool (3rd–7th) takes action against individual CP members inside the party.
Ninth Congress of CPGB in Salford (8th and 9th).

Nov– Visit of CPGB leaders to Moscow to hear 'new line'
Dec: proposal from Stalin and Bukharin.
Trotsky expelled from CPSU.

Dec: Fifteenth Congress of Russian CP (3rd–19th) declares a new period of revolutionary upsurge, and criticises the CPGB's relationship to Labour Party.

1928

Feb: Ninth ECCI Plenum (9th–25th) which held a British Commission to review the tactics of the CPGB in relation to the Labour Party. Majority, minority and solo (Murphy) reports submitted for discussion.

Mar– Fourth RILU Congress (17th March–3rd April) which
Apr: denounced existing trade unions and called for 'independent leadership'.

June: Cook-Maxton manifesto issued criticising the class collaboration of the Labour Party and union leaders.

July– Sixth Comintern Congress (17th July–1st Sept) at which the
Sept: 'new line' was officially approved, to be implemented by respective CPs. Argument involving CPGB leaders over colonialism.

Aug: Fifth National Minority Movement Conference (25th–26th).

Sept: Third National Left Wing Movement Conference agrees to support communist parliamentary candidates against Labour.

Oct: Labour Party conference introduces series of disciplinary measures against the CP.

1929

Jan: Tenth CPGB Congress in Bermondsey (19th–22nd). The 'new line' is proclaimed inside British party, and campaign against leadership fomented.

Feb: 'Closed letter' from ECCI to CPGB (27th) calls for more drastic implementation of the 'new line'.
Mar: National Left Wing Movement dissolved.
May: General Election in Britain (30th). CP stands candidates against Labour.
       First Five Year Plan launched in Russia.
       CPGB Political Committee summoned to Berlin to meet Comintern representatives to admit their failure to whole-heartedly embrace 'new line' and to make changes in the composition of CPGB leadership.
June: Formation of second minority Labour government.
July: Tenth ECCI Plenum (3rd–19th) at which social democrats are denounced as 'social fascists' and CPGB is again criti-cised for failure to implement the 'new line'.
Aug: Sixth National Minority Movement Conference (24th and 25th) agrees to 'independent leadership'.
Oct: Wall Street Crash in USA.
       Labour Party conference extends its ban to members of organisations 'ancillary or subsidiary' to the CP, including the National Left Wing Movement.
Nov–   Eleventh (special) CPGB Congress in Leeds (30th
Dec: November–3rd December) finally approves 'new line' and elects 'left' leadership.

1930
Feb: Enlarged Presidium of Comintern.
Aug: Fifth Congress of RILU.

1931
Mar–
Apr: Eleventh Plenum of ECCI (26th March–11th April).
Sept: Japanese invasion of Manchuria.
Oct: General election following the betrayal and collapse of the Labour government with the defection of MacDonald, Snowden and Thomas to form a 'National' government with the Tories and Liberals. CP stands candidates against Labour.
Dec: ECCI sets up another British Commission at which Pollitt extricates the CPGB from the 'independent leadership' line of the RILU.

1932

May: Murphy leaves the Communist Party and joins the Labour Party.

Aug–   Twelfth Plenum of Comintern (27th August–15th
Sept: September).

Oct: Socialist League formed by group of left MPs and intellectuals.

Nov: Twelfth CPGB Congress in Battersea.

1933

Jan: Hitler takes power in Germany.

Apr: Murphy joins the Socialist League.

Oct: Socialist League again makes some gains at Labour Party Conference in Hastings.

Nov–   Thirteenth (and last) Plenum of ECCI (28th November–
Dec: 12th December).

1934

Sept: Russia enters League of Nations.

Oct: Socialist League resolutions defeated at Labour Party conference in Southport.

1935

Feb: Thirteenth CPGB Congress in Manchester.

July–   Seventh (last) Congress of Comintern abandons the 'new
Aug: line' and proclaims the need for a 'united front' against the threat of fascism and war, in practice later translated into a Popular Front.

Oct: Italian invasion of Abyssinia.

Nov: General election.

1936

June: Popular Front wins elections in France.
    Murphy leaves the Socialist League.

July: Start of Spanish Civil War.

Aug: First Moscow Show Trial.

1937

Jan: Socialist League disaffiliated from the Labour Party.
    Second Moscow Show Trial.

Mar: Labour Party ruled membership of the Socialist League not compatible with membership of the LP, and Socialist League disbands itself.

1938

Mar: Third Moscow Show Trial.

1939

Aug: Hitler–Stalin non-aggression Pact in which Germany and Russia agree to be neutral to each other (23rd August) leads CP to completely reverse its previous support for war against fascism to opposition to 'the imperialist war'.

Sept: Start of Second World War.

1940

May: Churchill takes over as Prime Minister of coalition government, and includes leading Labour Party figures Ernest Bevin and Clement Attlee as Ministers of Labour and National Service.

1941

Jan: People's Convention in London.

June: Hitler invades Soviet Union and CPGB reverts to full support for the war, demanding the invasion of Europe to open up a second front against Hitler.

1945

May: End of War.

July: Labour general election victory.

1953

Mar: Death of Stalin.

1956

Feb: Khrushchev's secret condemnation of Stalin to CPSU Congress.

Oct: Hungarian Uprising.

1965

May: Death of Murphy (13th).

Preface and Acknowledgements

The Italian revolutionary socialist Antonio Gramsci[1] argued that the working-class movement needs the services of what he termed the 'traditional intellectuals', theoreticians like Marx, or indeed himself, who had been trained in bourgeois academic skills but were willing to break unequivocally with the ruling class. But Gramsci also insisted that every class needs its 'organic intellectuals'. In the case of the capitalist class, these include the managers, civil servants, journalists and politicians who organise its rule on a day-to-day basis. Similarly, the working class also needs its own 'organic intellectuals' if it is to seriously challenge the power of the capitalist class. Thus, the key task for a revolutionary party, Gramsci explained, is to weld together and develop such a layer of 'organic intellectuals' *inside* the working-class movement.

There is no doubt that during the 1920s the leadership of the British Communist Party bore all the hallmarks of the worker-intellectual polymath Gramsci saw as necessary. A whole generation of shopfloor trade union militants emerged, such as Harry Pollitt, Willie Gallacher, Arthur MacManus, Tom Bell, William Paul, Johnny Campbell, Wal Hannington, Harry McShane and J. T. Murphy, who educated themselves within the socialist movement before and during the First World War, and then went on to become leaders of the Communist Party. The energy and determination of such worker-intellectuals were displayed in their extraordinary hunger for reading books and the pursuit of knowledge, albeit outside the established institutions of learning.[2] It was characteristic that J. T. Murphy's agitational pamphlet on shop steward organisation[3] should list the famous writers, playwrights and poets Lewis Morgan, Havelock Ellis, Walt Whitman and Henrik Ibsen among the further reading recommended. Experience of religious doubt and an interest in materialism, against the background of a growing radicalisation of the working-class movement, helped to shape the intellectual curiosity of these autodidact trade union militants and led them on the road to Marxism. But significantly, they became committed to understanding the world not merely for its own sake, but in order to *change* it, so as to overthrow capitalism and establish an entirely different social order.

J. T. Murphy was one of the most gifted of these self-taught worker-intellectual figures of early twentieth-century British labour history. As a leader of the First World War National Shop Stewards' Movement, Murphy more than anybody else developed and expounded the novel theory of independent rank-and-file organisation, a carefully thought out plan for the formation of a national network of Shop Stewards' and Workers' Committees able to act independently of official trade union structures. Then after the war, profoundly influenced by the impact of the Bolshevik Revolution in Russia, Murphy went on to draw out the full revolutionary implications of the shop stewards' militant wartime activities, and to conceive the Workers' Committees as embryonic *soviets*, the institutional form through which the working class could take control of society. He subsequently made a far-reaching contribution to the formation and early development of the British Communist Party, serving as a full-time central committee member with responsibility for the party's industrial activities and as editor of its theoretical journal *Communist Review*. In addition, he helped launch the Red International of Labour Unions and served on the Presidium of the Executive Committee of the Communist International (Comintern) based in Russia. A prolific writer, Murphy made a distinctive theoretical contribution to several controversial trade union and political debates, displaying a fiercely independent analytical ability which often led him into conflict with mainstream party policy. Eventually in 1932, he left the Communist Party, becoming a strong critic of the organisation he had helped construct. After a spell as the general secretary of the Socialist League, a left-wing ginger group inside the Labour Party, he called for an all-class Popular Front alliance against the threat posed by Nazi Germany and in support of the allied war effort during the Second World War. His reflections on the crucial period in the history of the British working class movement in which he played such a prominent role were recorded in *Preparing for Power* and in his autobiography *New Horizons*, both of which remain classic texts.[4]

Yet although the experience of the shop stewards' movement has been well documented elsewhere[5] the remarkable role of its foremost English leader, Jack Murphy, has received relatively scant attention. Moreover, whilst the activities of some other British Communist Party leaders such as Pollitt and Palme Dutt have been highlighted,[6] an examination of the singular intellectual and political contribution made by the much neglected figure of J. T. Murphy is long overdue.[7] This book aims to fill that gap. But it seeks to do so not merely to rescue him for the historical record. Significantly, focusing on the specific development of Murphy's individual life and politics helps to throw considerable light on the general fortunes of the early British revolutionary movement. This is because Murphy was at the centre of the shift from pre-war syndicalism to post-war communism, the eventual marriage of home-grown Marxist organisation with the imported ideas of Russian Bolshevism, followed by the subsequent degeneration of the Communist Party in Britain from a genuinely revolutionary party into a loyal instrument of the rising Stalinist bureaucracy inside the USSR. Therefore, the book aims to combine a political biography of Murphy with a historical review of the early British revolutionary movement, exploring the inter-relationship between the working class, the Communist Party, the Comintern and Murphy himself. This fusion of the personal and the general, the biographical and the historical, is necessary because of the nature of the active political commitment to which Murphy's life was devoted.

In particular, the study locates the important specific debates and controversies in which Murphy intervened within the broader historical context of the general political dilemmas confronting the revolutionary socialist movement. These include issues such as the nature of the relationship between rank-and-file workers and full-time trade union officials; the interplay between shopfloor industrial activity and general socialist politics; the argument between parliamentary reform and social revolution; the significance of the post-1917 division of world socialism for Britain's labour movement; and the problems of building a revolutionary socialist organisation outside the Labour Party. Both the tremendous strengths, as well as the ultimately debilitating weaknesses, of Murphy's pioneering contribution to the analysis of such issues are explored. Through the prism of Murphy's life and politics it becomes possible to critically re-evaluate the historical and social significance of this British revolutionary tradition and the heritage it left behind.

Moreover, despite the collapse of the so-called 'communist' regimes in the USSR and eastern Europe, these pivotal issues which preoccupied Murphy remain of enduring relevance to many contemporary debates. Even where his analysis and initiatives proved misconceived, as much can be learnt from the mistakes as can be from the successes on other issues.

It will be clear to anyone familiar with the revolutionary left in Britain that the view of Murphy presented within this book derives from the theoretical tradition of the Socialist Workers Party. Its starting point is a basic orientation on the rank-and-file, on the self-activity of the working class, on socialism from below, rather than the socialism from above of the Labour MPs and trade union leaders. Of course, these notions of rank-and-filism and the self-emancipation of the working class are at the very heart of revolutionary Marxism. Significantly, they were also at the centre of the political outlook held by the First World War Shop Stewards' and Workers' Committee Movement and the early 1920s Communist Party within which Murphy played such a prominent role. In this sense, the analysis which is presented of Murphy is set firmly within the tradition which he himself helped to forge in practice and to formulate in theory, despite the fact that he veered away from such rank-and-filism in later years. Consequently, it also contains a sharp critique of the impact of Stalinism inside both the USSR and the Comintern on Murphy's political development, as well as of his subsequent abandonment of revolutionary Marxism in favour of left reformism and, later on, popular frontism.

Not surprisingly, a consideration of Murphy's political development from the standpoint of revolutionary Marxism has also involved challenging the prevailing historical interpretation of the early years of the Communist Party of Great Britain (CPGB) produced by many orthodox communist, conservative and academic commentators alike. The most common core assumptions held by such writers can be summarised thus. First, the formation of the CPGB and the development of 'British Bolshevism' were flawed because they represented an artificially imposed Russian transplant which was intrinsically alien to British political culture and to the previous experience and tradition of the socialist movement.[8] Second, the attempt to build a mass revolutionary party in the 1920s and 1930s, against the backdrop of a decline in working-class struggle in which the General Strike was merely the last hopeless stand of a labour movement which had been outmanoeuvred and defeated years earlier, was bound to push the party into the opportunist and sectarian political ghetto into which it became locked.[9] Third, so long as a much bigger party (in the shape of the Labour Party) existed with hopes of government office and access to real authority, the CPGB could never have been more than a 'ginger' group unless it had succeeded in directing its energies through the structures of the bigger organisation and within the mainstream of working-class politics.[10]

Of course, the complete rejection of the history of the British Communist Party as an error, is a viewpoint that many Cold War liberal historians long held.[11] But since the disappearance of both the USSR and the CPGB in the early 1990s, a new school of sympathetic and ex-communist historians committed to a reassessment of the party's role in British political life, and its part in the history and development of the British labour movement, has emerged.[12] Ironically, most of these historians have ended up drawing exactly the same conclusions as their erstwhile political adversaries. Thus, they also hold the view that the party mistakenly tried to implement a Leninist revolutionary strategy that may have been appropriate to Tsarist Russia, but was totally inappropriate in a developed parliamentary democracy like Britain. Notwithstanding the energy, self-sacrifice and enthusiasm of party activists, in the long run all its strategies were bound to run into the sand. Ironically, this is essentially the view that Murphy himself came to hold after he had left the CPGB. This study seeks to challenge and refute such basic assumptions by re-examining the history of the British revolutionary movement from within the Marxist tradition to which J. T. Murphy himself initially contributed so much.

METHODS

The research process involved a variety of data-gathering methods. Initially, the book relied heavily upon, indeed could not have been written without, the work of those scholars whose pioneering writings on the British revolutionary movement inform these pages and are cited regularly. The most useful texts included *The Revolutionary Movement in Britain* by Walter Kendall, *The First Shop Stewards Movement* by James Hinton, *The British Communist*

Party by L. J. MacFarlane, *A History of British Communism* by Brian Pearce and Michael Woodhouse, and *Marxism and Trade Union Struggle: The General Strike of 1926* by Tony Cliff and Donny Gluckstein. However, at the same time, I have tried to illuminate those episodes and events concerning J. T. Murphy about which such secondary literature remains elliptical, as well as to substantially revise our understanding of some major political issues.

Meanwhile, I carried out a detailed examination of a range of primary and documentary material relating to Murphy, which is deposited in libraries and centres across Britain. Foremost amongst this material were Murphy's own prolific writings in over 300 newspaper and journal articles, 13 pamphlets and nine books, as well as his (relatively minimal) personal papers containing correspondence with a variety of leading figures and some unpublished manuscripts and notes. Murphy was an extremely insightful and talented writer and, in concentrating on his political contribution, I have taken the liberty of quoting extensively from his published writings. In particular, I have drawn upon his autobiography *New Horizons*, which combines a sketchy outline of his life until the Second World War with some vivid personal reflections on political events in both Britain and the USSR. Unfortunately, the book is infuriatingly silent on a wide range of important political dilemmas that Murphy had to confront. Moreover, written shortly after he left the Communist Party in 1932, the reminiscences are somewhat coloured by a political evolution away from the revolutionary politics that had engulfed his life for the previous 25 years. Similar problems are attached to the unpublished autobiography of his wife, Molly Murphy, actually ghost-written by Murphy himself in the early 1960s; this unpublished manuscript, which has only recently been brought into the public domain, also provides some important new reflections on his activities during the 1920s and 1930s.[13]

A much more substantive source of primary material on Murphy was found in communist archives in both Britain and Russia. Since the collapse of the USSR, following the revolutions which swept Eastern Europe during 1989–1991, a considerable amount of completely new communist archival material has suddenly become accessible to external researchers for the first time. These include the archives of the Communist Party of Great Britain, during its lifespan between 1920 and 1991, which are located in the National Museum of Labour History in Manchester, and important new material on the Communist International and the CPGB located in the Russian Centre for the Preservation and Study of Documents of Recent History (RTsKhIDNI) in Moscow. Contained within these archives are the minutes of the closed and confidential CPGB Central Committee and Political Bureau meetings throughout the 1920s and 1930s,[14] and the proceedings and declarations of every leading body of the Comintern, as well as various organisational reports and substantial new documentation on the activities of Murphy in both Britain and Russia. Given that Murphy was elected to virtually every leading body of both the CPGB and Comintern in the 1920s, this rich archival material, much of which has never before been published, proved invaluable to the process of constructing a three-dimensional picture of his political development.

In addition, I conducted extensive tape-recorded interviews with a variety of individuals who knew, or were friends of, Murphy towards the end of his life, including his son, Gordon. Such oral testimony was particularly useful for filling in the gaps of Murphy's activities after the Second World War.

Finally, it is necessary to make a methodological point about the biographical nature of the text. One of the crudest versions of ruling-class history focuses on the deeds of 'great men', and very occasionally women. These 'great men' turn out to be mainly kings, emperors, generals, capitalists and politicians, and any explanation of history is sought in the personalities of such heroes and villains. An alternative view of ruling-class history focuses on great ideas. Often the ideas themselves, rather than the philosophers who develop them, are seen as history's prime movers, and there is little if any consideration of where the ideas came from and what material conditions gave them their appeal. Both versions of ruling-class history have two things in common. They view history from the top down and see the mass of working people as essentially passive, as objects, not subjects, of the historical process. By contrast, although I have focused on a single labour leader, I have endeavoured to firmly anchor and evaluate the development of Murphy's political ideas and activities within the broader context of the changing contours of working-class struggle in both Britain and the USSR. Whilst the text provides neither a standard biographical narrative (with irrelevant details of personal idiosyncrasies) nor an all-encompassing chronological history of the British labour movement (although it necessarily assumes some prior knowledge of the period), it does seek to understand and assess the dynamic process through which Murphy's distinctive political contribution helped to influence the early revolutionary socialist tradition in this country.

ACKNOWLEDGEMENTS

I wish to express deep gratitude to the many people who assisted me during the four years I worked on the study. The research was financially assisted by a number of bodies. The Christopher Hale Fund of the University of Salford provided initial support for visits to libraries across Britain. Another grant from the Barry Amiel and Norman Melburn Trust enabled me to visit Toronto in Canada and be the first ever researcher to examine what remains of Murphy's personal papers, before having them transferred back to Britain. A further grant from the British Academy (BA–AN1821/APN2133) and a personal donation from Lord Alan Sainsbury provided my expenses for two extensive research visits to the Comintern archives in Russia, as well as numerous other trips across Britain. I am very grateful for the assistance I received from Andy Flinn and Stephen Bird at the National Labour History Archive and Study Centre in Manchester, from Edmund and Ruth Frow and Alain Kahan at the Working Class Movement Library in Salford, and from George Matthews at the Communist Party Picture Library in London. The archivists at the British Museum Periodical Library in London and the Russian Centre for the Preservation and Study of Documents of Recent History in Moscow were also very helpful.

I owe a special debt of gratitude to Murphy's son, Gordon, and his wife Nadia, who provided me with their support and encouragement, and to the following who provided me with valuable information and advice: John Arnold (Arnold Polak), John Archer, Michael Foot, Monty Johnstone, Walter Kendall, Kevin Morgan, Bill Moore, Alison and Jack Macleod and Mike Tyldesley. I also extend my thanks to a number of individuals who read drafts of the book and offered their comments, forcing me to defend, qualify and elaborate my views on the issues raised. These include Gregor Gall, Duncan Hallas, Helge Hoel, Silvia Holden, Dave

Lyddon, Al Rainnie, and Jack Robertson. Needless to say, any mistakes and shortcomings remain my own. I would also like to thank Carol McFarlane for her insightful comments and love and support. The book is dedicated to my mother.

PHOTOGRAPHIC ACKNOWLEDGEMENTS

All of the photographs appearing on the following pages of this book and on the cover are reproduced by courtesy of the National Museum of Labour History, Manchester.

Third Comintern Congress, Moscow, 1920. Standing from left: a US delegate, Newbold, Fraina, another US delegate, Ramsay, Reed, Quelch; seated: Murphy, Gallacher, Tanner, Reinstein (translator), McLaine, Pankhurst, S. Morgan

Commission on tasks of Comintern, 1920. At left: Murphy, Levi (at end of table); at right: Lenin, Pak, McLaine

Comintern Congress delegates, 1920. In front line: Murphy, Melianchansky, John Reed, Mustapha Pasha

British Communist Party leaders in the early 1920s. Left to right: Arthur MacManus, J. T. Murphy, Albert Inkpin, Willie Gallacher

Murphy, with wife Molly and son Gordon and Officers of the Seventh Samara Cavalry Division of the Red Army in Minsk, December 1926

On Lenin's tomb, tenth anniversary of the Russian revolution, 1927. Left to right: Rykov, Bukharin, Kalinin, Uglanov, Stalin, Tomsky; at back: Murphy and Gordon

Communist Party election campaign, Sheffield, January 1930. Back: Murphy and George Fletcher; front: Molly and Tom Mann

Council of the Socialist League, 1933. Left to right: I. Davies, unidentified, J. F. Horrabin, Murphy, L. Anderson Fenn, Sir Stafford Cripps, G. R. Mitchison, W. Mellor, M. Wrigglesworth, G. Hopkins

Chapter One

The Early Years in Sheffield, 1888–1917

Born in 1888, the son of an Irish Catholic father and an English Baptist mother, John Thomas Murphy was brought up with an older and a younger sister in a 'back-to-back' terraced house in Wincobank, a small village on the outskirts of Sheffield. The family was poor, not least because of his father's drinking bouts and habit of leaving his work as a blacksmith's striker to take an alcoholic tramping holiday for several weeks each spring. To supplement the family income, Murphy's mother took in lodgers and baked and sold bread and cakes, which, from the age of seven, young Jack was given the task of hawking from door to door before and after school. He also worked for a local farmer on a milk round each morning and evening throughout the week, which enabled him to buy clothes which the family could otherwise not afford. It seems to have been a relatively happy childhood despite the fact his various jobs and strict Methodist upbringing meant he was only able to snatch half an hour here or there to play with his friends. Sundays were a particularly busy day:

> I started with the milk delivery and then my sister and I toddled off to the Primitive Methodist Sunday School at nine o'clock. At ten thirty we went to the chapel service until noon. Sunday school again at 2pm until 3.30pm and at 6pm we accompanied mother to the evening service.[1]

The young Jack Murphy received his elementary education at the Wincobank Council School and took his studies seriously, although the formal teaching of the 'three Rs' appears to have been designed above all to turn out 'a good Christian boy who would be ready and anxious to be a good wage worker'.[2] Like many other children of the period, he left school at the age of 13: in Murphy's case to work at the Vickers engineering factory in Brightside, Sheffield. He constantly agitated to be moved around the different workshops to get an all-round apprenticeship training, with the result that in the space of a few years he had worked on

1

almost every machine and on all classes of work in the factory. His original ambition was to eventually get out of the plant and enter the Civil Service. Indeed, at the age of 18, after undergoing an intensive correspondence course of study lasting almost two years with Pitman's College, paid for in instalments from the extra money earned from night shifts and piece work, he prepared to take the entry examination to become a second division clerk. But by a quirk of fate he was forced to abandon his plans at the very last moment when his father was sacked and he became prematurely the family's chief breadwinner. In retrospect, we may be grateful for an accident which forced Murphy to resign himself to engineering and his work as a lathe turner in Vickers, thus preserving for the British working-class movement a man who was to become one of its most prominent intellectuals of the twentieth century.

After his disappointment, Murphy remained studious, but his attention now turned towards theology. He became a superintendent at the local Sunday School and a preacher in the Primitive Methodist Church, where he zealously studied theological questions and Christian doctrine. Experience as a local preacher undoubtedly enhanced Murphy's natural abilities, enabling him to acquire some fluency and proficiency in public speaking and skill in the art of persuasion and advocacy. But he was not unaffected by the general debates and arguments which raged at this time as Christianity came under attack from philosophers for its supernaturalism, and the social implications of the Gospels were challenged by the rising labour movement. Murphy recalled:

> It was in this period that I approached young manhood armed with the evangelical teachings of my childhood and unquestioning faith. The first challenge had come from the Socialists in the factory. The very violence of their attack only steeled me in the beginning to equally violent resistance. But I felt that I must henceforth be able to rationalise the faith that was in me. It was no longer satisfying to say 'I believe'. I must now be able to say 'I know' and prove it.[3]

This search to prove the validity of his Christian doctrine led him to read numerous books on evolution and astronomy, as well as the philosophical writings of Thales, Pythagoras, Aristotle, Spinoza, Kant, Locke, Hume, Berkeley, Hegel and Spencer. Murphy claimed Spencer's *First Principles* was the main influence in gradually stripping him of his long-held religious beliefs. Finding himself in the middle of a sermon one day, he realised he did not believe a word of the Christian message he was exhorting.[4] As a result, instead of going on to the ministry, he resigned his position as a local preacher and became a non-believer. Although not jubilant about the decision, as he did not feel he had found a complete alternative, he now recognised that 'whatever the future held, I could no longer worship the God of yesteryear'.[5]

It was not long before Murphy was attracted to a new 'faith': militant trade unionism. But before proceeding, it is necessary to appreciate the industrial and political context in which Murphy's new-found commitment to trade unionism was to be formed. During the nineteenth century the trade unions were craft-based and had continued, in the main, to be controlled by those who accepted the liberal ideology of the partnership of labour and capital. But in the late 1880s, shortly after Murphy's birth, a series of dramatic struggles, most notably the London Dock Strike of 1889, had produced a massive growth of 'New Unions', of unskilled and previously unorganised workers. Militants with socialist beliefs, although tiny in number, played a leading role. Many of them were associated with the Marxist Social Democractic Federation (SDF). Whilst the upsurge of organisation had been made easier by an expansion in trade and industry, after 1890 conditions worsened and unemployment increased sharply, and many employers, taken by surprise at the new unionism, took the opportunity to counter-attack. The new unions were badly placed to resist: within two years they had lost half their members and in the adverse economic climate, union survival seemed to depend on reaching some accommodation with employers. The original militancy increasingly gave way to a restrained and even passive stance in which sectional interests rather than broader class questions came to the fore, with the new unions in many ways beginning to parallel the old craft unions they had once bitterly opposed.[6]

With industrial militancy repulsed, some socialists looked towards political organisation in parliament as the way forward. They responded by taking the initiative and setting up the Independent Labour Party (ILP), which aimed at creating an independent political bloc to end the traditional link between the trade unions and the Liberal Party, in which almost all of the handful of working-class MPs were 'LibLabs' (that is 'Labour' representatives supported by the Liberal Party). And in the wake of a number of industrial and legal attacks, some of the leaders of the main trade

unions joined with the ILP (and SDF) in 1900 to set up a Labour
Representation Committee (LRC), which in 1906 was renamed the
Labour Party. In so far as it represented a direct entry of trade
unions into political affairs, rallying workers against the established
and openly capitalist Liberal and Tory parties in favour of one
claiming to represent working-class interests, the formation of the
Labour Party was a significant step forward. But with the emphasis
on parliament it also represented a retreat from militant trade
unionism, from the belief that collective organisation could
defend workers' interests. Electoral considerations also meant it
sacrificed the socialist ideas of its left-wing (the SDF soon withdrew
as a result) by stressing the need to smooth over class conflict and
reconcile the interests of employers and workers. So radical liberalism rather than socialism dominated the Labour Party at the outset,
with an unofficial agreement between the Liberals and the LRC not
to stand candidates against each other during general elections.
Although its nominal parliamentary presence grew from 26 MPs in
1906 to 42 in 1910, the new party continued to rely heavily on the
Liberals and effectively acted as an adjunct to the post 1906 Liberal
government.[7] However, with real wages undergoing a continual
decline, there was an increased turning towards trade union organisation, with unions growing in size, between 1905 to 1908, by 25
per cent to a total of two-and-a-half million members.

Owing to the grim financial circumstances afflicting his family,
which Murphy had tried to alleviate out of his weekly wage packet,
he was unable to afford to join the Amalgamated Society of
Engineers (ASE) when he completed his apprenticeship, and it
was not until the age of 22 in 1911 that he finally became a trade
unionist. Nonetheless, his membership coincided with a massive
revival of industrial militancy, the great workers' struggles of 1910–
1914 known as the 'Labour Unrest', which were marked by an
upsurge of aggressive, sometimes violent and often unofficial strike
action that was to hit virtually every industry. In 1910 there were
strikes in the mines and the shipyards and a lock-out in cotton. In
1911 a strike of seamen spread to dockers and from there to the
railwaymen of the north-west until the railway union's executive
felt compelled to call a national strike. In Liverpool there was a city-
wide transport strike to which the government responded by
sending gunboats down the Mersey and flooding troops on to the
streets to break up an 80,000 strong demonstration. Later two

strikers were shot dead by the military. In 1912 a million miners were out for five weeks and there was a London transport workers' strike. Nor was there to be any abatement of the wave in 1913; more and more workers with little experience of trade unionism were drawn in, as with a rash of strikes by unskilled workers in the Midlands engineering industry. Trade union organisation was completely transformed by this new insurgency, with total union membership growing from two-and-a-half million to four million in just three years, and conservative and bureaucratic union leaders found themselves increasingly challenged by a radicalised rank-and-file membership.

It was in this militant trade union context that Murphy, having shaken off his attachment to Christianity, now found himself becoming interested in the practical problems of the world of labour. Whilst previously he had deemed the wrongs of the world to be due to the moral shortcomings of the people and consequently had preached repentance and individual redemption, he now began to realise that people suffered poverty, exploitation and degradation because of the way in which society was organised. However, he rejected the ideas of the reformist socialists in the Vickers plant, who advised him to help build an independent Labour Party that could be elected into parliament to bring about an improvement in working conditions and effect a gradual social transformation. For Murphy, as for many other trade union militants at the time, concern with the improvement of the terms and conditions of employment and disappointment at the Labour Party's continued dismal parliamentary record of alliance with the Liberals persuaded him that politicians could not do much for workers, and that workers should rely instead on their industrial organisation and the strike weapon. The direct intervention of the state in the bitter industrial disputes that arose also encouraged him to view the state as merely an instrument of the employers. And he rejected nationalisation and 'bureaucratic' state control of industry. Instead, it was his syndicalist associates in the local ASE branch, with their schemes of industrial unionism and class war principles of outright opposition to employers and the state, who most influenced Murphy.

The appearance and development of the syndicalist movement in Britain was rather meteoric. At the heart of the syndicalist doctrine, first developed in France at the end of the nineteenth century and launched in Britain by Tom Mann and some other prominent trade union leaders in 1910, was the notion that the emancipation of the working class would be achieved by direct industrial action. Syndicalism represented a reaction to the perceived shortcomings of parliamentary politics and conciliatory trade unionism.[8] It grew out of the feeling of revulsion for the incorporation of the Labour Party leaders in parliament and the increasing alienation between the full-time trade union leaders and the rank-and-file.

There were two main aspects of syndicalist activity in Britain. First, there was a remarkably widespread and influential propaganda drive designed to make workers appreciate the need for industrial unity and the class struggle against employers. Second, syndicalists took a leading part in various trade union activities such as strikes and the campaign to amalgamate the existing unions into industrial unions, with the ultimate objective of abolishing capitalism and laying the foundations of a completely new social structure based on workers' control. Although it probably only ever organised a few thousand hard-core activists, Tom Mann's powerful and tireless oratory and dynamic leadership, combined with the wave of strikes that swept the country during this period of 'Labour Unrest', ensured support for its methods grew and contributed to the notoriety of the syndicalist movement in the public eye, making 'syndicalism' a household word in Britain. The Amalgamation Committee Movement, a national unofficial rank-and-file movement active in the engineering industry, was the main vehicle of syndicalist propaganda among Sheffield engineering workers in the pre-war years, and in 1911 Murphy joined the local Amalgamation Committee, and later became its secretary.

In the years immediately preceding the First World War, the engineering industry, employing over one-and-a-half million workers, comprised many grades of crafts and skills with lines of demarcation very sharp and class solidarity often weak or absent altogether. The trade union structure reflected these divisions within the labour force, with about 200 craft unions and others for semi-skilled and labourers. Various remedies to this fragmentation were advanced by different groups. Some hoped to bring about the amalgamation of existing unions through official channels and appealed to union leaders to open negotiations for fusion. Others, in the tiny Socialist Labour Party, renounced the existing trade unions altogether as being hopelessly reformist and set out to establish new revolutionary unions. Finally, there were those in the Labour Party who turned towards political activity for the solution of the main problems facing the workers. For Murphy it became clear that none of these courses was likely to succeed. This was because the ASE's official proposal for amalgamation of different unions put before the Federation of Engineering and Shipbuilding Unions was flatly rejected; the policy of setting up new revolutionary unions, attempted on the Clyde, proved to be an ultra-left failure; and political action through parliament appeared another dead-end.

The ground was thus prepared for Murphy's attraction towards Tom Mann's syndicalist formula of working inside the existing unions and campaigning to amalgamate them on a revolutionary basis until the principle of 'one union for one industry' was achieved, with industrial organisation of all workers on the basis of class, not trade or craft. The syndicalists believed no help could be expected from official circles, and in fact saw the attitude and conduct of full-time officials as one of the major obstacles to amalgamation. Amalgamation would only be achieved as a result of unofficial rank-and-file action. At the same time, they were particularly keen to disprove the notion that industrial unions would necessarily lead to the growth of bureaucracy and over-centralisation: safeguards were suggested such as control of policy to be vested in a rank-and-file annual conference, thereby limiting the role of officials and executive members to 'administering' policy and ensuring a large measure of local autonomy. The industrial unions would include all workers 'without distinction of craft or skill, grade or sex'. 'Solidarity' and 'direct action' were their main slogans, and their purpose was to fight for immediate improvements in working conditions, to challenge the existing social system, and eventually to take over the complete control and ownership of industry.

The appeal of these syndicalist ideas was such that in Sheffield the local Amalgamation Committee was able to sell 1,000 copies in less than a month of the pamphlet *One Union for Metal, Engineering and Shipbuilding Workers*,[9] as activists like Murphy systematically set about taking their views to trade union branches by addressing meetings. For Murphy:

> A new world of activity thus began to unfold itself. It was a very real world—of the earth. The questions under discussion were very practical—the encroachments of unskilled workers on to skilled workers

jobs; the new machine processes and the division of labour that was going
on apace in the workshops; the wages question, the hours of labour;
overtime and the speed-up; and our organisational weaknesses.[10]

During the evenings and on Sundays he attended numerous
meetings in Sheffield addressed by well-known socialist speakers
such as Keir Hardie and H. M. Hyndman. The range of his
activities was further increased following his election as a delegate
to the local District Committee of the ASE and a member of the
executive committee of the Sheffield Trades and Labour Council.
In addition, when the Daily Herald League was formed to support
the newly launched radical labour newspaper associated with
George Lansbury, he became secretary of its Sheffield branch.

The wave of industrial militancy of the period reached its high
point during the six-month 1913–1914 Dublin lock-out, when
employers made a determined attempt to stem the tide of militant
trade union advance. A strike on the tramways in support of higher
wages was countered by the dismissal of all employees, and sympathetic action by other workers opposed by a general lock-out of
25,000 union members throughout Dublin and surrounding areas.
The employers demanded that workers repudiate the Irish Transport and General Workers Union led by Jim Larkin and James
Connolly. Like other union activists on the mainland, Murphy was
inspired by the tenacity of the Irish workers and the aggressive
syndicalist aims of the Transport Union. In the wake of a mass
solidarity demonstration in Sheffield addressed by Larkin and
Lansbury, Murphy travelled to Dublin where he met the Irish
revolutionary James Connolly, a man who was to have a profound
influence on his early political development. He wrote of his meeting: 'The only other man I have met who affected me in the same
way was Lenin ... behind his words was the sureness of conviction
and knowledge. I came away from him wanting to know all that this
man had ever said or written'.[11] Commenting on Connolly's
syndicalist views Murphy added: 'He was not propounding a new
theory in this respect, but the ability of his exposition made him its
foremost exponent. He described a political party as a propaganda
body, "the John the Baptist of the new Redemption" '.[12] Murphy
was enormously impressed:

Presented thus, the Syndicalist Socialist case seemed to be clearer and
more precise than anything I had read or heard from other socialists. It
invested the daily work of the trade unions with a vision and a purpose

that made it worth while. It appeared to me that here was the way to make democracy real and to ensure individuality in co-operation, the way in which men, individually and collectively, could really be masters of their fate. I now had a faith and reasons for the faith that was in me.[13]

Thus, by the outbreak of war, Murphy, now aged 25, had become a 'syndicalist socialist', a firm convert to Connolly's ideas. Despite having to work a 53-hour week turning propellorshafts and gun barrels at the Vickers plant, he managed to achieve the not inconsiderable feat of reading revolutionary socialist literature by Marx, Connolly and others 'for hours at a stretch', with the size of the lathes effectively hiding him from the view of the foreman.

'SYNDICALIST SOCIALISM'

At this point it is worth critically examining in more detail the nature of the syndicalist politics outlined by James Connolly (and originally formulated by the American socialist Daniel De Leon) to which Murphy was so attracted. This is particularly important given that Connolly's conception of the role of the industrial union in the struggle for socialism constituted the mainspring of the wartime shop stewards' thought, as reflected in Murphy's own writings. In addition to a number of newspaper articles, Connolly wrote a pamphlet entitled *Socialism Made Easy* in 1908, a major theoretical work advancing the case for syndicalism (although, confusingly, he used the term 'industrial unionism'). This pamphlet was widely distributed in Britain by the Socialist Labour Party (SLP), the organisation which Connolly helped to found and of which he had been the first chair. It began by stressing the importance of industrial unions for a socialist strategy, advancing two reasons why workers should organise along these lines. First, the growth of reformist politics and the general political confusion among workers were directly attributable to divisions on the industrial field between different sections of workers. Industrial unionism, therefore, would bring a new political clarity: 'As political parties are the reflex of economic conditions, it follows that industrial unity once established will create the political unity of the working class'.[14] Second, industrial unionism performs an ever higher function than simply overcoming political problems within capitalism. One of the purposes of the pamphlet was to show:

> How they who are engaged in building industrial organisations for the
> practical purposes of today are at the same time preparing the framework
> for the society of the future...
>
> Every fresh shop or factory organised under its banner [of industrial
> unionism] is a fort wrenched from control of the capitalist class and
> manned with the soldiers of the Revolution ... On the day ... [we]
> proclaim the Workers' Republic, these shops and factories will be taken
> charge of by the workers there employed ... the new society will spring
> into existence ready equipped to perform all the useful functions of its
> predecessor.[15]

Connolly was arguing here that the framework of the industrial
republic could be built up inside the shell of capitalism. It was a
matter of workers organising through their industrial unions to
encroach gradually on the powers of management at the workplace.
In this way they would push back the 'frontiers of control' so that
the employer's ownership and prerogatives became mere formal-
ities.[16] No political revolution would be possible, Connolly considered, until the socialist industrial union was in a position to take
over the decisive industries. Thus, *industrial* organisation was
primary, *political* organisation secondary. 'The fight for the conquest of the political state', he declared, 'is not the battle, it is only
the echo of the battle.' Political issues receded into the background.
'All actions of our class at the ballot box are in the nature of mere
preliminary skirmishes ... the conquest of political power by the
working class waits upon the conquest of economic power and must
function through the economic organisation'.[17] In Connolly's eyes
the struggle for socialism became a battle fought primarily on the
economic field, and what to others seemed merely an industrial
struggle appeared differently to Connolly:

> The power of this idea to transform the dry detail of trade union
> organisation into the constructive work of revolutionary socialism and
> thus to make of the unimaginative trade unionist a potent factor in the
> launching of a new system of society cannot be overestimated. It invests
> the sordid details of the daily incidents of the class struggle with a new
> and beautiful meaning and presents them in their true light as skirmishing
> between the two opposing armies of light and darkness.[18]

However, one of Connolly's distinguishing marks within the
syndicalist tradition was his defence of the role of the political party.
He believed that the party had two functions. It had the task of
producing general propaganda to educate the working class in the
period when industrial unity, and therefore full political conscious-

ness, had not been fully formed. It should also stand for elections and try to win seats in parliament to support, albeit in an auxiliary fashion, the industrial struggle.

But *Socialism Made Easy* rests on major theoretical weaknesses.[19] First, there is its crude deterministic materialism. Connolly argued that workers' consciousness is shaped by the form of industrial organisation they adopt. If workers are organised in industrial unions then class consciousness would permeate upwards. Connolly assumed that a trade union view of the world and socialist consciousness were one and the same. In fact, this is not necessarily the case. Industrial unionism can show workers, through their own experience, the need to unite against a particular set of employers. However, it does not automatically clarify the role of the state or indicate the way workers should relate to other elements in society. Connolly's view of working-class consciousness led him to some practical conclusions. Reformism, for example in the shape of the Labour Party, no longer needed to be dealt with by *political* struggle. It was to be defeated by union activity. In the longer run this would undermine his belief in the need for a separate revolutionary socialist party. Furthermore it also reinforced the view that particular issues outside the sphere of economics and narrow trade union activity barely warranted discussion by socialists. Both these factors profoundly affected Murphy's own political outlook within the wartime shop stewards' movement, as we shall see.

Second, *Socialism Made Easy* underestimates the role of the state in maintaining the domination of capital. Marx had argued that the state was a product of class anatagonism and an instrument of class domination: 'political power, properly so called, is merely the organised power of one class for oppressing another'.[20] Therefore, the working class could only triumph by overthrowing the capitalist state. The *Communist Manifesto* declared that 'the first step in the revolution by the working class is to raise the proletariat to the position of the ruling class'.[21] Thus, instead of the conquest of the political state being the 'echo of the battle' as Connolly suggested, Marx set this question before the working class as the first fundamental task of the revolution.

Third, there is an image of labour as an army with a great uniformity in the ranks where both industrial divisions and varying levels of consciousness among workers have disappeared. It reflects a mechanical view of social development in which the movement of the working class towards a revolutionary position was seen as an automatic reflex to the development of capitalism. However, in many respects the argument for a revolutionary socialist party rests precisely on the *unevenness* inside the working class, and on the need for the socialist minority to organise independently to win over the majority of their fellow workers by providing leadership on day-to-day issues. By failing to recognise this, Connolly's advocacy of a political party from within the syndicalist tradition, viewed as merely a propagandist agency or 'John the Baptist of the New Redemption', was necessarily limited.

Significantly, Murphy's embrace of Connolly's 'syndicalist socialism' did not include his attachment to a political party. It seems likely this was because he felt alienated from both main revolutionary socialist organisations in Britain at that time. Although the British Socialist Party (previously known as the SDF) was well rooted in Sheffield, it had come to regard trade union work with contempt and concentrated on making socialist propaganda and standing in elections. By contrast, the SLP, the party associated with Connolly, had no real base in Sheffield, and combined a highly sectarian version of the BSP's propagandism with the 'dual unionist' belief that because the existing unions were reformist and bankrupt, new revolutionary unions had to be formed. Rejecting both these organisations, Murphy instead became one of the many thousands of unaligned syndicalist activists who eschewed political parties in favour of militant trade union activity and the campaign for the amalgamation of the existing unions.

Whatever the limitations of Murphy's early political development, his identification with Connolly's brand of revolutionary syndicalism expressed the rising level of organisation, confidence and class consciousness in Britain at that time. Moreover, syndicalism was a qualitatively more advanced theory of political mobilisation than the parliamentary reformism against which it reacted, that of identifying politics and the achievement of socialism with elections and reforms *from above*. In contrast, what distinguished syndicalism was its emphasis on working-class self-activity, militant industrial struggle and its belief that socialism could only be achieved through revolution *from below*. In its deep antagonism towards the capitalist state and its vision of a new, classless society, syndicalism was close to Marxism, albeit with its own distinctive outlook.

OUTBREAK OF WAR

The wave of patriotism which the outbreak of the First World War produced, and the departure of hundreds of thousands of men for military service, caused an inevitable lull in industrial militancy. Like their counterparts in the rest of Europe, the leaders of the Labour Party and the TUC supported their own state's war effort. In March 1915, the ASE and other unions concluded the Treasury Agreement with Lloyd George, the Liberal Chancellor of the Exchequer, accepting an unprecedented sacrifice of trade union conditions for the 'duration of the war'. They agreed 'there shall in no case be a stoppage of work upon munition and other work required for a satisfactory completion of the war', and to abandon all restrictive practices, and suspend all objections to overtime, nightwork and Sunday working.[22] In June 1915, the Munitions Act gave the terms of this Treasury Agreement the force of law. Strikes were declared illegal, restriction of output made a criminal offence and a system of 'leaving certificates' was introduced which prevented any worker on 'war work' from leaving their job except by permission of the employers. In return, the trade unions received a pledge that their sacrifices would 'not be allowed to increase profits', a pledge which was not kept. Whilst national trade union leaders were being co-opted into the machinery of the state, the workers in the factories felt themselves increasingly deserted and defenceless. Those skilled workers paid by the hour now found their income greatly exceeded by that of unskilled and semi-skilled workers reaping the benefit of liberally established piece-work rates. Recruitment of non-union labour constantly threatened union conditions, whilst long hours and bullying foremen who could threaten recalcitrant workers with prison or fines added to the growing ill feeling.

The war undoubtedly affected the engineering industry more profoundly than any other. Its successful prosecution required enormous quantities of all kinds of armaments, and in order to meet the demands for these materials the engineering industry was radically reorganised and greatly expanded, thereby thrusting its workers almost overnight into a position of exceptional importance.[23] For skilled engineers like Murphy, the problems of regulating hours, defending existing patterns of wage rates and conditions of employment and protecting trade union organisation in the workshop became essential. It soon became clear such grievances could not be adequately expressed through the established trade union hierarchy. When disputes arose, workers found their unions unwilling to support them and their full-time officials dragged out negotiations indefinitely. This meant new measures and new methods of organisation were required.

From the turn of the century the practice of electing a rank-and-file trade unionist within the workshops to represent the skilled workers had begun to occur within some engineering plants, although there were few of these 'shop stewards', with duties usually limited to union recruitment, dues collection and safeguarding the 'trade' from encroachments by other sections of labour.[24] Awareness of the possibilities of shopfloor union organisation had been further developed by pre-war syndicalist propaganda and the formation of Amalgamation Committees composed of members of competing engineering unions in the localities. However, amalgamation of the unions, difficult enough to achieve in normal times, was made almost impossible by the enlistment of huge numbers of trade unionists in the army, effectively suspending the Amalgamation Committee Movement's activities in the first years of the war. Trade union activists were forced to turn their attention to other methods of promoting a militant industrial policy. Significantly, as the war progressed, the incoherent and unregulated tendency towards co-operation amongst different grades of workers and members of different trade unions in the workshop itself, in the form of shop stewards' organisation, was given a considerable fillip.[25]

It was on Clydeside that a powerful shop stewards' organisation initially emerged.[26] In February 1915 an overtime ban for a two pence an hour increase became an unofficial all-out strike after employers at Weirs had brought in American engineers on higher wages. The shop stewards at the factory, who had built an impressive organisation in the years before the war, led an immediate walk-out. Factory after factory on the Clyde followed until 10,000 workers across 26 different companies were out. Local and national ASE full-time officials refused to back the strike and ordered a return to work. But the solidarity held and the strikers organised their own committee. Stewards' organisation spread from the stronger to the weaker companies and when the strike was over the informal network of stewards' organisation continued. A few months later, when the employers attempted to crack down by imposing fines and prison sentences on engineers taking sympathetic action, the Clyde Workers' Committee was born. It united around 250–300 stewards, met on a weekly basis and was led by revolutionary socialists, members of the SLP and BSP such as Willie Gallacher, Tom Bell, Arthur MacManus and Harry McShane. The revolutionary agitator John MacLean also played a key supportive role. The movement's attitude towards full-time trade union officials was summed up by the famous statement:

> We will support the officials just as long as they rightly represent the workers, but will act independently immediately they misrepresent them. Being composed of delegates from every shop and untrammelled by obsolete rule or law, we claim to represent the true feelings of the workers. We can act immediately according to the merits of the case and the desire of the rank and file.[27]

In fighting to defend their members' wages and conditions in a series of strikes, the Clyde Workers' Committee rejected the jingoism of the official union leaders and employers' pleas to 'pull together for victory'. However, the government, skilfully exploiting the stewards' failure to put forward a *class* policy that could unite skilled and unskilled workers, was able to arrest, imprison and deport all the leading militants and effectively crush the Clyde Workers' Committee by the end of 1916 (although it re-emerged in a new form about a year later). But the flame of shop stewards' organisation soon flared up again in Sheffield.

THE SHEFFIELD WORKERS' COMMITTEE

It is notable that the rise of the shop stewards' movement, designed to overcome, on the one hand, the stumbling block of national trade union officials who were more concerned with winning the war than with following up local grievances, and on the other hand, the difficulties of negotiating quickly on workshop problems affecting members of many different unions, is commonly treated as a development centred on the Clyde. It is too often forgotten that it was actually in Sheffield where the movement achieved some of its most notable successes, and which gave birth, in the writings of J. T. Murphy, to the only thought-out shop steward philosophy and proposals for a complete national structure. Certainly, Sheffield was the only centre apart from Glasgow to maintain a fully developed Workers' Committee for any length of time, and it effectively shared the national leadership of the movement with the Clyde.

The key Sheffield shop stewards differed somewhat from their counterparts on the Clyde in that there had not been before the war the same kind of revolutionary socialist agitation. Many Sheffield workers were solidly committed to Labour Party politics. Instead of the SLP or John MacLean it was the syndicalism of the Amalgamation Committee Movement which formed the ideological basis from which Murphy, Ted Lismer and other leading Sheffield stewards approached shopfloor issues during wartime. However, co-operation between the different craft unions was much better than on the Clyde and the organisation of the semi-skilled was also stronger.[28]

Underlying the Sheffield stewards' strength was the cohesiveness of the local engineering industry. Even before the start of the war, Sheffield had been involved in armaments production, and within the heavy metal trades of steel, arms and machinery, the dominance of the arms firms in the city was more clearly marked than in any other munitions centre. On the outbreak of war, the large factories in Sheffield's East End were turned over entirely to the production of munitions of war. By 1916 some 45,000 workers were employed by the five main arms firms, with the largest plant Vickers, where Murphy worked, employing over 10,000. In many respects, the Sheffield engineering workers were drawn together by this integrated local industrial structure, rather than fragmented as on the Clyde. Moreover, not only did they work together, they also lived together. In 1918 only two of the 15 Sheffield ASE branches were located outside the East End residential areas on the hills overlooking the Don valley. The isolation of a militant section from the engineering workers as a whole was therefore far less likely to occur in Sheffield than (it had) on the Clyde. For the same reason, the need for a rank-and-file movement that could act independently of the *local* official trade union machinery became much less acute.[29] Nonetheless, the working class population of Sheffield had to bear all the burdens of war imposed elsewhere. Altogether about 50,000 men from the city joined the Forces and there were food and housing shortages, numerous local casualties, and many other grim reminders of the costs of total war. In addition, the rapid expansion and transformation of the local munitions industry, the absorption of thousands of female workers and the abrogation of trade union rules created special problems for the workers in the heavy metal industries not experienced to the same extent in other industries.

The first tentative steps towards independent rank-and-file organisation in Sheffield had been taken in late 1915, when skilled *time*workers set up an unofficial Day-Workers' Committee within the local ASE to pursue a wage grievance to maintain their relatively privileged position vis-à-vis less skilled *piece*workers. Through its success in initiating direct negotiations with the Ministry of Munitions, the Committee persuaded the Sheffield ASE to secede from the local Allied Trades body (which linked all engineering unions) in subsequent wage movements. Although the Committee subsequently petered out, it helped to encourage ideas of independent workshop organisation. Shortly afterwards, the ASE District Committee launched a systematic campaign 'to ensure that in every department there shall be fully accredited representatives of the men, empowered to take action on their behalf and recognised as part and parcel of the union's machinery'.[30] Already, before the war, Murphy had put forward a suggestion to the Sheffield Amalgamation Committee that, whilst they waited for amalgamation of the unions to take place, something could be done with the machinery of the shop steward system. The idea was that 'All the trade unionists in any shop should have shop stewards, who should form themselves into a committee to represent the workers in that shop, regardless of the trade unions they belonged to, and thus make the first step towards uniting the unions'.[31] The suggestion had been welcomed, but it was not until 1916 that Murphy and his syndicalist associates were able to gain official support from the Sheffield ASE District Committee and to put the plan into effect. Launched in the midst of a campaign against the Munitions Act and the government's subsequent introduction of conscription, the drive to elect shop stewards went, according to one report, 'like wildfire. The rank and file knew they were divorced from the officials and that the officials were linked with the government so far as the war was concerned. The rank and file wanted to express themselves and this was their medium'.[32] Murphy recalled:

> It was proposed that every branch of the union [ASE] should make a registration of its members under the auspices of the District Committee. This registration secured the information concerning the place of

employment of every member of the union in the District and the number of shop stewards in every workshop. The District Committee on the basis of this registration had to undertake a systematic attack on each factory, until every factory wherein there were members of the ASE, had its quota of shop stewards. The other skilled workers unions ... began to do likewise. This paved the way for the election of workshop committees representing all the shop stewards in each workplace.[33]

This was the real first attempt by an ASE District Committee to come to terms with the wartime boom in workshop organisation, and the Sheffield rules for shop stewards extended their role from dues collection, recruitment and reporting grievances to include direct day-to-day negotiations with management.[34] Murphy himself, still only in his twenties, was sufficiently highly regarded as a shop steward at Vickers to represent workers in discussions with directors of the company. By the autumn of 1916, a local Engineering Shop Stewards' Committee was formed to link up the individual shop stewards from different factories, and Murphy was elected secretary. Though still limited to the ASE, this Committee provided the basis from which an independent rank-and-file movement could be launched on the model of the Clyde Workers' Committee.

It was over the issue of conscription of skilled workers that the Sheffield Workers' Committee was finally brought into being. In October 1916 a time-served fitter, Leonard Hargreaves, employed in the same department at Vickers as Murphy, was suddenly conscripted into the army in breach of the government's pledge to exempt skilled workers who had volunteered for munition work. Murphy immediately reported this clear case of victimisation to the other shop stewards and news spread rapidly throughout the workshops. Coming soon after the horrors of the Battle of the Somme, everyone knew this meant a virtual death warrant. The issue was then relayed to the local trade union branches, the ASE District Committee, and the national executives of the ASE and other engineering unions. But despite these protests, weeks went by without redress. Finally, on the prompting of Murphy and other activists on the Sheffield engineering shop stewards' body, the ASE District Committee called a mass meeting on Sunday 5 November 1916, attended by 3,500 workers. Skilled workers of all trades were invited to attend, a significant step forward given that up until this time shop stewards' organisation had been confined to engineers in the ASE.

The chair was taken by the District President of the ASE, who announced that because it was bound by official union policy of opposition to strikes during the war, the District Committee had decided to suspend its meetings and hand over the business of dealing with the conscription issue to the shop stewards' committee. In practice, this did not entail much change on the platform as Murphy and many of the leading shop stewards were themselves members of the District Committee. But it was a clever manoeuvre which enabled a flexible combination of official and unofficial tactics to be adopted. After hearing a report from Murphy, the mass meeting voted in favour of a resolution threatening an all-out strike of Sheffield engineers unless the government returned Hargreaves to civilian life within seven days.[35] A joint strike committee was elected consisting of the 36 members of the District Committee and over 100 shop steward delegates. Under Murphy's direction, the strike committee then dispatched telegrams to the Prime Minister, the War Office, the Munitions Ministry and their own trade union executives, giving news of their decision. The Sheffield engineers were well aware of what they faced in threatening illegal strike action, and the efforts of the militants to perfect the shop steward organisation now 'developed like magic'. As Murphy recalled: 'In a week or ten days prior to the November strike the number [of shop stewards] rose to more than 300'.[36] In addition, the transfer of authority to the unofficial body facilitated the broadening of the stewards' committee from the ASE to involve members of other skilled unions.

The deadline for Hargreaves' release expired at 4.00pm on Wednesday 15 November. At a mass meeting of 200 shop stewards it was reported that no reply from the government had been received and that the ASE had merely telegraphed to say they would put the case before the Manpower Board. The stewards, not inclined to accept any vague offers, voted to organise strike action the next day unless Hargreaves was returned to Sheffield in person. Excellent organisation ensured some 12,000 workers, probably the complete membership of all the skilled engineering unions in Sheffield, walked out of the factories en masse. A fleet of motor cyclists was dispatched to all the main munitions centres across the country to break the press censorship, enlist support for the strike and try to arrange for joint action. 'In the annals of the war', commented the *History of the Ministry of Munitions*, 'no strike showed so few signs of indecision or half-heartedness'.[37] On the third day of the strike, thousands of engineers in the Vickers company town of Barrow-in-Furness, Cumbria, came out in sympathy, and the government, faced with the threat that the strike would spread still further, was forced to capitulate. On Saturday 18 November, Hargreaves was hurriedly released from the army and escorted back to Sheffield by two waiting shop stewards to another mass meeting of 10,000 engineers, at which the strike was triumphantly called off.

Although the strike had not been against conscription as such, but only against skilled workers being conscripted, the victory of the Sheffield engineers struck a severe blow to the government's ability to use its conscription powers as it saw fit. That same weekend, as a direct result of the Sheffield initiative, the government negotiated a Trade Card Scheme which gave the ASE and other skilled unions the right to issue exemption certificates to its members, thereby granting the immunity the Sheffield workers demanded. These were achievements of a remarkable order, indicating the power the shop stewards were able to wield despite the opposition of full-time officials of the ASE. In no other war-time struggle did the shop stewards challenge the government so successfully. The victory enormously strengthened the authority of the Sheffield stewards and the influence of the revolutionary syndicalist minority among them. 'For the time being', commented Murphy, 'the shop steward committee became the dominant authority. The men felt it was only through this new form of organisation that the unions could now justify themselves in the least as defenders of the interests of the workers'.[38]

Early in January 1917 the stewards called a mass meeting to consider the way forward. Such was the prestige of Murphy and the other leading stewards that they were able to get a unanimous decision to attempt to extend stewards' organisation to include *all* workers in the factories, including skilled, semi-skilled and unskilled, men and women. Their plan was for each department in a factory to elect a workshop committee comprised of shop stewards endorsed by their trade union, but wherever possible representing all grades of worker. Each workshop committee would then elect representatives to a factory committee, which in turn would be represented on a city-wide workers' committee. The plan was accepted and the engineering stewards' committee which had led the strike now reorganised itself as the Sheffield Workers' Committee, giving formal recognition both to its unofficial character and to the allegiance of workers other than those in the ASE. It aspired to be a class-wide organisation, even though in practice it remained primarily confined to the skilled trades. By the spring of 1917 the factories of Sheffield were covered with a network of workshop committees similar to those that had emerged on the Clyde, and the Sheffield Workers' Committee, chaired by Murphy, grew in power and influence until some 20–30,000 engineering workers were represented. The Committee produced its own newspaper and even issued associate membership cards, although at no time were there more than a few thousand regular subs-paying members.[39]

Under the impact of wartime conditions, Workers' Committees also gradually began to spring up in other munitions centres across the country, including Barrow, Coventry, Woolwich, London, the Tyne, and on Clydeside again. Shop stewards' leaders, their outlook similar to that of Murphy, were being brought to the forefront as a result of the growing tensions of the war. But national organisation and co-ordination of the shop stewards' bodies were still rudimentary and were soon put severely to the test. The first challenge came in March 1917, when 10,000 Barrow engineers walked out on strike and called for sympathetic action from other engineering centres. After almost two weeks no other centre in the country had followed Barrow's lead, although the Sheffield stewards felt under a special obligation to reciprocate the solidarity they had recently received. Because the issue of premium bonus payments on which the Barrow engineers had taken action hardly affected Sheffield, it required ten days of agitation and the coincidental advent of an unexpected local issue, the removal of the chair of the local Munitions Tribunal, before the Sheffield stewards were able to win a vote in favour of sympathetic strike action at a mass meeting. But confronted with the threat of imminent arrest and the apparent lack of national support, the Barrow strikers returned to work before the Sheffield decision was actually put into operation.

Shortly afterwards Murphy found the sheer pace of union activity over the previous hectic months had proved too much and his health deteriorated through physical exhaustion. Ted Lismer, the President of the Sheffield Workers' Committee, and other shop stewards instructed him to go away to the seaside to rest and not to return until his health had recovered, and presented him with £30 which had been collected in the workshops on his behalf. Murphy agreed to go to Llandudno in North Wales to recuperate. But after only a few days' rest he read in the newspapers about the outbreak of a massive strike by Lancashire engineers against an attempt to repudiate the Trade Card Scheme and to extend 'dilution' (the substitution of less skilled for skilled labour) to private work in violation of existing national agreements. By the second week of May 1917 the strike had spread throughout England, involving 200,000 engineers in 48 towns, with the exception of the Clyde and the Tyne. The strike, originating without prior preparation, was self-evidently a manifestation of the growing concern regarding the continuation of a bloody war which it appeared would never end. Murphy rushed back to Sheffield to a mass meeting which had been called to consider joining the strike. But as he entered the hall Ted Lismer seized him by the arm, pulled him into the corridor and told him: 'The lads sent you away to get well and not to come back looking half dead. If we can't run a strike without you then all your work of recent years isn't worth a damn'.[40] The stewards refused to let Murphy near the platform or where he could be seen by the audience, and because the excitement proved too much he found himself in the doctor's hands that same night. As a result of his illness, Murphy missed what turned out to be the biggest engineering strike movement of the war, which eventually crumbled when the government imprisoned a number of the unofficial leaders.

Murphy recovered some weeks later amidst the hills of Snowdonia with 'no interruptions but the sunshine and the breeze', and returned to work at the Vickers plant. However, his mind remained on the world at war and nations in the throes of revolution. As he commented: 'Socialism as a gospel had now taken completely the place in my life hitherto occupied by Christianity. I suppose I was what some people call a fanatic in my complete absorption in the service of these ideas.'[41]

By this time news was filtering through about the first Russian revolution of February 1917, widely heralded as a foretaste of the coming triumph of the labour cause amidst the growth of widespread disillusionment with the war. Murphy recalled:

> The effect of the news that Czarism had been overthrown and that the masses had begun a revolution electrified the labour movement. I remember the effect in the workshop where I was engaged. Men would

stand around the machines talking about this new event ... To learn, in the midst of all the gloom of war, that this great triumphant thing, revolution, had sent the Czar's crown toppling and swept the ruling class from power, was something which was new inspiration to the workers and they wanted to know all about it. I was an active shop steward ... and I found it impossible to get on with ordinary activities for answering questions to my fellow workers concerning this event ... What did it mean? Would the revolution spread? Would it reach Germany? ... From that time onward there was hardly ever a mass meeting that this question of the Russian Revolution [did not] come up for discussion.[42]

A national convention to welcome the February Russian revolution and call for an early 'people's peace' and the establishment of what were termed 'workers' and solidiers' councils' was held in Leeds in 'June 1917, attracting 1,500 delegates from the trade unions, Labour Party, shop stewards' movement, the Independent Labour Party, British Socialist Party and Socialist Labour Party. Very little came of the conference, partly because of government repression, and partly because the Labour MPs who headed it were more concerned to. demonstrate the need to adopt an independent foreign policy than to advance the revolutionary movement. Nonetheless, revolutionary tendencies inside the working class were undoubtedly strengthened, and this would be further reinforced by the second, or Bolshevik Revolution, in October 1917, although as we shall see (in Chapter Three), it was not until after the war that the full political significance of the events in Russia for shopfloor activity in Britain became apparent to Murphy.

A NATIONAL SHOP STEWARDS' MOVEMENT

One of Murphy's first acts after recovering from illness was to help to establish a national Shop Stewards' and Workers' Committee leadership. An initial attempt to establish a national organisation had been made in November 1916 under the initiative of the Clyde Workers' Committee and Arthur MacManus. But few other Workers' Committees were represented and the meeting did little more than elect a provisional committee to arrange a second conference. This met in Manchester in May 1917 with more delegates than previously, but before the conference could come to any definite conclusions it broke up, owing to the outbreak of the engineering strikes sweeping England. Although many of the local strike leaders were already in touch with each other through the engineering Amalgamation Committee Movement, the informal links between them were insufficient to spread the strikes to all the major engineering centres across Britain. Therefore, it was not until 18 and 19 August 1917 that the first broadly representative conference of shop stewards' organisations, with delegates from 23 Workers' Committees, assembled in Manchester.

The most important question discussed at the conference was the problem of leadership. Whilst the strike in May had shown the need for a strong national committee to give leadership to the movement, the majority of those present were influenced by syndicalist ideas of rejection of all leadership and came out against a national committee with *executive* powers. George Peet (representing the Manchester Workers' Committee), supported by Murphy (representing the Sheffield Workers' Committee), moved that the national committee should have purely *administrative* functions, essentially concerned with such matters as issuing shop steward cards, instructions on forms of organisation and propaganda on behalf of the movement, whilst referring all important decisions back to the rank-and-file for ratification. This proposal was accepted and a National Adminstrative Council (NAC) was elected with Arthur MacManus as chair, George Peet as secretary, and Murphy as assistant secretary.

Significantly, although Workers' Committees were established across the country, outside the Clyde, Sheffield and, for a short period, Manchester, fully-fledged Workers' Committees, representative of workshop organisation and capable of leading mass strike action in defiance of the trade union officials, were never to emerge. In recognition of the limitations of many of the Workers' Committees, Murphy advised:

> Hence, whilst defining the nature of the organisation we [are] aiming at, we ask for the affiliation [to the NAC] of all shop stewards' committees regardless of their degree of development towards the class organisation. This means we have to manifest a degree of tolerance both locally and nationally for the sake of getting unity of action wherever possible.[43]

Nonetheless, in estimating the potential of the shop stewards' movement, full account must be taken of the links provided by the NAC and the national conferences, and between groups of militant trade unionists throughout the country who identified with the aims and tactics of the Workers' Committees. Thus, over 30 different

localities were represented at the four national conferences held by
the movement between the summer of 1917 and the end of the war,
and the shop stewards now began to fill the vacuum which had
appeared between rank-and-file workers and their increasingly
distant union officials. Contacts gained through the Amalgamation
Committee Movement, the Plebs League, the SLP and BSP, helped
to bring the shop stewards' leaders together and create a nationwide
movement expressing the growing level of industrial discontent.
Murphy was soon to emerge as the chief theorist of this nascent
Shop Stewards' and Workers' Committee Movement.

After his election on to the NAC in August 1917, Murphy was
recruited to the Socialist Labour Party by Arthur MacManus, NAC
chair and executive committee member of the SLP. The central role
of the SLP in the industrial agitation of the war years, and the fact
that MacManus and many of the leading members of the Clyde
Workers' Committee were members, must have been influential
factors in Murphy's decision to join the party. Ironically however,
up until this point the official attitude of the SLP towards the Shop
Stewards' and Workers' Committee Movement (SS&WCM) had
not been unqualified support. Whilst it had welcomed the shopfloor
militancy that characterised the movement, it had also criticised its
preoccupation with the practical problems of the day and failure to
form a new revolutionary industrial union. But, confronted with the
spontaneous growth of workshop organisation and the fact of its
own leadership of rank-and-file militancy on the Clyde, the SLP
abandoned its previous attachment to a 'dual unionist' approach.
'This is no time for intolerant doctrinaires, this is no place for
bigoted critics', wrote the editor of their paper *The Socialist* in July
1917, urging that the propaganda of industrial unionism could now
be translated into concrete form, not in antagonism to the trade
unions but by building all-grades organisation within the workshops. Thus, the industrial unions of the future would grow
spontaneously out of the existing trade unions, not alongside
them. As Murphy, newly recruited to the SLP, declared: 'Our
policy must be a natural development from within the trade union
movement'.[44]

Meanwhile, despite his full-time job at Vickers and activities as
chair of the Sheffield Workers' Committee and assistant secretary of
the SS&WCM, Murphy now began to write prolifically for a
number of revolutionary working-class publications. An important

series of articles on the structure and policy of the Workers' Committees appeared in *Solidarity*, a monthly paper which became the mouthpiece of the English shop stewards' movement, and *The Firth Worker*, which was produced by the Firth shop steward's committee in Sheffield but was later used by the local Workers' Committee for propagandist and organisational purposes. In addition, he contributed regularly to *The Socialist*, the paper of the SLP.

During the autumn of 1917 Murphy also wrote the famous pamphlet *The Workers' Committee*, which is generally recognised as the chief theoretical statement to emerge from the shop stewards' movement in Britain. It expounded the theory of independent rank-and-file organisation, a carefully thought out plan for the formation of shop stewards' committees outside official union structures, and indicated how shop steward activity could be transformed into a weapon for the overthrow of capitalism. The pamphlet, representing an important development on the strategy of pre-war syndicalism, was first published by the Sheffield Workers' Committee and in January 1918 was adopted by the NAC of the movement as its official statement of policy and organisational principles.[45] By March 1918, 25,000 copies had been sold[46] and Murphy later claimed that the total sale reached 150,000.[47]

The pamphlet argued that a permanent tension existed between the interests of the rank-and-file and those of the officials in the existing trade unions. Trade union officialdom was subject to different pressures and a different rhythm of life which were conducive to bureaucracy. The trade union officials lived remote from the workshop atmosphere and, whatever their intentions may have been, did not succeed in retaining or understanding the actual spirit and feelings of the workers in the shops. Therefore, policy ought to be determined, not by a handful of leaders or official trade union representatives, but by the actual will of the members: 'Real democratic practice', Murphy urged, 'demands that every member of an organisation shall participate actively in the conduct of the business of the society'.[48] The pamphlet also noted the defects in the structure of trade unions, in which union representation was organised within the branches based where people *live*, rather than based on workshop branches where they *work*. In the branch, workers were sharply divided from one another, craft by craft, section by section, and men from women, whereas workshop organisation could be used to bind them all together in a common fellowship and solidarity.[49] The pamphlet advocated the new units of workshop, industrial and class organisation which could overcome such problems and invigorate the labour movement with a real democratic spirit.

The structure consisted of six main forms. First, Murphy argued for a 'Workshop Committee', composed of shop stewards elected by the workers in each individual section of a factory and representing all grades of workers (including skilled, semi-skilled and unskilled) and irrespective of different trade unions, with one shop steward to not more than 15 workers. Second, all the workshop committees within a factory should elect representatives to a 'Works Committee' which would provide coherent leadership on those questions which affected the workplace as a whole. Third, 'Local Industrial Committees' should be elected from full shop stewards' meetings in each city (as in Sheffield) or wider locality (as on the Clyde or Mersey), which would co-ordinate the efforts of all trade unionists across the different factories within specific industries (such as engineering). Fourth, all the Local Industrial Committees should unite to form a 'Local Workers' Committee', on a basis which would include all the workers in the area. These Local Workers' Committees would be 'similar in form to a trades council, with this essential difference—the trades council is only indirectly related to the workshops, whereas the Workers' Committee is directly related'.[50] Fifth, there should be 'National Industrial Committees' to match their counterpart in the local structure, grouped into 12 geographical divisions, with the aim of focusing on questions of a national character relating to the particular industry. Sixth, a 'National Workers' Committee', composed of two delegates from each national industrial committee, would be concerned with questions which affected the working class as a whole. Murphy summarised the structure thus:

> Working in the existing organisations, investing the rank and file with responsibility at every stage and in every crisis; seeking to alter the constitution of every organisation from within to meet the demands of the age; working always from the bottom upwards—we can see the rank and file of the workshops through the workshop committees dealing with the questions of the workshops, the rank and file of the firms tackling the questions of the plant as a whole through the plant committee, the industrial questions through the industrial committees, the working class questions through the working class organisation—the workers'

committee. The more such activity grows the more will the old organisations be modified, until, whether by easy stages or by a general move at a given time, we can fuse our forces into the structure which will have already grown.[51]

Whilst Murphy's pamphlet confined itself mainly to questions of method and structure, it was clear that the objective was nothing less than a complete transformation of the industrial system. The Workers' Committees were conceived of as revolutionary bodies, aiming at the overthrow of the capitalist system in industry and playing their part in the substitution of capitalism by 'workers' control'. Of course, the complicated scheme of organisation set out in the pamphlet was never fully realised in practice. As Murphy himself acknowledged in 1919:

> Nowhere in this country can we find a factory organised completely as described, and no one recognises more clearly than the revolutionist that such industrial organisation with its corresponding methods and principles will not come generally into existence prior to the destruction of capitalism.
>
> But persistent efforts to approximate to it are forced upon the workers by the development of industry and the intensification of the struggle. And, whether viewed from the standpoint of power, directness of contact with the workers, democracy in method or potentialities for control, it is difficult to see what other form of organisation could supersede it once it had become established'.[52]

Clearly, there were important disparities between the principles outlined in Murphy's organisational scheme and the actual practice of the stewards' movement. Even though by 1917 a multitude of shop stewards' committees had come into existence, they varied in character from town to town. Some of them were simply craft committees, some a combination of trades committees, and only a few included all workers, skilled and unskilled, as well as women workers. Even when it appeared there was a unified body, antagonisms prevailed because stewards tended to approach questions from the point of view of their individual craft or union. In fact the distinction Murphy drew between Industrial Committees and the theoretically all-embracing class-wide Workers' Committees was hardly necessary, since the movement in practice remained very largely confined to engineering workers. Only after the war, when unemployment had broken the power of the engineers' movement, was any real effort made to establish organisation in other industries, such as mining and the railways. Nonetheless, it is important to recognise that the underlying ideas of Murphy's *Workers' Committee* pamphlet were to spread a good deal further than the specific organisational forms on which it placed its emphasis. The shop stewards' movement played an extremely important role in the development of engineering trade unionism, and trade union officials, employers, and even the government, were forced to reckon and negotiate with it. Never before or since has an unofficial rank-and-file movement exercised such power and influence in this country. Moreover, the importance of the movement lies also in the fact that it made a lasting contribution to the development of the revolutionary socialist movement in Britain. Murphy's role in this was to prove central.

Chapter Two

The Shop Stewards' Movement, 1917–1919

Significantly, as the historian of the movement has pointed out, the tenor of the wartime shop stewards' thinking was organisational and its innovations lay in the field of industrial tactics, not of political strategy as such.[1] By and large, its leaders were practical figures whose thinking, so far as it rose above everyday matters, was more concerned with elaborating tactics than debating the long-term strategy or ultimate goals of the class struggle. Even Murphy, probably the most intellectually able of them, did not, at least during the war years, progress beyond tactical thinking, important and often original though that was. Nonetheless, the practice of the shop stewards' movement and its theory of rank-and-file organisation as set out in Murphy's *The Workers' Committee* and other writings did represent a decisive advance on the pre-war syndicalist tradition. Whilst it was only after the war that the full revolutionary implications of his wartime practice became clear and the transition from syndicalism to communism became complete, a full appreciation of Murphy's subsequent political development is impossible without first tracing his pioneering wartime attempt to advance revolutionary tactics on the shopfloor and within the unions.

ATTITUDE TOWARDS THE UNIONS

Initially, Murphy attempted to clarify the revolutionary attitude towards the unions. He argued that the growing level of class struggle and the dynamic changes of the war period meant trade unions were increasingly becoming a transitory form of labour organisation, which would tend to disappear as industrial processes became more social in character. In particular, he believed the structure of the unions had become an obstacle to the development of the natural unit of organisation in industry, which was the workshop or industrial group. But under the pressure of the 'march of events' or historical development of society, new organisations would emerge that would better fit the needs of the working class, namely Shop Stewards' and Workers' Committees, which would lead to an industrial form of union organisation.[2]

As we have seen, the critique of existing unions and advocacy of a new Industrial Union was not an entirely original contribution. Syndicalists had been using similar arguments for some years. The distinctive feature of the policy of Murphy and the other leaders of the SS&WCM was their suggestion for overcoming the defects of existing unions and achieving the new Industrial Union. Before the war, there had been two attitudes towards the unions by those revolutionaries prepared to engage in industrial work. The SLP denounced the existing unions as rotten props of the capitalist order and advocated the formation of new revolutionary industrial unions outside and in opposition to the old. The syndicalists, on the other hand, had sought to transform the existing unions from within into industrial unions as the embryo of a future socialist state. In the pre-war years Murphy had tended towards the latter view. However, the practical realities of building the wartime shop stewards' movement led him to reject the assumption that it was necessary to make a principled choice between *either* 'dual unionism' *or* 'amalgamation'. Instead, he borrowed elements from both these traditions and fused them into a novel synthesis.[3]

On the one hand, he rejected the 'dual unionism' of the SLP. Thus, he vigorously opposed an attempt by the Amalagamation Committee Movement (ACM) to establish a new national engineers' union in competition with existing ones. The ACM had collapsed after the outbreak of war, but from the beginning of 1916 it revived and became increasingly linked with the growing power of the shop stewards' movement, although unlike the stewards' organisations the Amalagamation Committees were purely propagandist bodies with no foothold in the workshops. In November 1916, infuriated by the sluggish attitude of engineering union officials towards amalgamation, and encouraged by the growing power of the shop stewards, the ACM presented the union executives with a three-month ultimatum to amalgamate, failing which a new industrial union would be formed. Paradoxically, just as the SLP was abandoning 'dual unionism' owing to its members' experience in the shop stewards' movement, the syndicalists pointed to the power of the shop stewards as their justification for swinging away from their pre-war policy of amalgamation. When their ultimatum ran out, W. F. Watson, since 1910 the leader of the ACM, wanted to press ahead with the formation of a new engineering union. The shop stewards' leaders, most of whom were themselves members of the Amalgamation Committees, opposed Watson's plan,[4] and Murphy addressed an 'Open Letter' to an ACM conference in March 1917:

> Remember it is not only the amalgamation of unions you require, but the amalgamation of the workers in the workshops ... Let your propaganda take concrete form by transforming the Amalgamation Committee into the Workers' Committee. Make the amalgamation of unions incidental, the amalgamation of the workers fundamental.[5]

The conference compromised, agreeing to defer, although not abandon, Watson's ultimatum. But when the issue was debated at the ACM national conference in October 1917, a resolution from the Sheffield and Manchester Workers' Committees for the fusion of the two movements was carried, 'That the members of the Amalgamation Committee unite with the Shop Steward and Workers' Committees with a view to concentrating activity at the point of production', and a merger took place at a special joint conference in January 1918.[6]

On the other hand, although Murphy was opposed to 'dual unionism', he also shifted his ground on the question of amalgamation. As we have seen, during the pre-war years he had viewed the existing trade unions as inadequate agencies of revolutionary transition because of their generally bureaucratic, sectionalist and collaborationist character. He believed that through propaganda activity amongst the rank-and-file they could be persuaded to amalgamate into new industrial unions which could be won over to a revolutionary perspective. But his shop steward wartime experiences now led him to believe it was doubtful whether the sectional interests of individual unions and their bureaucratic leaders could ever be overcome to get them to agree to amalgamate, and unlikely that the character and goals of the unions could be transformed merely through amalgamation of official structures:

> 'Amalgamate! Amalgamate!'. Scores of officials have won to office on that ticket and yet it does not come. Constitutions and constitutionalism stand in the way. Varied contributions, vested interests, varying benefits, and so on, all hamper the proceedings.

And more fundamental still, the form and character of many of the
organisations are such that without a revolutionary change in outlook and
purpose amalgamation is an absolute impossibility.[7]

Murphy now came to the view that the pre-war tradition of
seeking union amalgamation could not answer the immediate
needs of the moment. It was not sufficient just to pass resolutions
in the branches urging amalgamation. Militants ought to take the
initiative in constructing the new industrial unionism from below
in the workshops. In the past, Murphy explained, amalgama-
tionists 'sought for a fusion of officialdom as a means to the
fusion of the rank-and-file. We propose to reverse this procedure'.[8] The formation of workshop committees, he argued, would
render the trade union machinery more and more responsive to
the needs of the members at the point of production and would
facilitate the desired trend towards amalgamation. The workshop
committees, composed of shop stewards representing all the
workers in the shop, irrespective of craft differences, would
emphasise the social character of production and create a class
outlook among workers, unlike trade union organisation which
split up groups of workers and maintained artificial distinctions
between them. The spread of such workshop organisation, linked
by local Workers' Committees, from engineering to the rest of
industry, would ensure an all-encompassing *class* organisation on
a national scale.

I think that now is the time for those who believe in Industrial Unionism
on a class basis, to let the craft unionists run the craft organisations,
federate and amalgamate and chase the lost fancies of the past, whilst we,
confident that the historical developments are making *class* organisations
a more imperative need as the days pass, build up the class organisation
with class conscious men and women who have in view [not] ... 'the
permanent improvement of the relations between employers and employees', but the overthrow of capitalism and the bringing into being of the
Socialist Republic.[9]

This did not mean Murphy abandoned the long-term aim of
constructing a revolutionary industrial union. On the contrary, as
we have seen in *The Workers' Committee*, he envisaged the fusion of
the different industrial unions into 'One Big Union', albeit depart-
mentalised according to industry.[10] But he recognised that such an
Industrial Union, which would grow spontaneously out of the
existing trade unions and not separate from them, would only

emerge through practical experience of united class organisation from below:

> I advocate the formation of Workers' Committees, springing from the workshop ... The workshop demonstrates the weakness of craft organisation, but the prejudices of the past, the instinctive conservatism holds men to the old [unions]. They must grow out of the old and into the new. This can only happen where there exists the new into which they can grow. You cannot impose a system from above. It must grow from below ... The best way to proceed therefore, in my opinion, is to introduce machinery which in its very activity will produce the kind of thinking we believe to be necessary. The way to produce thinking industrial unionists is by the Shop Stewards' movement.[11]

Once such workshop organisation had been achieved, the reorganisation of national union structures on industrial lines would follow naturally, enabling workers to make the transition from the old form of trade unionism to industrial unionism based on class. He later distinguished two phases 'of our development as revolutionary agitators in the trade union movement':

> The first phase [pre-war] was that of propagandists of industrial unionism, amalgamation of the unions, ginger groups within the various organisations. The second [wartime phase] was characteristically the period of action, the attempt to adopt industrial-unionism principles to the immediate struggle, and to take on the direct responsibility for the conduct of the fight against the bosses and the state.[12]

In other words, in building up the Workers' Committees for practical and immediate purposes, Murphy began to register, although with no sophisticated theoretical explanation, his rejection of both amalgamation and dual unionism. Murphy's scheme was that instead of seeking exclusively to either reform or replace the existing unions, it was necessary to concentrate on developing the SS&WCM until in the process it completely superseded the unions by transforming itself into the Industrial Union. He left it an open question how far in the ultimate process of building such industrial unionism the existing trade unions would be compelled to weld themselves together and remould their internal structure or find themselves ignored in the industrial struggles of the future and effectively be 'cast on the scrap heap': 'That which is capable of responding to the demand of the hour will survive. That which is not will be destroyed ... unresponsive organisations and institutions [will be] swept away, and new ones brought into being'.[13]

Thus, in combining the best elements of both the SLP and the amalgamationist traditions, the practice of the shop stewards' movement and its theory set out in Murphy's *Workers' Committee* pamphlet and other writings, represented a decisive advance on both previous trends of pre-war syndicalism.[14] However, when it came to discussing the transition to socialism they still remained firmly locked within the syndicalist tradition.

WORKERS' CONTROL

From its origin the SS&WCM was committed to the revolutionary goal of workers' control of production and abolition of capitalism. A fundamental premise was that the emancipation of the workers must be achieved by the workers themselves, and as Murphy explained, the Workers' Committees were the only way 'towards the goal of our endeavours—the complete control of industry by the workers, for the workers'[15] Once this organisation was established it would first overthrow and supersede capitalism and then take over the whole industrial and social machinery. However, during the war, Murphy and other shop stewards failed to consider in any detail how this workers' control of industry would be achieved or exercised. The underlying vague syndicalist assumption, in the tradition of James Connolly's pre-war writings, was that the workers would gradually extend their control on the shopfloor, with the management of particular enterprises passing into the hands of workshop committees, until the employing class were completely expelled, overthrown or expropriated on a national scale. But this was a very oversimplified view that took little account of how fierce opposition from employers would have to be confronted or broken. It also assumed the struggle for control would remain confined to the industrial sphere. This analysis, in the light of the state's role in prosecuting the war effort, was particularly naive. It completely neglected the role of the state in maintaining the domination of capital and overlooked the central question of the conquest of political power by the working class. As Murphy later acknowledged:

> The shop stewards did not discuss it. Had this question been clearly understood then a totally different attitude would have developed on the question of union organisation and 'control of industry'. It would have

been realised that the unions will never be reorganised to control industry
until the working class has conquered political power. Every step in the
direction of industrial unionism is of value to the extent that it facilitates
the massing of the workers for common action in defence of their
economic conditions against the increasing pressure and exploitation of
the capitalists, but 'workers' control of industry' without 'workers
ownership of industry' is utterly impossible. The change of ownership
is a political question, indeed the outstanding political question of our
time, involving a complete and fundamental change in the relation of
classes[16]

In addition, during the war period, Murphy seemed to take it
for granted that, in the new social order, control of industry would
be exercised by the industrial union based on workshop organisation. But this raised the problem that as an organ of industrial
administration the union's role would be largely incompatible with
its character as an organisation designed to protect and represent
workers' interests independently of management. This contradiction could survive only because Murphy and the other leading
stewards during the war did not believe themselves to be operating
in a revolutionary situation. Because workers' control was an
ultimate goal rather than an immediate demand, it did not seem
urgently necessary for them to clarify their position. Only after the
war, when the demand for workers' control was subsumed into a
theory of the struggle for soviet power, would the confusion be
resolved[17]

UNION OFFICIALDOM

Meanwhile, Murphy also developed the critique of trade union
bureaucracy which had been made five years earlier in *The Miners'
Next Step* pamphlet produced by the syndicalist Unofficial Reform
Committee in the mining valleys of South Wales.[18] His analysis
went further by advancing the theory of independent rank-and-file
organisation as an effective counter to the bureaucratisation of trade
unionism. To begin with he identified the existence of a separate
stratum of trade union officials who had become removed from the
rank-and-file. 'One of the most noticeable features in recent trade
union history is the conflict between the rank and file of the trade
unions and their officials'. He continued: 'Everyone is aware that
usually a man gets into office on the strength of revolutionary

speeches, which strangely contrast with those of a later date after a period in office'.[19] Murphy pointed to the material and social pressures that can make union officials become bureaucrats:

> Now compare the outlook of the man in the workshop and the man as a full-time official. As a man in the workshop he feels every change; the workshop atmosphere is his atmosphere, the conditions under which he labours are primary ... But let the same man get into office. He is removed out of the workshop, he meets a fresh class of people and breathes a different atmosphere. Those things which were once primary are now secondary ... Not that he has ceased to feel interested, not that he has become dishonest, not that he has not the interests of labour at heart, but because human nature is what it is, he feels the influence of new factors, and the result is a change of outlook.[20]

In addition, he highlighted constitutional factors:

> The constitutions invest elected officials with certain powers of decision which involve the members of the organisation in obedience to their rulings. It is true to say that certain questions which have been referred to the ballot box are decisions that have been arrived at; but it is unquestionably true, also, that important matters have not been so referred, and increasingly insistent has been the progress towards *government by officials*. They have the power to rule whether a strike is constitutional or unconstitutional, and accordingly to pay or withold strike pay. Local business must be referred for executive approval, and, where rules are silent, power to decide according to their judgement is theirs.[21]

Murphy explained that the growth and consolidation of this stratum of union official meant 'a desire for their own security, a permanent office or a parliamentary career, and a "cushy" government job becomes more attractive as the days pass'.[22] Acknowledging that the passivity of ordinary trade unionists reinforced such bureaucratic tendencies, he argued the need for every rank-and-file member to become actively involved in union affairs and for all important decisions to be referred to the members for discussion and ballot vote within the workshops. It was necessary to make officials act as delegates on behalf of the rank-and-file rather than allowing them to '[speak] and [act] as if the workers were pliable goods, to be moulded and formed according to their desires and judgement'.[23] At the same time, Murphy saw the need to concentrate on developing, both *within* and *outside* the official union structures, rank-and-file organisations that would be capable of fighting independently of the bureaucracy wherever necessary.[24]

The Workers' Committees created in Sheffield and elsewhere were seen as the model of organisation. They represented the establishment of a situation of 'dual power' between trade union officialdom and independently organised militant sections of the rank-and-file.

It should be noted that whilst Murphy and the other leading shop stewards emphasised the need for rank-and-file control of union officials, they refused to centre their activity on contesting and capturing official positions in the unions (at least beyond the level of shop steward). The need for independent rank-and-file organisation was argued from the structural inadequacies of engineering trade unionism. The multiplicity of sectional trade unions stood in growing contradiction to the needs of workshop organisation. In these circumstances, Murphy argued, it was folly to expect that 'by the capturing of official positions we can change the nature of the organisation ... A craft organisation conserves a craft psychology or outlook and everything is determined in similar terms'.[25] Moreover, if the stewards tried to capture official union positions there was the danger, despite the best of intentions, they would themselves become bureaucrats removed from the rank-and-file:

> The policy of capturing the trade union movement is full of danger and is on a par with the idea that the workers will achieve their emancipation by sending representatives to Westminster ... Our policy must be to control and direct, and we can do that effectively by strengthening our workshop organisations. Our power lies in the works. In our willingness to work or not. That is the essential fact on which our movement exists and if we centre our activities on capturing the trade union movement, instead of capturing [the workshop organisations], we will be captured by the Official movement ... A man is governed by his environment, and we should very definitely oppose any member taking any office in a trade union that will take him away from the shop or his tools.
>
> The time calls for a movement full of life and energy, where responsibility rests on each individual, and not a body of glorified officials. Use the trade union movement, but do not let us waste our time trying to capture it[26]

This abstentionism derived from Murphy's syndicalist approach to the whole problem of leadership (an approach which is explored in some detail later in this chapter), but it also arose from the specific nature of the engineering industry within which he operated. On this question, Murphy differed from the experience of the syndicalist Unofficial Reform Committee which had laid out within *The Miners' Next Step* their objective of reforming trade unionism through the official machinery.[27] The contrast between the two movements is instructive.[28] In the mines workers were members of one union, the Miners' Federation, with union branches, or lodges, corresponding to individual workplaces. This meant that the grievances of the rank-and-file tended to be channelled directly into the Miners' Federation official machinery. But whilst this situation allowed for greater rank-and-file influence within the union, it also inhibited rank-and-file action independent of the official machine. By contrast, in engineering, there were more than 200 unions[29] and the unit of organisation of these numerous unions tended to be the poorly attended geographical union branch, not the workplace, and did little to express the immediate concerns of the mass of workers on the shopfloor. These were more effectively dealt with by shop stewards who, for much of the time, had to operate independently of the official structure in order to represent workers on day-to-day issues.

Therefore, reflecting the practical achievements of the shop stewards' movement, Murphy pointed to the possibilities of independent rank-and-file organisation based in the workshops rather than in the ill-attended local union branches, as an effective counter to the bureaucratisation of the unions. *The Workers' Committee* proposed a complete national structure which, unlike that proposed by *The Miners' Next Step*, was an *alternative* source of authority to the existing unions and their leadership. Such a position was logical for stewards faced with the multiplicity of engineering unions and their craft jealousies (just as the Unofficial Reform Committee's ideas were logical in terms of the mining industry and union). Whilst the miners aimed at *reforming* officialdom, the engineers attempted to *bypass* it where necessary. Thus, because the value of participation in the official union machinery necessarily appeared to be limited to Murphy and the engineering stewards, no organised effort was made to capture trade union positions, though this was never ruled out as such by some in the movement.[30] They believed the growth of all-grades workshop organisation and of Workers' Committees might force the existing officials to 'remould their internal structure and accept the workshop as the basis of the organisation', but they did not intend to encourage this process by capturing official positions and fighting for such a reconstruction of trade unionism from above as well as from below. They were content to rely on putting pressure on the trade union officials from the strongholds of independent rank-and-file organisation, confident that if the officials failed to respond to this pressure the existing unions would eventually be 'thrown off' and replaced in all their essential functions by the Shop Stewards' and Workers' Committees. As Murphy later reflected: 'We did not conduct the fight so much against the officials, but rather ignored them and fought the employing class directly'[31]

This refusal to campaign directly for union office has been attributed by some commentators as a fatal mistake on the part of the movement's leaders[32] Murphy himself, many years later, was very critical of 'the anti-official outlook [which] stultified any real organised effort to replace reactionary leaders by revolutionary leaders ... [and which] diffused the energies of the revolutionaries and made their movement into a ferment rather than an organised force fighting for a new leadership'.[33] He even went so far as to claim: 'It is quite certain that had the leading shop stewards of that period, when the workers were supporting them, really made a planful effort to win the leadership of the engineering unions they could have succeeded in the course of a few years'.[34] However, despite Murphy's later optimism, it is far from certain that the revolutionary shop stewards could have made any substantial inroads into trade union officialdom had they tried. Certainly, in most areas, apart from Sheffield, the appeal of their distinctive policies was limited to a minority of workers and only in strike situations did they really gain mass support. But trade union elections could not be expected to occur only, or even predominantly, at such moments. Given their minority position and the nature of the industry, it was highly appropriate and justifiable that the shop stewards should have concentrated their energies on enlarging the effective size of the rank-and-file movement in the workshops, rather than building an electoral machine which, because of its branch base, would have been valueless for fighting purposes.[35] Nonetheless, Murphy was mistaken to have taken a *principled* stance of opposition to the standing of candidates for union office, and failed to appreciate that in certain circumstances it may be *tactically* advantageous to utilise official union elections for propagandist purposes with official union positions being used as a (albeit subsidiary) means of encouraging rank-and-file self-activity.

Although the movement failed to seriously contest trade union positions, it did participate in the official union machinery at a *local* level wherever possible or appropriate. Thus, whilst the relationship between the SS&WCM and the official union machinery at a local level was in some cases antagonistic, in others there was a great deal of co-operation. At one extreme was the Clyde Workers' Committee which represented only a minority of the engineering workers and consequently could not control the local ASE District Committee. As a result, the rank-and-file movement tended to stand outside and in opposition to the official structures of trade unionism in the area. By contrast, the Sheffield Workers' Committee, representing the great majority of engineering workers, worked closely with the local District Committee, the two structures acting as 'official' and 'unofficial' wings of a single organisation. *The Workers' Committee* pamphlet, which drew heavily on the Sheffield experience, naturally stressed the possibilities of working *within* the unions, proposing shop steward rules for adoption by the District Committees which would make it possible for the workshop committees to operate as 'part of the official movement ... The means are then assured of an alliance between official and unofficial activities by the official recognition of rank and file control'.[36] In an article for *Solidarity*, Murphy explicitly stated that the local Workers' Committees 'should not usurp the functions of the local trade union committees but attend to the larger questions embracing all trade unions in the industry'.[37] However, at the same time, he made it clear the Workers' Committees should retain their distinctive entity and independence of the unions, essentially adopting a 'partly official, partly unofficial' stance.[38] In a conference report written in 1920 he explained that 'they would act officially or support officials of the unions when they moved in the right direction and move independently when they did not; they would press for the fusion of the unions and internal changes of organisation on the one hand and on the other build independently as near as possible the structure of industrial unionism'.[39] In practice, most of the local workshop and Workers' Committees adopted this flexible approach towards the unions.

POLITICS AND THE WAR

Meanwhile, one of the most important limitations of Murphy's syndicalist outlook during this time was the anti-political stance he adopted in relation to the war. Clearly, although the shop stewards' movement had established itself through workplace struggles, the wider political question of the war was central. It was important not only in the trenches but at home where rationing, changes in workshop practices and the outlawing of strikes were the direct result. But the shop stewards' syndicalist tradition of separating *politics* and *economics* meant that, although their leaders included a number of revolutionary socialists like Murphy, they did not, as yet, have a theoretical grasp of the importance of connecting industrial agitation with socialist politics. They were still in the habit of treating politics as something *external* to the factories and shopfloor unrest as simply an economic issue.

Murphy's own position, influenced by Connolly's 'syndicalist socialism', exemplified the problem. Unlike many other trade union activists in Sheffield who rallied to the patriotic flag in 1914, he opposed the imperialist war. His membership of the SLP from 1917 onwards reflected such anti-war convictions. But one could never have guessed this from his writings for the wartime stewards' movement. Incredibly, *The Workers' Committee*, the chief theoretical statement to emerge from the shop stewards' movement, made absolutely no mention of the war and the political issues it raised. Indeed, not one newspaper article he wrote between 1914 and 1918 openly called for an end to hostilities. No doubt Murphy denounced the war at SLP meetings, and it seems likely that he formed part of the small anti-war minority that gradually became a majority within the Sheffield Trades and Labour Council. But he made no attempt to propagate his views *publicly* amongst the rank-and-file in the factories for fear of losing support, remaining content to merely defend workers against the threats to their organisation brought about by the war. In effect, he wore two hats, one reserved for his SLP activities, the other, a shop steward's hat, to be worn as a representative of the rank-and-file, many of whom were pro-war.[40] Writing many years afterwards, Murphy remarked:

> None of the strikes that took place during the course of the war were anti-war strikes. They were frequently led by men such as myself who wanted to stop the war, but that was not the actual motive. Had the question of stopping the war been put to any strikers' meeting it would have been overwhelmingly defeated. The stoppages had a different origin and a different motive. They arose out of a growing conviction that the workers at home were the custodians of the conditions of labour for those in the armed forces, as well as themselves.[41]

But the fact was that every issue facing workers, every dispute over wages, conditions or military conscription was profoundly political, since all arose out of the government's determination to win outright victory in the war. This meant it was virtually impossible to oppose the government consistently without questioning its political assumptions. Of course, it is true only a minority of workers were fully conscious of the relationship between the attack on craft conditions and conscription on the one hand, and the war and the capitalist system on the other. Nonetheless, Murphy and the leading shop stewards had the opportunity to broaden the struggle by basing themselves on this militant minority. By doing so they could have attempted to raise the level of consciousness of the majority of workers to that of the most advanced. Certainly, the extreme political circumstances of the war, and the abject failure of the trade union and Labour Party leaders to defend workers' wages and conditions in the face of an all-out attack by the employers and the state, opened the way for socialist arguments that cut across the skilled engineers' craftist and nationalist ideas.

A major opportunity to link politics and mass militancy was provided in early 1918. The Bolsheviks had taken power in Russia and withdrawn from the war, and in Germany workers had staged several mass strikes. In Britain, in circumstances of profound unrest caused by food shortages and general war weariness, the government introduced a new Military Service Bill with wide powers of conscription, which had the effect of fuelling intense anti-war agitation. At the eleventh hour the shop stewards' leaders, greatly strengthened by the revival of the Clyde Workers' Committee, belatedly decided to organise against continuation of the war. A national conference decisively rejected any narrow defence of engineers' privileged exemption from conscription and put an ultimatum to the government demanding it scrap the new conscription laws and consider the Bolshevik peace proposals. National strike action was recommended, although delegates were instructed to consult the rank-and-file in the districts about what form this action should take.

It is possible that if the shop stewards, instead of preparing a form of national referendum, had gone straight back to the workshops with plans for a strike whilst the impact of the government's proposals was still strong, action might have been taken. Instead, the result of the national canvas of the rank-and-file, reported to a fresh conference held one month later, proved disappointing. Despite the fact that delegates from London and the Clyde claimed strong support for a strike, their reports were undermined when it was revealed that in the former there had been no workshop ballot and in the latter the vote had been fairly evenly divided. But the decisive reports came from Manchester and Sheffield, where the views of the rank-and-file had been tested in workshop meetings: they were opposed to strike action against the war. In Sheffield the movement had collapsed. A Trades Council meeting on 15 January displayed the solidarity of the skilled and unskilled on the issue of a democractic peace. However, during the same week, the ASE District Committee held an aggregate meeting attended by about 3,000 workers. An official, writing in the union's monthly journal, was able to claim:

> The meeting was one of the best I have ever attended, and the whole position was discussed from all points and with a full responsibility of the situation, without any excitement or attempt to introduce any other matter apart from the refusal of the Government to discuss the breaking of their agreement with the ASE.[42]

In other words, not only had the skilled engineers entirely neglected the political aspect of the conscription proposals, but their unofficial leaders like Murphy had made no attempt to enlighten them. When the Sheffield Workers' Committee met on 19 January it took its cue, not from the anti-war resolution passed at the Trades Council, but from the ASE aggregate meeting, threatening 'drastic action unless all men who have started in munitions factories since the commencement of the war are taken first, irrespective of their trade unions, and that unless ASE apprentices are to be taken thereafter in proportion to others'[43] It seems the workshop meetings went against strike action to end the war. Perhaps not surprisingly, many rank-and-file engineers who had not seen Murphy and the other stewards' leaders agitate against the war beforehand responded with little enthusiasm to suggestions for a strike that represented a direct political challenge to the state; and the Sheffield Workers' Committee retreated into mere defence of the skilled engineers' craft privileges in relation to conscription.

When the reports from Sheffield and elsewhere were presented to the shop stewards' National Administrative Council they faced a difficult tactical decision. A strike called to force the government to open peace negotiations would, it seemed, be easily sidetracked into a struggle by the skilled engineers in defence of craft privilege. But a strike solely on the narrow issue would have invited the hostility of other sections of organised labour, and capitulated entirely to the craft orientation of the rank-and-file.[44] The NAC decided to resolve the dilemma by abdicating responsibility, a decision that proved a fatal blow from which the shop stewards' movement was never fully to recover. Ironically, immediately after this decision, 400,000 German engineers struck against the war, only to find themselves isolated internationally.[45]

With expectations of a national strike abandoned, the NAC turned initially to an ambitious scheme designed to swing the whole working-class movement into action in favour of a referendum on the question of an immediate armistice without annexations and indemnities, hoping to force a general election. But like the strike plan this scheme quickly failed after the unexpected success of a new German offensive on the Western Front considerably undermined resistance to the government's proposals. When some delegates to a national stewards' conference in April 1918 continued to press the case for a general peace movement, Murphy countered with a proposal to concentrate purely on the industrial arena:

> When the programme was drafted there was a possible chance that it might succeed, but the great offensive had changed the temper of the people. Events were moving very rapidly and before long there might be a better chance for an advanced programme. In the meantime, we should discuss workshop organisation.[46]

The conference endorsed Murphy's line and the opportunity to initiate revolutionary action against the war was not to recur.[47]

It has been argued that in seeking the cause of the failure of the SS&WCM it would be wrong to exaggerate the subjective failure of leadership.[48] Both the collapse of the May 1917 strike movement and the failure of the strike call of January 1918 were more deeply rooted in the level of consciousness of the working class, including its advanced sections. But the problem with this analysis is that it completely absolves Murphy and the leading stewards of responsibility for their failure to openly and politically oppose the war. The war threw into sharp relief the contradictory nature of the shop stewards' movement. Thus, there was the *negative* element, the merely sectional struggle for craft status against the encroachment of less skilled workers, and there was the *positive* element, with resistance to changes in workshop control encouraging a generalised political opposition against the employers and state. But what this meant was that the only hope for a successful long-term resistance to the government lay in trying to harness the strength of the engineers' craft-based workshop organisation to the wider interests of the working-class movement, a class-wide agitation for militant trade unionism fusing immediate economic issues with politics into a struggle against the war.[49] In the event, instead of seeking to broaden the movement to deal with the political issues lying behind the strike, Murphy and the stewards' leaders restricted it to narrow trade union questions, thus cutting off the movement from its main sources of external support.

THE QUESTION OF LEADERSHIP

A related problem was Murphy's anti-leadership views. During the war the shop stewards' movement consistently experienced betrayal at the hands of the Labour Party and trade union leaders and, in rejecting their sell-outs, looked to develop workers' own organisation and confidence on the shopfloor to counteract this. But Murphy and the other stewards tended to blame the failures of the official labour leaders not merely on poor direction and wrong-headed policies but on the very institution of leadership itself. From the fact that shopfloor workers tend to become corrupted once they were elected to full-time union office, they concluded that *all* leadership, whether from official *or* unofficial sources, was bound to stifle the independence and initiative of the rank-and-file. As Murphy explained in *The Workers' Committee*:

> It matters little to us whether leaders be official or unofficial, so long as they sway the mass, little thinking is done by the mass. If one man can sway the crowd in one direction, another man can move them in the opposite direction. We desire the mass of men and women to think for themselves, and until they do this no real progress is made, democracy becomes a farce.[50]

His principled antipathy to leadership became almost an article of faith. As he later reflected:

> I had no ambition to be a leader or to be other than a worker in the factory. In fact the thought of stirring people emotionally to follow me or elect me to any position of authority over them was repugnant. I wanted men and women to stand on their own feet, think with me if they agreed with me, and regard all positions as administrative posts for carrying out

work agreed upon by the people who elected the administrators. I hated anybody's attempting to exercise authority over me, no matter what their position. Authoritarianism of any kind, whether of doctrine or social position, was an abomination to me.[51]

The essence of Murphy's and the leading stewards' attitude was that control of policy should be vested in the rank-and-file and that leadership as such was undesirable. Thus, the SS&WCM remained a very localised movement with only a loose national structure, never more than a federation of autonomous groups of militants. The central body of the movement, the National Administrative Council, as the name implied, held no executive power and was intended to function as little more than a reporting centre for the local committees, with no policy initiatives being taken independently of the membership. The movement had no paid officials, no organisers and no offices. Similarly, in *The Workers' Committee*, Murphy insisted the functions of the local committees 'should be such that instead of arriving at decisions *for* the rank-and-file they would provide the means whereby full information relative to any question should receive the attention and consideration *of* the rank-and-file, the results to be expressed by ballot'.[52] The point was further underlined in an article he wrote in *Solidarity*:

> One of the first principles of the shop stewards' movement and workers' committees, they obey the instructions of the rank and file and not *vice versa*. This repudiates the charge of the press and those good clear-thinking people who refer to those wicked shop stewards who bring men out on strike. Shop stewards do not 'bring' men out on strike, the shop stewards' duties do not involve 'leadership'. As a matter of fact the whole movement is a repudiation of leadership.[53]

This meant that fresh leadership, whether it was provided by full-time union officials *or* shop stewards, was not the answer to workers' grievances. The very act of leadership involves 'acting as if the workers were pliable goods, to be moulded and formed according to [the leaders'] desires and judgement'.[54] By contrast, Murphy constantly emphasised the self-activity and revolutionary potential of the working class.

Of course, such anti-leadership prejudice did not arise entirely from the principal shop stewards' abhorrence of trade union bureaucrats and parliamentary politicians. It was also bound up with the syndicalist theory of the automatic movement of workers towards the seizure of industry. From this perspective, the very

spontaneity of the movement made powerful centralised organisation and leadership unnecessary; all that was needed was a loose
body with local autonomy and democratic control to stimulate the
thinking of the rank-and-file along the right lines. In addition, there
was the fear that any powerful national co-ordination of the
SS&WCM would be indistinguishable from the establishment of
a 'dual' union. As Murphy explained: 'It must be clearly understood that the national industrial committee is not to usurp the
functions of the executives of the trade unions. Power to decide
action is vested in the workshops so far as these committees are
concerned'.[55] But, of course, in practice, Murphy and the wartime
shop stewards *did* provide a form of leadership to workers on a
number of occasions. Certainly, it was leadership they gave when
they suggested initiatives which involved the workshops in taking
action. The role of Murphy in the November 1916 Sheffield strike
was a vivid illustration of this. As Murphy acknowledged in a
private letter written many years later:

> It is quite true that the shop stewards and I very definitely were
> repeatedly frustrated and inhibited by the 'rank and file policy of
> administration' instead of executive authority to lead. But we did lead . . .
> and we did move masses into action against the war . . . every one of the
> wartime strikes were engendered and developed by the anti-war socialists
> and syndicalists who were seizing upon any and every grievance arising
> from the conduct of the war.[56]

During the war Murphy was the victim of a hidden contradiction in his own thought and action. Ideological considerations
and experience of the trade unions and Labour Party had led him to
reject the idea of leadership as reactionary. Yet the lesson of the
Sheffield strike and the other national disputes was that without
some form of centralised organisation the movement wasted its
strength, exerting its massive power to limited purpose. The
extreme concentration of economic and political power in the
hands of the wartime state demanded that the shop stewards reply
with a similar centralisation of their own forces. Instead, at every
crucial moment Murphy and the stewards' leadership effectively
waited on the mass of workers and lagged behind the progress of
events. This was further confirmed after the war in early 1919 when
100,000 Clydeside workers, including all its engineers, struck for a
40-hour week. The shop stewards' NAC, with its haphazard
attitude towards centralised organisation, proved unable to initiate

sympathetic action and the government sent troops into Glasgow to break the strike. Writing after the event, Murphy explained that the 'greatest mistake' of the Clyde Workers' Committee 'lay in the fact that it had done nothing to prepare the movement beyond the Clyde. Although it was represented on the National Committee of the Shop Stewards, it had not even acquainted this committee of its plans.'[57] Ultimately, it was the principal shop stewards' inability to accept the role of leadership which events forced upon them which prevented the movement reaching its full potential. Their anti-leadership convictions meant there was little attempt made to plan or provide centralised policies which could overcome the uneven-ness in organisation and consciousness within the workshops, and the movement also failed to establish genuine contact with rank-and-file movements in other industries.

ECLIPSE OF THE SHOP STEWARDS' POWER

During the war the shop stewards' movement suffered from con-stant police surveillance. In 1916 a number of agencies for reporting on 'labour unrest' had been established. These became partly unified into what was later termed 'a machinery of industrial espionage, with agents provocateurs of workshop sedition'[58] In October 1917 the War Cabinet had called for a special report on the danger of revolution and felt the need 'to be assured the police are doing something'.[59] Early the next year, Murphy was offered £5 a week for supplying regular information on both the causes of unrest in industry and the shop stewards' movement by a suspicious 'Mr Brown' from London, who said he represented people inter-ested in securing industrial peace, but who did not wish to be named. Murphy promptly took the proposals, of which he obtained a written copy, to the Sheffield Workers' Committee. It was decided he should appear to agree to the terms, albeit supplying no information that was not public knowledge, until sufficient evidence of 'Mr Brown's' real connections had been obtained, when the whole matter would be publicly exposed.

For a period of about ten weeks, a local committee supervised all Murphy's correspondence with his contact and took charge of all money he received. But after it become clear suspicions about 'Mr Brown's' connections with Scotland Yard's Special Branch could not be proved, the link was severed.[60] The stewards then took a copy of all the correspondence to a Labour MP who 'raised the matter in the House of Commons. The evidence was also taken to the National Administrative Council of the SS&WCM, where it was investigated by the highly respected labour figure Tom Mann. Although Murphy viewed the 'Mr Brown' case as an honest attempt to expose espionage within the British working- class movement, and could feel assured that neither the shop stewards' bodies nor the SLP questioned his integrity, he subsequently became open to slander and insinuation by others, against which the SS&WCM had to defend him in the *Daily Herald* in 1919,[61] and the case was to have several sequels.[62]

Meanwhile, early in 1918, continuing the policy of his apprenticeship days of attempting to advance his own knowledge of his craft, Murphy voluntarily left Vickers and moved from Sheffield to Southport to work at the Vulcan Motor plant, which at that time produced munitions. But after only three weeks employed in the tool room he was sacked on the pretext of bad timekeeping when the manager discovered he had 'an agitator' on his hands.[63] There was a fairly strong shop stewards' body in the plant and 1,000 workers immediately walked out on strike to win his reinstatement. The solidarity displayed was extraordinary, with men and women, and apprentices, acting in unison. The strike lasted two weeks, with threats of sympathetic action from several Manchester plants and many other parts of the country, including Barrow and Sheffield, before management were forced to reinstate him. Ironically, not long afterwards, realising his activities in the SS&WCM could not be carried on from such a distance, he returned to Sheffield and got a job at the Brightside Foundry, where he stayed until the end of 1918.

The end of the war brought a fairly rapid decline in the power of the shop stewards' movement in engineering. Paradoxically, this was despite the fact that 1919–1920 saw a massive upsurge of workers' militancy in many different sections of industry that had semi-revolutionary possibilities (this post-war workers' offensive is examined in some detail in Chapter Three). First, the unexpectedly smooth process of 'restoration' of pre-war industrial practices within the engineering industry greatly reduced the need for shop-floor bargaining, and this cut at the roots of the workshop organisations. The trade unions, with their rights fully restored, resumed the initiative in trade matters and took up many claims originally formulated by the shop stewards' movement. The 1919 engineers' Shop Stewards' National Agreement worked in the same direction. A workshop organisation with greatly reduced powers and functions was now officially recognised by the unions and the employers. Second, the rundown of munitions production led to a very high level of unemployment, with Murphy, like many thousands of other engineers, forced on to the dole queue. Already in July 1919 Murphy could state: 'At Vickers, Sheffield, it is questionable whether there is a single active shop steward or literature seller left in the place. They have practically all been cleared out under the cloak of unemployment. The same applies to many prominent people on the Clyde.'[64] Third, employers in many engineering districts took the opportunity to dismiss the leading shop stewards. The absence of strike action had a particularly demoralising effect and the stewards that remained were forced to accept official union discipline over their activities.

As a result of these factors the SS&WCM, from being a movement which could draw hundreds of thousands of workers into action, dwindled into militant propagandist political centres that acted as ginger groups within the official union organisations. Whereas in the war the affiliates had mostly been workshop committees, by the early 1920s they became groups of shop stewards, or even individual militants operating in the trade union branches. Meanwhile, the crumbling of the local Workers' Committees led to a corresponding growth of importance of the national organisation, with the NAC ceasing to be merely an administrative body. In fact, between conferences the movement hardly existed after the war outside the activities of its NAC and the propaganda of its two papers, *The Worker* in Scotland and *Solidarity* in England. By 1921 the SS&WCM had become simply the National Workers' Committee Movement, a belated recognition that the insurgent workplace activism which had launched the movement had long since been contained or dissipated.

However, for two or three years after the war the shop stewards' movement still retained considerable prestige within the engineering industry. Moreover, its influence spread throughout the trade union movement, as many groups of workers during 1919–1920 became involved in strike action and won significant concessions from the employers. After having successfully achieved a merger with the unofficial forces organised around the Amalgamation Committee Movement, the shop stewards then united with the miners' reform committees and the railwaymen's 'vigilance' committees at a conference organised by the NAC in Sheffield in April 1919 (to which Murphy contributed much of the preparatory work and drew up the proposals for discussion), and later the movement was extended to other industries. At the same time, the shop stewards began to see some of the fruits of their efforts. By the autumn of 1919 six of the skilled workers' unions, including the ASE, had merged into a new Amalgamated Engineering Union (AEU), and the issue of 'workers' control of industry' became generally accepted as the aim of most unions. The stewards also played a key role in ensuring the government's 1918 proposals for the establishment in each industry of permanent joint bodies of employers and union representatives (known as 'Whitley Councils'), aimed at countering the independent workshop committees, were met with considerable scepticism and had very little effect outside the sphere of government and municipal service. The most thorough critique of the Whitley Reports was to be found in Murphy's pamphlet *Compromise or Independence*, which was published by the Sheffield Workers' Committee and distributed across the country.[65] He later recalled:

> The essential difference between the Government's scheme and ours lay not in the formal structure but in its aim and content. It aimed at making capitalism work. We wanted to end capitalism. Its workshop committees were to be joint committees of employers and workmen. Ours were independent workers' committees against the employers.[66]

In conclusion, it is important to emphasise the significance of Murphy's contribution to the development of the shop stewards' movement. He helped make workshop organisation in Britain a reality for the first time on any large scale. He courageously and consistently fought for the unity of the working class under very difficult conditions, breaking down the barriers between skilled and unskilled, and fighting against every encroachment the war machine of British capitalism made in the workshops. Sheffield was probably the best organised district in the country, with a powerful Workers' Committee under Murphy's leadership. It provided a vivid example of how rank-and-file workers could create their own collective organisation, overcome the conservatism of the union leaders and act directly in their own interests against the employers. Moreover,

Murphy played a central role in shaping the fortunes of the national shop stewards' movement, a movement which at its height could count on the support of more than 300,000 workers.[67]

Of course, there were a number of other key stewards' leaders, including Willie Gallacher, Arthur MacManus, Jack Tanner and Harry Pollitt, all of whom were important agitators and organisers. But Murphy was unquestionably the shop stewards' movement's chief theorist, even if, during the war, it was mainly limited to organisational questions. Despite important limitations to Murphy's political outlook during this period, he made a significant contribution to the analysis of trade unionism and union bureaucracy, and to the development of revolutionary tactics on the shopfloor and within the unions, most notably through the theory of independent rank-and-file organisation. It was a formidable achievement for somebody who was aged only 29 at the end of the war. Moreover, immediately after the war and profoundly influenced by the impact of the Bolshevik Revolution in Russia, Murphy went on to play a central role in drawing out the full revolutionary implications of the Workers' Committees. In the process he made possible a complete transcendence of the limitations of syndicalism that would be crucially important to the postwar development of the revolutionary left in Britain.

Chapter Three

Towards Bolshevism, 1919–1920

After the war Murphy was only just able to survive on the meagre unemployment benefit he received by selling some furniture and books and with financial support from his mother. However, freed from the constraints of work, he was able to throw himself into full-time activity as chair of the Sheffield Workers' Committee and assistant secretary of the National Administrative Council of the SS&WCM. He also became active in the Sheffield branch of the Plebs League, which organised study classes among trade unionists, and gave two weekly Labour College lectures on Marxist economics and industrial history. In addition, after being elected an executive committee member of the Socialist Labour Party (SLP), he went on to play a central role in reshaping the party's policy and in conducting socialist unity negotiations with other revolutionary groups that eventually led to the formation of the British Communist Party.

Of major significance during this period of 1919–1920 was his political evolution from syndicalism to communism, as he combined his own wartime shop steward experiences with the events in Bolshevik Russia to develop a new form of revolutionary socialist politics. This involved three main features: an appreciation of the soviet as the chief agency of socialist revolution and the need for the working class to conquer state power; the central role of a vanguard political party; and the relationship between revolutionary socialists and the Labour Party. He also further developed his wartime analysis of the trade union bureaucracy.

THE THEORY OF SOVIET POWER

It was only after the war, in the context of the Russian revolution and revolutionary turmoil throughout Europe, including massive

54

labour unrest in Britain, that the full revolutionary implications of their own wartime practice of independent rank-and-file organisation came to be appreciated by Murphy and the others shop stewards' leaders.[1] Aided by theoretical developments within the SLP and the BSP, which their own practice helped to promote, the stewards' leaders initiated a new burst of theoretical activity during the autumn of 1918 which was to extend beyond the concept of rank-and-file independence to the idea of the seizure of state power by the Workers' Committees, which were now conceived of as embryonic 'soviets', the economic and political nucleus of a future workers' state similar to that which existed in Russia.

During the wartime industrial unrest the SLP had deviated from the rigidity of its 'dual unionist' views when several of its members on the Clyde became leading shop stewards, and Murphy had joined the SLP in Sheffield. The party's significance during this period was quite out of proportion to its small size (of about 1,250 members) and it was effectively the main political force within the shop stewards' movement, although the BSP also played an important role. Whilst the majority of the official leaders of the British labour movement had seen the October Revolution in Russia as a complete disaster, the SLP gave it their complete and unreserved blessing, seeing it as vindicating the policy and tactics of the party. The triumph of the Bolsheviks, combined with the rising industrial struggle in Britain, acted as a great stimulus to the growth of the SLP, BSP and other revolutionary socialist groups and to attempts to forge a common unity between the different organisations.

However, the more far-sighted of the SLP leaders realised it was not sufficient merely to applaud Russia from the sidelines; the whole basis of their socialist thinking needed to be re-examined if the lessons of the Bolshevik Revolution were to be successfully applied to Britain. The individuals who were most conscious of this need, Murphy, along with Arthur MacManus, Tom Bell and William Paul, came to the forefront towards the end of 1918. These four men, who would later become powerful figures in the Communist Party during its early years, set about reshaping the policy of the SLP. As Murphy later explained:

> When I became friends with Mac and Bell [Arthur MacManus and Tom Bell] and Mac persuaded me to join the SLP, reminding me that Connolly was its first chairman, I made it perfectly clear that I did not subscribe to the pure De Leonist IWW conception of Industrial

Unionism then prevalent in the SLP, but they were as ready as I to re-draft the constitution ... I was responsible for [redrafting the section] which referred to our industrial unionism in practice.[2]

Murphy and his comrades tried to bring traditional SLP theory, a mixture of Marx, De Leon and Connolly, into harmony with the experience of the Russian revolution and the shop stewards' movement in Britain. At the beginning of 1919 they published their *Plea for the Reconsideration of Socialist Tactics and Organisation*, which represented a major breach with past SLP ideas.[3] It committed the party to adherence to soviets and the dictatorship of the proletariat; to parliamentarianism only as a means for agitation to develop revolutionary consciousness; for mass action culminating in open revolutionary struggle for power; for working within the trade unions to challenge the union bureaucracy by means of creating extra-union organisations such as shop stewards and Workers' Committees; and to denunciation of the Labour Party as a hope-lessly reformist body. This programme was adopted as the basis for a new party constitution by a special SLP conference held on 11–12 January 1919, and was sent to both the BSP and the Independent Labour Party (ILP) with the proposal that it should serve as the basis for a merger between the different socialist organisations.

The most important aspect of Murphy's and his co-thinkers' ideological achievement at this point was to substitute the local soviet representative of all industries for the national Industrial Union as the basic unit of working-class political power.[4] Pre-viously, as we have seen, Murphy had envisaged a national In-dustrial Union enabling the working class to break through the shell of the capitalist political state and usher in an entirely new social and industrial order. Before the war he thought such an Industrial Union would emerge through amalgamation of existing unions, during the war that it would be built out of the Shop Stewards' and Workers' Committee Movement. In contrast, he now found in the local Workers' Committees the embryonic form of a proletarian state power, of the organisation of the workers as 'the ruling class'. 'The striking masses have spontaneously created the Workers' Committees, the basis of a workers' state', declared *The Socialist* at the end of January 1919: 'These committees representing every department in every mine, mill, railway, or plant, contain the elements of an organisation which can transform capitalism into a Soviet Republic ... All Power to the Workers' Committees'.[5]

The enthusiasm with which Murphy and his SLP comrades took up and developed the idea of soviet power was to be explained not only by understandable enthusiasm over the Russian revolution, but also by the fact that it was the logical development of the theoretical position already reached as a result of their own wartime practice of independent rank-and-file organisation. Indeed, Murphy saw a direct parallel between the Workers' Committees and the Russian soviets. If, at first, he explained, 'we knew next to nothing about how the Workers' and Soldiers' Committees were constructed, and had the vaguest ideas as to the conditions in which they could and should be formed',[6] by the end of the war the experience of the Russian revolution, relayed through the SLP paper *The Socialist*, had gone some way to familiarising him with the idea of soviet power. As he wrote years later:

> To me and many others, the shop steward movement assumed a new significance in the light of what we now learned of the structure of the soviets and the part the Russian workshop committees were being called upon to play in the control of production. The ideas I had outlined in connection with the development of the workshop committees, the demands we had made for the workers in industry, all appeared to me at that time to be the foreshadowings of the fuller structure which came into being with the revolutionary changes inherent in the crisis we saw ahead.[7]

Again, in a letter written towards the end of his life Murphy recalled:

> After the Russian revolution in 1917 we of the SLP thought there was considerable similarity between our conception of Workers' Committees composed of shop delegates and the soviets and saw in them the means to mass revolutionary action and these committees as the forerunners of British soviets.[8]

Murphy and the other SLP shop stewards formulated a 14-point party programme for the December 1918 general election in which Murphy, MacManus and Paul stood as SLP parliamentary candidates. In addition to championing the Russian revolution, their election platform called for the formation of Workers' and Soldiers' Councils in Britain and the taking over of the means of production as 'the communal property of the people' by transferring power from Parliament to a 'Federal Congress of People's Councils'.[9] Murphy stood in the Gorton constituency of Manchester against John Hodges, the Labour Minister of Pensions in the coalition government, with George Peet, national secretary of the shop stewards' movement, acting as his election agent. Seeking election to parliament only as a means of providing a platform for socialist agitation, he received 1,300 votes.[10] *The Socialist* made Murphy's position quite clear: 'We are denounced as "British Bolsheviks". We do not seek to conceal our views. We are proud of the title. The SLP is the only political organisation that stands wholeheartedly and uncompromisingly for the Soviet idea. Let it be known. We are the British Bolsheviks',[11] although in fact, other revolutionary groups, including the BSP, also began to uphold the soviet as the agency of social revolution.[12]

It is important to appreciate the context in which Murphy's political ideas were developed. The Russian revolution had lit a flame which flared all over Europe, with revolutions in Germany, Austria and Hungary. Britain in 1919–1920 was part of this rising revolutionary wave.[13] As the First World War had come to its bitter end the belief that past conditions could no longer be tolerated had become widespread. Prime Minister Lloyd George's promise of a 'land fit for heroes' evaporated fast in the aftermath of a general election which had returned a reactionary government bent on thwarting the aspirations of the masses for genuine peace and reconstruction. The period immediately following the end of the First World War was one of economic upturn, of sharply rising prices and wages and of a rapid increase in trade union and Labour Party membership. In these boom years which lasted until the end of 1920, the working class was on the offensive against the employers.[14] At the beginning of this period the struggle centred mainly around the question of hours of work. In almost every trade, the unions demanded the eight-hour day or the 48-hour week, and in most organised industries these demands were won during the first part of 1919. Strike days, having averaged 4.5 million a year during the war, soared to 34.5 million in 1919.

In January 1919, Glasgow and Belfast were brought to a standstill by general strikes for a shorter working week, although neither strike was supported by the national union leaders who were able to isolate both struggles. Meanwhile, in the coalfields agitation for a reduction in hours, an increase in wages and the nationalisation of the mines under some form of workers' control, produced a six to one vote for strike action. A pre-war agreement for joint action made between the leaders of the miners, transport and railway unions, known as the 'Triple Alliance', was revived.

Formed on the initiative of the Miners' Federation, under pressure from their rank-and-file militants, it promised to be a powerful alliance for mutual aid. With a desperate coal shortage, and with the other unions of the Triple Alliance themselves negotiating for demands similar to the miners, the government faced the prospect of a general strike with revolutionary potential. But Lloyd George managed to stave off this threat, on the one hand making it clear troops would be used against the miners, on the other by appointing a Royal Commission (the Sankey Commission) to investigate the situation in mining. The Miners' Federation leaders postponed strike action, thereby giving the ruling class the breathing space it needed. Although the miners obtained the seven-hour day and some wage increases, by the summer the government felt strong enough to reject the Commission's recommendation for nationalisation.

Meanwhile, having successfully prevented the railwaymen's claim against wage cuts coming to a head simultaneously with the miners', by a policy of deliberately dragging out negotiations, the government provoked a strike at the end of September when it thought itself most likely to win. The railwaymen's union leader Jimmy Thomas did his best to cool the situation by refusing to call for solidarity action by other members of the Triple Alliance, but the strike remained absolutely solid and the government, which had miscalculated, was forced to concede defeat after ten days. Mutinies in the army and a strike by the police in London and Liverpool rounded off the year.

The working class movement continued to be on the offensive through into 1920. In the summer, widespread sympathy for the Russian revolution led to a 'Hands Off Russia' movement pledged to prevent intervention by allied troops against the Red Army in Poland, with London dockers refusing to permit the *S.S. Jolly George* to sail with munitions for use against Russia. After some 350 Councils of Action had been formed across the country pledged to organise direct action, if necessary, against any further British attacks on the Russian revolution, a conference of trade union executives was forced to threaten a general strike if this occurred. Meanwhile, the industrial struggle also continued. In October the miners put in a further demand for wage increases and called upon the other members of the Triple Alliance to back them up. But the government's policy of using concessions to enable it to take on one section of workers at a time had its effect, as the leaders of the other unions rejected the miners' call (although a ballot of railwaymen showed a considerable majority for strike action). After a few days' strike action by themselves, the miners settled for a compromise which gave them a temporary wage increase.

However, although it was not apparent at the time, by the summer of 1920 the economic boom had broken and the semi-revolutionary challenge posed by the working-class movement in Britain had been exhausted. Although concessions had been forced out of the employers in industry after industry, in the absence of any powerful co-ordinated alternative political leadership to that of the trade union and Labour Party leaders, the ruling class had survived one of the most trying periods in its history with its power intact. And within a year the employers were able to launch a counter-offensive against the workers' gains on a terrain of their own choosing (see Chapter Four). Nonetheless, for Murphy, the period of 1919–1920 was 'a year of conferences, meetings, agitation and propaganda in the midst of a developing storm of disputes'.[15] He recalled:

> It was an intoxicating period for those who, such as myself, had become absorbed by the question of the workers' revolution. It appeared to us that events were sweeping us forward to that goal at a tremendous speed. All around us capitalism appeared to be on the retreat before the advancing workers. Now it seemed clear that the Russian revolution was no mere national event peculiar to Russia, but was the beginning of the World Revolution. Had it not already swept Germany into the throes of revolution? Were not thrones tumbling down and crowns rolling in the dust? Was not this tremendous wave of mass action in Britain but the prelude to revolutionary storms that would grow in force and power?[16]

In anticipation of such revolutionary storms, Murphy warned of the dangers of the trade union bureaucracy who were attempting to defuse workers' militancy.

THE TRADE UNION BUREAUCRACY

During 1919 some national trade union leaders, riding the massive wave of rank-and-file militancy in a number of industries, moved significantly to the left. Faced with the impotence of the parliamentary Labour Party, they began to talk the language of 'Direct Action', of the political general strike to force parliament to respond to the workers' demands. Thus, several unions threatened to take

Direct Action to enforce the nationalisation of the mines, the ending of conscription and the withdrawal of troops from Russia and Ireland. The formation of the 'Triple Alliance' and the replacement of the old ineffective Trades Union Congress (TUC) Parliamentary Committee by a General Council were seen by many union militants as the potential leaders of the political general strike and the final confrontation with the power of capital when such a mass struggle materialised. In the event, although formed in response to militant rank-and-file demands for greater unity in action, the Triple Alliance was dominated from its foundation by the union bureaucracy's desire to contain rather than to lead militancy, and, where this was not possible, to keep industrial disputes within the bounds of trade union sectionalism rather than broaden the struggle to challenge the state.[17]

Whilst Murphy and the other stewards appreciated the revolutionary possibilities of the political strike, they approached the rhetoric of 'Direct Action' with caution, developing a clear analysis of the inadequacy of left-wing union officials as leaders of a potentially revolutionary situation.[18] Thus, amplifying on his wartime analysis of the union bureaucracy, Murphy warned about the dangers of the growing centralisation of power in the hands of the union bureaucracy:

> One of the most dangerous developments in the industrial organisations of the working class demanding the serious attention of every worker and student, is the growth of an official class with its own vested interests and an excessive control over all the movements of the workers. Centralisation is proceeding apace, and as it does so the officials fasten themselves in office for longer and longer periods, and become the veritable rulers of the organisations. Centralisation is not necessarily bad: but centralisation which takes away all power of initiative, turns the rank and file of a movement into sheep-like beings devoid of individuality, and makes them blind worshippers of their rulers is a vicious development which must be checked.[19]

At the same time, Murphy warned about the illusion that the formation of a TUC General Council could succeed where the Triple Alliance had already failed:

> The call comes for a General Staff for the labour hosts [the General Council], and again the principal thought impressed is conservative and reactionary. The General Staff of officialdom is to be a dam to the surging tide of independent working class aspirations and not a directing agency towards the overthrow of capitalism.[20]

The clarity of Murphy's identification of the limitations of a 'general staff of labour' from above rested upon his understanding of the inevitable ambivalence of the trade union bureaucracy. The formation of a conservative labour bureaucracy is inherent in the very nature of trade unionism under capitalism. Because trade union struggle is concerned with improving the terms on which workers are exploited, not with ending that exploitation, a division of labour naturally emerges between the mass of workers and a layer of full-time union officials, with the latter seeing their role as being to negotiate the compromises between labour and capital within the limits of capitalist society. The officials become reluctant to use the weapons of economic class struggle for fear of disrupting their relations with the employers. So again and again they intervene to prevent those struggles from getting out of control and end them on terms which fall short of their members' aspirations. This in turn can create a conflict of interest with rank-and-file workers who have an interest in reducing, and ultimately abolishing their exploitation by employers. The outcome can be rank-and-file organisations which fight independently of the officials.[21]

The pre-war syndicalist tradition had acknowledged the conservative and bureaucratic nature of union officials, but in urging the possibility of reconstituting the unions within capitalism as the chief agencies of a socialist revolution, had failed to grasp the true nature of the trade union bureaucracy. Murphy, building on *The Workers' Committee*, now developed a much more sophisticated analysis of union officialdom. First, he explained that centralised collective bargaining under capitalism necessarily involved the creation of a 'big specialised official army' who, because of the need to strike bargains, take on certain disciplinary functions over their members on behalf of the employers and tend 'to run the organisation in oligarchical or caucus fashion' detached from democratic control.[22] Second, collective bargaining tends to produce a leadership incapable of seeing beyond compromise with capitalism:

> When it is remembered that Trade Unions are limited, constitutionally, to narrow channels of activity, and that officialdom is a product of this limited activity, it is only to be expected that the official leaders are essentially conservative in outlook and action. Today they have a nineteenth century psychology with which to face twentieth century problems. We have entered an era of revolution, demanding revolutionary leadership: we get in response pathetic appeals to do nothing

which will disturb the equilibrium of the existing order. Issues are confined to narrow channels. Sectionalism becomes a virtue to them and class action a dreadful nightmare. The unity we have appealed for becomes a unity to stop action by the mass rather than a unity which shall lead them to victory.[23]

Because their whole function was to negotiate, the trade union official comes to see collective bargaining procedures not as a temporary truce but as a permanent peace with capitalism: 'The whole machinery of the trade unions is constitutionally directed into channels of adaptation ... to the capitalist system'.[24]

Trade unions ... are organised bodies for the modification of the existing system, accepting the capitalist idea of society. They simply bolster up or modify part of the capitalist system itself...

I do not mean for a moment that these organisations will not play a part in the destruction of capitalism, but the revolutionist does recognise the limited part which they will play ... performing what I would call a conservative function, continually modifying the outlook of the workers by their limited scope.[25]

From this argument it followed that the only way to finally defeat the bureaucratic and collaborationist tendency of trade unionism was to overthrow capitalism. Of course, in a period of revolutionary upheaval, it might be possible for the workers to replace collaborationist leadership with revolutionaries and to re-mould the structure of the unions on industrial lines. However, unless the revolution was successfully carried through, the same tendency to bureaucracy and collaboration would rapidly assert itself amongst the new leadership. Thus, Murphy acknowledged that even the achievement of Industrial Unionism and the replacement of the branch by the workshop as the basis of the union could not ensure democratic control over the officials. Independent rank-and-file organisation, not the reconstruction of trade unionism as a whole, was the key to working-class advance, with the perfection of Industrial Unionist structures probably proving to be a post-revolutionary task.

THE STRUGGLE FOR POWER

Significantly, during the war, independent rank-and-file organisation had been developed primarily as a counter to the bureaucratic and collaborationist tendencies characteristic of trade unionism within capitalism, with no *immediate* revolutionary intent. But in the context of the revolutionary optimism of 1919, the larger implications of wartime practice came to be understood. Increasingly the purpose of the Workers' Committees was seen as independent *revolutionary* action, not the organisation of a strike for immediate demands, but the transformation of a strike into the final struggle for power. In the aftermath of the national railway strike of October 1919, Murphy and the other stewards' leaders came to believe that any large strike would take on the character of a confrontation between the working class and the state, a confrontation which could only be resolved either by the complete defeat of the unions or by revolution:

> Every strike of recent history has re-emphasised the futility of sectional strikes even when on so large a scale as the railway strike. Every strike now becomes a definite challenge to all the forces of the Government, and to attempt to fight these forces with anything less than all the forces of the organised working class is to deliberately place ourselves at a disadvantage. To accept the challenge of the governing class is to accept the responsibility to take out of the hands of the capitalist class its power to rule over us. These are the issues officialdom is shirking. These are the issues we must be courageous enough and audacious enough to tackle.[26]

Thus, it became necessary for the movement to be ready to try to convert any passing opportunity into a revolutionary situation. This required more centralised leadership than had seemed necessary or desirable in the less cataclysmic struggles of wartime, with more attention to forging an alliance with revolutionary elements in the mines, railways and other industries, and the construction of a working-class alliance from below, superior to the top-heavy Triple Alliance. Above all, the function of the Workers' Committees was redefined as involving not only the leadership of strike action but also its direct development into the revolutionary seizure of state power. By the end of 1919 Murphy was describing how soviet institutions capable of taking control over society would come into being:

> For example, suppose in a town like Coventry, Sheffield or Manchester ... to the there are masses of workers who want to solve a particular problem, and in the course of development you have a negative action, the stoppage of production. The issue changes, and a general strike committee is formed, not particularly dominated by the trade union

outlook, but by the psychology of the situation, and the fact that all are working with one particular object in view. Yet the objective becomes subordinate to the demand to satisfy their immediate wants, as we saw was the case in Limerick and Belfast. What is the demand? First of all probably, for light for hospitals. What happens then? At once the strike committee has to take upon itself positive functions; it sends men back to the electricity stations for the production of electricity, and it may send others to work too. They thus take upon themselves positive functions, and in doing so they immediately step into the arena of the control of industry and of distribution. The longer they are on strike the more insistent becomes the demand for food. We are faced with another problem and have to find the solution to it. Where are the bakers? Are they with us? Can we control them? Can the bakers provide sufficient food for the needs of the people? Again the strike committee has to function, and it becomes a positive work to control the millers to mill the flour and the bakers to bake the bread, and so right in the centre you have a strike committee as a committee controlling industry in various directions. Such a situation is, obviously, revolutionary, and may lead to complete revolution, and therefore I say that these are the particular elements which point to the development of the new industrial system during a revolutionary crisis, and at the same time make clear the limitations of trade unions as such.[27]

Murphy also rejected his previous notion that workers' control could be achieved by 'encroaching control' in the workshops and the piecemeal supersession of capitalist power. He now understood that there could be no peaceful and gradual evolution from capitalism to the new social system. The establishment of workers' control would involve a revolutionary struggle for the conquest of state power. This commitment to the notion of soviet power was reflected in the resolutions passed at the national shop stewards' conference called in January 1920 and attended by 63 delegates claiming to represent 77,000 workers. The conference was asked by the chair, MacManus, to look on the Workers' Committees as the equivalent of Russian soviets, as instruments for the overthrow of capitalism and the building of socialism. 'It required a revolution in Russia', he said, 'to unseat the capitalist from the saddle and it will require one in this country to accomplish the same task'.[28] The conference called on trade unionists to instruct their delegates to the next TUC Congress to demand a general strike against intervention in Russia, to affiliate to the Third (Communist) International, and to be represented at its Second World Congress in Moscow. It elected Murphy, along with Ramsey, Gallacher and Tanner, as their delegates.

Thus, the essential contribution of Murphy and the shop stewards' leaders to the ideological development of the revolutionary left during 1919 was that, in going beyond the purely propagandist activities of the syndicalists within the existing unions, while yet rejecting the attempt to establish rival Industrial Unions to take over the essential functions of trade unionism within capitalism, they laid the foundations for the replacement of the syndicalist by the soviet idea of revolution. While syndicalists continued to exaggerate the revolutionary possibilities of the left trade union bureacracy and industrial unionism, Murphy pointed out that however 'reconstructed', the trade unions and their leaders must continue to operate as the machinery of compromise with capital until the revolution was accomplished. At the same time, the identification of the Workers' Committees as the agency of working-class power also marked a decisive break with Labour Party notions that political change could occur through parliament.[29]

However, from the outset Murphy and the shop stewards' development of the theory of soviet power had rested upon an objective contradiction. It was the intensified industrial struggle of 1919 which, together with the international revolutionary crisis centred in Russia, had inspired them and their allies in the SLP and BSP to explore theoretically the revolutionary implications of the practice of the Workers' Committees. At the same time, however, the revolutionary optimism on which this exercise rested was being undermined by the collapse of the shop stewards' power within the engineering workshops. No struggle for soviet power was actually launched in Britain. The Workers' Committees only came to be defined in terms of such a struggle after they had been defeated as a mass force. Having no equivalent influence among the miners or railway workers who now led the industrial struggle, the shop stewards' theoretical advances of 1919 appeared not as an organic reflection of the immediate needs of the struggle but as a commentary from the sidelines. It is in this context of defeat that the political development of the rank-and-file movement after the war must be understood. Nonetheless, the experience of the Workers' Committees, which Murphy so eloquently theorised, was to be crucially important to the postwar development of the revolutionary left in Britain.

UNITY AND FRACTURE OF THE LEFT

Although Murphy had come to recognise the political potential of rank-and-file organisation, with Workers' Committees as embryonic soviets, he was not as quick to draw another lesson from the Russian revolution. The soviets had come to power under the leadership of the Bolshevik Party. Murphy did not appreciate how a revolutionary socialist party acted to overcome the divisions inside the working class, linking together different struggles and focusing them on the battle, not simply with individual employers, but with the capitalist state itself. As a member of the syndicalist SLP, he retained his view of socialist parties as essentially a propaganda outlet for purely industrial activity. It was the launch of the Communist International (or Comintern) in Moscow in March 1919 and the Bolsheviks' subsequent attempt to advise and assist revolutionaries worldwide which would be instrumental in bringing together the various groupings of the British revolutionary left and the leaders of the SS&WCM to form the Communist Party of Great Britain on the Bolshevik model.

Immediately after the launch of the Comintern, Bell and Mac-Manus were contacted by the Russian Communist Party and urged to organise all the separate British revolutionary socialist groups supporting the new Soviet state into a single party that could become a component of the new International.[30] Acting on this initiative, and in the wake of the January 1919 SLP conference endorsing the party's change of policy, Murphy, along with Mac-Manus, Bell and Paul, were appointed to a 'Unity Committee'. They were empowered to act on the SLP's behalf to pursue unity talks with the British Socialist Party (BSP), Independent Labour Party (ILP), Workers' Socialist Federation (WSF), and the South Wales Socialist Society (SWSS). Unity negotiations between the different groups took place throughout 1919, although the ILP soon withdrew. But it became clear that the old sectarian traditions of the separate revolutionary groups could not readily be overcome. The key issues dominating the debate were the importance to be attached to parliamentary activity and whether the new Communist Party should affiliate to the Labour Party.

Following the February 1917 Russian revolution, the Labour Party leaders had broken from the coalition government in order to demonstrate their own independence and to harness and ride out the growing socialist and anti-war feeling. They established a quasi-independent platform of 'democratic' war aims, hoping to rally pro-war reformists in Britain and among the allied powers and to express solidarity with the efforts of the Menshevik government to keep Russian workers and peasants in the war. But the October Revolution scuttled such schemes and showed a direct way of ending Russian involvement in the war: revolutionary defeatism. It also showed a way to socialism which was not through parliament but through the conquest of political power by workers overthrowing the capitalist state and taking full control over society themselves, a prospect which alarmed Labour Party leaders as much as it did the British ruling class. Their answer was crude denunciations of 'Bolshevik dictatorship' combined with a calculated attempt to hold back the militancy of British workers and divert it into parliamentary channels.

To do this Labour attempted to cultivate a 'left' image, and in 1918 adopted the now famous Clause Four into its constitution, committing the party to common ownership of the means of production, distribution and exchange. At the same time a reorganisation of the party created local Labour parties and a system of individual membership to complement the system of affiliated bodies that had operated hitherto. But Labour's apparent conversion to 'socialism' had little to do with activity outside the House of Commons but instead was designed to channel workers' energy into ordered social change through constitutional means. As Labour leader Arthur Henderson wrote: 'One good reason for beginning now to build up a strong democratic party in Parliament, with a programme of social and economic reforms carefully thought out [is] to prove that political methods are effective ... The Labour Party can rehabilitate Parliament in the eyes of the people'.[31] It marked the reconstruction of the Labour Party into a mass reformist party, which would in time be in a position to challenge for government office.[32]

The 1918 reorganisation led many Marxists to look anew at the Labour Party, some seeing it as a potential means for achieving radical social change, others as an out-and-out reformist body that had to be denounced. Lenin had already made it clear to British revolutionaries that whilst he was in favour of participation in parliamentary elections and for affiliation to the Labour Party, disagreement with his views should not delay the establishment of the Communist Party in Britain. But events were to prove much more complicated. The Comintern's main agent in Britain, Theodore Rothstein, played an influential role encouraging the left to see the BSP as forming the nucleus of the Communist Party, with other groups playing a subordinate role and merging with it.[33] The largest of the Marxist groups (with about 6,000 members), the BSP had undergone considerable change during the war years: its chauvinist policy had been overthown in favour of a pacifist position; it gave complete endorsement to the October Revolution; and there was the rise to prominence of that section of the membership who actively participated in the shop stewards' movement, including Willie Gallacher of the Clyde Workers Committee. But, as far as Murphy and the SLP were concerned, the BSP's commitment to parliament and its continuing affiliation to the Labour Party, loyally working within it and striving to push it in a leftward direction, were signs of the BSP's essentially left reformist outlook.

They pointed out that because the BSP aimed to gain the trade union block vote at Labour conferences, it was reluctant to criticise union bureaucrats who uttered left phrases but failed to match their words with deeds. Not wishing to antagonise the union leaders, the BSP was not officially in favour of building rank-and-file organisations within industry to challenge the union bureaucracy, something which for the SLP was a vital part of the struggle. As a consequence, the SLP believed the BSP had to be purged of its reformist notions before there could be any real revolutionary unity between itself and the other groups, and their opposition to the BSP had its counterparts in the leadership of the shop stewards' movement, the WSF and the SWSS. Nonetheless, recognising the urgent need for the revolutionary groups to forge closer links, Murphy wrote 'An Open Letter to Socialists' appealing for unity:

> It is true that during the last six months strenuous efforts have been made, sometimes locally, sometimes nationally, to obtain socialist unity, and it is true that most of these efforts have failed to arrive at their objective ... I write this open letter to you in the hope that some effort will immediately follow to remedy this state of affairs.
>
> A review of the position of the various parties will reveal that whatever the factors that prevent a fusion of forces, there is a great percentage of the members of every party who agree that the soviet ... is the only alternative to Parliament ... The main squabble turns on Parliamentarianism. The SLP believes in the use of elections for the creation of the revolutionary spirit, and even in getting members to Parliament for the

purpose of revolutionary Parliamentary activity. The BSP and ILP subscribe to Parliamentarianism of the reformist brand to legislate us by ameliorative legislation to socialism. Whatever the virtues of any of these tactics may be, the fact remains that so far as the objective is concerned ... there is a large measure of agreement. It may not be possible to get a complete fusion of all these forces into one party, but I do suggest, in view of the immense amount of propaganda that has to be done relating to the points on which we all agree, in view of the overwhelming importance of the building of the organisation which alone can effect and maintain a social revolution, that there can be a fusion to the degree to which we are in agreement and a retention of identity and independent action on those matters where there is disagreement. The situation demands a degree of tolerance amongst socialists on points of disagreement for the sake of the mightier things on which they do agree. Is it too much to ask in times like these? I think not.[34]

In June 1919 it seemed a basis for unity had been found when a joint meeting of the executive committees of the BSP, SLP, WSF and SWSS decided to consult their respective members on the question of merging the four organisations into a united Communist Party, committed to the soviet system of government and the dictatorship of the proletariat. On the vexed tactical question of affiliation to the Labour Party, it was agreed to recommend this should be decided by a referendum of the membership of the new party three months after its formation. This compromise proposal, put forward by Bell on behalf of the SLP delegates,[35] seemed to open the way to the formation of a united Communist Party embracing the main socialist groups to the left of the ILP. But before the unity negotiations could be reopened, internal troubles developed in the SLP when a new national executive committee was elected on which the 'unity' supporters found themselves in a minority. The new executive voted by a small majority to reject the compromise terms on Labour Party affiliation that had been agreed by Murphy, MacManus, Bell and Paul, and to dissolve the Unity Committee. They then proceeded to carry out a referendum of party members, organised in such a way that it inevitably produced a majority *for* merger of the left groups but *against* Labour Party affiliation. Given that affiliation had been a condition of BSP participation, the SLP now effectively decided to take no further part in the unity proceedings.

Despite this setback, Murphy, MacManus and Bell decided to proceed with the negotiations and they attended the BSP confer-

ence in January 1920 in a personal capacity. In an attempt to placate
the delegates they explained: 'they came unofficially, as a guarantee
of their personal good faith towards the representatives of the other
bodies. They were keenly regretful of the hitch that had arisen.
They did not accept the view that the vote of the SLP was adverse
to unity, and would use every effort to induce the SLP to fall into
line'.[36] But their attendance at the conference only further an-
tagonised the official, and uncompromising, new leadership of
the SLP. Thus, by the end of January 1920, the unity proposals
agreed on the initiative of the Comintern had still not come to
fruition.

They were further delayed following the decisions of a conference convened by the Comintern's West European sub-bureau in
Amsterdam, which was controlled by S. J. Rutgers and other
members of the ultra-left Dutch Communist Party.[37] The English
delegation to the conference comprised two BSP delegates, Pankhurst from the WSF, and Murphy, who had stopped over en route
to the forthcoming Second Comintern Congress in Moscow,
officially representing the shop stewards' movement but also unofficially representing the SLP. The chief resolutions agreed were
hostile both to participation in parliamentary activity and to work
inside the existing trade unions; the conference issued an appeal,
against the wishes of the BSP delegates, for British revolutionary
left groups to unite on the basis of 'no affiliation to the Labour
Party' and 'rigorous separation of the Communists from the social
patriots'.[38] Surprisingly, it seems that Murphy, presumably influenced by the ultra-left milieu in which he found himself, became
convinced of the need to abandon his previous support for unity
talks with the BSP. It is likely that when he heard news of the
attempt, in his absence and without his approval, by MacManus,
Bell and Paul to organise themselves into an unofficial 'Communist
Unity Group' with the aim of splitting the SLP and taking the
majority of members with them into a new united organisation with
the BSP, it only encouraged his fears that the tiny revolutionary
elements within the SLP would be swamped within a new reformist
BSP-dominated party.

After the Amsterdam conference, Murphy travelled illegally and
at great personal risk to Berlin with the professional Bolshevik
revolutionary Mikhail Borodin. He found the German capital
totally paralysed by a general strike in response to the Kapp

Putsch, an attempt by a Prussian general to overthrow the newly formed democratic (Weimar) republic set up in the wake of the German revolution. After proceeding to Hamburg with the American communist Louis Fraina, Murphy wrote a series of letters to *The Socialist* expressing his support for the uncompromising position being taken by the new SLP executive towards the BSP.[39] The most important of these letters, 'The SLP and Unity: An Open Letter to the Party', written on 20 April 1920, was published in *The Socialist* on the 6th May.[40] In it Murphy contemptuously dismissed the BSP's latest call for all trade unions to strike together to overthrow capitalism.

> It implies that the overthrow of capitalism can be attained by the general strike alone, a further proposition repudiated in history. No finer example of a general strike can be cited than the recent strike in Berlin. But it did not achieve the social revolution. More than a strike was required—real communist leadership, the seizure of arms, an open united military struggle for power. The repeated limitation of mass action to direct action (a syndicalist limitation) by the BSP is either an indication of lack of insight into the needs of revolution or moral cowardice expressing itself in a fear of an open declaration that revolution cannot be carried through without a resort to arms.

In the same article Murphy outlined the fundamental differences he saw between the two parties:

> It should be observed that the Russian revolution has affected the SLP and BSP differently. The Communist programme of the Third International partly accepts and partly supplements the principles and programme the SLP has fought for since its inception. Its uncompromising waging of the class war, its advocacy of industrial unionism, and its insistence on the impossibility of using the parliamentary state to accomplish the revolution, and the realisation of the need for an intermediate Soviet state with the dictatorship of the proletariat. This is a development of first principles. The BSP, on the other hand, in adherence formally to the Communist International, has had to reverse its former policy. Trailing with all the traditions of the SDF [Social Democractic Federation—forerunner of the BSP], its opposition to industrial unionism, its reformist parliamentarianism, it has had to pass through a process, and it has still to pass through a further process of internal change.

In Murphy's opinion, whilst the BSP gave formal adherence to the Communist International, it remained, in essence, true to its reformist spirit: 'There must be no compromise with the BSP. Better a Communist Party without the BSP than a party with the

BSP trailing with it in a spirit of compromise to hamper the party or its revolutionary character.[41]

He then provided the most cogent and powerfully argued case against the tactic of the new Communist Party attempting to seek affiliation to the Labour Party. His arguments against affiliation, which were later elaborated in a lengthy assessment of the state of the British left which he sent to the Comintern in Moscow in preparation for the forthcoming Second Congress,[42] are worth examining in some detail, particularly in the light of Murphy's subsequent, constantly changing, attitude towards the Labour Party.

1. The advocates of affiliation argued that the Labour Party represented the organised working class and that it was essential for the Communist Party to be within the Labour Party to maintain contact with the mass of workers. Murphy replied:

> The Labour Party is not the working class *organised as a class*, but the political reflection of the trade union bureaucracy and the petty bourgeois. Contact with the working class is not, and never has been, dependent upon contact with the Labour Party.

2. Supporters of affiliation argued that the organisational structure of the Labour Party differed from that of other social democratic parties and thereby permitted Communist Party affiliation. Murphy insisted that the only difference was that the Labour Party contained a more federalist structure and that federalism was anathema to communist principles.

3. It was suggested that affiliation to the Labour Party was analogous to the Bolsheviks being in the soviets when they had been dominated by the Mensheviks. Murphy replied:

> In no sense is there a parallel in the two situations. The soviets are the instruments of revolution, the future governmental machinery of the proletariat. The Labour Party is a parliamentary body, an instrument of reaction, a body to be destroyed. The soviets were created in the heat of revolutionary struggle. The Labour Party is a product of counter-revolutionary conciliation with capitalism.

4. Supporters of affiliation thought belonging to the Labour Party would provide the Communist Party with a public platform. Murphy countered:

> The workers are always accessible in the workshops, the streets, the unions, and the creation of an independent communist platform is better than going hand in hand to the Labour Party for a hearing.

5. It was argued affiliation would provide the Communist Party with an opportunity to influence the Labour Party through participation in its annual conferences and by getting socialist resolutions passed. Murphy answered:

> This implies that the Communist Party is either intent on capturing the Labour Party or passing revolutionary resolutions to carry out. If the first, the policy is fundamentally wrong because the Labour Party, in composition and form, is not a revolutionary organisation; its members are neither communists nor revolutionaries, and it is structurally incapable of mobilising the masses for revolutionary action. It is a product of capitalism, and is to be used only for the maintenance of capitalism. If the second, then the masses are betrayed and their revolutionary fervour used to strengthen the forces of reaction. This proposition also indicates that the BSP does not clearly understand the functions of a Communist Party in the struggle for power. It is evidently content to be a spur to another party for whose actions it refuses responsibility instead of being a strong revolutionary party leading the masses into action.

6. Another argument used by those favouring affiliation was that Trades and Labour Councils constituted the nuclei of soviets. Murphy denied this:

> The Trades Councils are not the nuclei of Soviets. Their ineptitude in industrial disputes provides ample proof of this. They possess no executive power over the unions and action comes either through delegates from the workshops, etc, or the local district committees of the unions, which improvise strike committees composed of stewards and district committees, leaving the Trades Councils in the background or playing a reactionary part. It is in such a manner that the Soviets will be formed and not through Trades Councils as suggested.

. To the argument that affiliation might provide a chance for electing communist MPs on the Labour Party ticket, Murphy retorted:

> This is sheer parliamentary vote-catching opportunism and a repudiation of independent political action. It is also confusing the masses. The Communist Party must go into elections not on vote-catching excursions, but for revolutionary agitation and to familiarise the masses with itself as the Party of Revolution.

8. Affiliation to the Labour Party, some argued, might lead to the overthrow of its leader Ramsay MacDonald. Murphy's answer was that, even if true, this was irrelevant. Given conditions inside the Labour Party, even if MacDonald were overthrown another

MacDonald would arise and take his place. The task was to destroy the Labour Party, not to capture it.

9. Those supporting affiliation contended that it would not involve accepting Labour Party policy. Murphy replied:

> This is an argument of political tricksters. The masses do not follow the winding paths of politicians and are confused by such practices. The masses reason more simply, and think that those in the Labour Party are of the Labour Party and responsible for its deeds. The Communist Party can best make its antagonism to the policy of the Labour Party clear to the masses by being neither in it or of it.

10. Finally, by way of justification, it was argued that affiliation would only be temporary, because when the Labour Party gained power, the Communist Party would have to separate. Murphy argued:

> This acknowledgement indicates that there is a fundamental antagonism between Communism and the Labour Party policy and programme, otherwise there would be no reason to part company at such a moment. Such a policy is not only confusing, but it weakens the confidence of the masses by encouraging hopes that cannot be realised. It is far better to make clear the antagonism now and build the Communist Party strong and independent, so that, instead of having to explain to the masses why the party retired at such a moment, it can proceed with revolutionary vigour and confidence to attack the Capitalist-cum-Labour Government as it attacked its predecessors.

Clearly, Murphy's 'Open Letter' was designed to stymie further unity talks between the SLP and BSP in the belief that revolutionary principles had to be maintained from reformist dilution, even if the price of this was a considerable reduction in the potential members of the new Communist Party. As he acknowledged in a letter to S. J. Rutgers: 'I expect it will cause a row in the BSP'.[43] The problem with Murphy's analysis was that it assumed the Labour Party was simply 'an instrument of reaction'. This meant he denied its reformist role, the fact that whilst the Labour Party defended the interests of capitalism it was also the central political focus for the majority of workers and therefore obliged to sometimes channel protest against capitalism, albeit through parliamentary means. As a consequence of his desire to 'destroy the Labour Party' Murphy ignored the need for revolutionaries to relate to Labour's rank-and-file supporters and address their political ideas. The sectarian and syndicalist traditions of the SLP, combined with his own inexperience in tactical questions of a political nature, were sharply revealed. But his position was to change completely when he finally arrived in Russia for the Second Comintern Congress.

A PARTY OF THE BOLSHEVIK TYPE

Murphy's trip to Russia in 1920 was to become a turning point in his political development, profoundly influencing his views on revolutionary strategy and tactics. After smuggling aboard a ship bound for Reval (Tallin) on the Baltic coast, disguised as a returning Russian prisoner of war, Murphy travelled by train across the Russian frontier on to Petrograd[44] with thousands of other men, women and children packed into the carriages of the trains. He recalled:

> The scenes of this day and the feeling of relief I experienced as we crossed this frontier are unforgettable. What a joy it was ... To those who had never dreamt of the day when there would be no more landlords and capitalists the crossing of the Russian frontier was only a matter of curiosity. But to me, one of the millions of workers who had been thrilled by the dramatic events of the revolution and to whom the revolution appeared to be the harbinger of the world's great social transformation, this was the moment of a lifetime, to be remembered for ever.[45]

In Petrograd he went to the International Hotel which accommodated the Comintern delegates who had travelled from across the world: 'Workers and intellectuals, journalists and politicians, white and brown, black and yellow, syndicalists, trade unionists, socialists, anarchists, all drawn from the ends of the earth by the magnet of this revolution'.[46] He met John Reed (the American journalist and author of the famous book *Ten Days that Shook the World*), Emma Goldmann (the anarchist) and many other revolutionaries. The next day he went to the Smolny Institute, the venue of the opening of the Second Comintern Congress, where 200 delegates from 37 countries were given an enthusiastic welcome by the Bolsheviks. Alongside all the other delegates, including Lenin, Radek, Bukharin, Zinoviev and other Russian leaders, Murphy marched in procession to the opening ceremony at the Uritsky Theatre, accompanied by thousands of Petrograd workers. After this first session, he travelled on to the Kremlin in Moscow, where the remainder of the Congress was transferred.

The circumstances in which the Second Comintern Congress took place need to borne in mind. The inspiration of the Russian revolution combined with the conditions of political and economic crisis that accompanied the end of the First World War produced a wave of revolutionary struggle that swept across Europe. In November 1918 a revolution in Germany overthrew the Kaiser and brought the social democrats to power. This was followed in January 1919 by the unsuccessful Spartakus rising in Berlin. In the spring of 1919 the short-lived Hungarian and Bavarian republics were formed, and in the summer Italy embarked on its two 'Red Years' of factory councils and occupations. It was the first international revolutionary situation since 1848, and far and away the most powerful challenge to world capitalism ever presented by the world working class. As we have seen, even in Britain capitalist power was more under threat than ever before.

The formation of the Communist International was both a product of this dramatic situation and a response to it. The Second Congress of the Comintern met in the summer of 1920 'in a mood of all-conquering faith and hope'.[47] Murphy recalled:

> We thought of ourselves as at the centre of the revolution which would spread and spread, wave on wave. Yes, there would be setbacks here and there which might make a difference of a year or two, but these would be incidental to the onward movement of the great army of the workers and oppressed.[48]

Lenin had advocated a new International since 1914, with the collapse of the Second International into reformism and nationalism. But now it was possible to make the aspiration a reality. The Comintern set itself the task of encouraging and sponsoring the building of revolutionary parties of the Bolshevik type in every country. It differed substantially from its predecessors. The earlier Internationals were loose federal bodies, allowing more or less complete independence for their national sections and embracing a wide range of different political tendencies. By contrast, the Comintern aimed to be a single centralised world party and exclusively communist, that is revolutionary Marxist. The form of organisation reflected a conception of the whole world as a single battlefield on which the class war was to be waged with one army and one high command. But achieving the transformation of the Comintern into a mass force was not a simple operation. What the Comintern had to do was to draw together all the existing communist and revolutionary tendencies, including syndicalists, uniting them into parties that embodied the Bolshevik experience. At the same time it had to win over as many as possible of the leftward moving rank-and-file of the old social democratic parties and detach them from their reformist leaders. The main obstacle to this process were 'centrists', workers' leaders who preached a very radical rhetoric and favoured affiliation to the International, but were unwilling to make a clean break with their old reformist ways. Nonetheless, mass organisations were won, against the opposition of their leaders, to affiliate to the International, for example in Germany, Italy and France.

In addition to establishing itself as a serious revolutionary force, the Comintern had to act as a school of revolutionary strategy and tactics for the new and inexperienced parties who inevitably contained many fine revolutionaries, but also ultra-left sections, some of whom wanted to march straight to revolution by boycotting parliament and the trade unions. There was little doubt that as leaders of a successful working-class revolution the Bolsheviks were in a unique position to offer this training. Murphy described the impact of the deliberations of the Second Comintern Congress:

> The Congress lasted three weeks. They were weeks of such intensive political discussion as I had never experienced. The proposals of the Russian representatives were for a centralised international party with an Executive elected by the congress continuously sitting in Moscow and directing the work of the national sections ... the national sections of this International Party were to be modelled on the Communist Party of the Soviet Union and subordinated to the Executive Committee of the Communist International—the World Communist Party. There must not be more than one section or party of Communism in any one country. Such proposals constituted a revolution in the conceptions of every party and every non-Russian delegate in the Congress.[49]

All of the British delegates embraced the Congress's declarations on the need for socialist revolution and establishment of soviet power. But the insistence on the need for a Bolshevik-type party, which in structure and character differed radically from the traditional social democractic model, was fiercely resisted by the shop stewards' delegates. Jack Tanner, the leader of the London Workers' Committee and editor of the paper *Solidarity*, explained how the nature of the wartime struggles in Britain had led the shop stewards' movement to give the Workers' Committees a revolutionary programme, as well as to support the Russian revolution and the Communist International from the start. But he insisted their action had always developed outside the confines of a political party, some of whose leaders were the same people they opposed in the trade union struggles.[50] Thus, he saw the Workers' Committees as the organisations most capable of carrying through revolutionary action. The most conscious and able minority of the working class could, on its own, direct and lead the mass of workers in the struggle for everyday demands as well as revolutionary battles. There was no need for any new type of Bolshevik political party in Britain. Significantly, even Murphy, who as a member of the SLP *did* accept the need for a socialist party, had not envisaged its role as extending beyond orthodox propaganda, accompanied by occasional participation in elections. As he later acknowledged: 'None of us saw the political party as anything other than a propaganda body for the spread of Socialist ideas'.[51] 'Before 1917, the revolutionary socialist parties "preparing for the day" were not conceived of as parties of insurrection. Rather did we conceive ourselves as "John the Baptists of the New Redemption"'.[52]

But in Russia Murphy's previous conceptions were quickly transformed. Lenin, who drafted the main Congress theses and participated throughout the Congress in the sessions and commissions, had a profound influence on Murphy. He argued that because of the unevenness in the organisation and consciousness of the working class, the most advanced politically conscious minority had to organise to fight to win the majority to the struggle for socialism. A Bolshevik-type party, defined by the common political outlook of its members, and bound by unity of action and organisation, was necessary to provide a lead to workers' struggles and to link industrial agitation with socialist politics, the fight for immediate demands with the battle to overthrow capitalism. Already, on his arrival in Moscow, Murphy had been given a copy of Lenin's pamphlet *Left Wing Communism—An Infantile Disorder* to read.[53] The pamphlet, which had been explicit written to counter both 'centrism' and 'ultra-leftism', outlined the role of the revolutionary party. Murphy commented:

> In my opinion the book is one of the most profound pieces of writing on revolutionary theory in relation to questions of strategy and tactics ever written, and it has probably influenced my own political development more than any other book in the armoury of revolutionary Socialism and

Communism. It was a remarkable introduction to the proceedings at Moscow.[54]

Meanwhile, after only two days in Moscow, Murphy was invited to meet Lenin in the Kremlin, where he found not a 'hard, ruthless fanatic' who sought to overwhelm him with authority, but a man who convinced him by his powers of reasoning.[55] Murphy talked for an hour, answering a range of questions about the trade unions, the shop stewards, the Labour Party and the different trends of opinion in the ranks of the socialist groups in Britain:

> I gave him an account of the Shop Stewards Movement and he was alarmed when I told him of our conception of the role of a political party. He set himself to explain the kind of party he thought was necessary to lead the workers in the struggle for power and later gave much attention to this question when he met other shop stewards.[56]

Such arguments were further reinforced at the debates that took place within the Congress sessions and commissions (at which Lenin and other well known Bolshevik leaders played a leading role), and in the informal discussions which went on until late at night between the foreign delegates. In addition, Murphy's preconceptions about the limited role of political parties were challenged following a visit he made to the giant Putilov engineering works in Petrograd, where he witnessed hundreds of Communist Party members discussing factory management and the organisation of production. He learned it was a preliminary meeting, called to help communist workers lead participation in these tasks by the workers as a whole.

> Here for the first time I found that the political party played an entirely different role in affairs from what I had hitherto thought possible. Here was an organisation holding itself responsible and being held responsible by the workers, those who were members of it and those who were not, for leading the work in every department of economic, social and political activity throughout all institutions ... I got a new conception of the functions of a workers' political party.[57]

Gradually, under the force of Russian argument, prestige and experience, Murphy and the other British delegates, including Tanner, Gallacher and Ramsey from the shop stewards' movement, came round to accepting the Bolshevik party model: a new type of revolutionary political party that would be capable of *leading* in struggle the mass of the working class:

> First, I realised that a party must be something more than a propaganda body. Second, that it should be composed only of those individually

pledged to a programme ... Third, that a programme as understood by Communists was much more than a series of demands, constituting an aim, in that it really embodied a philosophy of history and methods of achieving the aim set forth.[58]

News arrived in Moscow of the foundation of the Communist Party of Great Britain at a conference held in London in July, formed around the core of the old BSP and a section of the SLP. This further encouraged the British delegates to commit themselves to the task, on their return home, of fusing the various remaining revolutionary groups into a single party based on the principles decided during the deliberations of the Congress. Meanwhile, there were three other important debates which involved Murphy and the British delegates to the Congress: the question of whether communists should participate in the existing trade unions; whether they should participate in parliamentary activity; and whether the future Communist Party in Britain should affiliate to the Labour Party.

The trade union debate was long and animated. John Reed, the American revolutionary, and some of the British delegates argued that trade unions were a by-product of capitalism; that like the parties of the Second International, they had betrayed the cause of the workers in 1914 by supporting their respective national governments; and that they were by nature incapable of a revolutionary role. On the basis that it was impossible to win the reformist trade unions to communism, revolutionaries should boycott them and form new unions. By contrast, the Bolshevik leaders argued that rather than splitting away from the existing unions and thereby isolating themselves from the working class, communists should enter the unions and revolutionise them by leading the mass membership in revolt against leaders who no longer represented their true interests. The aim must be to bring the trade unions under communist leadership. Murphy agreed with the Bolshevik leaders and helped to convince his British comrades to support the majority Congress decision to participate in the trade unions. Nonetheless, he would have been well aware that the Congress left open and unresolved complex problems concerning the nature of the relationship between the SS&WCM and the trade unions, the attitude of revolutionaries to the trade union bureaucracy, and the question of whether the unions could be won over to communism en masse prior to a socialist revolution.[59]

The debate about whether revolutionaries should participate in parliamentary activity was also very lively. Participation was strongly opposed by Gallacher, the other British shop stewards' delegates (except Murphy), and by Pankhurst from the WSF. They believed that parliament was corrupt, and that no matter what measures were taken, elected MPs could not under capitalism be controlled or recalled. In any case it was through industrial action and not through parliament that socialism would be achieved. Given that the revolution in Britain was on hand at any moment, running candidates for parliament would be a sheer waste of time whose only effect would be to bolster up a dying institution. Of course, Murphy, who had stood as an SLP candidate in the 1918 general election, believed in revolutionary parliamentary action. Therefore, he supported the BSP delegation's resolution on the issue, despite believing that the BSP completely underestimated the reactionary nature of the Labour Party leadership by maintaining it could be changed by mass pressure. But he agreed with Lenin's view that whilst parliament had to be destroyed and replaced by soviets, this did not mean parliament could not be used as a platform for communist work, so long as the communists were not as yet strong enough to overthrow it.

Murphy accepted Lenin's argument that a categorical repudiation of any revolutionary participation in parliamentary activity reflected an ultra-left overestimation of the revolutionary consciousness of the working class. The majority of British workers still believed in parliament and followed the lead of right-wing reformists. Therefore, it was not possible to undermine such illusions merely through abstract condemnation of parliament. Instead the workers had to learn through their own practical experience the real nature of reformism, the way in which a Labour government would invariably accommodate to capitalist power by containing protest and opposition within the established 'rules of the game'. This meant it was necessary for the Communist Party to stand their own candidates for parliament, utilising this as a revolutionary platform from which to encourage mass working-class extra-parliamentary activity. Murphy strongly refuted the arguments of Gallacher who accused the Comintern leaders of becoming 'opportunist' and of advocating a policy of 'subservience' to democratic methods:

On the question of parliamentarianism I do not agree with my colleagues from the Shop Stewards who spoke this afternoon. I believe that all the attacks that have been made against parliamentarianism today, and all the criticism that has been directed against it, referred to bourgeois parliamentarianism and not revolutionary parliamentarianism.

It is true that many representatives of the socialist movement who have entered parliament have become traitors. But that it not sufficient reason to condemn any activity at all within parliamentary institutions. I have never yet heard anyone claim that the tactics that Comrade Liebknecht followed in the German Reichstag and the Bolshevik representatives in the Russian Duma produced anything other than good results for the revolutionary movement.[60]

But undoubtedly the main source of division amongst the British delegation to the Congress concerned the question of communist affiliation to the Labour Party. The BSP delegates argued the case in favour of affiliation on the basis that the Labour Party was the political expression of the trade union movement, and that by operating within it Labour could be won to revolutionary socialism. All the other British delegates opposed affiliation on the basis that the Labour Party was a right-wing organisation that had to be destroyed. The new Communist Party had to be kept clean and untarnished. Any relations with the Labour Party were bound to compromise and discredit it in the eyes of militant workers. Meanwhile, Lenin, who chaired the special committee on the 'British question' that dealt with the issue, opposed both right- and left-wing attitudes of the British delegates. He disagreed with the BSP's view of the Labour Party as a political party of workers:

Of course, most of the Labour Party's members are working men. However, whether or not a party is really a political party of the workers does not depend soley upon a membership of workers but also upon the men that lead it, and the content of its action and its political tactics. Only that determines whether we really have before us a political party of the proletariat. Regarded from this, the only correct point of view, the Labour Party is a thoroughly bourgeois party, because although it consists of workers, it is led by reactionaries, and the worst kind of reactionaries at that, who act fully in the spirit of the bourgeoisie.[61]

Lenin accepted the SLP view that the Labour Party would never lead the workers to socialism and had to be replaced by a Communist Party. On the other hand, he agreed with the BSP that the Labour Party was a different sort of party from the continental social democratic parties and that it was necessary to take advantage of the unique feature of the Labour Party constitution which permitted the affiliation of trade unions and socialist parties. In order to relate to Labour's reformist-influenced followers, Lenin proposed the tactic of Communist Party affiliation to Labour, albeit on the basis of complete freedom of revolutionary propaganda against the policy and leadership of the Labour party. After much discussion and argument, Murphy finally accepted Lenin's view on the question of affiliation and unceremoniously abandoned his previous hard-line opposition. He now accepted that British revolutionaries not only had to combat the all-pervading influence of reformism, but in doing so had to break with their own sectarian traditions that weakened their revolutionary activity.

Thus, by the end of the Congress, Murphy's political conversion to the principles of Bolshevism was complete. Gallacher and all the other British delegates felt likewise. As we have seen, before arriving in Moscow they had already come to an appreciation of the soviet as the chief agency of socialist revolution and of the need for the working class to conquer state power. But they now embraced the idea of a disciplined, centralised party, working in a planned and organised way in the trade unions and the Labour Party, and providing an alternative political leadership to the official leaders of the movement. They became convinced that Russian ideological and organisational conceptions were right not merely because the Bolshevik Revolution of October 1917 had proved their efficacy, but also because they appeared in many respects to fit their own positive and negative experiences in the shop stewards' movement. In particular, they now abandoned their previous syndicalist tradition of spontaneity, separation of economics and politics and anti-leadership views, and returned home to build the new Communist Party of Great Britain (CPGB) along the Bolshevik-type lines agreed at the Congress.

Murphy and the other shop stewards' delegates reported back from Moscow to an NAC meeting which decided to support a Communist Unity Convention to be held in Leeds at the end of January 1921 (and which finally fused together all the remaining different revolutionary groups into a united British Communist Party which adhered to the Communist International and agreed to seek affiliation to the Labour Party). But the relationship between the Communist Party and the shop stewards' movement was left undefined. One group, led by Tanner, advocated that the

SS&WCM should support the party as individuals and the movement should remain independent. The other group, led by Murphy and the Glasgow shop stewards, was in favour of a closer connection. The meeting therefore instructed the NAC to prepare a statement defining the relationship of the SS&WCM to the Communist Party and elected Murphy (and Campbell, Tanner and Klime) to meet the Communist Party executive to discuss relations. In the event, differences were overcome and the need for close co-operation between the organisations was agreed.

As Murphy explained to the Unity Convention, the NAC of the shop stewards' movement had played a very important part in the negotiations for the development of a united Communist Party. Of course, it was folly to think of the movement as a political party, or that it could perform the same functions, given that it embraced workers who were not Communists. However, he stressed the necessity for its active members to join the party, as had already practically every member of the NAC,[62] and in reciprocation he expected all industrial workers who were members of the Communist Party to participate in the work of the shop stewards' movement. It was necessary for both organisations to work closely together to further the interests of the revolutionary movement as a whole.[63] A national shop stewards' conference in April 1921 ratified this alliance with the CPGB by accepting a constitution which subordinated it to the political control of the party. Thus, the SS&WCM in engineering (although a shadow of its former self), now formally united with the newly-formed CPGB, brought within its scope the important unofficial movements which were developing in virtually all the major coalfields, the vigilance committees on the railways and the rank-and-file committees in the docks. It brought them in largely on the understanding that the party offered an effective way of organising the industrial struggle.

In conclusion, it should be noted that the view of some commentators that the CPGB was the brainchild of the Russians is facile and untrue.[64] Of course, the intervention of Lenin and the Comintern leadership in the affairs of the British revolutionary movement was vital for the creation of the CPGB. On one level this intervention was financial. For example, it is possible Murphy, MacManus and Paul received some monetary aid from Bolshevik agents in Britain to subsidise their SLP candidatures in the general election of 1918.[65] Certainly, Murphy's trip to Moscow, via

Amsterdam and Berlin, was beyond the limits of his own financial resources, and it is more than likely the 'whirl of exciting things' which foreign travel opened up to 'one accustomed only to the provincial life of the workers',[66] was only made possible through Comintern funding. But undoubtedly the main Comintern influence on Murphy and other British revolutionaries was of an ideological and political nature.

> The experiences I had had since leaving England at the beginning of the year, the countless discussions and conversations with all kinds of revolutionary leaders, in committees and out of them, had completely shaken up all my ideas on politics and life in general ... My experience in Russia as well as the discussions had shown me the real meaning of the struggle for political power ... Instead of thinking that a Socialist Party was merely a propaganda organisation for the dissemination of Socialist views, I now saw that a real Socialist Party would consist of revolutionary Socialists who regarded the Party as a means whereby they would lead the working class in the fight for political power. It would be a party such as Lenin had described.[67]

However, the ability of the Russians to teach their British comrades to transfer Bolshevik principles on to British soil was to meet with great obstacles. Murphy and the British revolutionaries had come to Bolshevism on the back of their own domestic traditions; there were strengths and weaknesses in this. The chief weaknesses were the propagandism and sectarianism engendered by small group politics. Whilst the Comintern leaders could help in the teaching of revolutionary strategy and tactics, the new party had to learn primarily from its *own* experience in struggle. This meant it was impossible to create real communist leadership overnight, and it took several years to transform the CPGB into a combat organisation orientated to workers' struggles. Of course, had the party been established in 1918 or 1919 it could have taken advantage of the unprecedented industrial and political struggles that had swept the country. But by 1920 and 1921 the working class was on the retreat and the shop stewards' movement in engineering was completely routed. The subjective weaknesses of the British revolutionaries compounded the disadvantages of the objective situation created by the belated founding of the CPGB.[68]

Chapter Four

The Communist Party and the Labour Movement, 1920–1926

On his return to Britain in December 1920 from the Second Congress of the Comintern, Murphy immediately went to visit his ex-girlfriend Ethel ('Molly') Morris in London. Molly had been active in the pre-war suffragette campaign as the organiser of the Sheffield branch of the Women's Social and Political Union (WSPU), involved in distributing leaflets, organising meetings and putting firecrackers into letter boxes. In 1913 she had sold Murphy a copy of the newspaper *The Suffragette* at an open-air meeting near Sheffield Town Hall, a regular meeting place for radical protest groups. Whilst Murphy was sympathetic to the suffragette cause, as a syndicalist he looked to industrial not parliamentary activity to achieve change. But it was the seller that attracted Murphy more than the paper and he became a regular visitor to the WSPU shop where Molly worked. Over the next two years he proposed marriage to her three times, only to be turned down on each occasion.[1] Their paths separated when she left Sheffield to train to become a nurse, although they remained good friends and wrote to each other occasionally. On his return from Moscow, Murphy visited her at the West London Hospital, and after relating his exploits travelling across Europe to revolutionary Russia and meeting Lenin, invited her to return to Moscow with him. She accepted the proposal and two weeks later they were married in Manchester, with George Peet (the national secretary of the SS&WCM) acting as best man. After only a week's honeymoon in Llandudno, they set off for the long trip to Russia, via Amsterdam, Berlin and Tallin. But they were in Moscow for only six weeks when Molly discovered she was pregnant, and shortly afterwards decided to return home to have the baby. Murphy stayed on for the Red International of Labour Unions Congress and Third Comintern Congress, before returning back to Sheffield in time for the birth of a baby boy named Gordon in December 1921. At a Socialist Sunday School naming ceremony for Gordon, everybody joined in expressing the fervent hope that 'he would grow up to become a good socialist'.[2]

In the late spring of 1922, Murphy moved to London with Molly, and over the next few years lived in rented rooms in Fulham, Hounslow, Ealing and then Golders Green. Molly recalls that Jack was a man of great energy and fanatical missionary zeal, ceaselessly active in practically every phase of the Communist Party's industrial and political activities.[3] Elected to the executive committee of the Communist Party in January 1921, he became a leading full-time political bureau member, with responsibility, at different times, as head of the Industrial and Co-operative Departments. He also served as the London correspondent of the Russian Communist Party paper *Pravda*, regularly contributing articles to a variety of CPGB and socialist publications, including *The Communist, The Workers' Weekly, Communist Review, Communist International, International Press Correspondence, All Power, Plebs* and *The Sunday Worker*. In addition, Murphy was elected by the party to attend the Third, Fourth and Fifth Communist International Congresses in Moscow in 1921, 1922 and 1924. Throughout the early 1920s he was also engaged in a variety of polemical debates with other party leaders, in particular Pollitt and Palme Dutt, in which he consistently made original contributions to the task of building the CP within the unions and Labour Party.

If the time-scale which the Russian communist leaders envisaged for world events had proved correct, had the degree of class tensions in Britain been as high as they believed, the CP after its formation should have grown rapidly. In fact, with the collapse of the brief post-war boom and the onset of the depression at the end of 1920, the immediate revolutionary tide was already on the ebb. As Murphy later commented: 'Had our estimate of the international situation at that time been correct ... A year, perhaps two years at the outside would, we thought, see the masses of the British Labour Movement deserting the opportunist leaders and following the Communist Party.' In fact, 'We were playing leap-frog with history and we did not know it'.[4] In 1921 there were a series of crucial defeats.[5] The first decisive struggle was in the mines. When the agreement of the previous autumn ran out, the government and mine-owners felt strong enough to counter-attack. The owners demanded wage cuts varying between 10 and 49 per cent, and locked out the miners from 1 April. Within the working class generally there was enormous sympathy for the miners and when the Miners' Federation appealed to its associates in the Triple Alliance, the leaders of the other unions felt they could not stand back and a general transport and railway strike was called for 12 April.

This time the government was determined to fight and an Emergency Powers Act was invoked to declare a 'state of emergency', reservists were called up and a special force, the 'Defence Corps', was formed. Machine guns were posted at pit heads and troops in full battle dress dispatched to large working-class areas. The leaders of the other unions had felt compelled to rally to the miners because they feared they were facing the first stage of an attack in which their own members would eventually suffer as well. But with the government behaving in civil war terms, no reformist union bureaucrat could go without hesitation into such a battle, which threatened to upset the whole process of 'constitutionally advancing' the role of the organised working class and its official leaders within capitalist society. Thus, as the day fixed for the general transport strike drew near, the leaders of the Triple Alliance became increasingly nervous and on Friday 15 April they announced that the sympathetic strike was called off. This betrayal became known throughout the labour movement as 'Black Friday'.

The way was now open for the employers' offensive to have its first success, and two months later the miners returned to work on the owners' terms. Not surprisingly, the collapse of the Triple Alliance meant that other groups of workers did not feel strong enough to fight back either. Engineers, shipyard workers, builders, seamen and cotton operatives all had to accept wage cuts. A year later came a second major assualt. In March 1922 the employers locked out members of the largest engineering union, the newly formed AEU, and of various smaller craft unions. Once again the employers had carefully chosen a time to fight when they were most powerfully placed. The immense funds of the AEU were drained as the battle dragged on and eventually the employers were able to secure an agreement to acceptance by the unions of their undivided authority on questions such as overtime working and 'managerial functions'.[6] At a time of high unemployment many militants did not get their jobs back and the power of what remained of the wartime shop stewards' movement was destroyed. As Murphy stated in a speech to the Fourth Congress of the Communist International at the end of 1922:

> In England we have had a powerful shop stewards' movement. But it can and only does exist in given objective conditions. These necessary conditions at the moment in England do not exist. How can you build factory organisations when you have 1,750,000 workers walking the streets?

You cannot build factory organisations in empty and depleted workshops, while you have a great reservoir of unemployed workers.[7]

The defeat of the engineers paved the way for acceptance of wage reductions by shipyard workers, dockers, builders, printers, railwaymen and cotton workers. Moreover, these defeats enabled the employers to force the unions into signing agreements that tied the union officials to the employers in new joint negotiating procedures. The previous militant industrial objectives—nationalisation, workers' control, recognition of shop stewards and 'Direct Action'—disappeared from the agenda, and trade union membership slumped from 8.3 million in 1920 to 5.6 million two years later. However, there was no rout of the working class. A solid core of organised workers remained waiting only for better conditions to return to a militant posture and, although the mass of workers might not feel strong enough to fight, they were far from accepting the ruling class ideology of 'national interest'. A sullen class consciousness continued to smoulder and could burst into flame on occasion.

Thus, it meant that the British Communist Party spent its formative years during the early 1920s trying to turn itself into a party of the Bolshevik type, along the lines laid down at the Second Comintern Congress, in conditions not at all favourable to its growth or expanding influence. Nonetheless, it succeeded in grouping together a network of militants from the engineering, transport and mining industries with widespread prestige inside the working-class movement and it made pioneering efforts towards building a Marxist party during this period. The broad strategy was to provide a militant lead in the trade unions and win over radical sections of the Labour Party by agitation and exposure of the leadership. However, as we shall see, by 1924 the party had effectively become tied to the left bureaucracy of the unions and the Labour Party, partly because of political weaknesses of the CPGB itself, and partly because of pressure emanating from the Comintern in Moscow. This chapter explores Murphy's involvement with the Red International of Labour Unions, his approach towards the 'Bolshevisation' of the party in 1923–1924, and his attitude towards the TUC General Council and the 'left' union leaders in the run-up to the 1926 General Strike. In addition, it considers his view of the relationship between the Communist Party and the Labour Party. An underlying theme is the influence of the Comintern, both on the CPGB generally and on Murphy specifically.

THE RED INTERNATIONAL OF LABOUR UNIONS

In its early years the Communist International was a power-house for the development of revolutionary strategy and tactics and drew on a wealth of Russian experience in many fields. But trade unionism was not one of these areas and the result was that in the years leading up to the 1926 General Strike, there was little aid forthcoming for the British CP in overcoming weaknesses in its own trade union policies. The Second Comintern Congress had affirmed the importance of communists working within the existing reformist-led trade unions and striving to win them to a revolutionary course. But apart from this general advice there was practically no guidance on how to operate inside the unions, and in particular the question of the union bureaucracy was barely touched upon. But before the Congress ended, Murphy was asked by Lenin to become involved in a major new initiative on the trade union front, the setting up of a Red International of Labour Unions.[8]

Early in 1920, Zinoviev, the President of the Comintern, had called for the unification of all revolutionary forces in the trade union movement into a new international union body. This was intended to rival the reformist-led International Federation of Trade Unions (IFTU), known as the Amsterdam International. The Comintern leadership based its proposal to launch a revolutionary trade union International on its assessment of the specific conditions in the labour movement at that time. Despite the Amsterdam International's recent growth, the authority of its reformist leaders had been severely damaged by their treacherous

conduct during the war in renouncing prior internationalist commitments, and workers in several countries were attracted to the
example of the October Revolution in Russia. On the expectation of
renewed social explosions and working-class revolutions in the
coming few years in Europe and elsewhere, a new, Red trade
union International, it was believed, could woo national trade
unions to break from their allegiance to the Amsterdam International and affiliate to Moscow.

At the Second Comintern Congress, a group representing the
Russian, Italian and Bulgarian delegations, and some members of
the British delegation, met to give their general approval to the
initiative. Following his meeting with Lenin, Murphy then played a
leading role in helping to set up the new organisation. He was
elected to a Provisional International Council of Trade and Industrial Unions, along with Mikhail Tomsky (head of the Russian trade
unions) and Alfred Rosmer (the French syndicalist), and helped
draft its first manifesto (which Lenin edited), as well as submitting a
plan for the construction of a British Bureau of this organisation. It
was then agreed he should travel home as quickly as possible to get
the British Bureau established, and then return to Moscow to assist
in preparations for the formal launch of the Red International of
Labour Unions (RILU) at a world congress the following year.

Arriving back in Britain at the end of 1920, Murphy carried with
him a considerable sum of Russian money with which to finance the
campaign for the new trade union international.[9] His main task was
to rally support for its founding Congress scheduled for Moscow in
May, although this was in fact postponed until July 1921 in order to
synchronise it with the Third Congress of the Comintern. The
British Bureau's 'Manifesto to the Organised Workers of Great
Britain' called upon all trade unionists to choose between Moscow
and Amsterdam:

> The world is now divided into great divisions and WE MUST MAKE
> OUR CHOICE as to which camp we belong. On the one side is the
> capitalist class with its ... 'yellow' Amsterdam International ... On the
> other side is the Communist International and all that is loyal and true to
> the working class ... All our minor issues ... are being thrust into the
> background as the mightier questions rise up demanding that we conquer
> capitalism.[10]

Murphy's arrival with a mandate to set up a British Bureau of
the Red International coincided with a series of meetings of the

NAC of the shop stewards' movement and a national SS&WCM conference held in January 1921. After hearing Murphy's report from Moscow, the shop stewards made arrangements for a national organising campaign to persuade British unions to sever their connections with the IFTU based in Amsterdam and to affiliate to the new Moscow body. Apart from providing Murphy with a regular income, the funds available were used to set up a dozen district organisers, to organise conferences in the principal industrial centres, produce leaflets and subsidise the shop stewards' papers *The Worker* and *Solidarity*, both of which carried regular supplements for the Bureau. Within a few weeks a national organisation had been created, with an executive committee composed of Tom Mann (the veteran strike leader and now general secretary of the AEU) as President, Ted Lismer (prominent member of the Sheffield Workers' Committee) as organising secretary, George Peet (national secretary of the SS&WCM) as corresponding secretary, and Murphy representing the Moscow executive. A number of prominent trade union leaders, including A. J. Cook and Robert Williams (leaders of the miners' and transport workers unions), were also represented.

Over the next two to three years the British Bureau of the RILU worked as the chief industrial arm of the Communist Party, effectively replacing the SS&WCM (which, although initially retained alongside the RILU, was finally submerged into it in June 1922). It provided the main political and organising forum for rallying militants within the trade unions during this period when the official union leaders were preaching retreat before the employers' offensive. Campaigning on a programme of action for different industries based upon militant economic and political demands, it produced a monthly paper named *All Power* with a circulation of 12,000 copies, to which Murphy frequently contributed. After the April 1921 disaster of 'Black Friday' and the Triple Alliance betrayal of the miners, it campaigned around the slogan of 'Stop the Retreat' (the title of a RILU pamphlet written by Murphy) which was a call to end the trade union leadership's policy of surrender to the employers' offensive, as well as the slogan 'Back to the Unions' which aimed at combating the haemorrhage of union membership.[11] Under the initiative of the Bureau, a number of new left-wing militant trade union organisations also gradually began to develop in particular industries, of which the most important was the Miners' 'Minority Movement' that started to spread from South Wales to the other coalfields.

Having got the British Bureau machinery up and running, Murphy returned to Moscow in June 1921 to attend the first Congress of the Red International of Labour Unions (as well as the Third Comintern Congress). The most controversial debate of the RILU Congress turned on the question of the relationship between the RILU and the Comintern, with syndicalists from a number of countries standing out strongly for trade union independence of any political organisation. Murphy spoke in favour of the Russian proposal for the Red International to be a constituent part of the Comintern.[12] Eventually it was agreed it would be structured as a separate organisation, but linked to the Comintern by fundamental political agreement, with 'real and intimate revolutionary unity' between the Red trade unions and communist parties in all countries.[13] Murphy then returned to Britain where he helped to organise the Communist Party's industrial intervention around the engineering lock-out of 1922 and the London dock strike of 1923, before travelling back to Russia again in 1924 for the Fourth Comintern Congress.

In fact, the RILU's optimistic expectations of rapid communist advance were soon to be confounded by the relative stabilisation of capitalism and the ebbing of working-class struggle across Europe. Thus, in Britain, despite Murphy's claim that it received the backing of hundreds of union branches and some district committees and trades councils, it actually proved unable to win the affiliation of any national union bodies nor able to build a real mass base in Britain.[14] In fact, with the exception of France, the RILU only really succeeded outside western Europe. Even Murphy criticised Rosmer's evaluation that the total membership of unions in the Red International was 17 million, suggesting the figures did not indicate the difference between actual union affiliations and estimate of minorities in unions.[15] Persistent rumours that it was about to be disbanded illustrated it was a far more hollow organisation than its leaders claimed. At the Fourth Comintern Congress in December 1922, the Bolshevik leader Lozovsky insisted 'the liquidation of the Profintern [RILU] would be a disaster'.[16] But three months later Murphy still had to 'dispose of the notion which has been running through the mind of many party members in this country, as in others, that there is an intention or ever was an

intention of winding up the RILU.[17] Only much later, at the Fifth
Comintern Congress in 1924, did Zinoviev admit:

> The [RILU] was founded at a moment when it looked as though we could
> break through enemy lines by a frontal attack, and quickly win over the
> trade unions . . . It was during the time when we thought that we should
> win over the majority of the workers in the shortest possible space of time.
> You know, comrades, that after that the movement was on the ebb. All
> the problems, all the tactical difficulties of the Comintern during these
> five years are rooted in the fact that the development was much slower
> than we had expected.[18]

However, the failure of the RILU in Britain, as elsewhere, was
not only due to the ebb of the revolutionary tide. It was also related
to the completely ambiguous nature on which it was set up. Murphy
commented: 'Had there been the slightest suggestion of splitting the
trade unions then, of course it would not have received the support
of Williams and Purcell [leaders of the transport and furnishing
workers' unions] or myself'.[19] Ironically, the incompatibility of the
proposal to call on communists to work within the existing
Amsterdam trade unions, whilst at the same time calling on these
unions to split from the Amsterdam International in favour of
Moscow, seems to have eluded both Murphy and the Russian
Comintern leaders. In retrospect the whole concept of the RILU
was fundamentally defective.[20] The strategy of attempting to be an
official mass union body committed to communism depended on the
hope that, in the short term, trade unions could be conquered
wholesale or substantial sections split off. It assumed that in a crisis
the unions could be turned into instruments of revolutionary
struggle, with union leaders either being forced to change by
pressure from below or being replaced by communists. But the
notion that the highly developed trade unions of western Europe
could be transformed *before* a socialist revolution and the conquest
of power completely undervalued the special role of the union
bureaucracy and its deep roots inside the labour movement. Certainly, the idea that the union leadership might play a central role in
defusing a revolutionary situation that threatened them was absent
in official pronouncements and discussions. Even Lenin and Trotsky did not appreciate the more deeply rooted nature of the trade
union bureaucracy within Britain compared with Russia and the
problematic nature of the RILU during this time. There is no real
evidence that Murphy, despite his own pioneering analysis of the

need for rank-and-file organisation to counter the treachery of union officials, raised any objections to the notion that the unions and their leaders could be won to communism wholesale, although the weakness of the CP and the British Bureau of the RILU actually made such a grandiose objective purely academic.

It should be borne in mind that the extent of Murphy's day-to-day practical influence on the British Bureau of the RILU and the party's industrial work during 1921–1923 was limited by the fact that he spent many months travelling to and from Moscow and attending the RILU Congress and the Third and Fourth Comintern Congresses there. Although he remained an RILU executive bureau member, it was Pollitt, Gallagher and Campbell who operated as its national secretaries. In addition, although Murphy was appointed to head the party's industrial department in October 1922,[21] his absence in Russia virtually immediately afterwards meant Pollitt had to deputise for him for some months. Nonetheless, Murphy was still a principal figure within the party's leadership during this period and was a central player in shaping the general thrust of its industrial intervention.

Whilst the British Bureau of the RILU served as an important rallying centre for militant trade unionism and helped to counteract the demoralisation inside the working class, it failed to build any real mass influence for the Communist Party inside the unions in the early 1920s. As Murphy himself was to acknowledge, there was a tendency to create overlapping machinery of propaganda with the Communist Party, thereby weakening the party's own industrial intervention.[22] Moreover, it seems the RILU effectively evaded central party control and to some degree became a rival body.[23] In the light of its complete failure to make any headway with the campaign for union affiliation, the British Bureau was finally liquidated into the National Minority Movement in 1924 (for an examination of the NMM, see later sections of this chapter), after the Comintern finally decided that it was not entirely suitable for carrying out communist activity in the trade unions.[24]

A 'GENERAL STAFF OF LABOUR'

Although the SLP and shop stewards' element within the new British Communist Party was in a small minority, they played a dominant role in the leadership in the first few years of its existence, and it was Murphy, along with MacManus and Bell, who helped to frame the first strategies for communist industrial work. The lesson of the wartime period that the trade union officials could not be trusted and the need for independent rank-and-file activity and organisation to counter this remained a central maxim. But at first Murphy and the other party leaders provided no detailed ideas on how the members should intervene in particular struggles or what strategy should be pursued, except for propagandist calls for Workers' Committees. These calls, against the post-war background of mass unemployment and working-class retreat, in which the power of the shop stewards' movement was completely undermined, proved to be totally unrealistic.

It was the shock of 'Black Friday' on 15 April 1921 which brought home to Murphy and the British communists that their approach to industrial work was unsatisfactory. The scale of the betrayal forced the CP to reconsider its industrial tactics. As Murphy explained:

> The situation is indeed serious. Ever since the memorable Black Friday of April 1921, union after union has been swiftly put hors de combat. The shadow of that fateful day hangs like a pall over the movement. We cannot escape it. Dodge, twist, turn as we may, no sooner do we attempt to think out any ways and means of struggle against the forces of capitalism than back we come to April's fiasco. Until that crisis is fully appreciated and its implications thoroughly understood, no apology is necessary for referring back to that period and the discussions arising out of it.[25]

The crisis forced Murphy and the CP leaders to think about the question of building a centralised leadership inside the trade union movement, so as to overcome the sectionalism of the different unions and betrayal of the existing leaders. This meant re-evaluating its attitude towards the union bureaucracy. Not surprisingly, with union strength on the shopfloor eroded by unemployment and victimisation, the focus of power and influence within the unions had shifted away from the rank-and-file to the full-time officials. The enormous growth in union membership immediately after the war (2.6 million in 1910, 8.3 million in 1920), the series of amalgamations which led to the formation of such giant general unions as the Transport and General Workers Union (TGWU) and the National Union of General and Municipal Workers (NUGMW), and the progress of national collective bargaining as opposed to the pattern of district settlements which had prevailed before the war, had further encouraged the development of full-time trade union bureaucrats, expert in negotiation rather than militant rank-and-file leadership. As Murphy explained, during the war years the shop stewards, who took on the direct responsibility for the fight against the employers and the state, had conducted the fight not 'so much against the officials, but rather ignored them and fought the employing class directly'. Yet whilst conditions during the war had been particularly favourable to this kind of activity, the post-war years had led to an important change in the objective situation which meant 'the officials cannot now be ignored. They have to be fought'.[26] Thus, in adapting to the new hostile post-war economic and industrial environment, Murphy and the other CP leaders understood it was necessary for industrial militants in different industries to concentrate more energies on working within the structures of the official unions to 'stop the retreat' and stem the decline in union membership.

But the question of providing leadership inside the trade unions provoked considerable confusion within the ranks of the party. Clearly, against the backcloth of economic slump and mass un-employment, a mass rank-and-file *movement* based on independent shop stewards' bodies was no longer possible. This left two very different approaches. One was to draw the lesson that no trade union leader could be trusted, and that it was necessary to attempt to do everything that was possible to encourage the self-confidence and fighting power of the rank-and-file, with the long-term aim of rebuilding shopfloor organisation from the bottom up. The other lesson was to concentrate on building strength at the top of the movement by trying to capture official union positions, filling such posts either with its own members or very close left-wing sym-pathisers, thereby overcoming the restraints of the bureaucracy to provide a central leadership inside the working class.[27] On the one hand, Murphy seemed prepared to put up some resistance to the second option, an orientation on trade union electorialism by the party. Thus, he wrote an article entitled 'On Leading the Masses' in *Communist Review* in February 1922, in which he posed all the problems of such a strategy and began elaborating some of the solutions. It started by criticising the pure syndicalist approach which Tom Mann had put forward in a recent article. First it quoted Mann's article:

'Refuse to allow executives to shape the policy for the rank and file. The membership must decide upon the objective and the policy by which it shall be achieved, and executive committees and officials must carry out the decrees of their members'. This is echoed and re-echoed throughout the land, both in the Red Trade Union International and the Workers' Committee Movement.

This form of protest will not do ... Leaders we need and leaders we must have. The democracy which the revolutionaries should aim at is the democracy which will enable the workers to do more than merely examine a ballot paper ... It must enable the workers to quickly remove leaders who will not lead. [But] the cry of 'Elect new leaders' sounds very much like an echo of the old socialist parties ... Elect new leaders by all means, but will anyone kindly calculate the number of years necessary for a formal ballot box removal of the reactionary trade union bureaucracy? ... The reactionary leaders will have to go. But they will have to be removed by a fight directly against them rather than through formal removal via the ballot box.

This does not mean that we should relax for a moment the attack through the union ballot box ... Indeed the ballot box method stands in the same category in relation to unionism, as parliament does in relation to the conquest of the state. Both are weapons to be used ... [But] in neither case have we control of the elected person. One of the elementary measures we should popularise ... is the right of having the power to recall the elected person.

Then we should consider greater measures of organised action whereby the masses will thrust aside the reactionaries as the struggle widens and deepens ... One section cries out for the One Big Union for One Industry, another for One Big Union, and some for Workers' Committees ... They side-track the masses into a formal debate concerning *forms* of organisation ... The swiftly changing phases of the struggle have swept away the condition which made the Shop Stewards' and Workers' Committees the natural mass expression of the requirements of the moment ... We need much more than propaganda for industrial unionism. We need *plans* of immediate organised action, definitely related to the existing organisational forces of the proletariat, the application of which will force them into action. For it is by action that situations are produced which offer the opportunities necessary for the revolutionary changing of leadership ...

We gave vigorous criticism of the leaders of the union movement in the crisis leading to Black Friday. We exposed them. We warned the masses to 'Watch their leaders'. We fostered the idea that the Triple Alliance would fail. But when it did fail the revolutionary movement was nearly as demoralised as the union movement in general. We had not, to any large extent, considered or advised the masses what they could do in such an eventuality. Yet everything cried out for the preparation of a new centre of leadership in the organisations involved, to which the masses could gravitate as the leaders moved towards failure. The lesson is obvious and exceedingly important. Immediately there is the slightest sign of action developing in any organisation the revolutionary movement, and especially the Communist Party, ought to immediately take the measure of all the forces operating, the potential of the situation, the limits of the organisation involved, and how the organisations can be used to drive the leaders along the revolutionary path or out of the way.[28]

Murphy seemed to be suggesting that effective communist work in the trade unions required the encouragement of workers' self-activity related to the level of the movement, with the aim of building a rank-and-file leadership to fight the bureaucracy rather than pursuing purely election campaigns or organisational reforms to remove them. But there was a different reaction amongst most party leaders to Black Friday and its aftermath. This was the call for the TUC General Council to be transformed from merely a co-ordinating body with no executive authority, into a centralised and powerful directing staff that could provide united leadership to workers' battles.[29] Ironically, although Murphy had previously poured scorn on this call for a 'General Staff of Labour', he was now clearly affected by the general sense of despondency inside the union movement and was prepared to change his tone. Thus, in an article in *Labour Monthly*, published in January 1922, one month before his *Communist Review* piece on the need for rank-and-file leadership, he put the emphasis on the need for a strengthened TUC General Council:

The crises of the last three years have delivered smashing blows at all our old conceptions of the struggle, and relegated the old slogans to subordinate rank ... No longer can there be any dubiety about the situation ... We are needing, as never before, a central authority that can command the respect and attention of the whole movement. True, we have all the leaders of the union movement nominally united in the Trades Union Congress and a central authority in the General Council. But actually there is no unity in the Congress or authority in the General Council. Each constituent part feels itself bound by its own particular constitution. So much is this the case that it is no exaggeration to say that the Trades Union Congress is only a reflex of the muddle of the union bureaucracy and not a live determining body holding the individual organisations subordinate to itself. Yet a Congress we must have, and a General Council we must have which shall function as a general staff. There is no union which can fight a winning battle on its own today. The massing of the unions and submission to a central lead is essential. This

can be obtained by investing the Trades Union Congress and the General
Council with executive power over all unions.[30]

The article went on to call for changes in the method of election of
delegates to the Trades Union Congress (TUC), with representation from trades councils rather than individual unions, and for the
General Council to be elected directly by the Congress, with the
latter having the direct power to remove unsatisfactory leaders.

In other words, in considering how a real leadership could be
created in the unions, Murphy effectively looked in two different,
and in many respects contradictory, directions. Whilst he continued
to advocate the need to rebuild shopfloor confidence in the factories
with the aim of encouraging rank-and-file organisation independent
of the union officials, he also now saw it necessary to reconstruct the
official union apparatus so as to provide a TUC general staff
empowered to lead workers' struggles. But by the end of 1922,
after the bitter defeat of the engineering workers' struggle, Murphy
began to tilt the emphasis much more towards the latter. Thus, in
an article in *The Communist*, analysing what would be the development of trade unions in a crisis, he still referred to the rank-and-file,
but they were relegated to secondary importance to the officials:

> To get the everyday results from wage negotiations etc, in an era of
> expanding capitalism (the era in which the trade unions made their
> greatest progress) became an art in which Mr. Thomas [the right-wing
> railway union leader] excels. It was in this era that practically all the trade
> union leaders of today came to power at the head of powerful
> organisations with strong vested interests binding the membership.
>
> Revolutionary leadership under these conditions could only be the
> exception and not the rule. Only when the general economic situation
> changes and forces the masses of leaders into revolutionary situations and
> policy can there be a general revolutionary change in leadership. Such
> change is rapidly taking place today and producing all the forces making
> for a change of leadership. The capitalists can no longer make the old
> concessions and the fate of the unions and the masses is now at stake.
> Under these circumstances it is useless and wrong to relate to the trade
> union leadership as a static unchangeable monument. It is subject to
> changed circumstances as is everything else. Nor can we assert that the
> change will come along a single track. This will operate in many ways. In
> some cases the union leaders will feel their fate bound up with the fate of
> their union and will fight even in a revolutionary fight. In others, new
> elections will throw up new leaders through the normal operation of the
> union apparatus, and still again, changes may be made through the
> organised pressure and activity of minority movements. To direct
> attention, therefore, to the central leadership of the unions is of

paramount importance, whatever its personnel may be. First, because it is a centre of authority controlling the masses; second, because it immediately focuses the character of the lead which is emanating from that centre, strengthening it if it is revolutionary, exposing it if it is not. And that is why the Communist Party directs attention to the leadership of the unions and makes its appeals to the leaders as well as to the masses.[31]

There were a number of reasons why Murphy began to shift his ground from his earlier position. To begin with, there was Murphy's own theoretical and political confusion in grappling with the problems of developing a revolutionary trade union strategy within unfamiliar and difficult objective circumstances. Thus, although the Bolsheviks' achievements in the Russian revolution had led him to abandon a generalised hatred of all leadership, the implications for revolutionary leadership in the trade unions had still to be thought through. Murphy had not recognised the fundamental difference between *revolutionary* leadership, the art of encouraging rank-and-file self-reliance, and *reformist* leadership, which consisted of spurring union officials to act on behalf of the rank-and-file.[32] The confused policy of the Comintern and the RILU, with its orientation on winning over unions wholesale to communism, compounded this lack of theoretical clarity by encouraging him to imagine some union officials might be prepared to fulfil the needs of the class struggle when the crisis of capitalism became critical. Finally, at a time when rank-and-file workers were lacking confidence and self-organisation was in decay, the campaign for the TUC to act as a 'General Staff of Labour' to lead workers' struggles, and trying to replace right-wing union officials with left-wingers, must have seemed a much more realistic option than concentrating purely on trying to rebuild rank-and-file organisation. Another party leader, Palme Dutt, attempted to refute the growing trend to see the TUC and union officialdom as the solution to the crisis in the movement and argued that class unity could not be achieved purely on a trade union basis but required political party leadership.[33] But by the end of 1922 the battle of ideas was over; Murphy and the other CP leaders increasingly tended to put the main emphasis on the need to 'capture' the central leadership of the British trade unions, or if that proved impossible, of finding left officials to co-operate with. In the process, as we shall see, they were to foster dangerous illusions in the union bureaucracy.

PARTY ORGANISATION

Although Lenin had expected quite a large Communist Party would be created as a result of the fusion of the various British revolutionary groups, the party had started off with a membership of only about 4,000 which dropped to 2,500 by the beginning of 1921.[34] Moreover, despite the overwhelmingly working-class nature of its membership, the quality of the party's organisation and leadership was far from satisfactory. First, the new party was afflicted with sectarianism, evidenced by the way its formal application to affiliate to the Labour Party was deliberately couched in terms that invited rejection (see section entitled 'Communists and the Labour Party' later on in this chapter). Second, there was a strong syndicalist approach to the party's industrial work. Thus, the CP's intervention in the 1921 miners' lock-out was fought out in purely economic terms with little political generalisation. Third, despite the CP's formal agreement to the principles of the Comintern, the organisation as it emerged in 1921 remained essentially that of the old type of socialist propaganda party, combining a loose, unco-ordinated structure of organisation with a federally-elected geographically-based leadership. This hampered both effective intervention inside the working-class movement and centralised leadership within the party.[35] As a consequence, at the beginning of 1922 there was a strong mood for radical change within the party, which was reinforced by behind-the-scenes pressure from the Executive Committee of the Comintern, who strongly criticised the failure of the party to depart from previous political practices and methods of work and to build a disciplined and centralised party of the Bolshevik type. As Murphy commented:

> We were of course far from having put into operation all that was required by the CI [Communist International] resolution to reconstitute the new Communist Party. We had made our political declaration of adherence to its principles, but it is one thing to accept a principle and another to apply it to life ... We had accepted the principles of 'democratic centralism' but had hardly begun to apply them to the general structure and work of the party. Naturally it would take time to transform parliamentary socialists, guild socialists, syndicalists, anti-parliamentarians and the like into fully-developed Communists of the standard set by the new Leninist conceptions.[36]

The growing dissatisfaction within the party, which inevitably began to take the form of criticism of the existing executive committee,[37] came to a head at the party's congress in March 1922 and expressed itself most clearly in the carrying of an amendment to the leadership's main resolution for the establishment of a special Commission to examine party organisation. The amendment established that the Commission to be appointed would be drawn from *outside* the membership of the executive committee, and be endowed with powers to conduct a detailed and drastic investigation of every aspect of party work and organisation. The Commission's report (prepared by Palme Dutt, Pollitt and Inkpin) was submitted five months later to the party congress in October 1922. Echoing Comintern criticism it noted:

> The Party has now been in existence for two years. They have been years of tremendous happenings, of great revolutionary significance, and of world-wide communist impetus ... Yet in these two years, with all these opportunities, and with the tireless activity and energy of individual workers, the Party has made no real progress either numerically or in terms of influence.[38]

Guided by the theses on organisation adopted by the Comintern's Third Congress, the report proposed a new party structure much more suited to intervention in the class struggle. Its main recommendations included: the party leadership to lead the work of the districts and branches; the formation of communist 'fractions' in the trade unions and 'cells' in the factories to give communist leadership to workers; the party's paper to be changed to appeal to factory workers; and the establishment of a system of political education. The party congress accepted the Commission's recommendations unanimously and proceeded to elect a leadership markedly different from the old in size, composition and power. As a result, the former SLP members Murphy, MacManus and Bell, who had previously played the leading roles in running the party, were excluded from the organising bureau which had the vital task of putting the report into operation (although Murphy and MacManus became members of the political bureau with responsibility for directing the party's general political activities).

Significantly, support for the *principle* of organisational reform by Murphy, MacManus and Bell masked a growing scepticism as to its practical feasibility. There was the belief that the question of party development was being treated in a purely organisational way divorced from the political work of the party and preparation of the membership, and that the very extensive organisational changes would merely produce an over-elaborate apparatus which would sap the resources of the party. Murphy, the most forceful and articulate of the critics, felt that many of the objectives were 'literally impossible'.[39] Certainly, he was justified in pointing to the absurd disproportion between the struggling British party and the attempt to impose on its (by now) 3,000 scattered members a highly cumbersome and bureaucratic system of organisation (with some 15 different departments attached to the central organisation and political bureau, and with numerous district party committees, local party committees, factory groups, and street groups). As a result of the resistance that the reformers (Palme Dutt and Pollitt, supported by Gallacher) encountered from Murphy and others within the leadership of the party, there was a slow rate of change in implementing the report. This led to the first serious crisis within the party, with sharp differences emerging amongst the leadership.[40]

It seems likely that Murphy's doubts were bolstered by a combination of interrelated factors that underlined the problems of party organisation within the sphere of trade union work. First, early in 1922 the Russian-American Comintern agent Mikhail Borodin had been sent to Britain (under the pseudonym of George Brown) to investigate the British Party's failure to win trade union support, and Murphy (whom he had previously met en route to the Second Comintern Congress) had acted as his personal secretary, writing up the reports he sent back to Moscow. Bypassing both the national and district leaderships of the party, Borodin had devoted a good deal of effort in South Wales and elsewhere encouraging communists and sympathisers to organise a left-wing trade union organisation or 'Minority Movement' in the mining unions. Moreover, he had publicly opposed the organisation report and engaged in a fight against its recommendations on the basis that the CP was too weak to live up to the Commission's grandiose objectives. Borodin's consistent alignment with the old party leadership, especially Murphy, quickly incurred the hostility of Dutt and Pollitt. Although Borodin was arrested and imprisoned in Glasgow before being deported as an 'illegal' after only six months in Britain, it strengthened Murphy's own public critique of the reformers' organisational measures. Moreover, as he was to discover, Borodin's approach had powerful supporters within the Comintern.[41]

Second, Murphy was influenced by the Comintern's adoption of the 'united front' policy, which had first been articulated at the end of 1921 and then reaffirmed at the Fourth Congress in November 1922 which he had attended. The leaders of the Communist International had recognised that the immediate revolutionary crisis that had swept across Europe had passed. The working class had suffered a series of disastrous political and economic defeats in Finland, Germany, Italy, Hungary and Bulgaria, ultimately because of the lack of mass Bolshevik-type parties, and capitalism had entered a (second) period of 'partial and temporary stabilisation' in which the conquest of power as an immediate task of the day was not on the agenda. As Trotsky admitted at the Third Comintern Congress in June 1921: 'Only now do we see and feel that we are not immediately close to our final aim, to the conquest of power on the world scale ... We told ourselves back in 1919 that it was a question of months, but now we say that it is perhaps a question of several years'.[42] Previously the task of the communist parties had been to provide independent leadership, aiming to lead the working class directly into a struggle for power based on factory organisation and soviets, and bypassing the reformist trade unions if they could not be won to the revolutionary struggle. In the new situation, revolutionaries had to recognise that they were merely a minority within the unions, and for the immediate future would remain so. This meant it was necessary to wean the workers from their reformist leaders by degrees. Communist strategy must now focus on the 'united front' with the reformists, making a determined attempt to force the leadership of the reformist organisations into limited co-operation on concrete issues by winning their followers for unity in action, not merely an attempt to draw those followers into action behind the communist parties. The implications of this strategy for the British party were spelled out by Lozovsky, the secretary of the RILU, at the Fourth Comintern Congress:

> As far as Britain is concerned, we see clearly that it would be disastrous if the party were content to organise its forces only within its little Party nuclei. The aim here must be to create a more numerous opposition trade union movement. Our aim must be that our Communist groups should act as a point of crystallisation round which the opposition elements will concentrate. The aim must be to create, to marshal, to integrate the opposition forces, and the Communist Party will itself grow concurrently with the growth of the opposition.[43]

In many respects, this proposal for the formation of 'revolutionary minorities' of communists and non-communist trade unionists represented a direct challenge to the British party's recently adopted organisational reforms, with their innumerable bureaucratic party committees that seemed to cut across any immediate priority of mobilising general resistance to the employers' offensive, and confirmed Murphy's doubts as to their efficacy.

Third, he was influenced by the specific criticism of the CP's industrial work levelled by the Comintern. A special Commission (which included Lozovsky and Borodin) was set up in June 1923 to investigate the party's trade union work and especially the lack of co-operation between the British Bureau of the RILU and the party. Simultaneously, the Comintern decided on the extraordinary step of inviting the entire leadership of the CP to an enlarged session of its executive committee in Moscow to discuss the progress made towards implementing the 1922 Party Commission's report on 'Bolshevisation'. Virtually all of the British communist leaders attended, with the exception of Murphy, who had only recently returned from the Fourth Comintern Congress and was therefore given responsibility as acting political secretary of the party in the interim.[44] The outcome of these discussions was mixed. On the one hand, the Comintern executive insisted on changes in the party's leadership to reflect the organisational changes introduced, which resulted in the establishment of an in-built majority for the reformers on the political bureau (from which Murphy was removed), which was newly conceived as the party's full-time executive authority. It marked a further reduction in influence of Murphy and the old SLP leaders, although they were not censured in any way and continued to serve the party in conspicuous and important positions. On the other hand, the reformers were obliged to acknowledge the need to set about the task of organising a national left-wing opposition movement in the trade unions. This proposal, pushed strongly by Borodin and Lozovsky, was based on the view that the British Bureau of the RILU was too closely identified with the single issue of affiliation to the Red International. What was needed was the formation of an opposition bloc by rallying all the various left-wing opposition currents and groupings in the trade unions.[45] To effect this industrial policy, Pollitt was made head of the party's industrial department (thereby formally taking over from Murphy), and Gallacher was made head of the British Bureau of the RILU with the instruction to organise a national conference to launch the 'Minority Movement'. In fact, because of the reformers' fears that such a movement might duplicate the work of the party or even become an alternative leadership, it was not until a year later in August 1924 that the first conference of the National Minority Movement (NMM) was held. The delay was later criticised by the executive bureau of the Red International in Moscow which now insisted the object of the British Bureau was:

> ... not to organise independent revolutionary unions or to split the revolutionary elements away from the existing organisations affiliated to the TUC and through it to the Amsterdam International, but to convert the revolutionary minorities in the various industries, into revolutionary majorities. Hence the British Bureau is not an organisation of unions but only of revolutionary minorities of unions.[46]

Significantly, whilst the Comintern's decisions were accepted by the majority of the executive committee of the CP, some members were still not convinced that the reorganisation of the party had been carried out along the right lines. The controversy was strong enough for open discussion to flare in the party's theoretical journal. In an important contribution to *Communist Review* in January 1924, Murphy, whilst careful to stress the positive achievements of the reorganisation, including the improved circulation of *Workers' Weekly* and the party's increased influence in the trade unions and the Labour Party, insisted that these had been achieved in spite of the mistakes in organisation. The party had come to treat the Commission's report as a 'Communist Holy Bible' and applied its proposals with little regard to the strength, resources and political development of the membership. Far too many full-time organisers and district party committees had been appointed, and these were a drain on the time and finances of the party. Aggregate meetings had become 'organisational washhouses' dealing with the demands and appeals pumped out by a remote executive. There was no time for party training or discussion and as a result members were politically ill-equipped to lead the struggles of the workers. Drawing attention to the lack of education and discussion in the party, Murphy wrote: 'Already the party lead is accepted too formally, and the voice of political criticism too seldom raised within our ranks'. He effectively summed up his critique of the reorganisation when he stated that: 'If I were asked what are the principal defects of the Party today, I would answer unhesitatingly, formalism, organisational Fetishism, and lack of political training'.[47]

Pollitt replied to Murphy's critique in the next issue of *Communist Review*, contrasting the influence and strength of the party in early 1924 with the position beforehand; the following month, E. W. Cant, the London district organiser, joined in the debate in support of Murphy.[48] It is clear from the report of the control commission to the party's Sixth Congress in May 1924 that the critics were eventually successful in persuading the majority of the leadership of the need for a whole number of 'organisational adjustments'. It was acknowledged that the implementation of the organisation report had 'led to an enormous increase in influence, but little change in the size of the party. These factors, along with overconcentration on the scheme of organisation, have resulted in the deterioration in the political quality of the party'.[49] One manifestation of the weakness of party organisation was the way in which during 1923 the industrial department had been bandied about from one executive committee member to another (from Murphy to Pollitt and back) and had failed to get down 'to the elementary task of ascertaining the strength and co-ordinating the work of the party nuclei in the trade unions'.[50] The party congress endorsed the critique, particularly the friction and lack of contact between the RILU bureau and CP executive and the failure to make any real attempts to set up a cohesive national unofficial rank-and-file movement. As a result, it was agreed to increase the size of the executive, appoint a small secretariat, and to elect Murphy back on to the political bureau despite his strong critique of the reformers in general and Pollitt in particular.[51] The net result was to change the overall composition of the leadership by restoring a rough balance between the 'old' ex-SLP group and those most associated with the organisation report.[52]

It is necessary to keep a sense of proportion about the controversy, in that the differences between the leaders at no time led to threats of resignation or splits in the party. Moreover, with the benefit of hindsight, it it clear the reorganisation of the CP marked an important step forward in breaking from the passive, sectarian, syndicalist and propagandist tradition of pre-1920 British Marxism. The discovery of centralised organisation and disciplined common action, the replacement of the essentially propagandist newspaper *The Communist* by the more agitational *Workers' Weekly*, and the establishment of factory branches all had the advantage of enabling the party to maximise the influence of its limited membership in the trade unions and led to an enthusiastic revival of party activity. Of course, the disadvantage, as Murphy had justifiably pointed out, was that, initially at least, the party inherited a bureaucratic, unwieldy party structure. It also took some time before systematic party training became established.[53] Nonetheless, even Murphy would have had to acknowledge that the combined impact of the transformation of the party's structure and the launch of the National Minority Movement (NMM), with Pollitt as national secretary, was to help bring about a marked improvement in its ability to intervene inside the trade union movement.

By the end of 1924, and against the backcloth of an important revival in working-class struggle (see next section) the party had grown to 4,000 members, rooted in numerous factory groups. The National Minority Movement was to have its main base within the mining industry, particularly in the South Wales area, although similar, less well rooted Minority Movements were built in engineering, transport and other industries. Individual militants who had made up the various unofficial movements of the previous dozen years—the shop stewards' movement and the amalgamation committees of the engineering industry, the 'viligance' committees of the railways and the miners' reform movements—were brought together around a single coherent programme for the first time. The NMM quickly became a prominent national body which injected new life into many trade union branches and trades councils around a fight for both economic demands (for wage increases and a shorter working week) and for turning the defensive struggles into an onslaught on capitalism. Its growing strength was shown at the second annual conference of the movement in August 1925, which mustered 683 delegates claiming to represent 750,000 workers, or more than three times the numbers of the inaugural conference a year before. But although it pulled together a substantial network of militant activists in a number of unions, the NMM was not really a *rank-and-file* movement in the same way as the SS&WCM had been. Instead, it saw itself as a ginger group acting in consort with left union officials where possible and pressurising them where necessary. As Murphy commented: 'It is not a question here, be it noted, of setting up a rival organisation. It is one of calling to officials and the rank-and-file alike to present a United Front against the capitalist offensive'.[54] In practice, the NMM tended to put the emphasis on looking towards left officials to provide leadership on behalf of the rank-and-file.

THE GENERAL STRIKE

If by 1924 Murphy, the CP and the NMM were already beginning to trail behind the left trade union leaders, a much more decisive shift to the right was spurred on by political developments inside Russia (known as the USSR from the end of 1923) and the Comintern. As we have seen, probably no lesser event than the Russian revolution and the advice and direction emanating from Lenin and the Comintern in Moscow would have been sufficient to unite the different British Marxist groups into the CP. Moreover, despite the difficulty in charting a detailed policy towards trade unionism that suitably fitted the experience of western Europe, the importance of a party of the Bolshevik type was never lost sight of and the first four Comintern Congresses were genuine schools of revolutionary strategy and tactics for the British communists. However, with the defeat of the German revolution in October 1923, it had become clear that the hopes of a socialist Europe coming to the aid of a backward USSR were gradually receding. The predominant view in Moscow was that the Russian revolution could not expect immediate assistance from revolutions abroad and would therefore, at least for a short period of time, be thrown back on her own resources. As a result, they began to look for allies and security from imperialist attack elsewhere. But the Russians' changing perception of the international revolutionary situation was to have extremely important consequences for the Comintern, as international diplomacy began to take precedence over the goal of world revolution. Thus, the Comintern leadership, impatient with the slow growth of the CPGB, began to seek alternative instruments for revolutionary policy in Britain.

The relative weakness of the CPGB seemed to be offset by the unique position of the British trade unions which enjoyed great influence and prestige, were the dominant power within the Labour Party and had shown more practical sympathy with the Russian revolution than any other British organisation. From the moment that the 'united front' policy had been proclaimed, the prospect of winning trade union support for Moscow, and thus gradually infiltrating the existing trade union structure, was judged to be more promising in Britain than in any other country.[55] Such a view was further encouraged by election of the first, minority, Labour government under Ramsay MacDonald in December 1923, and the widespread trade union disillusionment with the government which quickly set in. Zinoviev, the President of the Comintern, had become very impressed with the emergence on the TUC General Council of a left-wing set of leaders, notably Alfred Purcell of the furnishing trades, George Hicks of the building workers and Alonzo Swales of the engineers, who had articulated the disgust felt throughout the trade union movement with the policies of the Labour government. At the Fifth Congress of the Comintern (June-July 1924) which Murphy attended, Zinoviev, referring to the leaders of the CPGB, such as Bob Stewart and Arthur Mac-Manus, made a cryptic comment:

> In England we are now going through the beginning of a new chapter in the Labour movement. We do not know whither the Communist Mass Party of England will come, whether only through the Stewart-MacManus door—or through some other door. And it is entirely possible, comrades, that the Communist Mass Party may still appear through still another door—we cannot lose sight of that fact.[56]

By talking of this mysterious 'other door' Zinoviev implied that a mass revolutionary party could be built by the current around the left leaders of the TUC (and Labour Party), and there followed a policy of diplomatic manoeuvring. A delegation of Russian trade union leaders, including Tomsky, Melanchansky and Yarodsky, attended the TUC Congress in Hull in September 1924, and invited the General Council to send a delegation to the USSR. The Russians, all of whom Murphy had previously collaborated with in founding the RILU, stayed at his house in Ealing in west London. Molly recalled that Tomsky called on Jack to try to organise a meeting with sympathetic union leaders at the TUC to discuss the formation of a joint trade union body committed to building international unity between the movements in both countries and healing the breach between the Red and Amsterdam Internationals.[57] It seems highly likely Murphy had been involved in discussions about such an initiative at the Fifth Comintern Congress in Moscow from which he had just returned. Following a visit to the USSR by an official TUC delegation, an Anglo-Russian Trade Union Committee, composed of Russian trade union leaders and members of the TUC General Council (particularly its 'lefts', Purcell, Hicks and Swales), was established in April 1925.

But the Anglo-Russian Committee was a unity of the trade union *leaderships* rather than the rank-and-file. The rising Stalinist bureaucracy in the USSR, which had began to emerge in the internal power struggle that followed Lenin's death in January 1924, was in favour of this move for reasons of political expediency, although by 1926 it had even out-manoeuvred Zinoviev for political control of the Comintern.[58] In alliance with Bukharin, Stalin began to champion the idea of 'socialism in one country' which effectively ruled out any idea of extending the revolution beyond the USSR's frontiers. The implication was that the main task of the Comintern and foreign communist parties was to defend the USSR from the predatory attacks of international imperialism, not to foment revolutionary workers' uprisings. Thus, Stalin hoped a bloc with the left-inclined British unions would serve as a deterrent to western military aggression. Such developments were directly responsible for encouraging the British communists to maintain friendly links with the left trade union bureaucrats. But, on two counts, it was to have very damaging political consequences. First, the Committee granted the left-wing leaders on the General Council a false 'revolutionary' credibility at very little cost, which helped to cover their subsequent betrayal of the 1926 General Strike. Second, it inhibited the CP from making the necessary criticism of the General Council and its left leaders, and from attempting to encourage rank-and-file independence. Although there was no dramatic reversal of policy, gradually across the period between 1924 and the General Strike in May 1926 the Anglo-Russian Committee, as we shall see, served to confuse and neutralise the important steps which the CP had begun to take in implementing Bolshevik methods of work within the unions.

Significantly, a number of historians of the early Communist Party have argued that once the climax of 1919 had passed, a rank-and-file strategy whose objective was the creation of a mass revolutionary party was simply utopian during the 1920s, given the mass unemployment and consequent collapse of shopfloor organisation.[59] Certainly during the *early* 1920s a pure rank-and-file strategy, basing itself on the self-activity of the mass of workers, was bound to fall flat. But from 1924 there was an important revival of working-class combativity and a halt in the decline of trade union membership, as economic recovery and the consequent fall in unemployment gave workers greater confidence to take on the employers. The formation of the first Labour government under Ramsay MacDonald's leadership after the general election of December 1923 also helped to encourage a new spirit of resistance in the trade unions, although Labour fell from office after less than a year. During this period employers demanded wage cuts in industry after industry. But workers were now prepared to resist such cuts as they had not been in 1922–1923. The railwaymen, the dockers and the London tramway workers were all out on strike against wage reductions. Throughout the spring and summer of 1924 there were also a series of stoppages among ship repairers, railway shopmen and builders. The faint stirrings of a mass strike situation were becoming apparent, with unofficial strikes, lightning strikes, and strikes in one industry in one town, all building up. The overall number of workers on strike rose 50 per cent above the level of the previous year. The growth of resistance was encouraged by an important favourable external circumstance. The previous year French troops had occupied the Ruhr and as a result German industry was completely disrupted. Suddenly there were new markets for Britain's coal exports. This gave an unexpected strength to the Miners' Federation who were able to extract an agreement from the owners, to last for twelve months, which recouped many of the losses of 1921.[60]

The revival in workers' militancy was reflected in the way that a number of union leaders felt it necessary to give official support to carefully limited actions, if only to keep their leadership over the movement. This was mirrored by the emergence on the TUC General Council of an articulate and verbally very militant left wing, notably Swales, Purcell and Hicks, whose revolutionary class struggle language dominated the Trade Union Congresses of 1924 and 1925.[61] The launch of the National Minority Movement in August 1924 also reflected the renewed possibilities for creating a network of militant rank-and-file activists within the unions, particularly in the mines, engineering and on the railways. The influence of the NMM grew rapidly during this period, especially with the election of A. J. Cook as secretary of the Miners' Federation. The left wing mood led to the TUC's participation in the Anglo-Russian Trade Union Committee set up in the spring of 1925.

By far the most important arena of resistance was in the mining industry. In June 1925 the mine owners announced their intention of ending the National Wages Agreement fixed the previous year. This would have led to the break-up of national pay bargaining and to wage cuts. Fearful that the rest of the trade union movement would suffer the same treatment, with the employers and Conservative government attempting to repeat the same attacks that had followed 'Black Friday' in 1921, the TUC agreed, in an attempt to shake off their discredited prestige in the eyes of many rank-and-file workers, to support the miners by placing an embargo on the movement of coal. On 'Red Friday' 31 July 1925, the government was forced to back down, providing a nine-month cash subsidy to the mine owners and setting up a Royal Commission to investigate the industry. But it was clear the 'day of reckoning' had merely been postponed for nine months. Thus, from 1924 onwards there were a number of developments which began to open up significant new opportunities for the growth of communist influence inside the working class, even if the continued weakness of shopfloor organisation made the re-creation of a rank-and-file *movement* similar to that built during the First World War highly unlikely. However, Murphy and the other CP leaders tended to concentrate on marshalling this growing fighting spirit behind the left officials of the TUC.

In the wake of Red Friday there was a euphoric and widespread belief that the TUC could be relied upon to act firmly again when the postponed crisis finally came to a head in May 1926. The Scarborough Trades Union Congress in September 1925, with its militant speeches by Swales and other union leaders, and resolutions in favour of factory committees and against imperialism, helped to reinforce such a mood, even though the Labour Party conference that followed was the scene of vicious anti-communist witch-hunting. But at the very time when Murphy and the CP needed to criticise in a concrete manner the inactivity of the left trade union leaders in the face of the government preparations for a showdown, and to exert all its efforts to develop rank-and-file preparation *independently* of the TUC, 'left' as well as right, they were inhibited from doing so by fear of antagonising their allies on the Anglo-Russian Trade Union Committee. It should be noted some commentators have suggested that Murphy at first argued that no reliance could be placed on the TUC leadership.[62] Certainly, in September 1925, analysing the lessons of Red Friday and the fact that the government had nine months in which to perfect its strike-breaking organisation, he seemed prepared to acknowledge the potential revolutionary character of a general strike in support of the miners and to warn that the TUC leaders could not be trusted to lead such a battle:

> But let us be clear what a general strike means. It can only mean the throwing down of the gauntlet to the capitalist state, and all the powers at its disposal. Either that challenge is only a gesture, in which case the capitalist class will not worry about it, or it must develop its challenge into an actual fight for power, in which case we land into civil war. Any leaders who talk about a general strike without facing this obvious fact are bluffing both themselves and the workers.[63]

But despite this statement, the whole tenor of Murphy's writings during this period suggests his notion that the miners could only be defended by a struggle for state power was no more than a potential scenario which he believed was unlikely to occur in reality. Moreover, with the formation of the Anglo-Russian Committee, he clearly saw the party's chief task to be the pressuring of the TUC and its left leaders to lead the struggle in defence of the miners, regardless of their lack of revolutionary intent. To illustrate this we can consider his assessment of the Scarborough Trades Union Congress in September 1925. Re-elected head of the CP's Industrial Department in May, thereby taking over from Pollitt who had become preoccupied with the NMM, Murphy organised the party's successful intervention at the TUC Congress. The Congress passed a whole series of left-wing resolutions, including one which called for the development and strengthening of workshop committees as 'indispensable weapons in the struggle to force the capitalists to relinquish their grip on industry'. Murphy praised the adoption of this factory committee resolution as a major step forward in preparation for the anticipated General Strike.[64] Yet the whole context in which the resolution had been passed indicated that, for the General Council, it was merely a pious resolution not committing the TUC in any concrete way to the encouragement of committees of rank-and-file workers at workshop level. Significantly, as a leader of the wartime shop stewards' movement, Murphy had stressed the importance of workshop committees as an independent force in rank-and-file workers' struggles, and as a base from which the union bureaucracy could be fought. But he now advocated the whole initiative for their formation be placed on the General

Council and pleaded with the latter to live up to their Scarborough commitments:

> The initiative should come from the General Council of the TUC and its sub-committee of trades councils ... Both need, of course, the complete co-operation of the trade union executives and this ought not to be difficult to obtain if they are at all intent on defending their own interests.[65]

Even though over the next few months the CP and NMM did campaign for the formation of factory committees, and for trades councils to set themselves up as 'Councils of Action' to co-ordinate the General Strike at local level, they did little to break out of the limitations placed on the rank-and-file by the trade union apparatus. Indeed, Murphy could denounce any attempt to set up *independent* Councils of Action at local or national level: 'There should be no rival body to the Trades Council ... We should avoid rivalry and recognise the General Council as the General Staff of the unions directing the unions in struggle'.[66] Thus, the party's activities were mainly devoted to exhorting the TUC to act, not to challenging the largely verbal militancy of the left leaders or advocating the need for an independent leadership to the 'general staff of labour' on the basis that the TUC General Council was liable to betray the miners.

In the immediate run-up to the General Strike almost the whole of the CP's political bureau, including Murphy, was put out of action by a government crack down. In October 1925 the police raided the London offices of the Communist Party and *Workers' Weekly* and seized a mass of documentation.[67] Twelve of the leading figures of the CP, including Murphy, were arrested by the police on a charge of seditious libel and incitement to mutiny. The arrests, which occurred in the wake of Red Friday, were clearly designed to paralyse the party's activities in the lead-up to the General Strike, and a ten-day trial took place at the Old Bailey in November. As Murphy commented: 'We were quite confident that we were going to prison before ever we saw the jury: it was to us so obviously a political trial and part of a larger manoeuvre outside the court that we thought of the proceedings only in their effect on the outside public'.[68] Five of the accused, all of whom had previous convictions, were sentenced to 12 months in prison. The judge then turned to the others, including Murphy: 'You remaining seven have heard what I have had to say about the society to which you belong.

You have heard me say it must be stopped ... Those of you who will promise me that you will have nothing more to do with this association or the doctrines which it preaches, I will bind over to be of good behaviour in the future. Those of you who do not promise will go to prison'. One by one, beginning with Murphy, the judge asked: 'Will you be bound over?' Each of the seven accused answered 'No, I will not' and was sentenced to six months' imprisonment, evidently not for sedition but for refusing to leave the Communist Party.[69]

A broad national campaign of solidarity with the imprisoned communist leaders was mounted, and weekly demonstrations were held outside Wandsworth Prison. Murphy, who was by now 36 years of age, served his time working in the prison tailor's shop producing mail bags, reading novels by Conrad, learning shorthand and the rudiments of the Russian and German languages.[70] He was released from prison, with six of the other communist leaders, just before the onset of the General Strike in May 1926 and was greeted by a demonstration of 25,000 workers.[71]

From the beginning of the General Strike on 1 May the TUC leaders made it clear that they intended to keep a tight grip on the strike. First, the General Council decided that each union would organise its own individual campaign, thereby creating obstacles to unity across the working class at local level. Second, it decided workers would be called out on strike in separate 'waves', with industries to be hit picked on the most arbitrary basis, with the rest, including those in the postal service, not called out at all. By contrast, government preparations were much more extensive. Volunteers were asked to come forward and break the strike or to act as special constables. Public parks were requisitioned as supply dumps, two battleships were anchored in the Mersey, and battalions of troops marched through Liverpool as if for battle. At the same time, the Emergency Powers Act was implemented to give the police a whole number of new grounds for arrest. But despite the combination of half-hearted union leadership and government provocation, the response of the strike call, according to the TUC, 'surpassed all expectations'.[72] Three-and-a-half million workers became involved in the biggest single dispute in British history.

Trades councils were responsible for ensuring that local union branches kept to the General Council's instructions, drawing together representatives from the major unions and other sections of the labour movement in each area into 'councils of action'. Mass meetings were organised, local strike bulletins produced, pickets allocated (sometimes on a mass basis to stop all movement of strike-breaking traffic), and in a few places workers' defence corps were formed to protect workers from police attacks. But such activism in the localities was not matched by activism at the centre. A Strike Organising Committee was set up with the 'left' Purcell as chair-person. But it seems to have regarded its chief role as being that of restricting the activism in the localities. According to one historian of the strike: 'It was feared that in some provincial towns and cities extreme left-wing elements might take control and conduct the strike as a purely political affair. Hence the Strike Organising Committee tried from the first to maintain control over provincial activities which was simply unworkable'.[73] When the government started issuing its own daily paper, the *British Gazette,* the TUC replied with the *British Worker.* But there could hardly have been greater contrast between the tone of the two. The government proclaimed that the strike 'is not a dispute between employers and workmen. It is a conflict between trade union leaders and parliament'.[74] The *British Worker* lamely replied that 'The General Council ... wishes to emphasise that this is an industrial dispute ... The Council asks pickets to avoid obstruction and to confine themselves strictly to their legitimate duties'.[75]

The rebuff from Prime Minister Baldwin had forced the General Council to translate its threat of a mass strike into action. But once launched the TUC wanted to do everything to minimise the strike's effect. Their aim was to defend workers' interests *within* capitalist society, not challenge the basis of that society, and the ending of the strike showed that the TUC feared success even more than it feared defeat. On the fourth day of the strike the leadership of the TUC and Labour Party began secret negotiations with government ministers and officials on how to end it. Throughout, rank-and-file workers were kept in the dark, and on the ninth day of the strike, 12 May, the General Council called it off without consulting the miners. The agreement, which accepted wage reductions in the mines and provided no guarantees that other workers who had been on strike would not be victimised when they returned, represented a complete surrender. The decision of the General Council was *unanimous*, with not one left-wing voice raised against the proposal. Instead, Swales helped to formulate the agreement and Purcell pleaded with the miners' leaders to accept it.[76] The Miners' Federation, left abandoned, was to fight on alone for another six months, until it eventually returned to work on terms which included longer hours, wage cuts and a return to district agreements.

On his release from prison Murphy had immediately thrown himself into Communist Party activity in support of the General Strike in his old home town of Sheffield. But despite working with both the trades council's central disputes committee (which conformed strictly with the TUC's instructions) and with an unofficial CP/NMM strike committee (which raised wider political questions),[77] his equivocal attitude towards the TUC remained undiminished. Thus, three days before the General Strike commenced, Murphy spelt out his faith in the TUC leadership in an article that appeared on the front page of *Workers' Weekly* entitled 'Revolution Not in Sight':

> Our party does not hold the leading positions in the trade unions. It is not conducting the negotiations with the employers and the government.It can only advise and place its press and its forces at the service of the workers—led by others.
>
> And let it be remembered that those who are leading have no revolutionary perspective before them. Any revolutionary implication they may perceive will send the majority of them hot on the track of a defeat.
>
> Those who do not look for a path along which to retreat are good trade union leaders who have sufficent character to stand firm on the demands of the miners, but they are totally incapable of moving forward to face all the implications of a united working class challenge to the state.[78]

Such faith was completely unfounded. During the period from July 1925 to May 1926, whilst the government had carefully planned to break the miners' union, these 'good trade union leaders', who were supporters of the Anglo-Russian Committee, had made no preparation whatsoever for the inevitable conflict. Moreover, two weeks after Murphy's article appeared, the left leaders were to betray the miners as readily as Ernest Bevin, J. H. Thomas or any other right-wing member of the General Council. The unconditional nature of the surrender, and the failure of the left-wing members of the General Council to oppose it, came as a great shock to the Communist Party.

Trotsky, the only major figure in the Russian Comintern leadership to stand out against the British CP's opportunist drift, was far less impressed than Murphy with the left TUC leaders. His book *Where is Britain Going?* was published by the British Party in February 1926. Although it overestimated the revolutionary situation in Britain at the time and was factually wrong in some aspects, it emphasised again and again the dangers of trailing behind the left bureaucrats. Trotsky pointed out that the left nature of the Scarborough TUC remained 'left only so long as it had to accept no practical obligations' and that 'as soon as the question of action arises the Lefts respectfully surrender the leadership to the right'.[79] Trotsky's emphasis on the central importance of building a party of revolutionaries committed to the overthrow of capitalism ran directly counter to Zinoviev's hints that there might be some easier path to workers' power through alliances with left reformist leaders:

> The Communist Party will ... be able to take the lead of the working class only insofar as it enters into an implacable conflict with the conservative bureaucracy and the Labour Party. The Communist Party can prepare itself for the leading role only by a ruthless criticism of all the leading staff of the British labour movement.[80]

But Murphy completely rejected this analysis,[81] and in his *Workers' Weekly* article, written on the eve of the General Strike, implicitly attacked Trotsky's inflated hopes that a General Strike could lead to a revolution in Britain:

> To entertain any exaggerated views as to the revolutionary possibilities of this crisis and visions of new leadership 'arising spontaneously in the struggle', etc, is fantastic. Let us keep our feet well on the ground and our head clear.[82]

In a Sheffield CP bulletin published on the last day of the strike, Murphy repeated his view that the labour movement 'was totally incapable of measuring up to the revolutionary implications of the situation'.[83] However, even though the General Strike was not the revolutionary situation Trotsky hoped it would be, this did not mean the party could not have directed the attention of the most advanced workers to the dangers of reliance on the General Council and towards realistically exploring whatever independent rank-and-file initiatives were possible. Despite its numerically small size of 5,000 members, the CP, which had built a very large periphery of supporters and had considerable influence inside the unions via the National Minority Movement, played an energetic and heroic role in the strike, with hundreds of members arrested. But the party's slogan of 'All Power to the General Council' proved disastrous in feeding illusions that the TUC could be trusted to lead the strike. Of course, even if the CP had attempted to encourage some form of independent leadership it is unlikely it could have broken the control of the union bureaucracy. But it could have won a significant number of working-class militants to the ideas of communism and prepared them to learn from their experience, even in defeat, rather than suffer the shock of betrayal by the left leaders and consequent political demoralisation.[84]

Clearly, Murphy's political judgement was profoundly influenced by the Anglo-Russian Committee and Comintern. Of course, as some commentators have pointed out,[85] definite 'native' tendencies to trail behind the left TUC leaders had already become established inside the CP during the early 1920s and it is possible that left to themselves, Murphy and the party would have followed the same opportunist line. But the CP was part of a centralised world movement. In some respects it owed its very existence to the Russian revolution and its leaders and members were profoundly influenced and guided by advice and guidance from the Moscow centre. This was particularly the case with Murphy, who made regular trips to Russia and had close personal contacts with key Comintern leaders. In such circumstances, the line of the Comintern was bound to be decisive, and the tailing of the left union leaders was considerably spurred on by Moscow from 1924 onwards. Even though the Comintern made many left pronouncements, and in April 1926 even criticised the British CP for paying insufficient attention to the hesitation of the left leaders,[86] the logic of its search for allies on the TUC inevitably distorted the trade union policy of Murphy and the CP.

COMMUNISTS AND THE LABOUR PARTY

In many respects, Murphy's attitude towards the relationship between the Communist Party and the Labour Party during the early 1920s was a mirror image of and flowed directly from his changing industrial and trade union strategy. When the First World War began, the Labour Party was still only a trade union pressure group. But when it ended, an extraordinary transformation had occurred. As we have seen, Labour was relaunched as the chief opposition party with real prospects of government office. In addition to the adoption of the famous Clause Four, Labour's 1918 general election programme, 'Labour and the New Social Order', demanded the 'burial of capitalism'. Of course, as Murphy observed, 'The feet of the movement were shod with proletarian boots but its head was still Gladstonian wearing a little red cap which it liked none too well'.[87] But the impact of Black Friday, and the slump in trade union membership and the general workers' retreat during the early 1920s, saw Labour's vote and individual membership substantially increase. Trade union militants defeated on the industrial field increasingly began to transfer their hopes to Labour as a substitute on the political field. Thus, compared with 1918, Labour's vote in the general election of 1922 doubled to 4.2 million.

In the Russian leadership's calculations there could be no mass radicalisation of the British working class which did not express itself through the most powerful trade union movement in the world, and therefore through the Labour Party, since most of the large unions were affiliated to it. Thus, whilst Lenin had insisted on the *principle* of building a mass revolutionary party in opposition to Labour, he also proposed the *tactic* of the CPGB applying for affiliation to Labour. However, Lenin saw affiliation as conditional on certain vital factors.[88] First, 'the party of Communists can join the Labour Party only on condition that it preserves full freedom of criticism and is able to conduct its own policy. This is of extreme importance.' No continental social democratic party conceded freedom of criticism and autonomy, but Lenin believed that the Labour Party's unique structural link to the trade unions would permit such open revolutionary agitation. Second, the tactic was conceived in the context of the immediate prospect of European revolution. The Comintern thought the battle of revolution versus reform would soon be over. Affiliation was therefore a short-term policy for winning workers to the Communist Party, not a long-term one for becoming an integral part of Labour. Third, Lenin's proposal depended on a clearly demarcated Communist Party, able to *contrast* its politics with those of Labour before the working class. In other words, unlike the BSP, Lenin had no intention that the Communist Party should capture the Labour Party, nor that it should dilute its own revolutionary Marxism in order to stay inside.

As Lenin had explained: 'If the British Communist Party starts by acting in a revolutionary manner in the Labour Party, and if the Hendersons [the Labour Party general secretary] are obliged to expel this party that will be a great victory for the communists and revolutionary working class movement in Britain'.[89]

At the CPGB's founding congress the question of Labour Party affiliation was the most contentious issue, and although the delegates finally agreed to support Lenin's tactic, the reluctance of many of the party leaders to have anything to do with the Labour Party persisted. A letter applying for affiliation was sent to Labour's executive committee provocatively stressing the communists' belief in revolution and soviets. Not surprisingly, the application was rejected overwhelmingly at the 1921 Labour Conference, with similar rejections recorded in each of the next three years. It is possible that if it had been left to the CP's leadership, who thought that revolution was in the offing and that the Labour Party was doomed, this might have been the end of the matter. But the Comintern insisted on an ongoing campaign for affiliation, in the belief that any general radicalisation of the British working class would be channelled through the Labour Party (as yet untried and untested in government) and its trade unions.

Moreover, the Comintern viewed success on the question of affiliation as not resting on any conference vote; the campaign could help the CP raise its political profile of opposition to Labour's leaders, whilst at the same time relating to rank-and-file Labour Party members in the local branches. Thus, the affiliation issue came to affect every member of the party and became one of the principal forms of party activity. Moreover, with the adoption of the 'united front' policy towards the end of 1921, the British party was specifically advised to 'begin a vigorous campaign for their acceptance by the Labour Party'. Ironically, Murphy acknowledged that the new 'united front' tactic, which appeared to run counter to the idea of setting up a separate RILU in opposition to the Amsterdam International, came as a 'shock' to the CP.[90]

Over the next two years, during a period of mass working-class retreat on the industrial front in Britain, Murphy shifted his ground considerably on the question of the CP's relationship to the Labour Party. Thus, when the party's attempts to affiliate to Labour were rebuffed in 1922, and it looked as if the tactic was dead, Murphy proposed at the Fourth Congress of the Comintern that the attack upon the 'reformist fortress' must therefore be carried out by means of the 'open' penetration tactic of individual membership. He claimed the ability of CP members to work within local branches and through the unions at national Labour conferences had enabled them to wield significant influence, such that in some areas the communists had 'practically got control of the Labour Party organisations'. On this basis, affiliation no longer mattered. Instead, a direct effort had to be made to win over the Labour rank-and-file to communism.[91] In practice, the CP, which was, of course, primarily orientated on industrial organisation and struggle, pursued its Labour Party campaign by utilising both continued appeals for affiliation along with 'open' penetration on the lines recommended by Murphy.

It should be noted that despite Labour's rejection of Communist Party affiliation, communists were still eligible to become individual members of the Labour Party. During the first four years of the 1920s they became well integrated and accepted within the Labour Party, albeit as members of a separate organisation. A large proportion of the CP's membership had come from the BSP, which had been affiliated to the Labour Party both nationally and locally. BSP members had also represented their local trade union branches on the local Labour Parties and trades councils, and in a number of areas the leading figures in the local Labour Party had been BSP members. The numbers of such individuals, who now held Communist Party membership cards, and who retained their dual membership of the Labour Party, grew significantly. For example, Harry Pollitt was a well known communist who regularly attended the Labour Party conference as a delegate, and in a number of local Labour parties and Trades Councils, communists often exercised influence. In the 1922 general election six communist candidates actually enjoyed local Labour party support, and two were elected to parliament, J. T. Walton Newbold in Motherwell and S. Saklatvala in Battersea North. Moreover, irrespective of the formal policy decisions, an impressive list of local Labour party branches and unions repeatedly backed the demand for Communist Party affiliation.

Of course, the CP's strategy towards the Labour Party exposed party members to the risk of being influenced by Labour's reformist milieu even as they sought to win its rank-and-file for the revolution. A pull towards reformism was the price the CP had to pay for intervention, but it was worthwhile as long as the leadership understood the need to combat such tendencies towards political degeneration. However, the superimposition of the Comintern's united front policy on the affiliation tactic brought out an already strong latent tendency (especially among ex-BSP members) to adopt an equivocal attitude to the Labour Party. Thus, in early 1923 the Comintern was forced to insist that the CP maintain a sharply critical and independent standpoint,[92] and at the special meeting of the Executive Committee of the Communist International held in Moscow in July 1923 with the bulk of the CPGB leadership (except Murphy) the party was sharply criticised for its 'inadequate and aimless' application of the united front tactic. However, in spite of the lessons which had been drawn before the general election of December 1923 on the danger of viewing the advent of a Labour government as anything other than a capitalist bulwark against revolution, the election result (which led to the first minority Labour government) was greeted as 'a victory for the working class' by Palme Dutt, the editor of *Workers' Weekly*. He wrote: 'We are not fighting against the Labour government, which it is our concern to uphold and sustain against the attacks of the bourgeoisie'.[93] Murphy put the case for retaining a critical independent stance:

> ... if the voice of the working class criticism is silenced because Labour is in office while in a minority in parliament, and pursuing a Liberal policy, how are we to develop the class-consciousness of the workers and free them from the snares of capitalist Liberalism? It seems to me that this would be a surrender of the revolutionary movement to MacDonald on a par with MacDonald's surrender of the Labour Party to Nationalism.[94]

Further talks took place between representatives of the British CP and the Comintern in Moscow and on 6 February 1924 a joint declaration was issued by the two executives. The CP was urged to assist the workers to convince themselves of the 'utter worthlessness of the Labour leaders, of their petty bourgeois and treacherous nature, and of the inevitability of their bankruptcy'. The way to do this was by 'supporting the Labour government's programme' but at the same time pressing forward 'other immediate slogans calculated to mobilise the class-conscious sections of the working class for common action'. For its work to be effective, the CP had to 'maintain its ideological, tactical and organisational independence', whilst trying to 'come to agreements for such and such common action with "left" political organisations, as well as with local organisations of the Labour Party'.[95] As a delegate to the Fourth Comintern Congress in Moscow in November 1922, Murphy had been left in no doubt that the CP had to avoid the danger of fudging its differences with the Labour Party:

> The Communist Party of Great Britain came in for a little rough handling on this question by Comrade Radek, on behalf of the Executive Committee. The general election here has provided us with a fund of experience to test how far the party and its leaders have grasped the implications of the policy. Running throughout the party there appears to be the notion that the party exists only to become a Left Wing of the Labour Party, that we ought not even to criticise its leaders, that everything should be submerged to the idea of getting the Labour Party into power via parliament ... I have looked through the election material of members of the party, and in some cases it would be difficult to discover from the printed matter issued that they were members of the party. Had the Executive Committee of the Communist International received this election data before the Congress I am convinced that the criticism the Party received would have been much more stringent. We should neither aim at being a subterranean party existing to draft programmes on the quiet, or a party which has for its goal the election of a Labour government through a hush-hush policy. These things are not the application of the United Front policy but political confusion.[96]

In early 1924 he developed the same point:

> Already, danger is acute. The more progress we make in winning our way into the Labour Party, the greater the danger of absorption; the greater the need for political clarity, and the emphasis of first principles.

> The experience of the last twelve months fully justifies our warning. The United Front, for example, has too often been regarded as accommodation with the 'Right', instead of a means of struggle, involving the 'Right' in action, or exposure. The advent of a Labour government will accentuate this accommodation policy. Already, there are those in the Party, who contemplate the submersion of our programme to preserve the existence of a Labour government. These tendencies emphasise the need for sharpening our political criticism and a deeper regard for the theoretical equipment of our Party membership.[97]

The months of the first Labour government (December 1923–October 1924) were inevitably a complex and difficult period for CP-Labour Party relations. The CP had to maintain a principled critique of reformism and Labour's opportunist leaders whilst striving to develop the broadest rank-and-file Labour unity to force the Labour government to adopt a more anti-capitalist course of action. It had to continue to fight for affiliation to the Labour Party whilst more and more decisively criticising the Labour leaders. But the Labour government was given no time to demonstrate conclusively its impotence to solve the capitalist crisis; electoral defeat occurred in the midst of the infamous 'Campbell affair' (with the government attempting to prosecute the editor of the *Workers' Weekly* for an allegedly seditious article) and the 'Zinoviev letter' (in which the Tory press added to the growing anti-communist hysteria by forging a letter from the chair of the Comintern instructing the CP on how to control the Labour Party). When the Labour government fell in 1924 its right-wing leaders wanted scapegoats, and who better than the communists? The Labour Party conference of that year marked a turning point in Labour-communist relations when it agreed to exclude, not only the Communist Party as an organisation, but also individual CP members. It was to mark the final drive by the Labour leaders to ban communists from any kind of participation in Labour Party affairs, although it took another two years before the decision began to be implemented.

In the wake of these events during the end of 1924 and beginning of 1925, there were major differences of opinion inside the CP, revealed in the public controversy which took place within the journal *Communist International* between two of the party's leading theoreticians, Palme Dutt and Murphy. After having initially been carried away with the general euphoria of a Labour government, Palme Dutt now believed that the Labour Party was a 'broken instrument'. He thought that in the wake of the recent disillusionment, 'a process of separation of the workers and the Labour Party could be expected'. He predicted the growth of an opportunist left in the Labour Party but warned that the CP had to conduct an 'unceasing ideological warfare' against it; otherwise the masters of empty rhetoric would succeed in diverting working-class militancy. It was imperative that the CP maintain absolute independence from this phoney left which was bound to be discredited.[98] By contrast, Murphy argued that the Labour Party, far from being a decaying political force, was 'increasing in strength as the workers become more class-conscious', and was 'inevitably destined to be driven closer and closer to our party'. Moreover, he believed Labour's left wing should be seen as 'the indicator of where friendship for our party lies', and argued it was necessary to support the left-wing Labour leaders because 'if we attack the "left-wing leaders" we attack the mass with a similar outlook and drive them away from the party'. Therefore, he prescribed the maintenance of:

> ... a united front with the left-wing against the present leaders of the Labour Party, we should push this left-wing forward ... and use it as a vehicle for the dissemination of our revolutionary ideas among the proletarian masses until we shall have succeeded in transforming our own party into a mass party and eventually liquidating the Labour Party.[99]

Murphy also insisted it was not the task of the CP 'to split the Labour Party, although a split may be forced upon the Labour Party by the reactionaries, but certainly not by us'. Instead 'we are for the revolutionising of the Labour Party ... and against splits'.[100]

Although the next few years showed that Palme Dutt's forecast of the disintegration of the Labour Party was grossly mistaken, Murphy's stance effectively implied the subordination of the Communist Party to work inside Labour, even if Murphy, of course, did not envisage the disbandment of the CP. As Palme Dutt explained, the policy of the CP had to be based 'not on building up the Labour Party as the basis of the future revolutionary party, but on holding up the revolutionary mass movement within the Labour Party, which mass movement must develop to the mass Communist Party'. Murphy's view blurred the fundamental differences between the Communist Party and the Labour Party and reduced the former 'to a simple element of the left wing'. The lead could only come from the CP, not from the left wing leaders, who needed to have their ideological illusions and confusions exposed.[101] The controversy underlined wider differences generally inside the CP. On the one side stood those, like Palme Dutt, who stuck closely to Lenin's original thesis that the Labour Party was a 'bourgeois workers' party'. The task of building up the left wing was seen in terms of developing revolutionary class consciousness to the point where left-wingers realised that their aims could be achieved only by leaving the Labour Party and joining the CP. On the other side, there were many who saw the problem as Murphy viewed it, with its implication that a mass Communist Party could be built from an alliance with Labour's left wing.

There is no doubt that Murphy's stance was influenced by the notion of 'the other door' articulated by Zinoviev at the Comintern's Fifth Congress in 1924. Not only had Murphy attended this congress in Moscow but he had also sat on a British Commission which specifically dealt with the CPGB's relations with the Labour Party.[102] The 'other door' implied not merely the lefts in the TUC but also the left wing of the Labour Party, and the congress recommended the CP support and encourage this left wing to develop along revolutionary lines. As Zinoviev went on to say: 'I am quite aware of the fact that British leftists are still by no means revolutionaries, that they are still no better than the German "left" Social Democrats. But their appearance is an important event. We must understand this or we shall not be able to form a proletarian mass movement in Great Britain, much less bring about a proletarian revolution here'.[103] Zinoviev's statement reveals how difficult it was for the CP to adopt a consistent revolutionary attitude towards the left inside the Labour Party. By December 1924 the Comintern was insisting 'one of the most important prerequisites for the development of the Communist Party of Great Britain to a real mass party is to be found in the crystalisation of a left wing within the Labour Party. On this account the Communist Party should assist in the organisation of this Left Wing, which is the expression of the masses' desire for struggle'.[104] Over the next few months, it was Murphy's position that became dominant within the party. Thus, at a CPGB political bureau meeting in the spring of 1925, Murphy outlined the practical steps that needed to be taken to initiate a campaign for organising the left-wing elements in the Labour Party around a definite programme, and submitted a draft letter to be sent out by a sympathetic Labour MP calling for a national conference.[105] The initiative represented a gradual shift rightwards, away from what had essentially been a short-term affiliation tactic aimed at publicly exposing the Labour leaders as a means of building the Communist Party, to one where Labour was seen as open to conquest in the same way as the unions were supposed to be.

At the heart of the problem with Murphy's analysis was his view that as future mass workers' struggles pushed the trade unions to the left and either pushed the union leaders to fight or out of office, the Labour leadership would also inevitably fall to the left. As with the trade unions, he looked to the left in the Labour Party to lead the working class politically, imagining that Labour could be won to a revolutionary position. As he wrote in 1925: 'The Labour Party will grow in numbers and strength as the working class in increasing numbers awaken to political consciousness. In the process ... the bourgeois politics which dominate it today [will] be cleansed from its ranks.'[106] But this revealed a rather mechanical notion of political development. The problem was that the Labour Party, like the union bureaucracy, had a leadership with a vested interest in the preservation of existing society, a leadership which always looked at the wider movement as subordinate to parliament and the state. Moreover, Murphy was mistaken to see workers' struggles transforming Labour in their own image. In fact, the great advances in working class struggle, such as the wartime shop stewards' movement, had not led the most advanced workers towards the Labour Party but away from it. Labour's influence had only grown when the working class was in retreat. The assumption that Labour's right-wing leaders MacDonald and Henderson would be automatically cleansed from its ranks ignored the alternative strategy of unmasking false leftism by creating an independent revolutionary leadership free to initiate real action. Moreover, as Murphy had himself pointed out in 1920, it was wrong to suggest that because revolutionaries must be in the trade unions they should also stay in the Labour Party. Whilst the two are connected in terms of reformist politics, there is a qualitative difference between them in that only the trade unions are directly linked to collective struggle.[107]

Until the end of 1926 the CP's attention was concentrated more on the industrial than the political front. Nonetheless, when the Labour Party conference of 1925 reaffirmed its decision to proscribe individual communists from membership of the party, the CP, with Murphy taking a leading role,[108] pulled together a number of sympathetic local Labour parties which declared they would refuse to operate the ban, and shortly afterwards launched a National Left-Wing Movement (NLWM). The *Sunday Worker*, edited by a central committee member of the CP, became the movement's journal, with a peak weekly circulation of 100,000 copies. The NLWM's chief efforts were directed at getting the communist ban rescinded, the local Labour parties reinstated and at pushing the Labour Party to the left. Its proclaimed aim was 'not to supersede the Labour Party but "to remould it nearer to the heart's desire" of the rank-and-file'.[109] As with the unions, the CP adopted a ginger group approach, seeking to use the revolutionary political pressure of its supporters to force the left leaders to lead inside the

Labour Party. But just as the CP effectively abdicated leadership to the TUC lefts, so by putting all its efforts into a party tied to capitalism, it was giving way in political terms to left reformism. No doubt Murphy believed the National Left-Wing Movement would be a bridge to the CP for leftward moving Labour supporters. But why should they join the CP if the object was to 'remould' the Labour Party, especially as the CP said this was both possible and necessary? In reality, instead of helping to expose the Labour Party and build an alternative revolutionary socialist organisation, the NLWM actually worked to the advantage of reformism. Not only did it substitute for the Communist Party, it involved communists in sustaining a reformist left within the Labour Party.[110]

To conclude, by 1926 it had become increasingly difficult to separate Murphy's and the CP's approach to the Labour Party from that of the unions. In both they trailed behind the left bureaucracy, partly because of domestic political weaknesses but mainly because of the influence of the Comintern and its subordination of independent working class action to the search for reformist allies. Murphy's political development was to become even more skewed by Moscow over the next few years.

Chapter Five

The Comintern and Stalinism, 1926–1928

As we have seen, a crucial factor influencing Murphy's, and the Communist Party's, political development was the role of the Comintern based in Moscow. In turn, underlying the Comintern's role was the changing nature of the Russian workers' state in the first few years after the 1917 revolution. Indeed, it is impossible to fully understand the way in which Murphy and the CP operated inside Britain without placing their activities within the much broader context of the rise to power of the Stalinist bureaucracy inside the Russian state.

From the moment of its victory the Russian revolution had faced severe difficulties.[1] Marx and Engels had been clear that a socialist revolution could not be confined to one country because sooner or later it would be overcome by the pressure of world capitalism. Lenin, Trotsky and the other leaders of the Russian revolution shared this view, recognising that the economic backwardness of the USSR and its small working class in a predominantly peasant population would make the building of socialism especially difficult, and that everything depended on spreading the revolution to other more advanced capitalist countries. But the international revolution, although it came close to success in a number of European countries, failed to materialise, and the Russian revolution was left on its own. This enabled international capitalism to foment a terrible civil war in Russia between 1918 and 1921. So it was that a working class of just three million out of a total population of 160 million, racked by famine and strangled by an international blockade, faced 14 invading armies and domestic counter-revolution from the old ruling class. By the most extraordinary efforts the Red Army was victorious, but at an appalling cost. The country lay in ruins, industry was devastated and the working class, the class that had made the revolution, was effectively decimated with hundreds of thousands of the most politically conscious workers killed in the civil war. The working class lost the capacity it had established in October 1917 to directly control the newly formed state. In this situation, the ruling Communist Party, though its members still thought of themselves as Marxist, became transformed into an unaccountable bureaucracy standing above the working class. By 1921 what had emerged was, to use Lenin's words, 'A workers' state with bureaucratic deformations'.[2]

Because the only way of obtaining enough grain from the countryside to keep the towns and the Red Army on even minimum rations was by forced requisition, the Russian state was increasingly drawn into conflict with the peasantry, and Bolshevik rule, by force of circumstance, became harsh and authoritarian. As the civil war came to an end, revolt against grain requisition spread among the peasantry and a retreat became obligatory. The New Economic Policy (NEP) introduced in 1921 meant a partial return to capitalism in the form of private trading in grain. This had the effect of easing the tension in the countryside but it also increased the pressures on the ruling party to become a privileged elite, raising itself above the workers. As a result, bureaucracy grew apace both in the state apparatus and in the party, and, symptomatic of this trend, came the rise of the party's general secretary and chief bureaucrat, Stalin.

At the end of his political life, Lenin, who died in January 1924 but was too ill to be actively involved after the beginning of 1923, began to see the danger and fought a desperate rearguard action against bureaucracy in general and Stalin in particular. He sought Trotsky's aid in undermining Stalin's growing power. In the autumn of 1923 Trotsky formed the Left Opposition and outlined his ideas on how the bureaucracy, headed by the triumvirate of Stalin, Zinoviev and Kamenev, could be overcome. First, the revolution could only make progress in a socialist direction if the economic weight of the towns as against the country, of industry as against agriculture, was increased. Second, this industrial development, which would increase the size and social weight of the working class, had to be accompanied by increased workers' democracy, so as to end bureaucratic tendencies in both the party and state. Third, these first two policies could maintain Russia as a citadel of the revolution, but they could not produce that material and cultural level that was the prerequisite of socialism. The contradictions of a workers' government in a backward country with an overwhelming majority of peasants could only be resolved on an international scale through spreading the revolution abroad (as expounded in Trotsky's theory of 'permanent revolution'). For a brief period of time these ideas attracted significant support inside the Russian party.

It was the failure of the German revolution in the autumn of 1923, and Trotsky's critique of the inadequate leadership displayed by the German Communist Party and the vacillating advice provided by the Comintern (see next section), which brought to a head the sharp differences within the Russian leadership. However, the triumvirate soon fought back and an agitational campaign unlimited in its violence was launched against Trotsky. Every attempt was made to encourage the view that 'Trotskyism' had always opposed Bolshevism, and much was made of the fact that Trotsky had not joined the Bolsheviks until 1917. As Zinoviev and Kamenev later admitted, the myth of 'Trotskyism' was deliberately fabricated for the purpose of slander.[3] Lenin's will, revealed to the central committee in May 1924, and which called on the party to remove Stalin from the general secretaryship, was suppressed. Meanwhile, Stalin claimed to be the interpreter and faithful executor of 'Leninism' and took pains to justify his policies with quotations from Lenin's writings. By the autumn of 1924 the Left Opposition's challenge had been effectively broken. Triumphant, Stalin now declared the aim of the revolution to be 'socialism in one country', the idea that it was possible and necessary to build a complete socialist society in the USSR alone, without the aid of international revolution. It was an aim that represented a complete break with the Bolshevik tradition, although it represented perfectly the mood and aspirations of the rising bureaucracy who longed for business as usual, uncomplicated by a risky policy of international revolution.

Most historians have presented Stalinism as the inevitable consequence of Leninism.[4] In fact, as other writers have pointed out, it was Trotsky who kept the tradition of Leninism alive in his struggle against the Stalinist bureaucracy and the degeneration of the Russian revolution.[5] Trotsky's writings on the British General Strike of 1926 formed an important part of this critique of Stalin. At one stage he was joined by many other leading old Bolsheviks. Zinoviev and Kamenev, who had worked with Stalin in the first instance in order to drive Trotsky out of the party, briefly joined the new United Opposition, only to become reconciled with Stalin after he had succeeded in expelling them from the party as well. But by the end of 1927 Trotsky had been hounded out of the ECCI and Comintern.

Meanwhile, the rise to power of Stalin was to have a profound and lasting impact on the parties of the Communist International, including the CPGB. From the outset the Comintern had been dominated by its Russian section, as was only to be expected given that they were its founders and had the authority of the successful Russian revolution behind them. Murphy described the pupil-teacher relationship between the foreign communists and the Bolsheviks as it operated at the Second Comintern Congress in 1920: 'The whole Congress and especially its commissions were schools in which we immature socialists were being drilled into a theoretical understanding of Marxism as propounded by Lenin, Trotsky, Zinoviev, Bukharin and Radek'.[6] Nonetheless, during the first four congresses of the Comintern there was full and free debate and western communist leaders, particularly in Germany and France, felt able to challenge the Russians on certain aspects of policy, even if the latter's view generally prevailed. However, the defeat of the European revolutionary wave between 1919 and 1923 undermined the confidence of the western parties and emphasised their sense of inferiority to the seemingly victorious Russians. This, combined with the increased use of material aid and bureaucratic pressure, confirmed and intensified Russian domination of the Comintern to the point where it could be used to divert the International fundamentally from its original purpose of world revolution.

The ideological medium through which this shift was effected was the theory of 'socialism in one country'. If the main task, the establishment of socialism, could be achieved in one country, then the international revolution became a kind of optional extra or bonus, a distant goal to be rendered occasional homage, rather than an immediate necessity guiding practical activity. One consequence of this was a tendency to reduce the role of the communist parties to 'frontier patrols' for the Russian state.[7] Their first duty was to hinder any possibility of military intervention against the USSR and to this end they were induced to act as reformist pressure groups on their respective ruling classes, playing down revolutionary politics for fear of alienating potential friends and allies. One of the fruits of this orientation, as we have seen, was the subordination of the British Communist Party to the 'left' leaders of the TUC General Council who, posing as 'friends of the Soviet Union', subsequently betrayed the General Strike of 1926.

Thus, Russian state interests began to take precedence over the Comintern's original mission of world revolution and in the process the Comintern became a mere appendage of Stalin's foreign policy with extremely damaging consequences for its national sections, including the CPGB. This chapter explores the way in which Murphy (who was sent to Moscow immediately after the General Strike to replace Bell as the British party's representative on the Executive Committee of the Comintern) and the CPGB leadership wholeheartedly backed Stalin's fight against Trotsky inside the USSR and the Comintern, and the reasons for such loyalty.

THE ANTI-TROTSKY CAMPAIGN

At the Fifth Comintern Congress in June–July 1924 the slogan of 'Bolshevisation' was officially proclaimed, ostensibly signifying 'the application of the general principles of Leninism to the concrete situation of the given country'.[8] The crux of 'Bolshevisation' was the question of the relations of communist parties to the Comintern central bodies and to the Russian party. In practice, it played much the same role in the Comintern as was played by the cult of Leninism in the Russian party, with the struggle against Trotskyism being part and parcel of the same process. It had the effect of transforming the foreign communist parties along embryonic Stalinist lines, into parties that would be fiercely loyal to the Russian Communist Party majority and its bitter struggle against the 'Trotskyite opposition',[9] and which would gradually become highly bureaucratically centralist and disciplined organisations.

It has been suggested that the seriousness of the struggle for power within the USSR between Stalin and Trotsky did not become immediately apparent to the leaders of the British Communist Party, as reflected in the lack of discussion of this major controversy at the CPGB's Sixth Congress in May 1924.[10] But it seems much more likely that the differences within the Russian party, of which Murphy undoubtedly was aware as a result of his regular visits to Moscow, were effectively concealed from the CPGB membership by the leadership as being a purely internal affair of the Russian party, with no relevance to the work in Britain. It was only when the issues were transferred into the Comintern, and after specific pressure had been applied by the Executive Committee of the Comintern (ECCI), that a continued lack of discussion or comment on matters that had a major bearing upon the struggle in Britain became no longer tenable. Thus, the CPGB's delegation to the Fifth Comintern Congress, also attended by Murphy, was prepared to wholeheartedly support the Russian party's condemnation of Trotsky even before the matter had been raised with the membership.

But it was the publication of Trotsky's long essay entitled *The Lessons of October* in the autumn of 1924 that obliged the CPGB leaders to pronounce on the subject publicly.[11] Written under the influence of the recent defeat in Germany, Trotsky's essay re-examined the crucial points of the Russian revolution, and related the German events to the failure to grasp the lessons of the October revolution. The gist of the argument was that Germany had been ripe for revolution, but the German communist leaders had missed the opportunity because they had succumbed to the same kind of inertia and timidity as had been shown by Zinoviev and Kamenev (and Stalin, although he was not mentioned by name) in Russia in October 1917.[12] By implication, the Comintern leadership had also failed to provide adequate guidance, to encourage the decisive leadership crucial for the victory of the German revolution. Trotsky explicitly criticised Zinoviev, the President of the Comintern, for playing down the decisive role of the revolutionary party. Referring to Zinoviev's statement that in Britain the revolution could come through channels other than the party, he wrote:

> There has been some talk lately in our press to the effect that we are not, mind you, in a position to tell through what channels the proletarian revolution will come in England. Will it come through the channel of the Communist Party or through the trade unions? Such a formulation of the question makes a show of a fictitiously broad historical outlook; it is radically false and dangerous because it obliterates the chief lesson of the last few years. If the triumphant revolution did not come at the end of the war, it was because a party was lacking ...
>
> Without a party, apart from a party, over the head of a party, or with a substitute for a party, the proletarian revolution cannot conquer. That is the principal lesson of the past decade. It is true that the English trade unions may become a mighty lever of the proletarian revolution ... They can fill such a role, however, not apart from a Communist party, and

certainly not *against* the party, but only on the condition that communist influence becomes the decisive influence in the trade unions. We have paid far too dearly for this conclusion—with regard to the role and importance of a party in a proletarian party in a proletarian revolution—to renounce it so lightly or even to minimise its significance.[13]

In response, the central committee of the Russian Communist Party censured Trotsky for re-opening the internal faction fight which had officially been closed, and the Stalin group, needing the support of the international communist movement for its internal power struggle against the Left Opposition, obliged the Comintern sections in other countries to condemn *The Lessons of October*. Thus, in November 1924 a CPGB party council meeting endorsed the denunciation of Trotsky, even though they only had a summary of Trotsky's article to go on. Murphy, who had recently returned from the Fifth Comintern Congress, moved the main resolution:

> The Party Council of the Communist Party of Great Britain sees in the preface to Comrade Trotsky's book on '1917' an ... open attack upon the present leadership of the Communist International, which in the opinion of the CPGB, will not only definitely encourage the British Imperialists, the bitterest enemies of Soviet Russia, but will also encourage their lackeys of the Second International, and those other elements who stand for the liquidation of the Communist International and the Communist Party in this country.
>
> The Party Council and Executive Committee of the CPGB records its solidarity with, and implicit faith in, the Communist Party of Russia and the Executive Committee of the Communist International. Especially is this necessary in this most critical period when the world situation demands the closest co-operation of every member of the Communist International in carrying out the accepted policy of the International.[14]

When some party members questioned the hurried decision and asked for further information, a London aggregate meeting of 200 party members was held in January 1925. Again Murphy was central to the debate.[15] He argued that 'few of our party members would have thought of disassociating Lenin from Trotsky' because of the 'general ignorance of international affairs prevailing amongst the membership in Britain'. But, Murphy continued, Lenin and Trotsky 'had been in continuous opposition for 25 years', and Trotsky's policy would weaken the hold of the party and destroy the revolution. He answered those who criticised the action of the CPGB political bureau for their haste in bringing the issue before the membership with the assertion that 'the mere fact that Trotsky's action was a challenge to the International Leadership was a sufficient justification'. An amendment supporting the fight of the 'Left Wing Minority' in the Russian Communist Party against the bureaucracy received only fifteen votes.[16]

Meanwhile, early in 1925 a massive volume, *On Leninism*, appeared in the USSR. It contained fierce refutations of Trotsky's *The Lessons of October* in a collection of articles by Stalin, Kamenev, Zinoviev, Molotov, Kuusinen, Krupskaya, Sokolnikov and others. This work was translated, often in abbreviated form, into the main languages used within the Communist International. The English version, entitled *The Errors of Trotskyism*, was published in May 1925 by the CPGB, and contained an introductory chapter written by Murphy. He argued that *The Lessons of October* was completely mistaken because it dealt with the problems of leadership in the Russian revolution 'in a personal sense more than a party sense'. Whilst acknowledging the Russian party had become bureaucratised, he denied the current leaders 'were and are opposed to Party democracy'. But he insisted Trotsky's factional organisation stood condemned as 'the forming of a party within a party', and of 'Menshevik phrase-mongering':

> We cannot subscribe to Trotskyism on behalf of our party. We want not a 'subscribers' Party, but a 'working' Party. We want not a loose federation of conflicting factions, but a democratically centralised and united Party of the Proletariat. We want no policy of 'leading from below' which sets the rank and file against its leaders, but a living homogeneous party.[17]

The Errors of Trotskyism appeared on the weekend before the CPGB's Seventh Congress, and was meant to influence the delegates when the condemnation of the opposition came up. The Comintern was especially anxious to secure this, for it regarded the British Party as a model section, and the recent enlarged Plenum of the ECCI had praised 'the absence of factional struggles in the British Party'. The CPGB Congress accordingly declared 'complete agreement with the Central Committee of the Russian Communist Party in its estimation of the principles of Trotskyism and the measures taken to combat them'.[18] That such a condemnation could be made, without any debate or discussion whatsoever, justified the faith of the Comintern in its British affiliate, which effectively became a completely loyal devotee of the Russian Stalinist leadership before any other. In this respect, the CPGB offered a striking contrast to many other constituent parties of the Comintern. Thus, while the struggles by Trotsky and the Left Opposition during the mid-1920s provoked a sympathetic response among important sections of the major European parties, notably the French, Polish and German, the CPGB displayed an exceptional readiness to uncritically follow the latest Moscow line. It never seriously attempted to understand what was at stake in the struggles in the Russian party, and failed to grasp the disastrous international consequences of the theory of 'socialism in one country'.

A number of factors explain why Murphy and the other CPGB leaders were so unresistant to the process of Stalinisation. From the moment of the unification of the CPGB in 1920 the Russian experience had an overpowering influence on the development of the party. Whilst this influence was understandable given the prestige and authority of the Russian leaders, its impact was greatly accentuated by the fact that the British party, compared with other European communist parties, was a relatively tiny organisation of only a few thousand members. The theoretical weaknesses of the party, with a number of prominent British communists apparently indifferent to the issues of doctrine and theory which divided the leaders of the European communist parties, meant there was a tendency to rely for political guidance on the Russian leaders of the Comintern. Whilst this guidance, and the vast amount of financial aid which was provided,[19] was to be vital in directing the party into positive revolutionary work in the early 1920s, the party's dependent relationship on the Comintern ill-equipped it to resist the growth of Stalinism. In addition, the CPGB was pressurised by the ECCI into taking an orthdox line on Trotsky, without seriously debating the issues at stake or attempting to find out the reality of the situation inside the USSR. The problem for the CPGB leadership was that it either had to accept this situation or break with the Comintern, and the latter was not an attractive option as it would have meant breaking with the Russian revolution. But it was the legend of the Russian revolution, its solid and permanent substance, that gave Stalin his power over the CPGB, primarily because they were willing to serve a great cause which seemed to be of much greater magnitude than the internal feuds in the Russian Politburo. As Murphy commented: 'The longer I stayed, the more I saw, the less patience I felt with many of the critics of Russia and her Bolsheviks. The magnitude of the problems they had to solve was so stupendous that ... the more I ... felt the need for tempering criticism with understanding'.[20]

Moreover, Murphy had direct personal links with the Russian state and its leaders during the early 1920s. As we have seen, he made frequent visits to Moscow, helping to set up the RILU and participating in the Comintern congresses. He also corresponded with the ECCI secretariat[21] and wrote for the Comintern journal *International Press Correspondence* and the Russian party paper *Pravda*. In the summer of 1926 Murphy was sent to Moscow as the CPGB's representative on the ECCI and remained in the USSR for two years until his return to Britain at the end of 1928. Such close personal, organisational and political ties bound him firmly to the rising Stalinist group. As a result, he became convinced by Stalin's argument about the self-sufficiency of the Russian revolution, the view that the USSR could stand on its own two feet to complete the building of socialism in a single isolated state. Of course, he still looked forward to international revolution and was concerned to do what he could to further this in Britain and elsewhere from his position within the Comintern. But he came to believe that even if international revolution were to be delayed indefinitely, the USSR was capable of developing a fully fledged socialist society through its own efforts. Moreover, he accepted the Stalinist portrayal of Trotsky as somebody whose critique seriously threatened the security of the country at a time of imperialist threat.

POST-GENERAL STRIKE ARGUMENTS

The question of Trotskyism was raised anew in the CPGB during the summer of 1926 in connection with Trotsky's attitude to the role of the British communists in the General Strike. As we saw in Chapter Four, Trotsky's book, *Where is Britain Going?*, had warned of the danger of relying on the 'left' union leaders Purcell, Swales and Hicks. Trotsky argued that the CPGB could 'become the vanguard of the working class only insofar as it enters into an implacable conflict with the conservative bureaucracy and the Labour Party', and could 'prepare itself for the leading role only by a ruthless criticism of all the leading staff of the British Labour movement'.[22] Ironically, because it was couched in terms of future eventualities, instead of past errors, the leading group in Russia could see no threat to their policies, and the book went out to the CPGB, in effect with the agreement of the Comintern. But after the TUC betrayal of the General Strike, Trotsky criticised the Russian leadership and the British communists for not taking advantage of the situation.

At the heart of his critique was the role of the Anglo-Russian Trade Union Committee, and the way in which its 'left' British leaders had contributed to blunting the CPGB's criticism of the TUC General Council. He called for the Committee to be dissolved, so that the last shred of political respectability would be stripped away, and replaced with a strategy of seeking to strengthen the 'united front from below' with the maintenance of ties with the British miners' union.[23] In developing his critique, Trotsky referred to the CPGB as 'still politically very young' and needing to develop 'a spirit of irreconcilability towards opportunist leaders of all hues and varieties'. But he denied Stalin's deliberately malicious accusation that he regarded the CPGB 'as a reactionary organisation, an obstacle in the path of the working class'.[24] However, the CPGB was stung by Trotsky's criticisms, and when the Politburo of the Russian party met on 3 June 1926, Stalin denounced Trotsky for showing impermissible hostility to the British Communist Party. Meanwhile, an ECCI meeting held in June 1926, which issued a thesis on 'The Lessons of the General Strike', recorded that: 'by and large the CPGB passed the test of its political maturity. The attempt to present it as a "brake on the revolution" is beneath criticism. The ECCI was completely right when it unanimously approved the attitude of the CPGB'.[25]

However, Trotksy's critique was not completely ignored by the rising Stalinist faction within the Russian party and Comintern apparatus. Thus, the June ECCI meeting could not refrain from advising the CPGB to carry out ruthless criticism and denunciation of the left-wing TUC leaders who, it suggested, were 'chiefly responsible for the defeat' of the General Strike. Similarly, on 7 July 1926, the central council of the Russian trade unions felt obliged to publish a 'Manifesto on the General Strike' (which was sent to the TUC General Council) castigating not only the treachery of the right-wing Labour Party and trade union leaders, but also the capitulation of the left which had 'ingloriously trailed behind the ruling servants of capital'. In particular, it criticised the TUC's refusal to accept the financial aid (£1,250,000) collected by the

Russian trade unions in a gesture of solidarity with the striking British miners. But there was still, the manifesto declared, the 'necessity of a firm union between the workers of Britain and the USSR'. 'That is why', it continued, 'in spite of the fact that the Trade Union leaders have inflicted a heavy blow upon the British working class, upon the cause of international unity and upon the Anglo-Russian Committee, we not only do not propose the abolition of the Anglo-Russian Committee, but call for its whole-hearted revival, strengthening and intensification of its activity'.[26] At a time when Russian relations with the British government and with the TUC were precarious, the Stalinist leadership was reluctant to completely withdraw from the Anglo-Russian Committee as Trotsky and the United Left Opposition (including Zinoviev and Kamenev) now insisted they should.

Paradoxically, the Russian trade union manifesto was not at all to the liking of a majority of the political bureau of the British Communist Party who immediately protested to the ECCI.[27] The matter came up for discussion at a meeting of the Presidium of the ECCI on 7 August, and Murphy, representing the CPGB on the Communist International, put the British party's case. He strongly protested at the alleged unwarranted intervention of the Russian trade unions into British affairs, partly on the formal ground that any public reproof of the CPGB should have come from the Comintern or the RILU and not from the trade unions, and partly on the basis that it could be used by the TUC General Council to rupture the existing bloc with the Russian unions and lead to the break up of the Anglo-Russian Committee. Murphy told the ECCI Presidium there was:

> ... an overestimation of the revolutionary tempo of the British movement and an underestimation of the powers of the leaders of the British trade union bureaucracy. If the British workers had been on the point of overthrowing the General Council as a result of what they felt, then the manifesto would have been an excellent thing. But when the workers are not ready to do that, then the extremities to which you go in the manifesto simply strengthen the hands of the General Council and obscure the real lessons of the General Strike to the workers. I suggest that by doing so you are intensifying the difficulties of our work within the British trade unions, rather than making it easier to draw the revolutionary workers towards the unions of the USSR.[28]

It seems likely that Murphy's protest reflected the CPGB's general antagonism towards Trotsky's criticism of its stance

during the General Strike, and their specific anxiety about the Left
Opposition's call for withdrawal of the Russian unions from the
Anglo-Russian Committee, which it was feared would strengthen
the position of the British government at a time when it was
threatening to sever relations with the USSR. But it also underlined
the central problem of the strategy adopted by Murphy and the
CPGB, namely that in the process of attempting to foster a bloc
between the left leaders of the TUC and the Russian unions they
felt obliged not to go too far in criticising the former's role in the
General Strike.

However, Murphy's objection was demolished by Stalin, who
personally intervened in the Presidium debate. Stalin was able to
justifiably argue that the assertion that the Russian Trade Union
Council had no right to interfere in internal British matters was
exactly the same argument levelled by the British trade union
leaders. The manifesto had been issued in the name of the Russian
unions because they were more well known to British workers than
the RILU or Comintern, and had been published with their knowledge and approval. Whilst the TUC General Council might threaten to use the Russian Trade Union Council's criticism as an excuse
for breaking up the Anglo-Russian committee, they were unlikely to
do so in view of the assistance which was being offered to the miners
by the Russian unions. But Stalin acknowledged the Anglo-Russian
Committee was not an end in itself, and could not exclude mutual
criticism. Indeed, to keep silent simply to preserve the Committee
was not the way to bring Russian and British workers closer
together for mutual assistance, but to make the Russian trade
unions accessories to the treachery of the TUC General Council
in the eyes of the labour movement of the whole world.[29]

Stalin's rebuttal of Murphy's protest was accepted by the ECCI,
and shortly afterwards by Murphy himself, who apparently created
something of a sensation when he reported to the next meeting of
the Presidium that on reflection he had come round to the Russian
view on the question. He commented: 'It came as a surprise because
it had become by that time somewhat unusual for anyone to admit
mistakes, ie. in Communist International headquarters'.[30] Although
the official position which was adopted to a considerable extent met
Trotsky's earlier criticism of the failure of the Russian trade unions
to condemn the TUC, Murphy and the CPGB proceeded to
dutifully follow the Comintern's general anti-Trotskyist line with-

out question. Thus, the CPGB's political bureau subsequently 'condemned the suggestion of the Opposition that the Russian Trade Unions should withdraw from the Anglo-Russian Joint Advisory Council' as a course 'dictated either by despair or by an overestimation of the degree of revolutionisation of the British workers'.[31] The continued policy of tailing the TUC leaders was defended at the CPGB's Eighth Congress held in October 1926, where it declared: 'The attempt of the "Left" elements in the Comintern to get the Russian unions to withdraw from the Anglo-Russian Committee is absolutely incorrect. The Anglo-Russian Committee is not a union between the leaders, but a union between the millions of trade unionists of Russia and Britain'.[32] Ironically, only a few months later the Committee was finally disbanded when the TUC broke off relations with the Russian unions.

Despite the fact the CPGB's Eighth Congress admitted that in the task of unmasking 'the former "left wing" in the General Council' the party had 'missed one or two opportunities of driving home the criticism already begun in its first manifesto at the end of the general strike',[33] there was no mention of who had assisted them to gain this 'left' image, and the party assiduously avoided any real self-criticism of its line prior to and during the General Strike. This was despite the publication of a number of articles and pamphlets written by leading party members analysing the lessons of the strike. Thus, a lengthy pamphlet entitled *The Political Meaning of the General Strike*, originally written by Murphy for *Pravda* immediately after the strike, and published by the CPGB in September 1926,[34] confined itself to a broad overview of 'the greatest political landmark in the history of the working class in Britain', with any critical reassessment of the role of the 'left' TUC leaders or the Communist Party, noticeable by its complete absence.[35]

With the end of the General Strike, the British Communist Party had seen its main task as winning the miners' strike and securing a new leadership for the labour movement.[36] Working through the Miners' Minority Movement, it campaigned for a fighting policy and, in the process, developed some differences of opinion with A. J. Cook and other Miners' Federation leaders over the terms for a return to work. A number of prominent church leaders put forward the so-called 'Bishops' Proposals' which provided for a resumption of work under existing conditions for a period of four months, during which time if a national agreement was not negotiated an independent arbitrator would settle the issue. The proposals were accepted by the Miners' Federation executive (although rejected by Baldwin's government) and then recommended for acceptance to a delegate miners' conference. But the Miners' Minority Movement and the CP conducted a successful campaign in the coalfields against the proposals, which were rejected in a district vote by 786,000 to 333,000. Meanwhile, the Third Annual Conference of the NMM was held in August 1926 and attended by 802 delegates representing 956,000 workers who gave enthusiastic support to the fighting policy of the executive. The miners' section of the Minority Movement also met and was attended by a record number of 108 delegates. But when the Trades Union Congress met in Bournemouth in September, any hope of forcing a change of policy on the General Council was frustrated by an agreement reached between the Council and the Miners' Federation that there should be no full-scale discussion of the General Strike. A resolution moved by two prominent NMM members to refer back the General Council's report on the strike was lost after Cook intervened to urge that there should be no washing of dirty linen in public while the miners were still on strike. Cook's action and the failure of the left-wing members of the General Council to fight the right wing on a single issue at the Congress finally convinced the Communist Party that there was no hope for a new leadership in the trade unions outside the ranks of the CP and the NMM.[37] But when the party's Eighth Congress met in October it was triumphantly announced that since the General Strike, 5,000 new members had joined the party to give a membership of 10,730. The vast majority of the new recruits were miners who had turned towards the CP as the only party pursuing a consistently militant policy in support of their claims. And since the party's last congress the circulation of *Workers' Weekly* had risen to 80,000 and 100,000 pamphlets had been sold.[38]

The general self-congratulatory consensus within the leadership of British communism was only finally broken when Murphy and Robin Page Arnot wrote an important article in the journal *Communist International*, which argued that after the General Strike there had been 'vacillations to the right in the ranks of the British Communist Party or rather in its leadership'. Murphy and Page Arnot argued this right tendency in the party had been revealed by the opposition to the Russian Trade Union Council's criticism of the TUC, the 'mild' attitude towards 'left' leaders like Purcell, the failure to condemn the shift to the right of A. J. Cook, and the decision of the executive of the National Minority Movement to restrict themseves to a 'mild criticism' of the TUC General Council instead of a sharp denunciation of their treacherous conduct. As they commented: 'Such a position, shielding "generous" endeavours to preserve the Anglo-Russian Committee at any cost, objectively means aid to the opportunists'. This vacillation to the right, the authors argued, was also shown in the failure to appreciate the way in which the British working class had moved sharply to the left after the General Strike, as reflected in the development of a new left-wing opposition of 'unknown figures emerging from the real movement of the workers' at the Bournemouth TUC Congress held in September 1926.[39] Subsequently Murphy, in a single-authored article in the Russian party journal *Bol'shevik*, went even further in his criticism of the CPGB leadership, which he accused of adopting the standpoint of left-wing trade unionism rather than of revolutionary communist tactics.[40]

On the one hand, it might seem that Murphy, despite the earlier argument with Stalin, had undergone a significant political change of heart in finally recognising the deficiencies in the CPGB's attitude towards the TUC after the General Strike, even if this critique was not extended to the party's stance *before* and *during* the General Strike along the lines that Trotsky and the Left Opposition had emphasised. On the other hand, there were complex factors involved influencing his revised attitude. Significantly, the article by Murphy and Page Arnot carried an addendum to the effect that the authors' views were supported by the ECCI and the Moscow-based editorial board of *Communist International*. In fact, newly available documents within the Comintern archives reveal that Murphy (the CPGB representative on the ECCI) and Page Arnot (who was also resident in Moscow) were actually commissioned by the editorial board of *Communist International*, specifically by Otto Kuusinen, a leading ECCI Presidium member, to write the article.[41] In effect, they had been actively encouraged to argue that the CPGB had not been sufficiently critical of the 'left' TUC leaders as part of the general campaign being waged by Stalin's supporters to neuter the impact of the Left Opposition's criticism of the Anglo-Russian Committee and the CPGB line.

The CPGB central committee, stung by Murphy and Page Arnot's critique, issued an immediate reply which was published in the next issue of *Communist International*. They condemned the fact that such criticism had been made without consultation by two leading British communist leaders who had themselves shared in the responsibility for any errors the party had committed. (In fact, Murphy had sent a telegram acknowledging his share in the errors, which was published in the English but not in the Russian, French or German editions of *Communist International*.) Although a mistake was acknowledged on the question of the Russian Trade Union Manifesto on the General Strike, it was strongly denied this was part of any general right-wing trend within the leadership of the CPGB. On the contrary, the central committee claimed the party had consistently criticised the TUC's betrayal of the General Strike, the attitude of the sham left leaders of the TUC, and the errors of Cook in not breaking with the General Council. Moreover, they insisted the 'new' left opposition inside the British working-class movement was a figment of Murphy's and Page Arnot's imagination. It had been the CPGB and the NMM which were the 'active directing elements' of all the left-wing forces at the Bournemouth TUC congress.[42]

The question eventually came up for discussion at a specially enlarged meeting of the Seventh Plenum of the ECCI, held in Moscow in November–December 1926, at which Bukharin repeated Murphy's and Page Arnot's criticisms and mildly reproached the CPGB for 'an insufficiently consistent and determined criticism of the "Lefts"'.[43] However, although Murphy was chosen to introduce the debate on 'The Lessons of the General Strike', the mood of his report, notwithstanding the TUC betrayal of the strike and the subsequent bitter defeat of the miners after a six-month lock-out, was essentially one of triumph and congratulation. 'Our Party came through the General Strike with honours. The Communist International agreed on this, and so did large sections of the British workers.' Whilst he reiterated that, in the rapidly changing situation after the General Strike, the majority of the CPGB leadership had made some mistakes that represented a 'right deviation'—for example, taking exception to the Russian unions' manifesto and failing to criticise sufficiently the 'left' leaders of the trade unions—such mistakes were being corrected following comradely proposals from the ECCI, and 'we can say that our party in Great Britain has in the main conducted a sound line of action'. Moreover, he once more insisted that the alleged assertion by Trotsky that the CPGB was a 'drag on the revolution' had no justification whatsoever.[44] Thus, the final resolution, which was unanimously adopted by the ECCI Plenum, ended up complimenting the CPGB for its clear and correct leadership in the miners' struggle and specifically commending, instead of criticising, its exposure of the left leaders on the TUC General Council.[45]

The resolution was undoubtedly a compromise designed to avoid any major difference of opinion between the CPGB and the Comintern. Certainly, it would have been incongruous for the Communist International to have launched a major censure on the policy of the CPGB at the same time as it was condemning the Russian Left Opposition for, amongst other things, allegedly carrying out unwarranted attacks on the British party. Therefore, the CPGB's overall strategy during the General Strike was approved, albeit with some mild reservations about some subsequent tactics, and the resolution emphasised the favourable prospects which existed for the formation of a mass revolutionary left-wing movement in Britain under the leadership of the British Communist Party.[46] Despite Murphy's apparent change of position, there is no evidence that he drew any wider implications about the nature of the CPGB's trade union strategy or its role within the General Strike.

However, not surprisingly, personal relations between Murphy and the rest of the British Communist Party leadership became severely strained as a result of the internal dispute that had raged. A meeting of the CPGB central committee had unanimously condemned the manner in which Murphy and Page Arnot had lectured the party leadership as if they were not part of it, and insisted their article had been based on a complete misunderstanding of the situation and a lack of information. They also protested at the way the ECCI had endorsed their criticisms without first consulting the central committee.[47] Suspecting there had been behind-the-scenes involvement by the Comintern, Bob Stewart, acting secretary of the party, wrote to Murphy: 'Some of [the central committee] are satisfied that Arnot and you have merely been used',[48] and Murphy was threatened with being withdrawn as the party's representative on the ECCI. In response, Murphy bitterly complained that a number of articles he had submitted for publication in the party's press had not appeared, and that he had been subject to 'public vilification in a manner which is only adopted by the reactionaries of the Second International ... because of a clean straightforward political criticism'. Nonetheless, he clearly felt his position in Moscow to be relatively secure, given the official support he had received from the Comintern. As he commented: 'If you wish to withdraw me, then go ahead. It will be quite unique to be withdrawn from the central committee of the Communist International for carrying out a decision of the Communist International. I am quite sure the membership of the party would be very interested when the matter was fully explained'.[49] After the ECCI Plenum the acrimony of the dispute that had erupted in the wake of the General Strike finally died down, and Murphy, who was re-elected on to the central committee at the CPGB's Eighth Congress, remained as the party's chief representative in Moscow until the end of 1928. But the underlying deep resentment felt towards Murphy by the British communist leadership as a result of this episode was to remain, and to be rekindled in the months and years to come.[50]

WITHIN THE COMINTERN APPARATUS

Whilst in Moscow Murphy lived, along with practically all the representatives of the foreign parties, at the Lux Hotel on Tverskaya Street, a principal highway a few hundred yards from Red Square and the Kremlin. With his wife Molly and young son Gordon, Murphy occupied two rooms, one with a bathroom. Although the Russian leaders of the Comintern, Bukharin, Molotov and Manuilsky did not live in the Lux Hotel, they became frequent visitors, and several of the hotel's residents also became close friends of the Murphy's, including Thaelman (the German Communist Party leader), Katayama (the Japanese labour leader), Kuusinen (leader of the Finnish revolution and secretary of the Comintern), Roy (the Indian communist) and a number of American communist leaders, including 'Big Bill' Haywood, Duncan, Browder and Freeman. In addition, there were a number of British communist residents, including George Aitkin and George Hardy from the National Minority Movement. Despite the fact that Murphy engaged in sharp arguments and controversies over political issues with such figures, regular social evenings were held in each other's rooms with singing and dancing until late into the night.[51] Murphy fondly recalled the mix of characters to be found in the Lux Hotel:

> The Lux was the most interesting hotel in which I have ever stayed; it had Arnold Bennett's Grand Babylon beaten to a frazzle, not in its efficient service and external and internal grandeur, but in the human material which flowed through it. The stream was constant. The visitors came from the ends of the earth, workers, intellectuals, artists, ambitious politicians, revolutionaries, all vital, alive, intelligent, battling with ideas, some playing their own hand, others deputising for somebody else. Here were love affairs and tragedies, new political stars in the revolutionary firmament, damp squibs, fun, fights, storms, celebrations, conspiracies, disclosures, jealousies, the clash of national customs, and such a variety of appearance that variety itself became commonplace and hardly noticeable.[52]

Although by the end of 1926 Murphy and Molly had been married for six years, they had not spent a great deal of time together due to his repeated journeys to Russia, the spell in Wandsworth prison, and, even when nominally at home, the countless party meetings he addressed across the country. The time in Russia proved no real respite, with Murphy working in the headquarters of the Comintern during the day and then attending numerous meetings, writing up reports and drafting resolutions and theses in the Lux Hotel until the early hours of the morning. To begin with, he was put in charge of the Comintern's British section, which included not merely Britain but also Ireland, the Dominions, India and the colonies, and he later worked under the auspices of the Anglo-American Committee which included the United States. This involved systematically studying and analysing the economic and political situation in these countries and the position of their communist parties, and preparing reports for all the executive organs of the Comintern and its corresponding national sections.[53] He regularly met delegations from these countries to gather first-hand information and provide advice on specific problems. Later on, he sat on an Eastern Commission which dealt with the problems of China and Japan, again meeting numerous delegations from these countries and from Africa:

> Whatever else I may have been doing in these eighteen months I was receiving an education such as I could get nowhere else. I found it intensely fascinating to meet Koreans and Javanese, Japanese, Negroes from the Gold Coast and Chinese from Shanghai and Canton—and to

wrestle with them, often through two translators, over questions of theory and practice. It meant such an intensive reading of the history, geography, economics of the countries that there hardly ever seemed to be an hour free for social life, though somehow or other we managed to squeeze it in.[54]

Moreover, during his time in Russia, Murphy was taken into virtually every central body of the Comintern's apparatus. Thus, apart from serving as a member of the ECCI, he was subsequently elected to the Presidium and the Political Secretariat in December 1926, working alongside all the leading Comintern functionaries, including Bukharin, Kuusinen, Manuilsky and Piatnitsky.[55] In addition, he represented the ECCI on the directorate of the Lenin School, which provided international courses in the theory and practice of Marxism for leading members of the principal communist parties.[56] He was also made an honorary member of the Seventh Samara Cavalry Division of the Red Army based in Minsk following an official visit on behalf of the ECCI to inspect the barracks, camp and troops.[57] In the process, Murphy learnt to speak conversational Russian and a little German, as well as being aided by a secretary who was a brilliant linguist, although it seems the Comintern pioneered simultaneous translation of its main sessions into English and most declarations and documents were also published in English.[58]

Significantly, Murphy's direct involvement with the Comintern coincided with the consolidation of Stalin's rise to power. Of course, to the extent that the only party in the Comintern that had won power and held it was the Russian party, it was natural for it to be accorded great theoretical and political prestige and authority. Having failed to make a revolution themselves, Murphy and the other foreign communist leaders could not help but see extraordinary qualities in the Russians who had succeeded. The uncritical attitude towards the Russian party had showed itself at the Second, Third and Fourth Comintern Congresses. Thus, although delegates of individual parties had raised points about policy affecting their respective countries, they hardly touched on the Comintern as such, and in all the debates whilst the Russian delegates criticised other parties, the representatives of those parties did not once criticise the Russians. A remark by Murphy was well founded:

When a general or principal question was under consideration every delegation approached it from the angle of his or her own particular country. Only the Russians showed any real knowledge and sense of internationalism, though frequently they wore Russian spectacles when looking through the international window. We from England were very insular and knew little of the life of other countries and their parties.[59]

But this uncritical attitude towards the Russian leaders was dangerous. Almost from the Comintern's inception any major decision concerning tactics or personnel questions had been taken in advance by the highest ranking Russian party bodies, with the ruling communicated to the Russian party delegation at the ECCI which then ensured its passage through the Comintern.[60] In other words, the Russians effectively took charge of the whole policy of the Comintern, and in the process were given the credit for successes, and completely exonerated for the failures, which were always someone else's fault. But such problems became considerably aggravated after Stalin became actively involved in Comintern affairs after Lenin's death and extended to the Comintern the bureaucratic administrative methods by which he was moulding the Russian party into a monolithic body under his control. Thus, although the world congresses were supposed to be the 'supreme organ' of the Comintern, after 1922 it met less and less frequently, and its functions increasingly passed to its executive committee. The authority of the ECCI was in turn supplanted by that of its smaller Presidium. Even within the Presidium effective power soon passed to an even smaller Political Secretariat.[61] Such executive and administrative bodies, based in Moscow, were effectively run by loyal Stalin supporters. Thus, by 1926 Zinoviev had been removed from the Presidency of the Comintern and replaced by Bukharin, and other top Comintern officials who had come round to Stalin's way of thinking, such as Piatnitsky, Kuusinen and Manuilsky, were put into place. Protected by the aura of Bolshevism, such Comintern *apparatchiks* became increasingly high-handed in dealing with foreign communist parties. Instead of letting the leaders of the national sections learn by experience, they simply had them replaced at every point of crisis, thus preventing the leaders and cadres from gaining real experience and learning from their mistakes and successes. Instead, an obedient 'leadership' was gradually selected, with relatively little independence of judgement, self-reliance or capacity for self-criticism.[62]

It was against this background that Murphy's involvement with the higher echelons of the Comintern apparatus must be viewed.

Indeed, the very fact he was admitted into such positions was indicative of his degree of loyalty to, and the trust placed in him by, the rising Stalinist grouping. This was to be expressed in a variety of ways, notably his willingness to become a 'policeman' within the Comintern. Thus, at the Fifth Comintern Congress in 1924 Murphy was elected to the International Control Commission, which had the power to summon any communist before it and pass judgement on any real or alleged misdemeanours. It effectively became a disciplinary instrument in the hands of the ECCI for dealing with any 'deviation' from the official Comintern line by constituent parties. Although the sessions and decisions were generally kept secret, and no minutes taken, it seems highly likely that Murphy was involved in a number of special hearings aimed at quashing Left Opposition activities. Similarly, Murphy was intimately involved on a Comintern Commission on Internal Relations, which also concerned itself with the relationship between Moscow and the foreign communist parties. He reported to one session of the Commission:

> [We would] like to know from each party how it is reacting to the headquarters of the Comintern. How does it accept the instructions which are sent out from the centre to the parties? ... Is there an attitude in any of the parties which says—well, they may know a lot in Moscow but they do not know the situation like we know it. This is a common problem.[63]

Murphy was also elected to sit on a special commission, along with Stalin and Kuusinen (the secretary of the Comintern), to examine the troubled relationship between the ECCI and the French Communist Party, a considerable section of whose membership had sided with Trotsky.[64] Moreover, he personally moved the expulsion of Boris Souvarine, the French Oppositionist, from the Comintern at the ECCI Plenum in December 1926 for alleged 'counter-revolutionary propaganda'.[65]

Murphy's devotion to the policies Stalin pressed on the Comintern was also evident on the question of the Chinese revolution. Stalin and the ECCI had urged the Chinese Communist Party (CCP) to unite with the bourgeois anti-imperialist Kuomintang nationalists. This position reflected the view that the current stage of economic and social development in China precluded a rapid socialist revolutionary transition. The most immediate objectives in China, those of national independence and unification, would best be achieved through implementation of the Kuomintang pro-

gramme. Stalin set aside worries that the bourgeoisie might desert
the revolution and instructed the communists to curb the risings of
workers and peasants in the interest of 'national unity'. Chiang Kai-
shek was even made an 'honorary member' of the Comintern and at
the Seventh (enlarged) ECCI Plenum of December 1926, Murphy
moved a resolution on China, ending his speech with the robust
call: 'Long Live the united national-revolutionary front. Long live
the Chinese Communist Party. Long Live the Kuomintang'.[66]

But the result of the Chinese policy was to be Chiang Kai-shek's
massacre of his Communist allies in Shanghai in April 1927, and the
smashing of the Chinese revolution, with the creation of a right-wing
military dictatorship under 'Comrade' Chiang. Such a disastrous
turn of events in China was an almost intolerable blow to the Russian
and Comintern leaders in Moscow. It made them vulnerable to the
criticism of Trotsky and the Opposition, who had described the
participation of the CCP in the Kuomintang as an 'unequal' treaty
between the Chinese proletariat and the bourgeoisie, and had
advocated an independent class position. As Trotsky later wrote,
the subordination of the class struggle to the Kuomintang on orders
from Stalin, 'cut the throat of the Chinese revolution, and with it of
the young CCP, for years to come'.[67] Such criticism, and the events
in Shanghai, provoked some restiveness within the Comintern,
which Stalin and Bukharin were concerned to dispel. Yet whilst
they were obliged to acknowledge that the Kuomintang had ceased
to be a revolutionary force[68] they denied that the policy of an 'anti-
imperialist' bloc and collaboration with a national bourgeoisie had
been discredited, and exonerated the CCP and Comintern from any
share of the blame for the Shanghai massacre. Murphy also strongly
defended the Comintern's stance, and argued against an application
of Trotsky's theory of permanent revolution, which advocated a
necessary progression from the bourgeois-democratic revolution to
socialist revolution within Chinese conditions:

> At the recent meeting of the executive [of the ECCI] we again subjected
> our experiences [of the Chinese revolution] to a searching examination.
> This was urgently necessary in view of the important events of recent
> months, especially ... after the counter-revolutionary course taken by
> Chiang Kai-shek. It was especially necessary too in view of the challenging
> attitude of the Russian opposition who were recently grossly accusing the
> Communist International of betraying the Chinese masses and for
> responsibility for the bloodshed arising from the counter-revolution ...
> But comrades ... were we, in order to develop the unions to break with the

Kuomintang and endeavour to conduct a frontal fight against the bourgeois forces in the Kuomintang at the same time as we were fighting the war lords and the militarists? Such a proposition is absurd on the face of it. Yet this is the logic of the criticism of the Russian opposition.[69]

MOVING TROTSKY'S EXPULSION FROM THE ECCI PRESIDIUM

Undoubtedly the most graphic expression of Murphy's incorporation into the Comintern apparatus was the manner in which he was accorded the 'honour' of moving the Presidium resolution expelling Trotsky from the ECCI in September 1927. The stage had already been set to move against Trotsky by a resolution from the British, French, Italian, German, Czechoslovakian and American parties, accepted by the Eighth Plenum of the ECCI in May 1927, which gave the ECCI authority to expel him if he persisted in factional struggle. At the Presidium meeting it was Murphy, described by one historian as 'the insignificant envoy of one of the most insignificant foreign Communist parties', who moved the resolution to expel Trotsky and Vuyovitch[70] from the Executive Committee of the Comintern.[71] Although Murphy later claimed he had 'not come prepared to do this',[72] he was undoubtedly chosen beforehand by the Russians as an appropriate vehicle to take such an apparently audacious step. Murphy recalled that Trotsky was 'particularly truculent':

> Trotsky arrived about the same time as my secretary and I. We met in the corridor. It was 9pm and the night was cold with thick snow on the ground outside. Everybody had their heavy overcoats and fur hats, and the hat and coat rack in the hall was full. Trotsky was looking around, when Kharhan (my secretary) asked: 'Can I help you, Comrade Trotsky?'. Quick as thought he answered smartly: 'I'm afraid not. I'm looking for two things—a good Communist and somewhere to hang my coat. They are not to be found here.[73]

The meeting was opened by Bukharin and, after Trotsky, who Murphy acknowledged 'put up a masterly performance which lasted two hours'.[74] and Stalin had spoken, they were followed by other Comintern figures. Then Murphy's moment had arrived:

> I walked towards the platform . . . I knew now that Trotsky had come, not to defend or retract his case, nor even to take the best form of defence—attack. He had plunged into a naked battle for power, and it

was to bring about one of the strangest episodes in Russian history, when a comparatively unknown Englishman moved the expulsion of the second most powerful figure in the Russian state.

> But this is how it really went. From the platform I said the time had come for final decision. This was no longer an internal fight. It was a fight for control of the whole International. We had no option but to accept the challenge. 'I therefore move that Comrade Trotsky no longer be recognised as a member of the Communist International ...' For a moment the silence was almost tangible. Then they took the vote, and there were only two dissentients.... Trotsky marched out, his head held high.[75]

Murphy returned briefly to Britain in October 1927, on this occasion travelling by aircraft which only took a few days as opposed to the normal overland trip which took many weeks, to report back to the CPGB on the expulsions. He addressed a Sheffield party district conference which resolved unanimously to send an approving telegram to the ECCI 'demanding that speedy organisational measures be taken against the Opposition'.[76] He then reported on the anti-Trotskyist struggle to the CPGB's Ninth Congress, at which he accused the Opposition of attempting to set up another political party inside Russia, and a rival leadership and organisation within the Comintern internationally. He described their support as composed of 'a few university professors, shopkeepers, and middle class elements'.[77] A stiff resolution was adopted charging the Left Opposition with 'playing straight into the hands of counter-revolution', adopting an 'anti-Leninist and objectively counter-revolutionary role', and acting as propaganda agents of Churchill and Baldwin (the British prime minister) 'in making irresponsible and slanderous accusations against the leadership of the CPSU'.[78] On Murphy's return to Moscow he spoke at the ECCI Presidium in November 1927, and claimed:

> The English Party not only supports the exclusion of Trotsky and Zinoviev from the Executive of the International but pledges itself most emphatically behind the [Russian] CP and the International in every measure which is thought desirable in order to help the party of the Soviet.Union and the International to rid itself of their influence and even of their personality ... I attended conferences in London, Sheffield, and Glasgow, besides the party congress in Manchester ... and in not a single meeting did we hear a voice raised in support of the Opposition. This was the general attitude of the membership of our party.[79]

Clearly, in many respects Murphy's loyalty to the Stalinist grouping is to be explained by the nature of his position within the Comintern apparatus. Unlike many rank-and-file CPGB members who were starved of information about the fight for power inside the Russian leadership, Murphy was able to make an assessment based on first-hand observation of the key figures and issues at stake. As he later commented on the role played by Lenin, Trotsky and Stalin:

> I knew all three men over a period of years, and because of the part I had been called upon to play in international politics from 1920 to the end of 1927 I was frequently brought into intimate contact with all three. I was thus able, as it were, to study them at first hand. I have not only read all that each had to say about the other, but many of the things I have read I have also heard them say.[80]

As a result, the Stalin-Trotsky split was central to all his activities within the Comintern:

> There are those who say that Trotsky and the others never had an opportunity of putting their point of view before the Russian party and the people. It seemed to me that during the whole of this time from 1923 the Press, the meetings, the institutions, the universities and the Communist International were literally overwhelmed with perpetual discussion and the issuing of documents by all the protagonists. In the Communist International headquarters we were at it all the time from early morning and sometimes through the whole night. The Lenin University and the Lux Hotel offered no avenues of escape from Trotskyism, Leninism, Marxism and all the attendant deviations.[81]

Of course, despite such alleged intense familiarity, such discussion about Trotsky and the Left Opposition within the Comintern apparatus was conducted within an atmosphere of gross caricature, wilful distortion and bitter recrimination. As a consequence, Murphy was later to write of Trotsky as 'a supreme egotist and individualist', who was 'not an original thinker', but held a 'romanticised and dramatised [form of] Marxism'. Murphy condemned 'his egotism, his histrionic capacities, his reliance on spontaneity in the masses'. By contrast, he viewed Stalin as 'an organiser with unsurpassed tenacity of purpose', and marvelled at his 'life of poverty and ceaseless conflict' as 'a student of Marx, a disciple of Lenin, a superb organiser, a builder and a fighter' who was 'steel tempered in battle'. Murphy essentially justified the Stalinist purge of Trotsky and the Left Opposition as being 'the normal process of a party of Leninism', on the basis that a 'deviation from the programmatic line' was later translated into 'an alternative political policy' and then 'a struggle for power'. Thus, as Trotsky, Zinoviev, Kamenev and others challenged the policy of Stalin it was not unnatural for there to be some 'party cleansing'.[82]

Ironically, Murphy probably saw little of the true face of the situation inside Russia, since he effectively spent most of his time travelling to and fro between the Lux Hotel and the Comintern, insulated from reality by ideology and his professional cadre position, and as a consequence unable to react with a discerning judgement to events. Moreover, at the heart of Murphy's allegiance were his exaggerated hopes and dreams about what was being accomplished inside Russia. This is graphically illustrated by his account of the introduction of the First Five Year Plan on the occasion of the tenth anniversary of the revolution in 1927:

> The Congress of Soviets met about the time of the anniversary of the Revolution. It was held in St. Andrews Hall in the Kremlin, and I attended as a guest. Stalin outlined the Five Year Plan. Another speaker followed him, giving details with the aid of a giant illuminated map of the Soviet Union. On it were hundreds of small coloured electric lamps grouped and spread in varying ways across the background representing the vast territory of the Union. The speaker began to unfold his story and as he told of the number of new electric power stations that would be built in the course of the five years, brilliant red lights stood out from the map to show where they would be. Green lamps, yellow lamps, blue lamps and lamps of varying hue were flashed on in turn as he told of the mines that would be opened, the cotton fields that would be sown, the iron and steel plants that would be erected, the canals that would be cut linking the great waterways and cities to the five seas, the schools that would be built, and the collective farms that would be organised. As the speaker quietly went on one could feel the sense of achievement and victory rising in the audience. The last lamp flashed and the map looked radiant with colours, every one of which had its own specific message. One could feel the emotion in the great crowd of more than a thousand delegates from every part of the vast country. The speaker managed to say 'Comrades, this is Socialism'. Then the pent-up feelings found expression. Everyone rose by common impulse and the cheering echoed through the halls of the forgotten Czars.[83]

In fact, the Five Year Plan was to completely transform the USSR from a workers' state into a brutally exploitative and repressive state (see Chapter Six).

However, at the same time, in the belief that socialism could advance in the USSR without a revolution in the advanced capitalist countries of the west, Murphy was prepared to effectively turn a blind eye to the systematic denigration of the Left Opposition which replaced rational debate and argument within the leading organs of the Comintern. Thus, he was disposed to accept the manner in which meetings were 'packed', speakers shouted down and prominent Oppositionists likely to find themselves assigned to minor positions in remote areas, so as to discredit 'Trotskyism'. Certainly, there is no evidence that he was willing to systematically question Stalin's policies on any single issue, whether it was the causes of the failure of the German revolution, the impact of the Anglo-Russian Committee, the attitude towards the 'left' union leaders in the British General Strike, the causes of the failure of the Chinese revolution, or the general and bitter struggle for power between Stalin and Trotsky which formed the background to his eighteen-month residence in Moscow. In this sense, it is possible to identify a very marked contrast between Murphy's previously independent, self-reliant and critical judgement and his increasingly loyal and unquestioning subservience to Stalin and the Comintern hierarchy. Significantly, when he addressed the CPGB's Ninth Congress in October 1927, Murphy felt obliged to attempt to dispel allegations that the Comintern was merely a tool in the hands of Stalin.

> Let me say, in answer to those who seem to have the idea, or, at least, are very busy propagating the idea, that the Communist International Executive Committee is not an international body at all but some little organ of the Communist Party of the Soviet Union; that we simply sit in Moscow and listen to some directions from their Political Bureau, and automatically append our signature to them. Such a conception of the Executive Committee of the Communist International is a completely erroneous and false idea of this body.[84]

In reality, despite Murphy's protestations to the contrary, the concentration of power in the hands of the Russian party delegation to the ECCI was pivotal to the Comintern mechanism of functioning. But Murphy's loyalty to the USSR and to the strategy of building a single international communist movement gave it immunity from any fundamental critique, and made it impossible for there to be any substantive conflict between the interests of a national party and the Comintern, the latter being clearly seen to be the *real* party, of which the national units were no more than disciplined sections. Of course, it would have been extremely difficult for Murphy, given his position, to have withstood the tide of Stalinism that swept the USSR and the Comintern during this period. Virtually no other leading foreign communist official in a similar position did so either. But the very fact that Murphy was completely unquestioning towards Stalinism and played such an active role in its development was to have profoundly negative implications for his subsequent political development and the policy of the CPGB.

Chapter Six

The 'New Line', 1928–1932

During the period that Murphy was based in Moscow as the CPGB representative on the ECCI, his relationship with the British Communist Party leadership, already tense in the wake of the post-General Strike debate, continued to be very strained. Involved in monitoring the political situation in Britain and advising the CPGB on strategy and tactics, he gradually became embroiled in major arguments concerning a contrasting assessment of the political situation inside the British labour movement in the wake of the General Strike and the attitude communists should adopt towards the Labour Party, as well as over the question of the role of the national bourgeoisie within colonial countries in the struggle for national liberation. This internal party conflict was to culminate eventually in the party's adoption of an ultra-left 'new line' of refusing to collaborate with social democrats. Before exploring the nature of these arguments and their implications for the policy of the CPGB, it is necessary, as with the previous chapter, to understand the broader political context in which they took place, namely the internal struggle for power inside the USSR and the Comintern, and the way this profoundly shaped Murphy's role in the whole process.

THE RUSSIAN CONTEXT

By late 1927 Russia faced an immense economic and political crisis, a result of problems that had built up during the New Economic Policy (NEP) period.[1] Between 1921 and 1925 the NEP enabled the economy to grow at considerable speed. This was because both industry and agriculture were able, partially, to recover from the devastation of the civil war period. On the basis of this economic recovery, a stabilisation and improvement in social life in general occurred. But the very success of the NEP period hid from the rising Stalinist party leadership deepening problems below the surface, namely the weaknesses in agriculture (especially in grain production), a low per capita output of industrial goods, very high levels of unemployment in the cities, and a high rate of inflation. Also the low level of military expenditure left the country very poorly defended if one of the western states were to launch an attack. Such conditions made imperative more rapid industrialisation, but there were not sufficient resources to accomplish this.

At first the Russian party leadership tried to ignore these problems. They argued that the USSR could, in the words of Bukharin, proceed towards socialism in one country at a 'snail's pace'.[2] Their assumption was that somehow they would be able to muddle their way through, getting the needed resources from ad hoc measures internally and breaking out of isolation abroad by alliances with the trade union bureaucracy in the advanced countries (such as Britain) and the national movements in the biggest of the backward countries (such as China). The 'successes' of the Stalin-Bukharin leadership were great enough to secure its position even when the best known leaders of the pre-1917 party, Zinoviev and Kamenev, joined Trotsky in the United Opposition in 1926. But then the crisis suddenly erupted. Its immediate cause was a crisis in foreign relations. First, the faith which Stalin and Bukharin had placed in their alliance with the nationalist Chiang Kai-shek in China was rudely shattered when he turned on the cCommunist-led workers' movement in April 1927. Second, a new and still heavier blow was delivered by the British Conservative government when, for political reasons, it severed relations with the USSR and stopped virtually all trade. Britain had been, until then, the USSR's biggest trading partner. But suddenly any hopes of using foreign trade to ease the problem of finding resources for industrialisation were dashed.

This *external* crisis translated itself immediately into an *internal* crisis, as the authority of the Bukharin-Stalin party leadership was severely undermined and the influence of the United Opposition grew, notably during the tenth anniversary celebrations for the Russian revolution. This was compounded by the 'kulak' offensive, the grain strike of late 1927. The kulaks, the prosperous minority among the peasantry, controlled practically all the marketable grain in the USSR, the surplus over and above peasant consumption. Faced in any case with a worse than usual harvest, the kulaks attempted to force prices up by witholding grain from sale. In a country which was still overwhelmingly agrarian, the state suddenly was unable to feed the towns and sustain even the old level of industrial output, let alone raise it. The party leadership was driven to resort to forced requisitioning of grain in the spring of 1928, with massive repression by government police agents. This undermined the fundamental basis of NEP, provoking massive peasant resistance. It led in turn to the forced collectivisation of agriculture and to the adoption by Stalin of the Opposition's centrally directed industrialisation programme, though in a grossly exaggerated form (with Trotsky having advocated much lower growth targets and opposing the coercion of the peasantry into collective farms).

The First Five Year Plan (1928–1932) was launched, based not on any assessment of the real resoures available to the Russian economy, but on what was needed to build up the country's heavy industry and military defence capacity. The Plan was launched by Stalin, for the section of the party bureaucracy around Bukharin shrank from the massive brutal attack on the lives and working conditions of both the industrial workers and the rural population which was inseparable from implementation of the Five Year Plan. Indeed, controversy over such a policy became a struggle for power within the Russian leadership, between the Bukharinists and the Stalinists, until the latter's final victory over what was termed a 'right-wing deviation' from the party line. At the same time, on the left flank, the United Opposition was also politically destroyed, with supporters expelled from the party and only readmitted if they recanted. Trotsky, who had been expelled from the party in November 1927, was deported to Alma Ata in Turkestan in January 1928 and exiled from the USSR in February 1929 (although he maintained a revolutionary Marxist critique of Stalinism and organised an International Left Opposition of a small handful of supporters in different countries across the world).[3]

Over the next few years the USSR was to be transformed. The last remnants of what Lenin had called in 1920 'a workers' state with bureaucratic deformations' were swept away. As writers from within the Trotskyist tradition have argued, the bureaucracy became a self-conscious ruling class,[4] and a bureaucratic 'state-capitalist' regime was firmly established, its ideology being, of course, 'socialism in one country'. A vast network of forced labour camps was created, populated in the first instance largely by deported peasants, with their numbers soon supplemented by an influx of workers and officials accused of 'sabotage', pilfering and opposition of any kind. By the second half of the 1930s, forced labour—modern slavery—had become an important sector of the economy and a most powerful deterrent against any kind of resistance to the new despotism. Meanwhile, the working class was transformed, growing from 11 million in 1928 to 23 million in 1932. As a vast flood of ex-peasants was drawn into the towns and into the rapidly-expanding workforce, all residual trade union rights disappeared. Strikes were banned in 1928 and the unions effectively became state agencies for disciplining the workforce and speeding up output. This fast-growing workforce was atomised by vicious repression, with average real wages cut severely and huge differentials opened up within the workforce itself. As a political force the working class no longer existed.[5] The bureaucratic state-capitalist regime was consolidated.

Not surprisingly, the battle between the Stalinists and the Bukharinists during 1927–1928 was also carried over into a fierce struggle for control of the Comintern and direction of communist policy abroad.[6] Ironically, revision of the Comintern line had begun under Bukharin's own sponsorship in 1927 in the aftermath of the setbacks in China and Britain. The severing of relations between the British government and the USSR served to confirm the aggressive posture of the British in eastern Europe and was interpreted in Moscow as the preliminary to an imperialist intervention against the USSR, since relations with France were simultaneously deteriorating. These fears, deliberately fanned by the Stalinists, fuelled the 'war scare' which had been sweeping the country since early 1927 and which was now cynically used to condemn Trotsky and the United Opposition in the Russian party and their supporters in the Comintern. Bukharin had originally conceived of a leftward turn, less as a radical break but more as a moderate revision toward more independent communist activity and less high-level collaboration with European social democrats. But voices demanding a much greater leftward shift were raised. Uneasily aware of their vulnerability to attack from the United Opposition over the policy failures in Britain, and above all, China, Stalin and his supporters in 1928 directly undermined Bukharin's leadership of the Comintern to push through a more uncompromising tactical orientation.

The struggle over international policy inside the USSR revolved around conflicting estimates of the health of western capitalism and the likelihood of imminent revolutionary situations. The Stalinists now asserted that advanced capitalist societies were on the eve of profound internal crises and revolutionary upheavals. This led them to two tactical demands. First, foreign communist parties should prepare to chart a radically independent course, refusing any collaboration with social democrats and by creating rival trade unions. Second, they should in the process destroy reformist influence on the working class by attacking social democratic parties, which according to the Stalinists were passing from token reformism to 'social fascism', as the main enemy of the labour movement. All of this amounted to a sweeping repudiation of Bukharin's policies and was brought to a head during the Sixth Comintern Congress in July–September 1928, when, despite being its political secretary and titular head, Bukharin's authority and policies were completely undermined by Stalin's faction. As we have seen, the swing to ultra-leftism owed something to the need to weaken the impact in the communist parties outside the USSR of the Left Opposition's criticisms of the previous period's rightist policies of seeking diplomatic alliances with reformist leaders, especially after their disastrous outcome in Britain and China. But more important was the need to remove Bukharin's supporters from positions of influence inside the Russian party, the Comintern and various communist parties across Europe. 'The main danger is from the right', it was proclaimed, and the well-established techniques of bureaucratically eliminating inconveniently independent party members, pioneered by Zinoviev and developed by Bukharin, were now used ruthlessly against the latter's supporters.[7]

For Stalin, the Comintern now existed as a subsidiary agency for the defence of the process of Russian industrialisation and of the bureaucracy which directed it. Any external political upheaval, any upset in international relations, anything which might have adverse effects on the foreign trade of the USSR (for the Five Year Plan assumed a substantial increase in foreign trade), was the last thing Stalin wanted. His policy was conservative and aimed at avoiding the risk of foreign intervention. Paradoxically, the ultra-left 'new line' the Comintern now proclaimed fitted very well with this aim and had the desired effect, despite the fact that it might have been expected to have thrown the communist parties outside the USSR into conflict with the governments of their respective countries. In practice, the policy was so extreme that it effectively isolated the communist parties from the working-class movements, making them abstentionist and passive.[8] As a result, they posed no real threat to their ruling classes, and no danger to Russian foreign policy. In fact, the impact of the 'new line' on the CPGB was to push the party into the political ghetto.

MURPHY AND THE CPGB

As we have seen, the Comintern's influence over the policy and activities of the CPGB during the early 1920s had been extensive. But whilst Murphy was based in Moscow its mechanisms for gathering information about, and control over, the policy of the CPGB were developed even further. Forums through which Murphy operated were the British and Anglo-American Secretariats, which were sub-committees of the ECCI. These bodies drew detailed information on the CPGB from the regular confidential reports and minutes of the party's central committee and political bureau which were sent to Moscow, and from the publications of the British communist press. This was supplemented by dispatches from the permanent Comintern representative based in Britain and attached to the CPGB between 1924 and 1929, named Petrovsky (who operated under the pseudonym of Bennett). In addition, Murphy and Comintern officials met with a number of leaders of the CPGB who visited the Russian capital for special 'British Commissions'. This flow of information was then analysed and presented in the form of written reports by Murphy to the Secretariats and other ECCI bodies, which in turn decided on the detailed instructions that should be transmitted to the CPGB leadership on how to conduct future activities.

In the process, Murphy became preoccupied with a broad range of issues concerned with the CPGB's general political work in Britain. For example, a letter he wrote to the party's political bureau in January 1927 included advice on the following issues: the threat of war against the USSR and the CPGB's campaign against the breaking of relations between Britain and Russia; the political situation in China and the need for the party to bring the work of local 'Hands Off China' committees to the attention of the National Minority Movement; Indonesian affairs and the arrest of two comrades on British territory; the work of the party's

Co-operative Department; and the Baldwin government's proposals for new poor laws.[9] Of course, it should not be assumed there was a simple transmission belt in which instructions were conveyed from the Comintern or Murphy through to the CPGB leadership. In fact, as we shall see, tension between conflicting interpretations of the political situation in Britain surfaced over a number of important issues, as evidenced by the way in which Murphy, acting on behalf of the ECCI, increasingly found himself at odds with the CPGB leadership during his stay in Moscow. But in the course of such arguments the extent of the Comintern's power to impose its strategic line on the British party, and Murphy's own role in this process, became graphically evident.

At the heart of the problem was the failure of the CPGB leadership to understand the impact of the massive defeat inside the working class represented by the General Strike and the shift to the right inside the trade unions and Labour Party. The immediate aftermath of the General Strike had seen the introduction of the Trade Disputes and Trade Unions Act, 1927, by the Conservative government, which was explicity aimed at curbing strike action and weakening the bargaining power of the unions. Amongst other provisions, it prohibited various forms of industrial action, restricted the right of picketing and substituted 'contracting-in' for 'contracting out' in the payment of the trade union political levy (so that whereas previously a portion of union members' subscriptions was automatically used to pay a political levy unless they personally took the initiative to 'contract out', it was now obligatory for union members to 'contract in' before the unions could use some of the funds collected for political purposes). The main effect of this evidently partisan attack on the political levy was a cut in the Labour Party's income from affiliation fees by over 25 per cent between 1927 and 1929. This was followed by the Mond-Turner talks between employers and trade union leaders (headed by Sir Alfred Mond, chairman of ICI and Conservative MP, and Ben Turner representing the TUC General Council) to discuss how a drive for the 'rationalisation of industry' could be carried through more smoothly if there were 'industrial peace'. Not surprisingly, although (outside the textile industry) there was no repeat of the wage-cutting of the early 1920s, the immediate effect of the General Strike was to sap union militancy, with the number of days lost through strikes falling from a massive total of 162,230,000 in 1926 (or 7,950,000 in 1925) to a record low of 1,170,000 in 1927 and 1,390,000 in 1928. At the same time, the number of trade unionists also declined from 5.2 million in 1926 to 4.9 million in 1927 and 4.8 million in 1928.

Meanwhile, the trade union and Labour Party leaders, who had increasingly begun to see the Communist Party as a thorn in its side which needed to be removed, now used the downturn in workers' struggle to take the initiative. The Labour Party conference of 1924 had voted to deny communists individual membership of the party, a policy which was reaffirmed in 1925, but had not been implemented. This was because the degree of local autonomy exercised within the Labour Party enabled activists who were sympathetic to the fighting policies the communists stood for to successfully resist the leadership. Thus, by the end of 1926 as many as 1,544 Communist Party members still belonged to the Labour Party, with many others trade union delegates to local Labour parties and trades councils. And Pollitt was still being elected as a delegate to the Labour Party conference by the boilermakers' union in 1927. Nonetheless, after the General Strike, 27 local Labour parties which had refused to expel Communist Party members were disaffiliated and 'official' parties set up in their place. Meanwhile, the Labour leadership began the process of expelling individual communists, particularly in the London area where some 434 communists out of a total membership of 1,105 were active in their local Labour parties. The 1928 Labour Party Conference proceeded to introduce a new series of recommendations under the heading of 'party loyalty' which debarred trade unions from electing communists as delegates to Labour Party meetings and banned communists and non-communist members of the National Left Wing Movement from sharing platforms at Labour Party meetings. Simultaneously, the TUC General Council became intent on breaking the National Minority Movement by threatening to withdraw recognition from trades councils affiliated to or associated with the NMM, and a number of trade unions followed the initiative of the National Union of General and Municipal Workers in suspending communist members, disenfranchising communist-influenced branches and forbidding members of the CP or NMM from standing for union positions.[10]

As we have seen, in the months after the General Strike, 5,000 people had joined the Communist Party, almost doubling its membership to 10,730 by October 1926.[11] Many had joined in disgust at the betrayal of the TUC and the rightward drift of the Labour Party following the defeat of the miners. They were overwhelmingly working-class militants, many of them victimised, who were looking for a new lead to strengthen the working-class movement. Yet because the CPGB had assiduously avoided any self-criticism of its role during the General Strike, it was ill-prepared for the difficult times that now lay ahead, as opposition from the official trade union movement to the activities of the Communist Party and the Minority Movement gathered pace, whilst the influence of the left-wing movement in the Labour Party increased. By the time of the party's Ninth Congress in October 1927 the membership had fallen to 7,400. This drop of 30 per cent was attributed almost exclusively to a loss of members in the mining areas. But it also inevitably reflected a drop in influence generally, brought out clearly by the declining sales of the party newspaper. *Workers' Weekly* reached a peak circulation of 80,000 in August 1926; a year later its successor, *Workers' Life*, was selling some 60,000 copies a week and thereafter considerably fewer. Equally, the sales of party literature also fell heavily in the second half of 1927.[12]

On the one hand, despite the dramatically transformed political climate, the formal policy stance pursued by the party during this period was essentially the same as that adhered to since its adoption of the united front tactics in the early 1920s. Thus, the official leadership of the trade unions and Labour Party was attacked and attempts were made to build up a new alternative leadership based on and guided by the Communist Party. On the other hand, in practice, the party operated in what Trotsky termed a 'right centrist' fashion, in common with the line of the Comintern during the previous period. Thus, it was very defensive in its policy stance on a number of issues, effectively blunting its revolutionary politics in order not to 'split' the unity of the labour movement. In the process, the party lagged behind the militant minority who could have been drawn directly into the CP's orbit. It was this defensive stance which began to be called into question by Murphy based in Moscow, essentially reflecting the turn to the left of the Comintern.

One of the main initial arguments between Murphy and the CPGB leadership was over the attitude the party should adopt to the TUC General Council's decision in February 1927 to withdraw recognition from trades councils affiliated to or associated with the National Minority Movement. Behind this demand was the TUC's attempt to complete what the Trade Disputes and Trade Unions Act had begun—the task of forcing the Trades and Labour Councils to split into separate bodies, with trades councils confining themselves to purely trade union business and politics being dealt with exclusively by the local Labour parties. The TUC, determined to bring the trades councils under its own discipline and direction, issued the ultimatum to break from the NMM or suffer the penalty of expulsion. Although the CP and NMM vigorously protested against the policy, they did a complete somersault at the very last moment and issued instructions to their supporters to obey the TUC's edict and disaffiliate from the trades councils. Murphy immediately wrote a letter of protest to the CPGB leadership, which was endorsed by the Presidium of the Comintern.[13] In an article for *Pravda* he argued that if the trades councils had stood firm the TUC would have had the job of expelling practically all the most important trades councils in the country, but the NMM had made it easier for the TUC to operate its decision by acceding to its demands without a struggle.[14] Despite Murphy's rebuke of the CPGB leadership, no clear decision was reached by the Presidium, for the resolution later adopted by the ECCI Eighth Plenum in May 1927 merely urged the party to conduct 'with greater energy' the campaign to expose 'the disgraceful and unprecedented' ultimatum of the General Council 'with a view to this document being rescinded at the first opportunity'.[15] Nonetheless, some months afterwards, following further official Comintern endorsement of Murphy's critique, the CP publicly admitted its mistake.

THE NEW ATTITUDE TOWARDS THE LABOUR PARTY

Undoubtedly the most significant area of dispute between Murphy and the CPGB leadership was over the question of the communists' relationship to the Labour Party. Murphy played a central role in challenging the party's traditional stance towards Labour and advocating a more independent and sharply critical line. In some respects, his critique undoubtedly reflected the general sense of frustration and impatience felt in Moscow at the inability of the British Communist Party to break out of its marginalised position inside the British labour movement. It also represented a genuine and entirely justifiable attempt to reappraise the party's strategy and tactics in line with the changed political climate. It was clear to Murphy that the Labour Party and union leaders had comprehensively betrayed the interests of the working class, in government in 1924 and on the industrial field in 1926, and was now set on a course of still more comprehensive class collaboration. The left wing outside the Communist Party, such as the Independent Labour Party, a parliamentary socialist organisation which had helped set up the Labour Party and remained an affiliated but separate body with its own MPs, had proved vacillating and quite incapable of providing a real alternative to the right.[16] Moreover, the Labour Party was becoming effectively barred to communists, either as individuals or as representatives of their trade unions, thereby dramatically limiting its capacity for political intervention from within. As a result, the only way forward seemed to be independent workers' action, under communist leadership, against what appeared to be an increasingly monolithic and reactionary Labour and trade union apparatus. However, Murphy's stance was not arrived at entirely through an independent evaluation of the political situation in Britain. On the contrary, the role of the Comintern, and ultimately of Stalin, was absolutely central.

Thus, first intimations that the ECCI wanted a different political line had been contained in a telegram sent by the Political Secretariat to the CPGB in October 1927, urging the party to 'struggle against the bourgeois leadership of the Labour Party, against parliamentary cretinism in all its forms, and to prepare to take its stand at the forthcoming elections as an independent party with its own platform, and its own candidates, even in cases where so-called official candidates of the Labour Party will be put up against the candidates of the CP'.[17] As it happened, due to 'technical mishaps' the message failed to reach its destination in time for the CPGB's Ninth Congress that same month. But the demand for what amounted to 'a complete review of the tactics pursued by the party in regard to the Labour Party since 1920' led to major differences of opinion within the central committee. A delegation from the party centre went to Moscow in November 1927 to discuss matters with Stalin, leading members of the ECCI and Murphy. Whilst the delegation was in Moscow, Murphy reported to a meeting of the ECCI's Presidium on the CPGB's recent Ninth congress (which he had returned to Britain to attend). He argued that whilst the party had conducted some excellent activity during the previous year, there had also been some disquieting features, including the loss of over 3,000 members. Murphy insisted that despite some objective difficulties, notably the witch-hunt inside the unions and Labour Party, there were important political reasons underlying the loss of membership, factors that related to the party's mistaken general estimate of the situation and its political line. In particular, he criticised the party congress's decision to oppose the standing of CP parliamentary candidates against the Labour Party and contrasted it with the Presidium's advice to put up independent candidates wherever possible, even against Labour.

Murphy castigated Gallacher's view that the party should first of all help the Labour Party to gain office, and only when workers had become disillusioned with their performance, proceed to fight against them by putting up communist candidates in elections. He argued that the nature of the Labour Party had completely changed since Lenin's time and this meant there was a corresponding need for new tactics. The Labour Party leadership had moved to the right whilst the workers were moving to the left. In this situation, it was necessary for the CP to stand candidates to expose the Labour leaders and place the responsibility on their shoulders for the split inside the labour movement. Otherwise, he argued, the danger was that the CP would make itself culpable with regard to illusions in the Labour Party and assist in the CP's own liquidation.[18] Murphy's position was supported by the Comintern representative in Britain, Petrovsky (Bennett). However, most of the CPGB leaders were not convinced and offered strong resistance to any change of policy.

This debate was followed by an informal commission of the Presidium which met on 15 December 1927 specifically to discuss the British situation. Although no formal decision was reached, the party leaders were advised that 'as a rule, no votes should be given for Labour Party candidates', or that, where 'in exceptional cases' such votes were cast, they should be accompanied by 'a special declaration (exposing the Labour Party, etc)'.[19] Although Pollitt and Page Arnot were persuaded by such arguments, scepticism was still widespread amongst the majority of party leaders. On his return to Britain, Gallacher gave the CPGB central committee an account of the discussions in Moscow, and complained the Comintern had arrived at certain conclusions even before the discussions had commenced. He reported that these conclusions:

> ... were thrown at us quite unexpectedly and had the appearance of coming from nowhere ... I found that a very serious discussion had gone on and certain conclusions had been arrived at, and that the resolutions we had passed at the Party Congress had been condemned by these decisions. Murphy who had been with us at previous meetings was now condemning the Congress resolution.[20]

Implicit in Gallacher's comments was a recognition that underlying Murphy's demand for a radical change in tactics lay the influence of the Russians and the Comintern. In his defence, Murphy claimed that before the party congress he had held only a short discussion with the Comintern leaders Bukharin, Kuusinen and Piatnitsky 'wherein the question was raised of the necessity for sharpening the struggle and challenging the leaders of the Labour Party openly, but so far as a full review and political analysis of the situation is concerned, nothing of the kind took place'. It was only after he reported back on the party congress to the Anglo-American Secretariat that there 'was the first really full discussion which has now culminated in the Plenum proceedings and Gallacher was there'.[21] Nonetheless, this account of Murphy's lack of complicity in the Comintern's critique of the CPGB seems highly unlikely given his position within both the ECCI Presidium and Political Secretariat and his intimate familiarity with the changing political line that was beginning to unfold in Moscow. Significantly, at the Fifteenth Congress of the Russian Communist Party, which took place at the same time as the Presidium meeting on the British situation, Bukharin severely criticised 'the flagrantly opportunist errors' of the leaders of the CPGB. They had expressed dissatisfaction with the Russian trade union council for its sharp criticism of the TUC. Their attack on the leaders of the trade unions and the Labour Party at the recent TUC congress had been weak and not trenchant enough. Now they feared that new electoral tactics would 'mean too much of a "turn" to the Left'. The task of the Comintern was to 'correct all these errors'.[22]

Ironically, Bukharin's comments, which were aimed, in part at least, at undercutting the appeal of the Left Opposition's cogent criticisms of the Comintern's opportunist policies of 1925–1927, closely mirrored Murphy's own critique of the CPGB. They were more than justified. Certainly, the defeat of 1926 had clearly enormously strengthened the right inside the unions and this had strengthened the Labour Party against the CP. As we saw in Chapter Four, the CP had established the National Left Wing Movement (NLWM) in 1926 to fight, not only the expulsion of communists, but also the abandonment by the Labour leadership of socialist principles. However, increasingly isolated and too weak to affect Labour policy, the very existence of the NLWM, under obvious CP direction, had given the Labour Party leadership an excellent pretext for suspending local Labour parties who had held firm and refused to expel communists. In these unfavourable circumstances, the notion that a *revolutionary* left current could be sustained in the Labour Party was absurd. A more appropriate strategy would have been to close down the NLWM, pull out of the Labour Party as many militants as possible and concentrate on building the CP directly, whilst at the same time maintaining a united front approach to those rank-and-file Labour Party members who still had illusions that they could change the party from within. Whilst the CP eventually adopted the first position, it completely ruined it by rejecting the second. From gross opportunism it swung into lunatic ultra-leftism as a direct result of the policy that was to be imposed by the Comintern and Murphy.

A WORKERS' POLITICAL FEDERATION

The pressure for change that was placed on the CPGB leadership deepened the differences of opinion within the central committee. The outcome was a special Commission, set up during the Ninth Plenum of the ECCI and held in February 1928, to review the tactics of the CPGB in relation to the Labour Party. In preparation for this event, the CPGB central committee attempted to draw up a report.[23] The majority around Gallacher and Campbell argued in defence of the traditional party line against the new proposals from the Comintern. They insisted the experience of the first Labour government in 1924 had been too short to expose to all but the most politically conscious workers the true character of the Labour leaders. The unbridled reaction of the Conservative government now presented the first Labour government in a more favourable light and wide sections of the working class were more anxious than ever to return Labour to office. But despite Labour's refusal to agree to CP affiliation and its exclusion of communists as individual members, a genuine mass left-wing opposition in the Labour Party was possible in the near future if the CP continued with its policy of working within the Labour Party as Lenin had advocated it should do in 1920. This meant it was necessary for the party to fight to get the return of a second Labour government 'in order to help the workers by their own experience to convince themselves of the worthlessness of reformism'. At the same time, in no circumstances must the communists stand a candidate in an election where this might result in a Conservative being elected, for that would discredit them in the eyes of Labour-minded workers. Where no communist was standing, the party should support the official Labour candidate, whilst expounding CP policy and sharply criticising the Labour Party.[24]

A minority on the central committee, including Pollitt and Palme Dutt (both of whom, like Murphy, had close personal links with the Comintern apparatus), put forward alternative proposals which completely rejected the majority assertion that there had been no major political change in the period between 1920 and 1928. For them it was a period of 'increasing division between the mass of the workers and the reformist leadership, expressed in the leftward advance of the workers and the right wing consolidation of the reformist leadership'. Since 1924 the Labour Party had become a third capitalist party (along with the Conservative and Liberal parties) and had 'surrendered socialism', whilst the introduction of disciplinary measures and the expulsion of communists meant there was no longer the opportunity for affiliated parties to put forward separate programmes. Therefore, it was proposed that in the next general election the CP should *not* assist the official Labour Party leadership to return to office but should 'lead the revolutionary working class fight in open opposition to both the capitalist reaction and to the official Labour Party leadership'. The CP should enter the electoral field with the maximum number of candidates, and where there was no communist candidate and the Labour candidate refused to support the party's united front demands the party should call on the workers to 'refuse to vote'. The launch of such an independent fight meant the party should abandon attempts to affiliate to the Labour Party and should campaign for the trade union political levy (whereby trade unions maintain a separate political fund which is used to affiliate their organisations to the

Labour Party to provide financial support to Labour candidates in parliamentary and local elections) to be handed over to a communist election fund. At the same time, the National Left Wing Movement, which served only to foster illusions in the possibility of changing the Labour Party, should be dissolved and left-wingers in disaffiliated Labour parties be invited to join the CP. Finally, Palme Dutt and Pollitt accused the party of failing to provide the strong independent leadership which the new situation required; a failure which had largely been responsible for the serious decline in party membership which had set in at the beginning of 1927.[25]

Murphy also put forward a solo report, although the CPGB political bureau made an attempt to exclude him from participation in the ECCI Plenum, no doubt because of antipathy towards his role within the Comintern and persistent sharp criticisms of the party leadership. Murphy was forced to write a letter of appeal to the Presidium:

> First, formally I have the right to attend as a member of the Presidium. Secondly, and this is more important than the formal reason ... I represent a definite point of view on the questions under discussion in our party EC [executive committee] which will not be defended by the British EC if I am absent. On the contrary, my point of view will be subject to attack by our comrades. This I claim puts me at a distinct disadvantage which can neither be helpful to the discussion in Moscow nor to the party ... I therefore appeal against the decision of the Political Bureau and ask for your ruling on this matter.[26]

Murphy was eventually granted the right to attend the Plenum and present his own separate report. In it he accepted the main assertion of Palme Dutt and Pollitt that 'the masses were ready to be organised into class action against the Labour Party' and that the party must cease to function as a 'radical section of the Labour Party'. He also supported the proposal to put forward the maximum number of communist candidates and to drop the affiliation campaign, although in constituencies where there was no communist candidate he advocated voting for the Labour candidate. But the main interest of Murphy's report lay in his suggestion that, because the rival policy and organisation of the NLWM had inevitably led to its expulsion from the Labour Party, the disaffiliated Labour parties and left wing groups should 'organise themselves into a national anti-capitalist party'. He argued that the basis for such a 'second Labour Party or Workers' Political

Federation', under the leadership of the Communist Party, existed in the sympathetic forces that had been expelled from local Labour Parties. Moreover, it should be this new body, rather than the Labour Party, which became the recipient of the political levy paid by the trade unions.[27]

Murphy's 'third party' proposal reflected his concern that many of the left-wing members of the disaffiliated Labour parties, rather than accepting the invitation to join the Communist Party with its outright revolutionary politics, might end up being swallowed back into the Labour Party to avoid expulsion. Therefore, he advocated the creation of a new intermediary political party which, whilst endorsing the CP's parliamentary candidates and programme, would, he believed, be more congenial to such leftward moving sections of the Labour Party and would organise much wider forces than the CP could muster on its own. It seems likely he envisaged the possibility of future left-wing splits in the Labour Party, with the Communist Party ultimately becoming a mass organisation through its activities both inside and outside such a new Workers' Political Federation. However, in practice, Murphy's idiosyncratic proposal exposed him to the damaging charge of threatening to completely 'liquidate' the CPGB as an independent entity by effectively merging it into a broader rival political organisation. Paradoxically, it was Murphy's belated recognition that the National Left Wing Movement had effectively functioned as a parallel political party to the Communist Party, but one in which CP members had operated merely as a left-wing fraction, which led him to propose a Workers' Political Federation which would organise sympathetic forces 'around our party and under the leadership of our party'. But whilst Murphy's report had the merit of recognising that the NLWM had been a barrier preventing workers joining the Communist Party, the formation of a Workers' Political Federation would merely have recreated a similar barrier. Not surprisingly, this 'second party danger', as it became known, was rejected outright by the CP leaders. In fact, the proposal hardly figured in the debate at the Ninth Plenum after Murphy agreed to its withdrawal, although he later resurrected it in discussions amongst the CPGB delegation to the Sixth Comintern Congress in July–August 1928,[28] before finally abandoning the idea. Significantly however, it suggested some underlying ambiguities in his attitude towards the Labour Party.

Meanwhile, the principal argument at the Ninth ECCI Plenum was between the majority and minority reports, to the latter of which Murphy now lent his support. Significantly, tremendous pressure was placed on the majority to abandon their stance. Thus, two days before the Plenum opened, *Pravda* reiterated the criticism of the CPGB levelled at the Fifteenth Russian Communist Party Congress, and demanded changes in the party's attitude towards the Labour Party. It became clear that the Russian CP and Comintern apparatus would line up, in the main, behind the minority report, and this hardening of attitude towards encouraging the CPGB to make a sharp turn to the left quickly communicated itself to the British delegation on their arrival in Moscow. The result was that, after initially vigorously defending their position, the majority on the CPGB central committee retreated and agreed to accept the change in policy demanded by the Comintern, and supported by Pollitt, Palme Dutt and Murphy. Thus, after stressing the need to 'adopt clearer and sharper tactics of opposition' to the Labour leaders, the Plenum resolution laid down that the slogan in favour of a Labour government be abandoned and replaced by the call for a 'revolutionary workers' government'. It also agreed it was necessary to stand candidates against the dominant leaders of the Labour Party. However, on some questions the minority proposals were not accepted. First, the resolution laid down that it was 'inexpedient as yet' to abandon the slogan of communist affiliation to the Labour Party. Second, it agreed the political levy should be paid, although the party should campaign in union branches for local control of the money raised.[29] But on the questions of what was to be done about the National Left Wing Movement, and what the Communist Party should advise workers to do in places where there was a Labour candidate, there were no clear-cut answers at this stage, and there was considerable confusion within the CP as to the implications of the 'new line'.

The ECCI Ninth Plenum marked only the initiation of the 'new line', a sharp swing to the left by the Comintern. By the summer of 1928, when the Sixth Congress of the Comintern took place, the new policy had been elaborated and laid down as a guide for the parties of every European country. It was explained that the international working-class movement had now passed out of the period of gradual and partial stabilisation of capitalism into a 'Third Period'[30] in which all the antagonisms and contradictions of capitalist countries had become acute. This gave rise to an intensification of the class struggle with the mass of the workers swinging to the left and towards revolution, whilst the social democratic parties collaborated with the class enemy. Left-wing social democracy was denounced on the basis that in carrying out a counter-revolutionary policy 'the left wing is essential for the subtle deception of the workers'. Thus, the very people who had hitherto been regarded as left-wing allies of communists were now characterised as 'the most dangerous faction in the social democratic parties'. At the same time 'social fascist tendencies' amongst social democrats were attacked. Under these circumstances, of social democracy moving in one direction and the masses expected to move in another, it was useless any longer to talk of unity with the reformists or to try to maintain a common front with them. The communists should immediately pass over to more rigorous, independent tactics, presenting their revolutionary line directly to the workers without any united front tactic to dilute the message. At the same time, given that the trade union bureaucracy was 'social fascist', communists should seek to split the unions, establishing separate 'red' unions.[31] Although the Sixth Comintern Congress did not deal in any detail with the situation inside the British party, it endorsed the decisions of the Ninth Plenum, and Murphy recorded that discussions behind the scenes with the Anglo-American Secretariat had resulted 'in those of us who had stood for voting [in parliamentary elections] for the Labour candidate where there was no Communist, recognising we were wrong'.[32]

In other words, to fully understand the nature of the left critique of the CPGB's relationship to the Labour Party which Murphy articulated whilst he was based in Moscow, it is necessary to appreciate the Russian domestic situation and the key role played by the Comintern in advocating the 'Third Period' line. Murphy was directly influenced by the Russian-dominated Comintern machine of which he was part, and this was undoubtedly the primary factor shaping his attitude towards the CPGB's tactics, rather than any independent analysis based on observation of the British situation. As we have seen, within this general framework, Murphy was able to float his own 'anti-capitalist party' proposal, until agreeing to withdraw it for lack of support from either the Comintern or CPGB leaders. He also advocated an even more leftist and sectarian stance towards the Labour Party than the resolution which had been adopted at the Ninth Plenum, especially on the issues of the future of the National Left Wing Movement and payment of the political levy. The lack of detailed Comintern guidance on the practical implications of the 'Third Period' new line in Britain, possibly because of internal divisions within the Political Secretariat as they groped towards a new tactical orientation, provided Murphy with some leeway to develop his own emphasis on such issues. Nonetheless, the Comintern now deliberately sought to incite a left wing in the CPGB against the existing leaders, and gave their backing to Murphy in the battle to radically shift the party's stance. But before exploring Murphy's role in this process, it is necessary to briefly consider the argument on the colonial question he had with the CPGB delegation at the Sixth Comintern Congress and its impact on Murphy's relations with the British party leaders.

THE COLONIAL DEBATE

A large CPGB delegation, which included Murphy, Pollitt, Bell, Page Arnot, Rothstein and Petrovsky (Bennett), attended the Sixth Comintern Congress in July 1928. Although the affairs of the CPGB were not seriously debated in open session of the Congress, beyond repeating the injunctions of the Ninth ECCI Plenum on the party's relationship to the Labour Party, there was a major argument over the Comintern theses on the colonial question. The debate pitted virtually the whole of the CPGB delegation (with Murphy being the key exception) against the Comintern leadership and the other foreign communist delegates. On the surface, the point at issue was the question of 'decolonisation'. Stated simply, the British communist delegation held the view that the colonies, above all India, were being gradually decolonised by the imperialist power through a process of industrialisation carried through by the colonialists in alliance with the native bourgeoisie. Comintern opponents of this position claimed that capitalism had a vested interest in keeping the colonies in a condition of economic backwardness and dependence.

The debate, which raised the role of the national bourgeoisie within the colonial countries in the struggle for national liberation, was marked by extreme bitterness and acrimony. Murphy, who had been actively involved as member of the ECCI Presidium in drafting the main congress resolution on 'The Revolutionary Movement in Colonial and Semi-Colonial Countries', jumped to the defence of the official Comintern line and denounced his British colleagues for 'presenting a Menshevik picture of the colonial problem'.[33] The CPGB delegation, who were heavily defeated in the final vote, departed from Moscow issuing a statement which bitterly criticised the way the debate had been conducted:

> We wish to enter our emphatic protest against the tone and method of polemics introduced by Comrade Kuusinen and certain other comrades, which, if persisted in, can only have the effect of killing healthy discussions. The only possible method of discussion for the Communist International, in our opinion, is to debate questions upon their merits, with full freedom and encouragement for all sections and individual comrades to state their point of view freely, frankly, and fraternally. The method of hurrying to tie labels on comrades who hold different opinions, before a final decision has been reached, can only result in destroying independent thought and in robbing the Comintern discussions of much of their value.[34]

The British delegation had resolutely held firm, in spite of the opposition of the whole of the Sixth Congress who faithfully followed the official line. But this position could not be maintained once the decision had been taken. Ironically however, whatever the disagreements on *analysis*, few if any of the British delegation disagreed with the leftward turn in the Comintern *line* on India. This reproduced the essentials of the 'Third Period' new line as applied to advanced capitalist countries. Just as the one denounced reformists and left reformists as 'social fascists', so the other denounced bourgeois nationalists, especially the left nationalists, as collaborators with imperialism. In other words, the disagreement was not over what line or strategy to adopt, but simply over the analysis behind that line. But it was because of the serious political implications that were raised, albeit implicitly, by the CPGB delegation argument that Murphy felt compelled to react with such invective to his British colleagues. For the direct inspiration for the new colonial policy was the recent collapse of the Comintern's policy in China, where the communists had been allied to the nationalist Kuomintang until the latter turned against them. Stalin, who had been an enthusiastic supporter of the earlier policy, was now, mainly for internal reasons, switching the Comintern line from one extreme of subordination to the national bourgeoisie to the opposite extreme of total rejection. The reason the issue was so sensitive was because the Left Opposition had previously warned against the pro-Chiang Kai-shek line, and now the old line had to be dropped without admitting that the Left Opposition had been correct in denouncing it. This accounts for the extraordinary bitterness of the discussion in the Comintern and Murphy's own defensive position on the matter.

At a CPGB political bureau meeting back in Britain, Gallacher and Bell complained that Murphy's attitude at the Sixth Comintern Congress had been 'decidely fractional' and bore 'a sense of personal grievance'.[35] The matter came to a head following the appearance of an article critical of the CPGB which was written by Murphy for *Pravda*, and roundly castigated by Pollitt. Newly available documents within the Comintern archives reveal that it provoked Murphy's resignation from all leading positions in the party. In September 1928 he wrote to the political bureau and central committee:

> After serious consideration of my position in relation to the present leaders of the party, I have decided to resign from all leading positions that I hold ... I am well aware that on formal grounds resignations are impermissible, reprehensible, etc. On formal grounds they are untenable. But in actual life what is not always formally tenable is sometimes necessary as a means of retaining one's self-respect and rendering a much needed service to the party ...
>
> So far as I am concerned the personal attacks as distinct from the political attacks (although I am well aware that even the personal attacks have a political basis) at the Political Bureau during the last two days, brought matters to a head. I can no longer work in an atmosphere of dirty innuendo as to my personal motives which reached its height in the attack of Pollitt, who accused me of being willing to write for money in *Pravda* at £3 per time and unwilling to write for nothing in the *Workers' Life* and *The Worker*, etc.[36]

Murphy went on to argue that whilst political bureau members had written for *Pravda* on similar terms as himself, *Workers' Life* had refused to print articles he had submitted which were critical of party policy, and he had not been invited to write for *The Worker* since Pollitt had taken charge of it. He commented:

> The innuendo of Pollitt as to mercenary motives governing my writing is wholly unwarranted and contemptible. It is impossible to work with

people who fight out their political differences on these lines and I have no intention of attempting it further. Of course there are political roots to this matter. They lie in the fact that we have deep political differences and Pollitt and others become angry at every note of criticism.

Were Pollitt alone and this incident an isolated one the situation would not be so serious. But it has become characteristic of members of the Political Bureau. Gallacher I am informed made a similar personal attack on me at a [Comintern] secretariat meeting in Moscow before the plenum ... Horner accuses me of 'saying not one word to the British working class but speaking only to the stenographer with my eye on Moscow' in the discussion on reorganisation of the party. Rothstein accuses me of 'lack of good faith in carrying out Political Bureau policy' ... Bell says not a single word in Moscow while the delegation is there about my 'working in a fractional spirit' but unloads it here in a bitter personal attack...

All these incidents show that it is not a mere personal squabble ... but characteristic of the Political Bureau attitude and method of work which I refuse any longer to tolerate and to be associated [with] ... The political basis for the antagonisms lies I repeat in the attitude of our party leadership to party self-criticism revealed publicly for the first time on the occasion of the article of the ECCI in the *Communist International* signed by Arnot and myself. The anger which expressed itself on this occasion concentrated on we two because of a breach of formal procedure by the ECCI. This was made to appear to be a breach of faith on *our* part, for which we were castigated at the Party Congress. From this time onward our differences have increased and so has the reluctance of the Political Bureau to bring the difference before the party.[37]

Murphy also complained that his differences with the party leadership over the NMM/Trades Council decision and the 'decolonisation' issue had not been brought to the attention of the party members as a whole. He tendered his resignation from all positions within the party, although agreeing to work voluntarily within his local party branch and to write for the communist press. However, a few days later Pollitt wrote to the central committee to unreservedly withdraw any imputation that Murphy was prompted by financial motives, either in regard to his press articles or political line.[38] Murphy responded by withdrawing his letters of resignation 'not only because they constitute an impermissible act, but they are written in a spirit of bitter resentment and a tone of polemic which I do not wish to carry into the party'.[39] But the hostile recriminations, which had been sown as early as 1926, merely festered below the surface as the battle for the 'Third Period' new line now proceeded in earnest.

CLASS AGAINST CLASS

However convincing the 'Third Period' new line might have sounded in theory, in practice it raised appalling difficulties for the CPGB leadership and the attempt to implement it threw up so many contradictions that for nearly two years the members of the British party were embroiled in argument. As we have seen, the initiative for driving the policy of the party to the left came from the Comintern. But it was also to require a determined fight by a powerful minority within the leadership of the British party, in which Murphy, who returned to Britain after the Sixth Comintern Congress in September 1928 to become a full-time political bureau member, would play a pivotal role. Moreover, victory also depended to some extent on the support they received from important sections of the party's rank-and-file, who had increasingly become disillusioned with the apparent failure of the party's traditional united front stance and enthusiastically greeted the new line as a way to stem the tide of a continuing fall in membership, down from 10,730 in October 1926 to 5,500 by March 1928.[40] The increasingly implacable hostility of the right-wing TUC and Labour Party to everything that smacked of communism further reinforced the ready acceptance of the new line as a necessary response to the changed political environment. Most of those with substantial disagreement with the new directive left the party, whilst those members who were doubtful of its applicability had their reservations stilled by the belief that the Comintern's analysis and assessment of the possibilities could not fail to be superior to their own party understanding. They were assured that the masses would stream towards the party if only the line were applied firmly and consistently enough. For this reason Murphy's arguments landed on fertile ground inside the base of the party.

Nonetheless, the isolationist implications of the new line were soon to be dramatically revealed over the Cook-Maxton Manifesto issued jointly in June 1928 by the miners' leader A. J. Cook and by James Maxton of the Independent Labour Party, supported by John Wheatley, the most left-wing of the Labour Party's leaders. The manifesto launched a counter-blast to the Mond-Turner proposals, denouncing all forms of 'class collaboration' and calling for 'unceasing war against capitalism'. It announced a national campaign of conferences and meetings to recall the labour movement to its task of destroying the capitalist system. Although Gallacher had taken part in the drafting of the manifesto and the National Left Wing Movement officially greeted its appearance, Murphy soon denounced it as nothing more than an effort to create a pseudo-left opposition in the parliamentary Labour Party and trade union bureaucracy that diverted workers from the need to join the Communist Party. He called on the CP to have nothing to do with the campaign whatsoever.[41] But this ultra-left and sectarian stance only had the effect of divorcing the party from a significant layer of left-inclined rank-and-file Labour supporters, some of whom could have been won over to the Communist Party through joint action against the labour movement leaders.

However, the sectarian policy was to be considerably reinforced following the Labour Party annual conference decision in October 1928 to take even further disciplinary measures against the CP. A 'loyalty resolution' banned trade unions from electing communists as delegates to Labour Party meetings and prohibited communists and non-communist members of all organisations who opposed Labour candidates (such as the National Left Wing Minority Movement) from sharing platforms at public meetings convened by Labour parties. In many respects, these measures gave Murphy and the minority inside the CPGB the necessary opening for raising anew the whole issue of what attitude to adopt to Labour. Within a week of the Labour conference it was announced that a full discussion on policy would take place within the CPGB in preparation for its Tenth Congress to be held in January 1929. The main attack on the party leadership came from Murphy. No doubt anxious to retrieve his false start at the Ninth Comintern Plenum, he now made himself the spokesperson of the party Left and of the Comintern line in an article he wrote in *The Communist* with the foreboding title 'Is There A "Right" Danger in Our Party?'. The essence of his argument was that: '... we can no longer do a single thing to strengthen the Labour Party—neither affiliate to it nor pay [the political levy] to it, neither work for it nor vote for it'.[42] In this article, Murphy disclosed that the party leaders had already taken one step to the left away from the Ninth Plenum resolution. It had been agreed after discussion at the Sixth Comintern Congress that there could be no question of voting for Labour candidates where no communist was standing. Thus, three questions remained to be clarified: affiliation to the Labour Party, payment of the political levy and the role of the National Left

Wing Movement (NLWM). As to the first, Murphy said that after the recent Labour Party conference he doubted whether anyone in the party would still want to press for affiliation. If this was agreed, then how could the party urge the trade unions to affiliate to this discredited body by paying the political levy? To advocate paying the levy implied acceptance of the false notion that the trade unions could somehow or other reform the Labour Party. The fight to secure non-payment of the levy would serve a double purpose. It would provide another issue of conflict between the trade union bureaucrats and the party, and where successful it would free trade union branches from Labour Party control. As for the NLWM, Murphy repeated his argument that although it had begun as a united front movement of left-wing forces within the Labour Party, it now had all the apparatus of a 'centrist' political party within which the CP did not function openly as an independent body, but merely as a left-wing fraction. This had led to the situation where the NLWM was regarded as a 'camouflaged Communist Party':

> Our Party members are not quite sure when they should be recruiting for the Left-Wing and when for the Party. It appears that we can carry the programme of the Left-Wing in one pocket and that of the CP in the other, and, according to the audience we are addressing, use one or other without contradiction, for ... the Communist programme and the Left-Wing are identical in all essentials ... I am sure our Party members are unhappy about it, and cannot get results whilst such a policy exists. It neither builds a real left movement nor helps our party. It creates the illusion that there is no real need to join the CP whilst it does not develop as a real left movement because it functions as a Party which denies its own existence as a Party, and at the same time does not know what to do with itself as a left-wing movement.[43]

As a result the movement had become a 'laughing stock' and a burden to the CP. 'It ought to be liquidated, and would die in a fortnight if the Party ceased to support it.' In its place, Murphy proposed the establishment by the party of united front organisations on specific issues. Such organisations should not be allowed to develop into a political party, but would provide avenues into the Communist Party, not alternatives to it.[44] To those members who argued that the NLWM was the political equivalent of the National Minority Movement, Murphy replied that the party did not aim at the liquidation of the trade unions, but it *did* aim at the liquidation of the Labour Party. The political alternative to the Labour Party was the Communist Party:

The difference between the position of the MM and the NLW is obvious. The one has a basis in the trade unions for a working alliance of our party and non-party workers. The National-Left Wing has no basis in the Labour Party, and cannot have a basis. The CP is not in the Labour Party, and is the enemy of that party, whilst not being the enemy of the trade unions. There is, therefore, neither a basis for a National Left-Wing organisation nor a Communist Party within the Labour Party. We are forced by the nature of the changes that have taken place in the Labour Party to completely change our line of approach to the Labour Party. We are compelled to attack it from outside, and to win the workers away from it. A totally different proposition to our task in relation to the unions.[45]

Clearly Murphy, who had been opposed for some time to the role played by the NLWM, and having had his initial bizarre suggestion for transforming it into a separate Workers' Political Federation rejected by the Ninth Comintern Plenum, now saw no alternative to its complete liquidation.[46] He recognised the CP had functioned as merely the left-wing of the Labour Party, with the NLWM effectively serving as a 'one-way bridge' of communists to the NLWM. The left-inclined workers would find their way into the ranks of the Communist Party only if the NLWM was not there to intercept them en route, and the changes in the Labour Party meant there was no option but to disband it. Significantly, however, the ECCI did not approve of this proposal.

The CPGB central committee dealt with Murphy's arguments in a long resolution which was summarised in *Workers' Life*. It declared that by adopting new 'loyalty' resolutions against communists, the recent Labour Party conference had completely ended the conditions for communist affiliation, and that the trade unions should be urged to disaffiliate from the Labour Party. However, they argued against Murphy on the other main issues. First, the party should continue to fight for the right of union branches to send whom they liked as delegates to Labour Party committees and conferences. Second, the political levy should continue to be paid as the Communist Party could not give support to the reactionary idea that unions should not take part in politics; instead the party should campaign for trade union disaffiliation from the Labour Party and for half the political levy funds to be retained by union branches and used to finance locally elected union candidates for political office. Third, the party should continue to support the NLWM.[47] Thus, the main thesis to be considered by the Tenth Congress of the CPGB, representing the views of the majority in the party leadership, ran up against opposition from Murphy, who wrote another article, this time entitled 'There *Is* A Right Danger', which reiterated the arguments of his November polemic and spoke of himself and supporters of the 'Third Period' new line as an 'opposition' within the party.[48]

The draft resolutions were sent to the Comintern for comment, but no reply was received until just before the CPGB Congress met in January 1929, when it emerged that the ECCI did not yet approve of its left turn being followed to its logical conclusion, and was opposed to both the decision to drop the communist affiliation demand and to the recommendation to trade unions to disaffiliate from the Labour Party. Therefore, the results of the congress were inconclusive. It agreed to the continuance of the political levy, albeit under local control, and to stand independent communist candidates in elections, although there was no specific advice of how to act in constituencies with no communist candidate. A resolution that party members should leave the NLWM was narrowly passed against the opposition of the central committee, after vigorous speeches by Murphy and other left critics. Ironically, this decision (which led to the dissolving of the NLWM in March 1929) also went much further than the Comintern had desired. Meanwhile, following a tactical blunder, no recommended list of nominations for a new central committee was put forward, resulting in the leading figures of the 'majority' being re-elected back into the leadership of the party.[49]

The results of the congress gave little satisfaction to the directors of policy in the ECCI Presidium, who on 27th February 1929 issued a 'closed letter' to the central committee of the CPGB. It made a number of criticisms of its work and the 'practically unaltered' composition of its leadership. The Presidium called for the immediate introduction of new blood into the leadership and preparations for major changes at the next congress. The 'closed letter' concluded by calling for a campaign in the party press on the Presidium's proposals and the immediate circulation of the letter to all district and local committees of the party.[50] Thus, the 'closed letter' opened the door wide for renewed attacks on the existing party leadership by Murphy and the minority, with encouragement and backing from Moscow.

In this atmosphere of discord and disarray, the CP central committee finally decided to advocate abstentionism towards

Labour candidates in those areas where communists were not standing in the coming General Election of May 1929. At the same time, the party nominated 25 candidates, including Murphy, who was selected to stand against Herbert Morrison, the chair of the Labour Party, in the London constituency of South Hackney. Murphy drafted a special national party election programme entitled 'Class Against Class' which sold over 80,000 copies. The programme declared that 'class is against class. The Labour Party has chosen the capitalist class. The Communist Party is the party of the working class—the Labour Party is the third capitalist party.' It set out a programme of immediate demands which did not differ greatly from the much-maligned programme adopted by the 1928 Labour Party conference. However, the CP's long-term objective was a 'revolutionary workers' government', which would federate with the USSR. The election mainfesto put the CP's new electoral position very clearly:

> The CP, in pursuance of its independent policy, is putting up its candidates in a number of constituencies. Where no Communist candidate is in the field, and where the Labour candidate refuses to pledge himself to a programme of fighting for working class demands, the Communist Party advises the workers not to vote for any capitalist candidate, Tory, Liberal or Labour.[51]

In the general election a second minority Labour government under the leadership of Ramsay MacDonald was voted into office. Not surprisingly, given that industrially the working class had suffered a series of major defeats in the early 1920s, culminating in the betrayal of the General Strike by the TUC in 1926, many workers now looked to Labour electorally as a way to advance their interests. The Labour Party increased its vote by three million and emerged as the biggest single party in the House of Commons with 127 new seats, although without an overall majority it was obliged to rely on Liberal support. But the election proved to be a fiasco for the CP, whose total vote only amounted to 50,600, less than a third of the expected figure. Murphy, who only polled 331 votes and lost his deposit, received one of the worst results.[52] The CP's dismal performance, in part directly attributable to its ultra-left new line, vividly demonstrated that Murphy and the left critics were wrong to assume that a great mass of radicalised leftward-moving workers were streaming towards the Communist Party and were unwilling to vote for the candidates of the Labour Party. Ironically, as CP membership fell to 3,200 by December 1929, the voice of fanatical sectarianism grew even louder, with Murphy blaming the poor election results on the degree to which the party had been weakened as a result of its previous hesitation and wavering 'rightist' policy. Nonetheless, he claimed:

> There is no pessimism in the ranks of the party. There is, on the contrary, an enthusiasm generated by the conviction that the new line of the party and the Communist International is right, and the consciousness that the party has conducted a splendid campaign. It has now come before the workers definitely as an independent force. It has got its message across even better than ever before.[53]

Although the CP central committee failed to critically reassess the new line in the wake of the election, it took the decision to reduce the size of the political bureau from nine to five, excluding Murphy and Gallacher in the process. Since both had been, on different grounds, sharp critics of the party leadership, their removal was not welcomed in Moscow. The Tenth ECCI of July 1929, which gave final formulation to the doctrine of 'social-fascism', according to which fascism was in the process of being introduced in countries like Germany and Britain by the respective social-democratic parties, was the occasion of a major onslaught on the leadership of the CPGB. The miserable showing of the party in the general election left it wide open to attack. Manuilsky observed that the party had secured only 50,000 votes not because it had applied 'class against class' tactics, but because it had not applied them energetically and firmly enough. Ulbricht, the German communist leader, in a fierce denunciation of the 'wavering' of the CPGB, demanded a still sharper turn to the left, with the removal of any leaders who stood in the way of such a turn: 'Not only should the two comrades [Murphy and Gallacher] be taken back into the politburo, but also other revolutionary workers who would provide certain guarantees that they would consistently carry out the Comintern line'.[54]

The theses adopted by the Tenth Plenum called on the CPGB to 'eradicate from its ranks all remnants of right opportunist deviations'[55]. Murphy and the left critics now had the full authority of a Comintern Plenum for attacking the leadership and they immediately pressed home their advantage. In July, a meeting of the London district party discussed a motion censuring the party leadership for its failure to conduct an energetic fight against the 'right danger' in the party, and called for a special party congress in October to discuss the 'closed letter' and for the election of a new central committee. In August, the Young Communist League congress also called for changes in the composition of the party leadership and a wide party discussion on the 'right danger'. The party central committee eventually bowed to the inevitable. Its resolution on 'The Tasks Before the CPGB', published at the end of August, confessed that 'the chief cause of the present critical situation of the party is right mistakes committed by the leadership, which interpreted the new line as being mainly a changed electoral tactic, and failed to understand it as an entirely new tactical line: a struggle for the independent revolutionary leadership of the masses in all their struggles'. In this situation it was essential to 'carry out a decisive struggle for cleansing the party from all right wing and conciliating tendencies'.[56] In October, anticipating victory, Murphy wrote an article in *Workers' Life* which claimed:

> The fundamental cause of the the failure of the party leadership in recent years is founded upon a non-understanding of the period and an inadequate grasp of the essentials of Marxism and Leninism ... the history of the party from the General Strike is that of an increasing number of blunders which are being daily paid for in the loss of members, decline in circulation of the paper, etc.
>
> To think that any mechanical re-shuffling either at the centre or in the districts or locals will eradicate the Right Danger is therefore an obvious mistake. There must be a guiding principle underlying the changes. That guiding principle must be in my judgement—the selection of a leadership approximating as closely as possible in outlook and methods of thought to the line of the Sixth Congress of the Comintern and the Tenth Plenum of the ECCI.[57]

Not surprisingly, the Eleventh CP Congress held in November-December 1929 registered the final, total triumph of the new line in deeds as well as words, with only 13 members of the old central committee surviving on the new committee of 36 (although Murphy's proposal that trade unions should stop paying the political levy was defeated).[58] By January 1930, after being appointed the editor of *Communist Review*, Murphy began to warn, in line with the Sixth Comintern Congress prognosis, of the imminent danger of 'social fascism' in Britain.

> One of the most important 'Right' mistakes of the majority of the old central committee of our party was their complete failure to understand the evolution of the Labour Party into a Social-Fascist party ... There is

still considerable confusion and lack of understanding on this question [but] ...

The theoretical unity of Fascism and Social-Democracy is not difficult to establish. Theoretically the Fascist corporate State stands above classes subordinating all classes to the common interests of the national state, incorporating within itself the trade unions and employers' syndicates, enforcing class collaboration.

The British Labour Party regards the State as above classes for the subordination of class interests to the common interest of the State. It stands for class collaboration, for the British Empire, for the unions and co-operatives to play a subordinate role, but to be recognised as an integral part of the State apparatus ...

The fact Mussolini's black shirts seized power by a *coup d'etat* and that MacDonald and Co theoretically disapprove of this method does not alter the fundamental unity betwen them in respect to class relations and the role and character of the State.[59]

The term 'social fascist' was a grotesque description of right-wing Labour leaders, let alone left figures like Cook and Maxton, and utter political nonsense, as communists were to discover later and at appalling cost in Hitler's Germany when the real fascists turned on communists and 'social fascists' alike. Moreover, the implementation of the 'Third Period' new line proved to be extremely damaging, with the CP finding itself more and more isolated as a consequence of its sectarian policies, with membership continuing to fall to about 2,500 by June 1930.[60] Nonetheless, Murphy continued to insist that it was not the new line that was wrong, but the overestimation of capitalist stabilisation and the inability to see the development of the trade unions and the Labour Party towards 'social-fascism' by leading members of the party, which explained the CP's continuing weakness.[61] And when party membership shot up again to 6,279 by November 1931,[62] primarily as a result of the agitation against mounting unemployment organised by the CP-influenced National Unemployed Workers' Movement, it only reaffirmed Murphy's belief in the efficacy of the tactical stance adopted.

THE NEW ATTITUDE TOWARDS THE UNIONS

During 1928 Murphy was also central to the fight within the central committee for a changed attitude towards the trade unions. For many years the guiding aim of the party and the National Minority

Movement (NMM) had been to build up the existing unions, whilst working to win them away from policies of class collaboration, thereby transforming them into organisations genuinely fighting in the interests of the working class. But pressure on the CPGB leadership to change this attitude emanated from the Fourth Congress of the Red International of Labour Unions in April 1928, which insisted that it was no longer possible to change existing unions, since they were fast becoming part of the capitalist apparatus. This meant the CPGB and the NMM must develop 'independent leadership' on the factory floor which would, when the time was ripe, lead to the creation of alternative revolutionary trade unions. Unless and until this happened, work must continue within the reformist unions, but only in order to expose the treacherous leaders and win over the rank-and-file to the new revolutionary trade union opposition.[63]

Most of the CPGB leadership were resistent to RILU pressure to form new revolutionary unions, despite the fact that some members of the Young Communist League became convinced after the Sixth Comintern Congress that the fight to transform the existing unions into organs of genuine struggle was no longer the way forward. At the British party's Tenth Congress in January 1929 the main thesis warned against the dangers of dropping trade union work and establishing new unions: 'This policy would only lead to the isolation of the revolutionary workers from the great mass of the organised workers and play into the hands of the bureaucracy'.[64] However, just after this congress, the ultra-left and sectarian policy advocated by the RILU began to make some headway inside the party for a period of about 18 months, with Murphy's approval.

The policy was considerably reinforced after the CP set up a new union, the United Mineworkers of Scotland (UMS) in reaction to a breakaway right-wing union which had been recognised by the Scottish Executive of the Miners' Federation in place of the Fife Union in which communists had recently won official positions. The whole affair appeared to confirm the argument growing up in the party that the trade union bureaucracy would inevitably split the unions if their control was threatened, meaning communists would have to set up new unions. But if the formation of the UMS was inevitable, much more controversial was the creation of the United Clothing Workers in London, which arose out of a strike by members of the National Union of Tailors and Garment Workers (NUTGW) at Rego Clothiers in North London. The executive of the union refused to make the strike official and dismissed a leading London organiser (and a co-opted member of the CP central committee), Sam Elsbury, who had supported the strike. The London executive of the union refused to accept his dismissal and a meeting of the London membership enthusiastically agreed to form a new union, the United Clothing Workers Union (UCWU). Murphy and the CP's industrial committee supported the formation of the breakaway union and believed a majority of the membership nationally would join its ranks.[65]

The new union almost immediately became involved in another strike, this time at the Polikoff clothing factory in East London.[66] Although the overwhelming majority of workers in the factory joined the UCWU, management withdrew recognition when the new union insisted NUTGW members who applied for jobs in the factory would have to transfer membership to the new body. The new union's executive board met with Murphy and the CP's industrial committee and decided a strike call was necessary if the UCWU was to survive in the factory. After Elsbury pleaded the strike could not be conducted successfully without financial assistance, which the union did not have, he was promised a sum of £500 would be made available to meet strike pay, through local collections and a donation from the RILU. In return, it was agreed Murphy should work with the union's executive board. A strike was then called involving 700 workers, and Murphy, as communist parliamentary candidate for South Hackney, was co-opted on to the strike committee.[67] But arrayed against the UCWU were not only Polikoff, who took out court summonses against individual strikers for breach of contract, but also the NUTGW, the TUC General Council and the employers federation. Meanwhile, despite repeated requests from Elsbury, the CP central committee failed to provide the promised cash. Indeed the general isolation of the party at this time is indicated by the fact that although in the press they called for collections and Murphy spent most of his time attempting to raise money, the total collected nowhere met the sum needed. When Elsbury called a meeting of the strikers and confessed his inability to provide funds for the strike or to pay court fines, the strike was called off. They returned to work with membership of an unofficial union punishable by instant dismissal. Elsbury, who had attacked the party leadership for 'blowing hot and cold' on the 'new union', resigned from the party and was expelled.[68]

Thus, the breakaway union strategy proved to be a complete failure. The new union gained a foothold only in the London area and it became isolated from the rest of the labour movement generally. But for Murphy, the experience of the Polikoff strike reinforced the new union argument. In an editorial article in *Communist Review* he outlined the new perspective:

> That the officials will split the unions rather than struggle with the workers is obvious from what has already occurred. It is through this process that the new unions will inevitably come into being. This perspective must be ever before us from this time onward or we shall be dragging behind the workers instead of leading them ... the character and structure of the unions will be new—revolutionary in policy and industrial unions in structure based upon the factories. The period of new unionism in Britain has definitely opened and the pathway along which they are coming is the pathway of the direct revolutionary struggle arising at the foundations of the industrial life of the country.[69]

Following a letter from the executive bureau of the RILU to the National Minority Movement's August 1929 conference, the party moved further away from the concept of working through the existing trade unions to transform them into genuine instruments of struggle. This was now thought to be an illusion since the reformist bureaucracy would split the unions before this could happen. Instead, Moscow demanded that the National Minority Movement should attempt to wrest the leadership of strikes from the union machinery. Alternative strike committees were to be formed, composed of both trade unionists and non-unionists alike, on the basis of becoming factory committees that would be linked to the NMM as their revolutionary centre and eventually amalgamate to form new trade unions. Thus, the NMM was encouraged to lead the independent fight of workers against the capitalists and their 'social fascist' agents, the reformist trade unions.[70] Murphy explained what the new policy meant:

> ... the storm-centres of the struggle must be the factories. To confine the fight simply to the union apparatus is to narrow the front of the struggle, to play into the hands of the bureaucrats, to miss the significance of the militant spirit now finding expression even amongst the unorganised workers and the unemployed masses. Instead of the fight in the unions being the principal fight it is now an auxiliary struggle supplementary to

the direct leadership of the fight by the Party and the Minority Movement.[71]

In the early and middle 1920s the major industrial disputes had taken place in the mining and engineering industries where the Communist Party was relatively strong; in the late 1920s major disputes were concentrated in the textile industries where the party was much weaker. Moreover, in the textile disputes the CP suffered not only from a small membership, but from its new sectarian trade union policy which ruled out collaboration with the trade unions concerned. In the summer of 1929 Murphy was involved around a national cotton workers strike, when half a million workers were locked out by employers over protests against wage reductions and an extension of working hours. The party central committee issued a strike manifesto throughout the country to set up Textile Workers' Aid Committees to collect money, whilst rank-and-file lock-out committees were set up in Oldham and Burnley. When the unions agreed to an arbitration plan that reduced wages, the party called on workers to reject the award and Murphy made strenuous but unsuccessful efforts to get the workers at Dunlop's mill in Rochdale to strike against it.[72] But the real meaning of 'independent leadership' in practice was illustrated during a woollen strike in Yorkshire in the spring of 1930. Many thousands of mainly non-union workers, 60 per cent of them female, employed in mills concentrated in the Bradford area, took strike action to oppose wage reductions. The NMM organised a Bradford 'central strike committee' which included unemployed woollen workers and sympathisers outside the industry who wanted the workers to win, including Murphy.[73] But those members of the central strike committee who were strikers were not elected by the workers from their respective mills, but were present on their own initiative. Moreover, the committee's call for the formation of rank-and-file committees in each mill met with no response. The committee made a contribution towards maintaining solidarity and Murphy was central to the campaign of meetings held outside mill gates, and the recruitment of some workers into the party. However, when the union leaders authorised separate negotiations with individual employers for wage reductions, the strike quickly crumbled. The woollen dispute illustrated the CP's gross overestimation of the radicalism of the working class. It showed that rank-and-file committees did not emerge, as a rule, as a result of a generalised call from outside but depended on initiative from within. Moreover, a workplace committee which was separate from the existing trade unions in such circumstances did not provide a basis on which to build permanent organisation beyond the heat of battle.

Clearly, the party's decline into building new unions was dictated not by considerations of British conditions or a genuine spontaneous movement of British workers, but solely at the behest of Moscow. Whilst the party undoubtedly played a valuable role in stimulating resistance to wage cuts in several areas of the textile industry, its mistake was to try to conduct the struggles from outside the union, a mistake which flowed directly from its 'Third Period' new line. The impact was to isolate the party from the working class, even though it was able in January 1930 to launch a daily newspaper *The Daily Worker* with financial subsidies from Moscow, which gained a daily readership of about 11,000.[74] Even Murphy later felt it necessary to acknowledge that the creation of new unions depended on certain conditions and was not a prerequisite means of the revolutionary struggle, compared with the development of factory committees. Moreover, he conceded communists could not neglect the fight within the existing unions, despite their 'social fascist' bureaucracy:

> The masses are not social fascists, and we must not confuse them with the bureaucracy which cleverly harnesses their beliefs for counter revolutionary ends. We must keep in our trades unions, fight to oust the bureaucrats, expose tham at every step, and thereby strengthen our position in the factories.[75]

Eventually the Comintern appointed a commission to investigate the reasons for the CPGB's abject failure to break out of the political ghetto and, following a submission by Pollitt, approved the modification of its 'independent leadership' line within the unions. This gave rise to the so-called 'January Resolution' of 1932 which, whilst reiterating many of the unfounded assumptions concerning the 'radicalisation of the masses', made a significant change in direction in respect of trade union work. It spoke of the need to fight 'for the transformation of the trade union branches from organs of class collaboration into organs of class struggle', and it created the conditions in which genuine rank-and-file movements could be built in some industries, notably on the London buses and in the South Wales Miners Federation. The CPGB central committee endorsed the ECCI report in an 'open letter' to party members that admitted the party had taken a wrong turn: 'The whole basis of this work within the reformist trade unions ... must serve as a basis for drawing the most active workers in these [rank-and-file] movements into the ranks of the revolutionary trade union opposition'.[76]

To conclude, despite the view of some commentators,[77] there is no doubt the exaggerated expectations of an 'ascending revolutionary wave' and the lunacy of denouncing social democrats as 'social fascists' proved to be completely disastrous for the CPGB. The essential character of the British Communist Party was fundamentally transformed by the imposition and implementation of the 'Third Period' new line, just as the USSR was socially transformed by the First Five Year Plan with which it largely coincided. The end result was a party that had become thoroughly Stalinist and whose political line was determined by the requirements of Russian foreign policy. This was the real tragedy of the international effects of Stalinism on Murphy and the CPGB.

Chapter Seven

Towards Left Reformism, 1932–1936

As we have seen, there was a very strained relationship between Murphy and other leaders of the CPGB from the mid-1920s onwards. There had been the major argument immediately after the General Strike, with Murphy's polemical article in *Communist International* (with Page Arnot) attacking the party's failure to criticise the 'left' trade union leaders. Then there had been Murphy's critique of the party's acceptance of the TUC's instruction to trades councils to disaffiliate from the Minority Movement. This was followed by the bitter and protracted battle to gain the party's acceptance of the need for a sharp leftward turn towards the Comintern's 'Third Period' new line, exemplified by the political bureau's attempt to prevent Murphy attending the Ninth ECCI Plenum and Murphy's resignation from his leadership position within the party in September 1928.[1] Moreover, Murphy's proposal for a Workers' Political Federation, and his distinctive position on such tactical issues as the non-payment of the political levy, had even pitted him against those members of the central committee who agreed with the general thrust of the new line, such as Pollitt and Palme Dutt. Such tensions were reflected in a number of bitter exchanges within the political bureau during 1930 over a range of tactical issues, which resulted in Murphy's appointment to, and then removal from, the industrial department within the space of just a few days.[2] This chapter explores the way these tensions were further exacerbated in early 1931 over a conflicting assessment of the Labour Party's fortunes, which eventually culminated in May 1932 with Murphy's expulsion from the CP over an argument about credits to the Soviet Union. It also charts his subsequent political trajectory towards left reformism.

A 'DISINTEGRATING' LABOUR PARTY?

The conflicting assessment of the Labour Party was a major turning point. In early 1930 Murphy was appointed head of the CP's parliamentary department[3] and, as part of the political offensive against Labour, he stood as the party's candidate in a by-election in the Sheffield constituency of Brightside against the Labour candidate Fred Marshall.[4] Murphy wrote a special pamphlet entitled *The Labour Government: An Examination of its Record*, which explained how:

> Betrayal of the working class in the General Strike in the period when the Labour Party was in 'opposition' was not an accidental occurrence but in keeping with and a necessary part of the development of the Labour Party into a party of social fascism (ie, a party which binds the workers' organisations to the capitalist state and strives to transform these organisations, forcibly and otherwise, into instruments to serve the capitalists instead of to fight them). The expulsion of the Communists from the Labour Party and the trade unions was a necessary part of the process of fascist development, the recognition of which led to the complete change of line by the Communist Party in relation to the Labour Party. It meant the cessation of the Labour Party as in any sense an oppositional force to capitalism, and the Communist Party as the party of the working class has to fight the Labour Party as an enemy of the working class.[5]

Murphy's by-election campaign in his old home town was endorsed by the local AEU District Committee and supported by the veteran strike leader Tom Mann, and he received 1,084 votes. In a later assessment of the local campaign, he argued the party should only select constituencies to stand communist candidates where there would be a 'definite effort to win the seat', and that in a general election the party should concentrate its forces in a few places rather than dispersed across the country.[6]

Meanwhile, the second minority Labour government, headed by Ramsay MacDonald, had quickly disillusioned many of its working-class supporters. Hardly had the new government come into office when the Wall Street stock market crash of October 1929 had thrust the world economy into the worst slump in the history of capitalism, with unemployment in Britain soaring to 2.8 million by July 1931. In response, the government had cut back public spending. But when, in August 1931, the Chancellor of the Exchequer, Philip Snowden, demanded a 10 per cent cut in unemployment pay, the

Cabinet split under pressure from the TUC, and MacDonald, Snowden and a small band of leading Labour figures immediately defected to form a new 'National Government' with Conservatives and Liberals. At the October 1931 general election this national government, essentially a Tory administration though with Mac-Donald as prime minister, scored an extraordinary victory as the Labour Party's vote collapsed. Labour's share of the vote declined from the 37 per cent two years earlier to 33 per cent. In the process, it lost two million voters and won just 52 seats compared with 287 seats two years previously.

The election result forced Murphy to reassess communist strategy and brought him into collision with the party leadership once more. Previously he had assumed that Labour was effectively finished as a political force in Britain and would be rapidly over-taken by the Communist Party. Thus, after the September 1930 Labour Party conference he had reported: 'The Labour Party Conference was not the conference of an advancing party, but of a party in decay ... The Labour Party is a party in process of disintegration'.[7] But it was difficult for Murphy to take any real comfort from the 1931 general election result. Although Labour suffered enormous losses, its constituency organisation remained virtually intact and it still had a popular vote of six-and-a-half million. By contrast, the communist candidates could secure only 75,000 votes for their 26 candidates and were unable to win a single seat. Even Murphy, who once again stood in the Brightside con-stituency of Sheffield, only polled 1,571 votes.[8]

On behalf of the party leadership, Palme Dutt argued that workers had lost confidence in the Labour Party, that the high abstention rate revealed Labour was dying, and the CP was on the verge of becoming a mass party.[9] This official assessment aroused the wrath of Murphy, who effectively represented the only potential rival to the Dutt-Pollitt leadership inside the party. He poured scorn upon Dutt's optimism, enquiring what could be said for the CP with its 75,000 votes, if the Labour Party with six-and-a-half million votes was dying.[10] In an article submitted for *Daily Worker* which was not published, presumably for its 'pessimistic' prognosis, Murphy asked:

> Is it not a matter for alarm that after the General Strike, the years of the Baldwin government, and two and a half years of the Labour government, that the Tory Party is not weakened but enormously strengthened? And

let there be no illusions on the matter—by millions of working class votes too.[11]

But, Murphy continued, whilst the Labour Party had received a stunning blow, this was only a temporary phenomenon which could not be sustained, and a recovery of the Labour Party could not be underestimated as discontent with the national government grew in intensity. Therefore, it was necessary not to dismiss the Labour Party, as Palme Dutt had, but to *intensify* the CP's fight against Labour in the process of preparing and leading the mass struggles which were immediately ahead. In other words, Murphy's critique of the official line, and the party's poor showing in the elections, led him to adopt an even more *leftist* stance. (Further evidence of this ultra-left stance was provided in a pamphlet he wrote in early 1932, published by the Sheffield CP, in which he viciously denounced local Labour Party and trade union figures in a completely sectarian fashion as the 'Handrags of "Law And Order"'.[12])

Simultaneously during this period, within the central committee Murphy repeatedly drew attention to the failure of the party to succeed in building a mass base amongst workers, making the point that there was a distinct difference between acceptance of the party line and its correct practical application on the ground. The question of organisation could not be separated from the question of political understanding of the tasks, and only a handful of central committee members devoted any time in meetings to analyse and understand the politics of the situation in which they were supposed to be giving leadership. Instead, they became immersed merely in various tactical problems. The party centre had to assist party branches to gain a proper understanding of their particular locality, of when and where trade union branches met, and of what was happening in the local factories and Labour Party.[13]

But if the conflicting assessment of the Labour Party's fortunes and the critique of lack of effective leadership within the CP reopened the political differences, and personal animosities, between Murphy and the party leadership, it was an argument over a rather more obscure topic that brought matters finally to a head and led Murphy to break from the party entirely.

CREDITS TO THE USSR

Following Comintern intervention aimed at rectifying the CPGB's 'continuing isolation from the masses', a number of central committee members were transferred from headquarters in London to the various districts across the country to build the party from the bottom upwards. Murphy was sent to the Sheffield district. This left a small secretariat, headed by Pollitt, to oversee affairs in between bi-weekly political bureau meetings, for which members returned to the capital.[14] Newly available documents within the Comintern archives reveal that in March 1932, after only a few weeks of being posted to Sheffield, Murphy wrote a letter to Pollitt calling for a party campaign (in addition to the series of hunger marches which were being organised by the CP-influenced National Unemployed Workers' Movement against cuts in unemployment benefit and more means testing) to fight the rapidly increasing levels of unemployment, which now stood at almost three million or 22 per cent of the British workforce. He suggested the CP campaign for mass pressure to be placed on the employers and government to provide credits to the USSR for orders to be placed for industrial products from Britain. The objective was to provide some jobs for the massed ranks of the unemployed across the country. He made the point that in the Sheffield Attercliffe constituency, where there were 20,000 unemployed armaments workers, the Conservative MP was demanding work through armaments orders, and it was necessary for the CP to come up with its own practical proposals to fight closures and mass redundancies. He outlined the nature of his proposal:

> We have to raise the issue concretely of the mass demand that the employers open up relations with the Soviet government for engineering orders, shipbuilding orders, etc, for the fulfilment of the Five Year Plan. This we know at once raises the issue of credits and enables us to mobilise the demand for credits as a demand for work and transform our abstract propaganda about helping the workers of the Soviet Union into the bread and butter fight of every day.[15]

He explained that mass pressure on the employers to open up negotiations for orders could mean 'these engineering firms shall become instruments for the furthering of the industrialisation of the Soviet Union'. Moreover, he argued:

> The fight for work thus becomes a fight for the Five Year Plan, a fight against the government, a fight against war on the Soviet Union. It makes

> the workers see more and more how the fight for bread is bound up with
> the fate of the Soviet Union. It makes it increasingly difficult for the
> government to break off relations the more the manufacturers become
> tied to Soviet orders for work.[16]

In fact, Murphy's proposal was not an original one, but had
been argued for since the early 1920s.[17] After the 1927 decision by
the Baldwin Conservative government to break off diplomatic
relations with the USSR and to cancel an agreement to advance
credits on Russian purchases in Britain up to a total of £10 million,
the party had campaigned for the restoration of credits to break the
blockade on trade, as well as to provide more jobs for the unemployed in Britain.[18] Although the Labour government that resulted
from the 1929 election had resumed diplomatic relations with the
USSR and signed a trade agreement in April 1930, this in no way
softened the Stalinist bureaucracy's fears of an 'aggressive imperialist policy of war' camouflaged with 'pacifist phraseology'.[19] Thus,
during the 'Third Period' the CP's policy of calling for credits had
been dropped. It was also dropped because it was thought Russian
orders from Britain would stave off the revolution in Britain, and
because Trotsky, from his exile on the Turkish island of Prinkipo,
had written a pamphlet on the significance of trade credits being
given to the USSR and their relationship to unemployment in the
capitalist countries.[20] Murphy now called on the party to renew the
campaign.

However, Pollitt, on behalf of the political bureau, wrote back
unequivocally rejecting Murphy's proposal. Whilst he acknowledged it was necessary for the party to expose the hypocrisy of
the 'national' government cutting unemployment benefit on the
grounds of national economy at the same time as it refused to extend
credits to the USSR and provide work for the unemployed, he
argued Murphy's proposal of raising the demand of credits to the
USSR as a concrete party slogan was grossly mistaken. It would
only bring forward plans for the solution of the market crisis facing
British capitalism, effectively undermining the pressure of the
masses in fighting against the means test and unemployment by
demanding work or full maintenance.[21] Murphy replied to Pollitt
that if he agreed the party was in favour of trade relations with the
USSR, then 'why not say so and advocate them'. He went on:

> In effect you say 'It is very wicked of the shipping companies and the
> government to refuse credits ... but you must do nothing to force them to

rescind this decision, at least our party must not. You see fellow workers, whilst our party is very sorry for you and regards the companies and the government as a gang of hypocrites, if we demanded that they alter their decision our enemies would say that our party was only concerned with orders for the Soviet Union and that would never do. We cannot soil our hands with commerce. You must wait for the revolutionary way out. To get orders from the Soviet Union is to put forward plans to solve the market crisis of capitalism. So please go to the PAC [public assistance committee] for relief and wait for the revolution'. I wonder what the shipyard workers would say when you deliver that speech?[22]

Murphy refuted Pollitt's view that the call for credits brought forward a solution to the market crisis of capitalism on the basis that this would mean all demands for work would have to be ruled out. In addition, he rebutted the implication that a lack of orders would hasten the collapse of capitalism, saying this overlooked the fundamental character of the economic crisis of capitalism and its drive to war, the contradictions of which the placing of Russian orders would not solve. Indeed, otherwise they ought to be in favour of the breaking of relations with the USSR on the grounds that every order would bolster capitalism. Significantly, Murphy now also argued that the demand for credits for the USSR would impede the preparations for war at a time when the whole line of policy of western imperialism was to prepare for active intervention and war against the USSR. 'I am of the opinion that every order lost, every credit frustrated by the imperialists is the snapping of a thread which makes war on the Soviet Union nearer'. Finally, he remarked he was 'greatly disturbed by Pollitt's reply, and 'much as I hate the idea of a sharp political dispute with you ... it is essential we thrash the question out'. He requested his letters be circulated to the political bureau and discussed at the next meeting. Meanwhile, despite Pollitt's disapproval of his proposal, Murphy provocatively went ahead and publicly elaborated his views in an editorial article in the April issue of *Communist Review*:

It is not enough to shout 'Defend the Soviet Union' ... We must do more. We must also advance the demands for credits to the Soviet Union, for the building of Soviet ships in the British dockyards, for utilisation of the factories of this country on orders for the acceleration of the industrialisation of the Soviet Union, integrate the demand of the workers for work with the defence of the Soviet Union. We have been slow to grasp the full significance and bearing of the fight for work in its concrete relationship to the revolutionary way out and the defence of the revolution already victorious ...

> But bind the struggle for bread and for work close to the fate of the
> Soviet Union ... until the working class of this country feels and realises
> more and more that its fate and the fate of the Soviet Union are
> inseparable. This is fighting against the war. This is waging the class war
> as certainly and as decisively as the waging of a strike.[23]

Murphy's resort to the party press provided Pollitt with the
opportunity he needed to move against his long-time adversary
within the leadership of the CP. As soon as the editorial appeared,
the party secretariat met and wrote to Murphy that 'in our opinion
the conclusions of the article are in direct contradiction of the line of
the party and the Communist estimation of relations between the
socialist and capitalist worlds'. The letter made the point that
Murphy's proposal dampened the fight against the danger of
imperialist war against the USSR at the very moment when such
military intervention was becoming even more likely, arising from
the failure of the economic war against the USSR and the fact that
Russia's vivid economic triumph stood in sharp contrast to the
world economic crisis of capitalism. Furthermore, although
Murphy had prefaced his article with a vicious attack on Trotsky,
the secretariat went on to accuse him of being a 'Trotskyist': 'There
is little difference between your formulation and the Trotskyist idea
that the Russian economy represents an organised part of the world
capitalist economy'.[24]

A week later, following continuing pressure from the secretariat,
Murphy acknowledged he had made some mistakes in the original
formulation of his argument. First, he had made the fight for credits
the main line of the fight against war on the USSR.

> This is wrong because on the one hand it is impracticable and on the
> other hand which is more important, politically false because it gives the
> impression of the possibility of continuous peaceable parallel existence of
> the two worlds of socialism and capitalism. To create such an illusion at a
> time when a whole host of facts point in the opposite direction is a serious
> error.[25]

Second, he had given equal weight to the winning of Russian
orders as to waging strikes, which was also a mistake. Nonetheless,
despite these errors, he maintained the fight for credits was justified
as a part of the fight against war, and that many thousands of workers
could be mobilised on it both as an economic and political question.

> It is not so much the net result in terms of orders as the result in terms of
> the mobilisation of our class in class action that is important. That is what

> I meant when I wrote 'bind the struggle for bread with the fate of the
> Soviet Union'. It must be obvious that this is something different to
> advancing the idea that Soviet orders can solve unemployment. Such an
> idea is ridiculous. It is not as a solution to unemployment that I have put
> forward this proposition but as an important issue of the struggle.[26]

Finally, he claimed that the call for credits was not in opposition to
the fight against wage cuts, against production of munitions and
abolition of the means test, but complementary to it and a 'widening
of the class war front'.

EXIT FROM THE PARTY

Pollitt and the secretariat, sensing their advantage, now demanded
that Murphy write a public declaration admitting his mistakes in
the next issue of *Communist Review*, threatening that they would
officially repudiate his arguments themselves if he refused.[27] Rejecting this ultimatum, Murphy immediately took the dramatic and
unprecedented step of resigning from membership of the party. In
his letter of resignation he explained:

> I am sorry to part company with the Party after all these years of service
> to it, but I decline to go about subordinating myself to a policy I do not
> conscientiously accept, to be silent on questions which I conscientiously
> deem important, and subject myself to an authority which sees in every
> difference of opinion which arises a machiavellian manoeuvre to deprive
> the Secretariat of the Party of its power and prestige.
>
>   Therefore, from today I cease to be a member of the the Communist
> Party of Great Britain. Whatever of its policy I can continue to support I
> shall support to the best of my ability.[28]

At first, the secretariat refused to accept Murphy's resignation,
and wrote to remind him that, in accordance with the practice of all
sections of the Comintern, resignation was impermissible.[29] Instead,
he was instructed to attend the next meeting of the political bureau at
which he could state his case. Murphy immediately sent back a note
refusing to attend and informing them: 'I am no longer a member of
your party and therefore decline to obey your instruction'.[30] The
political bureau then took the equally startling decision to expel
Murphy from the party. Using unequivocal language the next issue
of the *Daily Worker* informed the membership of their action:

> The Political Bureau has been compelled to take the extraordinary serious
> step of expelling a leading member, J. T. Murphy, from the ranks of the

Communist Party. This decision, arrived at after lengthy and serious consideration, was taken on the grounds of the propagation of anti-working class views and the desertion of the working class fight against war, starvation and repression at a decisively critical stage in the class struggle...

Murphy's cowardly desertion of the revolutionary working class movement shows that his *Communist Review* article did not contain just wrong formulations, arising from lack of clarity, but was a deliberate attempt to utilise his post in the party in order to propagate anti-working class theories.

Murphy has passed over to the camp of the enemy. He has become a propagandist of the peace mission of capitalism, and an exponent of the inability of socialism to overcome capitalism.[31]

The political bureau simultaneously issued a statement refuting Murphy's *Communist Review* article. It attacked his idea that trading relations between Britain and the USSR could somehow lessen the danger of imperialist war and that capitalist and socialist economies could be 'integrated' one with the other:

Far from being an integration there is a decisive sharpening of the struggle between the two world systems, the menacing danger of war with the Soviet Union arises precisely because the capitalists, having failed to vanquish socialism by means of economic competition, are now resorting to the weapon of armed intervention, for which they have prepared during the whole period of trading relations.[32]

The statement also denounced the 'abandonment of the class struggle':

Murphy wants the Communist Party to abandon the policy of mass struggle against the capitalist warmongers and to make the question of fighting war into making proposals to the capitalists on how they should utilise their financial resources. To raise the demand for credits, he says 'is fighting against war', 'is waging the class war as certainly and as decisively as the waging of a strike'...

If this statement is allowed to pass without emphatic condemnation the greatest practical aim of the party in the present stage of the anti-war fight—the organisation of strike action against the making and transport of munitions for the war in the Far East—would be undermined and sabotaged.[33]

In addition, the statement castigated Murphy for his 'anti-working-class' stance:

He goes even so far as to claim that the execution of Soviet orders in Britain means that British workers are working on the Five Year Plan! According to Murphy British engineers working under capitalist slave conditions, intensely speeded-up, paid low wages, and without a vestige of control in the industry, are being 'integrated with socialism in the Soviet Union'!

This argument must be advanced by a capitalist anxious to persuade the workers to submit to his attacks, but it would never enter the head of a revolutionary worker. The fight for socialism in Britain is a fight against the British capitalists, who are exploiting the workers. Murphy's line means the sabotage of that fight.[34]

The CP leadership proceeded to open up a campaign of denunciation against Murphy, and for three weeks afterwards hardly an issue of the *Daily Worker* appeared without an article attacking him, or without one party branch or another joining in with a resolution endorsing his expulsion. The prominence of Murphy's erstwhile position within the party, and the fact that after the early 1920s no other leading figure had left the party as a result of a political disagreement, made it necessary to explain to the members in some detail why he had been thrown out. The political bureau also wrote a report to the Comintern to explain Murphy's expulsion. It claimed he had not become transformed overnight from a sincere revolutionary into an open enemy of the working class. In fact, during the party's existence, Murphy:

> ... had some important differences with the leadership of the party and these differences have revealed some important tendencies which can only be characterised as non-revolutionary and betray his reformist conception of the workers' struggle. In these controversies Murphy has revealed a lack of faith in the revolutionary will of the workers, a lack of faith in the party and an over-estimation of the strength of the reformists.[35]

The report then listed a number of examples of these controversies, including Murphy's reply to Palme Dutt in *Communist International* in 1924, when he had 'proposed a ginger group inside the Labour Party instead of a mass Communist Party as an alternative to Labour'; the 1928 Ninth ECCI Plenum proposal for a Workers' Political Federation, 'again revealing his lack of faith in the mission of the Communist Party and revolutionary temper of the masses'; and the debate over the 1931 general election, when Murphy once more had 'displayed a lack of faith in the working class'. Finally the report raised the spectre of Trotskyism: 'Like Trotsky, with whom he has much in common, he attacks the leadership of the party on grounds of bureaucracy, and the withholding of documents. This is the stock-in-trade of every renegade and particularly of the Trotskyists.'[36] Naturally, the question arises why did Murphy choose to resign from the party over the relatively obscure issue of credits to the Soviet Union? It seems this specific issue merely brought to a head the simmering general discontent which had been building up over a period of time. Ever since the 1926 General Strike in particular, Murphy had found himself at odds with the CP leadership on a variety of political and tactical issues, and despite the party's eventual adoption of the 'Third Period' new line, such tensions had prevailed during 1930–1932. As one political bureau member recalled:

> It is clear that for quite a long time he has been out of step with the Secretariat and the Political Bureau and felt that he had a grievance. On several occasions last year he indicated to me that it was no use bringing forward any point of view because there was a solid bloc in the Secretariat which would oppose and fight against the point of view of any other PB members.[37]

At the root of the problem was Murphy's disenchantment with the party's continuing isolation from the working-class movement and its apparent inability to break out of the political ghetto. The 1931 general election result had emphasised this isolation in graphic relief. Ironically however, Murphy did not draw the conclusion that the ultra-left new line had to be abandoned. On the contrary, he appears to have floundered politically. As we have seen, in relationship to the Labour Party, he advocated an even more sectarian version of the new line. But his proposal for credits, reflecting his passionate attachment to defence of the USSR, essentially represented an opportunist attempt to provide a solution to mass unemployment short of working-class struggle. Of course, that he should be accused of moving 'towards the camp of counter-revolutionary Trotskyism'[38] was doubly ironic, given he had consistently been one of the most vociferous opponents of Trotsky, and clearly had no desire whatsoever to be identified with his ideas on this issue, or indeed on any other.[39]

The real dilemma was that, having stumbled into a argument with the party leadership over the tactical question of credits to the USSR, he was unable to extricate himself, despite his partial retraction, without completely compromising his personal and political position within the leadership of the party. But the fact remains that his differences with the leadership were not formulated in any coherent strategic fashion, nor did he provide any overall political alternative to the official line. Such a critique and perspective were only developed afterwards, with the benefit of hindsight. In other words, it seems that although Murphy was unhappy with the CP's general isolation, he had not necessarily consciously anticipated an internal fight that might lead to his resignation and expulsion. Instead, he appears to have drifted into a confrontation for which he was ill-prepared, and his personal tempestuousness, evidenced by his earlier resignation from the central committee in 1928, merely reinforced his weak position.

Significantly, Murphy now found himself completely isolated within the party and received virtually no support. Thus, only one member of the central committee backed him, and this support was retracted at a subsequent meeting.[40] At a Sheffield party aggregate meeting attended by 76 members, his expulsion was endorsed with only two dissentients.[41] As the Sheffield organiser explained:

> Although our party members are politically backward there is one thing that Murphy nor anyone else can break—and that is loyalty to the party, for despite the effort Murphy made to circulate this document to party members, he has not had a single supporter ... All the comrades in Sheffield were shocked about it, but most comrades were prepared to give a unanimous declaration that the step taken by the Political Bureau was absolutely correct and necessary.[42]

Such lack of support seems astonishing, given Murphy's prominent position within the party as a political bureau member, editor of *Communist Review* and founder member of the party. However, there were a number of factors which explain how he could be removed with such near-unanimity. First, the nature of the disagreement between himself and the leadership was concealed from the membership for two months, and it was only his resignation and expulsion which forced the matter into the open. In fact, the paradox is that not one party member had even noticed or complained that Murphy's *Communist Review* editorial was 'anti-working class' before they heard he had been expelled. Moreover, Murphy himself, probably out of a sense of party discipline and because he saw the dispute primarily in personal terms, made no effort to engage in an open political struggle and to make a public appeal to the members directly on the question. This meant the party leadership was able to strictly control the flow of information that was provided once the issue had become public. A party member in East London recalled the extent to which the party went to prevent Murphy explaining his point of view after the expulsion:

> When J. T. Murphy was invited to speak at the Circle House in Aldgate,
> I helped to break up his meeting, so that no one would hear what this
> 'traitor' had to say. That's how things were. I feel ashamed of this action
> now ... During the next few weeks the *Daily Worker* gave a lot of space to
> attacking Murphy, using language which was usually reserved for use
> against Fascists.[43]

Second, there was the fact that most party members genuinely
disagreed with the substance of his proposals. Whilst they may not
have initially appreciated their significance, they became convinced
that, if implemented, they would lead the party down an opportunist path. Third, there was unanimous disapproval of Murphy's
'resignation' from the party in the face of opposition to his proposal.
As central committee member William Rust argued:

> Murphy stands condemned both because of the political theories he
> advanced and the way he deserted the party. What do the workers think of
> a leader who in a period of intense class struggle runs out of the party
> without having even the courage personally to face his fellow members of
> the Political Bureau or to defend his views before the party membership?
> ... He ran out of the party without resorting to the right which every
> party member has when political differences arise—appeal to the
> Executive Committee of the Communist International.[44]

Fourth, Murphy compounded his offence by publishing an
article entitled 'Why I left the Communist Party' in the 'counter-
revolutionary' Independent Labour Party journal *The New Leader*,
in which he stated: 'The slanderous and violent attacks, full of lying
imputations and distortions of my views and motives, are indica-
tions of the triumph of hysteria in the Communist Party leadership
... I refuse to be coerced into the acceptance of views I do not agree
with.'[45] Fifth, and perhaps surprisingly, there appears to have been
no support for Murphy whatsoever from Russia and the Comintern.
Significantly, he had been removed as the London correspondent of
Pravda only a few months before his expulsion, perhaps, although it
is impossible to confirm this, because of his critique of the official
party assessment of the 1931 general election result and his constant
battles with the Dutt-Pollitt leadership. But it is clear his advocacy
of 'integration' between capitalism and socialism was completely
contradictory to the line of the ECCI, which at its Eleventh Plenum
in March-April 1931 had brought out the unbridgeable antagonism
between the two social systems. In these circumstances, Murphy is
unlikely to have bothered to appeal to Moscow for support against
the party leadership, particularly given that the ECCI were clearly

unwilling, notwithstanding Murphy's loyal devotion in the past, to be seen publicly defending views that could in any way be linked to Trotsky. In fact, Murphy's personally close association with the Comintern apparatus provided no protection whatsoever at a time when many similar cadres in communist parties across the world were routinely being suddenly demoted or expelled against the background of a hysterical anti-Trotskyism. Moreover, Pollitt, as general secretary of the party, also had very close links with Moscow which he undoubtedly would have used to his advantage.

Sixth, there was the innuendo and personal 'dirt' that accompanied Murphy's expulsion. After returning to Britain from Moscow in 1928, Murphy had placed his young son Gordon in the private fee-paying Bedales boarding school in Petersfield, Hampshire. Not surprisingly, although Molly and Jack justified their action on the basis of being prepared to make a real financial sacrifice to obtain the best education for their son,[46] it was met with bitter disapproval from Communist Party colleagues who were, on principle, in favour of public education. It also meant that, after the expulsion, Pollitt was able to claim that Murphy's earlier removal as *Pravda* correspondent and accompanying loss of income which he received had meant he was unable to continue paying Gordon's school fees out of the £4 weekly wages he received as a party organiser, 'so he may think he is going to get a living as a freelance journalist'.[47] In future years, on the basis of resurrected stories of Murphy's involvement with 'Mr Brown' during the shop steward days of the First World War (see Chapter Two), there were even unfounded allegations that he may have been a police spy inside the Communist Party.[48] For some party members such innuendo seemed to more than justify the political bureau's decision to expel Murphy. Moreover, his apparent rather aloof personality, compared for example with Pollitt's gregarious relationship with party members, tended to provide fertile ground for such allegations.[49]

The manner of Murphy's unjustified expulsion highlighted in sharp relief the Stalinist nature of the Communist Party's organisation during this period. Despite the sometimes fierce nature of the controversies that had taken place during the early and middle 1920s, the party had retained a healthy democratic structure and atmosphere within which they could be freely aired and resolved. But by the late 1920s, with the adoption of the 'Third Period' new line, the party had become increasingly bureaucratic and monolithic in its organisation, dominated by a layer of full-time apparatchiks, and with little genuine internal debate. Nonetheless, Murphy's decision to leave the Communist Party, which for 12 years he had worked day and night to build and to which he had innumerable ties of political loyalty and personal friendship, must have been extremely difficult. As he commented:

> Had I been contemplating the prospect of leaving the Communist Party, I no doubt would have been better prepared for what happened. But it was not premeditated. The circumstances had been growing which made it inevitable, but the decision was made only at the climax of a crisis ... Nevertheless the act of leaving produced in me—and I am sure my own experience is not unique in this respect—a most profound psychological shock ... When I left the Church the Christians had merely walked on the other side of the street and passed silently by. But my Communist friends not merely cut our old friendship; they were far from being silent. Without having read a word of the controversy that had taken place, they almost with one accord, from the moment there appeared in the *Daily Worker* the announcement that I had been 'expelled' (resignations not being permissible), joined in a campaign of abuse and slander such as I had not before seen. One or two, like George Fletcher and Harold Wilde, expressed their sorrow that we had to come to the parting of the ways. The rest found the ordinary dictionary to be deficient in supplying terms of abuse.[50]

Concerned not to allow personal animosity to play a part in political activities, or to provide an opportunity for right-wing trade union and Labour Party leaders to jump on an anti-communist bandwagon, Murphy resisted the pressure to be dragged into bitter public recriminations with his erstwhile 'comrades'. But in a further twist of double irony, the call for increased trade with the USSR to alleviate unemployment, which had been official party policy before Murphy was denounced for it, became official policy again a few years afterwards.

THE SOCIALIST LEAGUE

Murphy now found himself completely ostracised from the party he had helped to construct. Financially the bottom dropped out of his political livelihood, with Molly forced to go back to work as a nurse, while Murphy strove to earn money as a freelance journalist. Over the next eighteen months he became primarily engaged in writing a book, which was published in 1934, entitled *Preparing for Power*.

The book was a critical history of the British working class movement during the first few decades of the century, focusing on the crucial period during which Murphy had played such a prominent role, the pre-war syndicalist upsurge, the wartime shop stewards' movement, and the immediate post-war years. Significantly, despite his continued defence of the USSR, Murphy now developed a vigorous critique of the Communist Party, not merely of the ultra-leftism of the new line period, but of the whole project of attempting to build a revolutionary socialist party in Britain (see below). Between 1932 and 1936 his political trajectory moved rightwards towards a form of left-wing reformism. Within a few weeks of leaving the CP he joined the Labour Party, and was later elected on to the executive committee of Islington Borough Labour Party. By April 1933, at the age of 44, he joined the Socialist League, a national left-wing ginger group inside the Labour Party committed to campaigning for the adoption of socialist policies.

Following the 1931 general election and the ignominious collapse of MacDonald's Labour administration, Labour Party activists had begun to engage in fierce in-fighting as some members reassessed the politics of parliamentary gradualism, the notion of a peaceful and constitutional transition from a capitalist to a socialist society through social reform enacted in parliament. Such doubts were further reinforced by Hitler's assumption of power in Germany in January 1933 and the impact of the world economic slump. The crisis forced some Labour left activists to recognise that capitalism could not be abolished gradually. As R. H. Tawney put it: 'onions can be eaten leaf by leaf, but you cannot skin a live tiger paw by paw; vivisection is its trade and it does the skinning first'.[51] These sentiments encouraged the growth of a new left-wing faction inside the Labour Party. During the period from 1918 until the fall of the second Labour government, the Independent Labour Party (ILP) had acted as the left reformist grouping within the Labour Party, until its breakaway in July 1932 had left a political vacuum on the Labour left.[52] In its place stepped a completely new body, the Socialist League, founded in October 1932 by members of the ILP who refused to leave the Labour Party along with other sympathetic left MPs and intellectuals.

Whilst its initial role was that of a socialist propaganda organisation which declared its resolute loyalty to the Labour Party, the League soon changed its position to one of vigorous antagonism in which it challenged the very basis of party policy.[53] Murphy claimed: '...the Socialist League is not merely the rump of the old ILP carrying on, but the organisation of revolutionary socialists who are an integral part of the Labour movement for the purpose of winning it completely for revolutionary socialism'.[54] Reflecting a mechanical conception of social development, Murphy had now become convinced that, despite its reformist limitations and right-wing leadership, the Labour Party was being propelled into a left-wing and revolutionary direction by sheer pressure of events.

> I have joined the Socialist League because I am a revolutionary marxist who is convinced that the working class of this country is facing an oncoming revolutionary crisis in which the Labour Party, of which the Socialist League is a part, will be called upon to play a deciding role...
>
> An increasing volume of opinion demands a break with the past and the immediate application of fundamental Socialist measures from the next Labour government. They are declaring that the next Labour government must be a revolutionary government. They are saying, and rightly so, that the propertied classes will resist the innovations of such a Government and that it must be prepared to fight and repress these defenders of profits, property and privilege...
>
> A great change is coming over the Labour Movement. It is as clear as daylight that the masses regard the Labour Party as the only serious opposition to the reactionary National Government, and that they regard all other oppositional movements as insignificant and incapable of rendering effective assistance. The workers ... are demanding a Socialist Government prepared to fight for Socialism against Capitalism.
>
> To make such a job possible is the job of every revolutionary within the labour movement ... I have joined the Socialist League in order to support every possible Socialist force within the Labour Party that is prepared to be as revolutionary in action and policy as Socialism is in aim.[55]

After working for the Socialist League as an organiser in the London area from May 1934, Murphy's political and organisational experience and abilities were further utilised by his appointment as the League's full-time national secretary towards the end of the year, thereby providing him with a regular income once more. The League's executive committee encompassed every shade and nuance of the left, from barely left-of-centre to near communist. Its chairman and most dominant figure was Sir Stafford Cripps, who was the most prominent Labour front-bencher after the new Labour Party leader George Lansbury. It brought together a number of other left MPs and intellectuals including G. D. H. Cole, Frank

Wise, William Mellor, Barbara Castle, Aneurin Bevan, Ellen Wilkinson, Harold Laski, Sir Charles Trevelyan, and D. N. Pritt. What united these disparate figures was the questioning of earlier assumptions concerning the efficacy of parliamentary gradualism as the means to achieve socialism. They demanded a future Labour government should embark, as soon as it assumed office, on a programme of nationalisation far more extensive than the Labour Party had ever put forward, including the Bank of England and the joint-stock banks. It also warned that a Labour administration, intent on the carrying out of such a programme, must expect fierce and, quite likely, unconstitutional resistance on the part of its ruling-class opponents in international capital, the armed forces, the House of Lords, the judiciary, the monarchy, and the press. Thus, they advocated the need for a future Labour government in the first few months of office to resort to wide emergency powers, including the abolition of the House of Lords, to beat off by sheer speed any capitalist counter-attack and to lay the foundation for a more extensive five-year programme. They also called for a coherent national plan and the introduction of workers' participation in management at the point of production to be administered by industrial unions.[56]

Murphy played a central role as national secretary in transforming the Socialist League into a highly structured political organisation. He organised lectures, conferences and weekend schools, and helped to build a national branch organisation. He also wrote regularly for the monthly journal *The Socialist*. Throughout its existence between 1932 and 1937, the League remained a small organisation, which at its peak in March 1934 could only claim 74 branches and about 3,000 members, most of whom were based in London. But against the backcloth of the effective defection to the Conservatives of some of the Labour Party's leading parliamentary figures and a widespread disillusionment over the policies which had been pursued by the second Labour government, the League proved to be an effective ginger group. Certainly, between 1932 and 1933 it enjoyed an influence out of proportion to its size and, despite stubborn opposition from the right-wing Labour Party leadership, succeeded in forcing through a series of resolutions and amendments at party conferences committing a future Labour government to 'socialist policies'.

However, such victories were only on paper. The panic

engendered in 1931 began to subside by the middle of the decade, with the empire cushioning British capitalism from the worst rigours of the slump. Britain did not have 33 per cent unemployment, like the United States, or six million out of work, as Germany did when Hitler took power. Parliamentary democracy survived and in the 1935 general election the Labour Party recovered much of the ground lost in 1931, with 8.3 million votes and a trebling of its representation in the House of Commons to 154 seats, although this still left the Conservatives with an unassailable majority. The right-wing Labour Party leadership discovered the left-wing blood-and-thunder of the Socialist League need be tolerated no longer. Significantly, whilst the League could mobilise constituency support and its links with the Parliamentary Labour Party (PLP) were quite strong, such support was less significant than it might have been at other times because the relative weakness of the PLP (with only 46 members between 1931 and 1935) had increased the power of the trade unions and their right-wing leaders within the party. The trade union bloc vote at Labour Party conferences totalled approximately two million whilst constituency parties, socialist and co-operative societies was approximately 400–500,000. Thus, however much the League could attract support for its arguments in constituency parties, the combined votes of some of the largest trade unions were large enough to dominate conference proceedings. The alliance between the leading personalities in the trade union bureaucracy and the dominant leaders of the PLP was sufficient to reassert its dominance at the 1934 Labour conference, and although the political perspective and language of the Socialist League still had great influence, the organisation was effectively crushed with official policy being pushed through. In 1937, after the Labour Party leaders had disaffiliated the League and made membership of the body incompatible with membership of the Labour Party, the League was dissolved.[57]

LEFT REFORMISM

Murphy's writings for the Socialist League between 1932 and 1936 reflected the nature of his new left reformist stance. At the centre of this new perspective was the view that fascism had become *the* main enemy in western Europe. Hitler's assumption of power in 1933, the installation of a semi-fascist regime in Austria in 1934, and the Italian invasion of Abysinia in 1935, all seemed to point to a rising tide of world fascism, and to threaten a new imperialist war which would enable the 'national' government to implement fascism at home. After 1933 the almost pathological obsession with the nightmarish possibility that the fascist tendencies of the capitalist class would lead them to attempt to seize power in Britain was common amongst broad sections of the left. Murphy wrote a pamphlet for the League entitled *Fascism: The Socialist Answer* which expressed some of the factors encouraging such fears:

> Within the Tory Party the Lord Lloyds, Churchills, Hoggs, Beaverbrooks, Rothermeres, Trenchards and Elliots are forcing the pace towards Fascism with the popularisation of Fascist personalities and ideas. They are introducing innovations of a Fascist character into the government of the country. The militarisation and class organisation of the police by Lord Trenchard, the talk of a 'National Party' ... the propagation of the fullest centralisation of industry and increased rationalisation and 'conditional protection'—all these demonstrate that the growth of Fascist forces and ideas within the ranks of the British Capitalist Class proceeds apace.
>
> The evolution of British Capitalism towards Fascism must not be measured by the number of people wearing black shirts, but by the extent to which Fascist ideas are finding expression among its leaders and in the plans they are advancing to meet the increasingly critical condition of its economy.[58]

Clearly, Murphy's understanding of the nature of fascism in Britain at this point, as a counter-revolutionary force within the state and capitalist class aimed at overthrowing parliamentary democracy and destroying all working-class organisation, was rather different from his previous ultra-left notion of 'social fascism' in which the Labour Party had been seen as effectively the main enemy of the working-class movement. He now argued that the imminent danger of fascism in Britain made the battle to win the Labour Party to socialism even more imperative:

> There are two courses which open up before the Labour Party—either the forces in favour of a decisive struggle for Socialism win the leadership and guide the Labour Party accordingly, or the conservative forces within it secure the ascendancy and bring about a defeat of the working class more gigantic than the defeat of the General Strike, split the Labour Party and make it easy for a period of fascist terror and war to dominate this country.[59]

The Socialist League was also concerned with what it saw as a sinister tendency towards the development of a 'Corporate State', which was seen as being synonymous with fascism. Thus, the Labour Party's plans for industry, based on Herbert Morrison's 'public corporation' model of nationalisation, became a key target of critique. It was argued such policies merely vested control in the hands of a state bureaucracy, whilst excluding workers from any power and responsibility. It also condemned advocates of a British 'New Deal', similar to that introduced in the United States, pointing to the allegedly 'fascist' implications of reformist remedies to unemployment. Murphy considered it necessary:

> ... to warn Trade Unionists that the propagation of 'Roosevelt Recovery Plans' for Britain represents unconscious support to Fascist plans for the 'Totalitarian' or 'Corporate State'. From a continuance of such an attitude will follow, is following, the unchecked rise of the power of Finance, the power of increased rationalisation, Public Corporations, which leave the claims of private property intact, class collaboration which keeps the workers subservient to the employers.[60]

By contrast, the League insisted only decisive and rapid action towards socialism by a Labour government could avert the fascist and corporatist threat. This would involve centralised economic planning with full industrial democracy and workers' participation. Of course, when the League talked of the need for centralised economic planning they believed the Russian model represented a real socialist alternative to the economic chaos and looming fascism they saw across western Europe. From 1932 onwards many activists on the non-communist left had began to look sympathetically towards the USSR as never before, essentially because the first Five Year Plan seemed to offer a planned and ordered system of economic progress as well as full employment which contrasted with the anarchy and chaos of western capitalism, particularly after the 'Great Depression' which began in the autumn of 1929. However, as we have seen, Stalinism and its centralised planning had its origins in the strangulation of the spirit of the 1917 revolution and in the breakneck accumulation of capital through the exploitation of the peasantry and workers. Although the Russian state bureaucracy still employed the rhetoric of Marxism, it did so only to cloak its intentions. Thus, the 'dictatorship of the proletariat' had been transformed into the dictatorship of the bureaucracy, the socialist planned economy had been changed into five-year plans for the forced industrialisation of a new 'state-capitalist' economy.[61]

However, the real Achilles' heel of the League's politics was its ambiguity on the question of *reform* or *revolution*. On the one hand, it stated its objective as being to secure a socialist parliamentary majority, enacting a peaceful rather than violent and revolutionary seizure of power. Yet there was little confidence in the amenability of Britain's political institutions to secure socialist change, especially since it was believed the capitalist class would sabotage the policies of a radical Labour government by extra-parliamentary means. On the other hand, therefore, some members of the League rejected the idea of the parliamentary road to socialism, and argued it might be necessary for socialists to defend their democratically won power by violence since others might choose to adopt unconstitutional methods of opposition. For example, even Stafford Cripps in his pamphlet *Can Socialism Come by Constitutional Means?*, suggested that to defeat its ruling-class enemies 'the Socialist government [should] make itself into a dictatorship'.[62] But it is clear from Cripps' writings and speeches at the time that such a statement remained little more than daring oratory on his part, and there was never a hint that workers' industrial power should be mobilised for political ends, with the encouragement of extra-parliamentary support to ensure the advance programme advocated by the Socialist League could be implemented in the face of ruling class opposition. On the contrary, his radical suggestion for the next Labour government to introduce Emergency Powers was firmly encased within Labour's parliamentary tradition.

On this question, Murphy's own writings reflected a distinct shift in position from his revolutionary socialist viewpoint towards left reformism. Previously, Murphy had argued that socialism could only be achieved through the smashing of the existing capitalist state apparatus, with parliament replaced by new institutions of workers' power, i.e. soviets or workers' councils. Furthermore, this socialist revolution required the mass action of workers from below led by a revolutionary party. But having joined the Labour Party, he now saw the election of a Labour government committed to socialist policies as a key step to the transformation of society, on the basis that only after workers had experienced the failure of a Labour government to introduce radical change would workers be prepared to take up arms against the capitalist state.

Whether the capitalist class of this country will emulate the capitalist class of Germany and Italy and destroy Parliament at the approach of a Socialist majority or make civil war when such a Government comes into being makes no difference to the fact that only by experience of one or the other kind convincing the millions of the working class will the latter turn to more desperate and decisive forms of struggle.[63]

However, he had no illusions that a Labour government could make a decisive break with capitalism merely through the single channel of parliament, given the level of ruling class resistance it would face. Thus, he wrote a damning critique of the 1932 Labour Party conference's attachment to parliamentarianism, notwithstanding its pledge to socialist measures:

The assumption that the British ruling class will passively allow parliamentary majorities to walk in for the purpose of putting *them* to sleep was the premise of all the 'advanced' resolutions and speeches at the Leicester Conference. Those who so argue, forget that parliamentary democracy is capitalist democracy, created by capitalism to serve capitalist ends, and that capitalism will discard it as soon as there is any likelihood of its being used for Socialist ends.

The tremendous disillusionment which has come over the Labour Movement regarding MacDonald, Snowden and Thomas, still awaits it with regard to MacDonaldism—which remains rooted in the Labour Party. The resolutions of the Conference made this abundantly clear ... "The Bank of England should be brought under public ownership and control ..." Who are the 'public'? Are the capitalists, landlords, investors, included? Apparently. Then where do the workers come in? The existing relation of classes remains.

The only Nationalisation of the Banks that will make any fundamental difference in this country is the nationalisation by confiscation, put through by a working class dictatorship expressed through its Soviet Government. But the resolution of the Labour Party Executive is along the lines of State Capitalism, and not Socialism ...

A similar line was taken in all the resolutions under the cover of Socialist phrases. But the sooner it is understood that Socialism is inseparable from the question of the power of the working class to dispossess the capitalist class the sooner will the illusions concerning the possibilities and limitations of parliamentary democracy be swept away.[64]

In other words, Murphy, despite his membership of the Labour Party, retained the view that socialism could be won not through parliament alone but would require mass industrial action from below to crush the resistance of the ruling class. Moreover, he was also keen to draw attention to the parliamentary limitations in the Socialist League's policies:

In a series of lectures, now published in pamphlet form, [the Socialist League] has begun to develop a programme which it hopes to see adopted as the mandate for the next Labour Government ... The fundamental defect of each of the pamphlets lies not in the working out of projects of socialism on the basis of having achieved a parliamentary majority, or in expounding plans for a socialised industry. Both are necessary. The defect lies, in my opinion, in the predominantly legalistic, instead of social-political, analysis of the situation. It is not wrong to aim at a parliamentary majority. The working class of this country will not attempt to reach socialism in any other way, until experience proves to them that this is closed. The folly is to shut one's eyes to what the enemy is doing and will do to prevent the workers from getting such a majority and to the measures the propertied classes will take against socialism. Their resistance will not be limited to the veto of the House of Lords. The ramifications and key positions of the ruling class are numerous. What of the press and of the class domination of the army, navy, air force, civil service, etc? The demand for a parliamentary socialist government is at bottom a demand for a bloodless revolution. Surely therefore the first job of a socialist government must be to disarm the capitalist class so that they cannot make war on the workers or violently obstruct the operation of socialist laws? ...

It is a Marxist axiom that the emancipation of the working class must be the act of the working class. Is this confined to voting for socialism? The writers of the pamphlets declare for Marxism. Very well, surely the first need is to be realistic in facing the tasks before us? Has not socialism its own state form? Are socialism and capitalism so much alike that the capitalist parliament will do for socialism? Yet the writers so far have only thought out a socialist scheme to be operated through parliament and it would appear that the workers have only to delegate powers to their MPs who will appoint socialist specialists to re-organise industry, etc.

The Socialist League will have to go much further along the path of Marxism.[65]

However, the logic of attempting to marry both parliamentary and extra-parliamentary struggle, under pressure from the Labour Party electoral machine to which he pledged his allegiance, quickly led Murphy to considerably modify his critical stance. Thus, by 1935, in a book which he wrote entitled *Modern Trade Unions*, Murphy considered the issue of workers' control by making a sharp contrast between the revolutionary and parliamentary roads to socialism. He explained the revolutionary view was that unless there is social ownership there can be no workers' control of industry, and that the question of ownership has to be solved by revolutionary means that does away with parliament and establishes a soviet or workers' council form of government based upon an industrial work franchise, with representatives from various departments of social activity. As an alternative, Murphy argued in favour of the socialist conquest of political power through a parliamentary labour majority, and the use of that power to establish the social ownership of the means of production and workers' control of industry, in which the trade unions would be transformed into industrial unions and become instruments of industrial administration. Murphy acknowledged that if the change from capitalism to socialism met the stubborn resistance of vested interests and the issue was settled by civil conflict, then the direct mass conquest of ownership by factory committees in a class political fight would have to precede the development of forms of administration of industry. But he believed that there was a possibility of a parliamentary socialist government coming to power, making the problem of administering industry in an entirely different way than in the Russian revolution.[66]

In this scenario, Murphy believed the socialist government should create a National Economic Council, representative of the socialised banks and industries, trade unions and co-operatives. This council would be responsible for the planning of industry and its administration, although its plans would have to receive the approval of parliament. This National Council would then appoint representatives within regional and district councils who would be responsible for carrying out the general plans. Such local representatives would be nominated by the trade unions, local authorities, co-operatives, the Labour Party and the government. Within each workplace there would be works councils to discuss with management the implementation of plans, with the popular elective principle at this level acting as a check on the selective principle in the appointments to special positions of responsibility. Thus, the works councils would be the industrial union at work, with essentially a regulatory function. Significantly, Murphy argued this general industrial structure would not supersede parliament, but be responsible to it. In other words, he now saw soviets or workers' councils as parallel to, or even 'supplementary' to, political activity in parliament:

> There is indeed, an intimate connection between the two forms of advance being made by the Labour Movement. They are not separate from each other as many people would have us believe. Nor are they alternative forms of action. They are both reflexes of the one struggle against exploitation, the character of which varies according to circumstances.[67]

Clearly, this left reformist position was a far cry from Murphy's previous advocacy of soviet power and his denunciation of the sham democracy of parliament, even if he still conceived workers' control of production as a central element. Basically, in line with official Socialist League policy, he now saw socialism as being introduced *from above* by a radical Labour government.

Meanwhile, Murphy's conception of the role of a socialist party was also transformed. He argued that although the class struggle had produced an independent organised working class movement, at no stage had it yet produced a permanent revolutionary socialist leadership with a policy and vision consistent with its struggles and tasks. Instead, 'The working class is led by leaders who carry within their heads the political equipment of nineteenth century Liberalism to wage the battles of twentieth-century revolution'.[68] The problem, as he saw it, was that rarely were revolutionaries elected to permanent posts in the trade unions and the Labour Party. The historical development of the labour movement was the key factor here. The Labour Party had grown out of the unions with an antipathy towards revolutionary Marxism, and the record of the BSP, SLP, syndicalists, shop stewards' movement and Communist Party was the pursuit of a sectarian policy which had left them isolated on the fringes of the working-class movement. For example, the syndicalists had stood aside from 'politics', the shop stewards had refused to stand for official positions in the unions, and the communists had formed a separate party as an alternative to the Labour Party when the masses were moving towards Labour, not away from it. Thus, the critique of the Communist Party which Murphy now developed was a radical one: the party should never have been formed:

> The split of the international working class movement which the war and revolution had carried to its completion in some countries was extended to all countries whether they were ready for it or not. The general revolutionary character of the world situation and the assumption of an almost imminent world revolution was made the basis for an international split extending with equal sharpness to every country.
>
> Had the [Second Congress of the Comintern] examined the situation in each country and decided upon the formation of communist parties in those countries where the internal position of the working class movement was ripe for such a decision ... it would not have thrust upon small immature groups of communists the tasks and responsibilities of independent parties and made it easy for the reactionaries to thrust them into isolation.[69]

In other words, if revolutionary socialists in Britain, instead of forming a separate organisation, had operated in effect as the left wing of the Labour Party, they would have been able to have made a significant contribution to the labour movement. By contrast:

> Those who attempt [to build a revolutionary party outside the Labour Party] will not merely be ineffective but in many ways hinder the development of the tide of revolutionary opinion within the working class movement which they wish to see developed. This has been demonstrated to me by experience in which I have participated.
>
> It seems to me obvious in the fact that the Communist Party is 50 per cent less than it was at its formation nearly thirteen years ago, and that six times as many people have passed through its ranks than it numbers at the present time. It is obvious, too, in the failure of the ILP to rally increased forces after its split from the Labour Party.
>
> Objectively it is a denial of the faith of the capacity of the working class to effect any transformation of its own organisations and its ability to bring forth leaders commensurate with its historic revolutionary tasks. To such sectarianism I will no longer subscribe. The greatest need of the working class is the closing of its ranks against its class enemies without and an internal revolutionary transformation of outlook, will, leadership and organisation. The Socialist League proclaims it to be its aim and purpose to work in this direction. Hence my decision to join it and my appeal for others to do likewise.[70]

From this analysis, Murphy concluded it was necessary for socialists to remain inside the Labour Party *today* to transform it into a revolutionary instrument *tomorrow*. He imagined that given time, revolutionaries would almost certainly assume leadership of the Labour Party and trade unions due to the pressure of events and the incompatability of the reformists position. However, ironically, as Murphy himself acknowledged in his book *Preparing for Power*, all the great waves of class struggle in British industrial history had been led by people indifferent or even hostile to parliamentary reformism. Thus, the Labour Unrest of 1910–1914 was led by industrial militants who repudiated dependence on parliament and the Labour Party in favour of workers' self-activity. The shop stewards' movement was in favour of soviets not parliament, and was followed in 1919–1920 by 'direct actionists' whose name showed how they saw Labour's efforts as futile. Moreover, the Communist Party, despite its Stalinist degeneration, had been at the centre of the 1926 General Strike compared with the Labour Party's hostile reaction. Clearly, whilst the role of revolutionaries was crucial to these mass struggles, their role was only influential to the extent that their extra-parliamentary activities fitted the mood of the most militant sections of the working-class movement. In fact, despite Murphy's new-found enthusiasm for the Labour Party, *Preparing for Power* actually presented a devastating critique of reformism. It showed it was not the policy of extra-parliamentary activity outside the Labour Party, or rank-and-file organisation independent of the trade union officials, that was mistaken *per se*. It was the relative weakness of the revolutionaries compared to the treachery of the reformist leaders.

At the heart of Murphy's viewpoint was his optimistic fatalism. Despite the past treachery of the Labour Party leadership, the return of a socialist Labour government would inevitably push the party to the left as millions of workers would join it in disgust at the betrayal of the reformist leaders. But Murphy ignored the way in which, amidst such circumstances, there would be an over-riding need for a powerful revolutionary socialist organisation that could offer an independent lead to workers' struggles in opposition to the Labour Party and union leadership. His notion that socialists, in the circumstances of the early 1930s, should remain inside the Labour Party merely helped to provide a left cover and breed false expectations in such leaders.[71] He could not have it both ways. It was incompatible to actively encourage workers to join a Labour Party unashamedly committed to reformism, whilst at the same time trying to destroy that party's reformist practice, pretending the Labour Party was the vehicle for radical change and then crying wolf when the leadership betrayed workers.

As the German revolution of 1918–1919 had demonstrated, the consequences of socialists staying inside a reformist party in a revolutionary period led inevitably to catastrophe.[72] Thus, Rosa Luxemburg and Karl Liebnecht had remained with the German Social Democratic Party (SPD) because they believed that small groups of revolutionaries could only win the mass support of workers if they were members of the traditional labour party. Whilst they argued fiercely against the reformist leadership inside the SPD, they never carried those arguments to their practical conclusion, to split organisationally as well as politically into an independent revolutionary party. Instead they believed the power of their arguments would be proved right in the long run, and when this happened the mass of workers would look towards revolution-ary ideas. In many respects this was the case, but it did not take into account that in a revolutionary situation many workers can still look to their old leaders and organisations unless they are offered an alternative revolutionary organisation, which has the potential to grow extremely rapidly into a mass party in such circumstances. Thus, although many German workers and soldiers moved towards revolutionary ideas, the old reformist leadership, for lack of an alternative, was able to strengthen the shattered state machine and destroy those workers' soviets that had been set up, smashing the revolution entirely. It was quite otherwise in Russia, where Lenin had built up a Bolshevik organisation that had split from the reformists many years beforehand, which related to workers' struggles against the reformist leadership, and turned a revolutionary opportunity into a revolutionary victory. The problem with Murphy's conception was that the Socialist League effectively acted as a buffer between the leftward-moving Labour Party members and the Communist Party, shielding the Labour leadership and 'rehabilitating' the Labour Party in the eyes of politically conscious workers.

Another major weakness was the Socialist League's lack of real links with the working-class movement, which as national secretary Murphy did little to change. This was a direct result of a primary orientation on transforming Labour Party policy. Since it always insisted that the *sine qua non* of the socialist revolution in Britain was a duly elected socialist majority in Parliament, the League's programme could be implemented only if it were accepted by the Labour Party. That meant it concentrated above all on operating inside the party machine to win conference resolutions to commit a future Labour administration to socialist measures. But primary emphasis on internal party policy militated against socialists moving outside their position within the Labour Party, to build connections with, and to offer leadership to, the working class in its struggle at the point of production. This self-adopted isolation from its potential working-class base, and its insistence that the relationship between the left wing of the Labour Party and working-class socialist militants should be almost exclusively an electoral one, had far-reaching repercussions on the character and degree of success of the Socialist League. Thus, it failed to encourage the strength and confidence of rank-and-file workers to act independently of the union officials, and to shape a powerful counterbalance to their bureaucratic and compromising leadership. The absence of such a mass base of support for its policies within the unions also denied the League any substantial influence within the Labour Party, since it meant the left represented little more than a minority strand even in electoral terms.

Of course, during the early 1930s many workers in Britain were demoralised and depoliticised as a result of mass unemployment. But from 1934, as some measure of prosperity returned to parts of the economy, there were occasional upsurges of militancy, particularly in the engineering industry, to which the League failed to relate. By contrast, despite its increasing Stalinism and the adoption of a 'Popular Front' policy (see Chapter Eight), the Communist Party still rejected Labour's parliamentary cretinism and had an orientation on the struggles of the working class. This meant it was able to attract a new layer of trade union militants and shop stewards who led the recovery in class confidence under the stimulus of rearmament, which took place during the second half of the 1930s. Thus, the CP played a prominent role in major strikes in the engineering and mining industries, encouraging new rank-and-file movements in transport and aircraft factories. The party also provided the dynamic behind the organisation of the hunger marches led by the National Unemployed Workers' Movement, much of the opposition on the streets to Oswald Mosley and the British Union of Fascists, and a great deal of the efforts that went to support Republican Spain in the Civil War.[73] Inevitably it also derived some benefit from the increased popularity which the USSR enjoyed on the left, which was seen as the only positively and actively anti-fascist power. As a result, the CP's membership rose from 6,279 in November 1931 to 17,750 by July 1939, and its political and social influence was considerably greater than these figures would immediately suggest. Thus, the *Daily Worker* increased its daily sales from 20,000 at the end of 1932 to between 40,000 to 50,000 by February 1939, with the weekend circulation (when party members were generally more available to sell it on the streets) increasing from between 30,000 to 46,000 in 1932 to betweeen 75,000 to 80,000 by 1939.[74]

Finally, the League deluded itself that by being inside the Labour Party it could avoid the political impotence of the ILP. Thus, Murphy described the League's objective as being to transform the Labour Party 'into the Party of the working class revolution'.[75] But the mere fact of the League's separate existence as a fully-fledged political party, in some respects comparable with the

CP except that it was determined to remain affiliated to Labour, aroused the antagonism of the official party leadership who feared the electoral damage which might be caused by having such an organised left-wing within its ranks. This was reflected in an agitated letter to the Labour Party's national secretary sent by a Socialist League member from South Wales, which reported that Murphy had made a disloyal speech attacking trade union and Labour Party reformist leaders, allegedly undermining mainstream support from the party.[76] The need to organise as a separate entity with its own programme was essential if the rest of the party was to be won to a socialist position, and yet separate left organisation made it open to party disciplinary procedures and even expulsion. As a consequence, there was intense pressure to fudge issues in the name of party unity, and to show its loyalty to the party's electoral ambitions by playing down the League's socialist programme. Thus it would not have been possible for Murphy to have remained a member of the Labour Party for long at the same time as putting his main emphasis on denying the possibility of a parliamentary road to socialism. Like it or not, he was obliged to publicly state that it was possible for a Labour government to make a decisive break with capitalism through parliament.

At the same time, the price of staying inside the Labour Party also affected the Socialist League's activities. This was graphically illustrated in 1935 when many active London branches and members of the League, recognising the need for working-class unity in the face of the rise of fascism at home and abroad, began to engage in united front activity with the CP and the ILP against the national government's Unemployment Act. In response, the League's national council, over the signature of Murphy, issued a circular prohibiting such action on the basis that they could not allow League branches to identify themselves with an activity initiated by outside bodies which could prejudice the League in the eyes of the Labour Party leadership and allow them to take action to expel them from the party.[77] As Murphy explained:

> The most important campaign conducted by the League has been on the Unemployment Act of 1934. This campaign has demonstrated what can be done through the Party when the Socialists within it act in an organised way.
> Such campaigns, of course, raise problems like that of the participation of the League in the 'United Front' of the CP and ILP ... One thing,

however must be clear: we cannot have it both ways—be in the [Labour] party and act as if we are out of it. This the National Council has stated clearly, and it has taken its stand on loyalty to the party.[78]

Although the Socialist League subsequently supported the application of the CP for affiliation to the Labour Party,[79] notwithstanding Murphy's opposition, it effectively remained a compromise between socialist objectives and the existing power structure of the party. Of course, this pressure to adapt to the right is a fundamental aspect of electoral politics, watering down radical policies and activities so as not to jeopardise votes. And Murphy and the Socialist League were caught by this dilemma. The only way to have overcome it would have been to abandon electoral politics and the parliamentary road to socialism, recognising that workers' ideas only change *en masse* in struggle, and that a real socialist alternative to the Labour leaders could only be built by attracting the minority prepared to fight to a party that was both politically and organisationally separate from Labour.[80] The problem for Murphy, was that in rejecting the critique of Stalinism presented by Trotsky and his supporters, he had no alternative theoretical and practical basis from which to assess his negative experience in the Communist Party other than through the prism of left reformism.

Chapter Eight

Popular Frontism and Re-appraisal, 1936–1965

A noticeable feature of Murphy's political trajectory after his expulsion from the Communist Party was his growing distance from the working-class movement in which he had earlier played such a prominent role. Thus, as a member of the Socialist League's national leadership, he found himself amidst a predominantly public school and university educated group of people. Amongst the 23 people who served as national council members between 1932 and 1937 there were two Etonians, three Wykehamists, and one old Harrovian. At least nine had been at Oxford or Cambridge, and four at London University. The formal education of only two, one of whom was Murphy, ended at elementary level.[1] Ironically, despite the fact the Labour Party had a primarily working-class membership, Murphy now mixed in a social milieu which was less than ideally suited to the task of enticing the labour movement from its inherent suspicion of left-wing middle-class intellectuals.

In addition, Murphy increasingly began to write for, and closely associate with, a number of liberal reformist journals which were linked to different middle-class groups and individuals. There was *Adelphi*, which was owned by John Middleton Murry who espoused a form of Christian communism and who grouped around him a number of young writers with a 'synthesis of aestheticism, post-Impressionism, Nietzsche, D. H. Lawrence and socialism'.[2] As well as writing for the journal, Murphy became particularly friendly with its editor, Sir Richard Rees, whom Murphy's wife Molly described as 'a typical representative of the English intelligentsia, a pacifist and well-dressed gentleman'.[3] There was also *New Britain*, a journal connected with a Bosnian Serb intellectual, Dimitrije Mitrionovic, who set up a national organisation known as the New Britain Movement (NBM) that operated between 1933 and 1934. It called for personal alliance (individuals consciously entering into unity with others to achieve a new unity), Monetary Reform, Industrial Guilds (which would run and control industry), the Three Fold State (separate parliamentary 'houses' for politics, economics and culture), and the Federation of Western Nations.[4] In addition, there was the House of Industry League, a successor body to the NBM, which formed in 1936. It sought collective ownership of industry in an Economic Chamber, to be known as the 'House of Industry', representatively based on national Industrial Guilds.[5]

Murphy was attracted to these three bodies essentially because they provided him with a platform to expound his analysis of the crisis of the labour movement and the need for workers' control of industry.[6] Notwithstanding that many of the intellectuals they contained were either mystic idealists or liberal reformists, Murphy retained his faith in Marxism and his belief that the fundamental question to be tackled was the abolition of private ownership of the means of production. Thus at a *New Britain* conference in March 1934, he declared from the platform: 'The New Britain of our aim must be a Socialist Britain free from the profit motive, free from financial swindlers, indeed, a classless Britain. Our task is to ensure the movement will dare to be Socialist and build a new Socialist Britain.'[7] This strident call for socialism was more than a little disconcerting to those who, in pursuit of their aim of transforming *New Britain* into a mass movement with wide political appeal, had been attempting to attract a number of business people into their ranks. When one speaker appealed to the conference to water down their antagonism to the capitalist class to guarantee the recruitment of 10,000 new members, Murphy cynically retorted: 'If you went a little further and turned it into a capitalist party, I could bring you in 50,000 new members!'.[8] In fact, the organisation split up as a result of disagreements about forming a new political party. However, Murphy's involvement with these groups helped to encourage his own political evolution towards the notion of an all-class alliance which he had initially found so distasteful. This chapter explores Murphy's shift from left reformism towards popular frontism and the embrace of a cross-class alliance, and his eventual abandonment of socialist politics altogether.

THE THREAT OF WAR AND FASCISM

The most dominant political issue in Britain during the 1930s was foreign affairs and the approach of war, and it was on the strategies and tactics to be used in the fight against fascism that Murphy was to find himself increasingly at odds with the Socialist League. In many respects, the question of social transformation had remained an academic one for the Socialist League, the Labour Party and Murphy alike, so long as the Labour Party lacked an electoral majority. The danger of fascism, on the other hand, was real and immediate, and threatened the very parliamentarianism in which all three, in their varying ways, placed their hopes.

The Japanese invasion of Manchuria in 1931, Hitler's assumption of power in Germany in 1933, the installation of a semi-fascist regime in Austria in 1934, and the Italian invasion of Abyssinia in 1935, all seemed to point to a rising tide of world fascism, and to threaten an imperialist war. The Labour Party's main platform was opposition to the 'national' government's appeasement of the expansionism of the German and Italian fascist states and, after 1935, support for military sanctions by the League of Nations against acts of aggression. But the Socialist League rejected the notion that the League of Nations, which it regarded as no more than a front for imperialist and capitalist interests, could offer any 'collective security' against war. It insisted any war undertaken against an 'aggressor' in the name of the League of Nations had to be resisted for two reasons. First, because it would inevitably be an imperialist war which would solve nothing, except possibly be used as a cover for an attack on the USSR. Second, because it would help the British national government to misuse its power to the detriment of the working class movement. Instead, the Socialist League called for international working-class solidarity action to oppose the war plans of both British and foreign governments, with a general strike in Britain in the event of war being threatened. The corollary of this view was that the government must be swept out of office as an essential condition for the prosecution of a vigorous policy of resistance to aggression. The League believed only a socialist government could be trusted with the possession of armaments, and if Britain happened to become socialist before other countries, it would organise its defence with the USSR. Murphy's initial commitment to this revolutionary socialist foreign policy stance was

illustrated by his insistence that the Socialist League conference
resolutions of 1933 be implemented in practice:

> The Conference ... supported the proposition of a general strike against
> war and the utilisation of such a situation for the overthrow of capitalism.
> With the revolutionary spirit of the resolutions of the conference there
> can be no quarrel. But have we not had similar resolutions many many
> times, from many organisations? Did not the Rome Conference of the
> International Federation of Trade Unions pass such a resolution
> immediately after the last war? And nothing has happened to prepare
> the workers to give effect to such resolutions.
>
> A general strike that is not prepared is doomed to defeat. A movement
> that is caught napping by the outbreak of war cannot call a general strike.
> A number of resolutions have been passed by local Labour Parties and
> Trades Councils calling on the General Council of the Trades Union
> Congress and the Executive of the Labour Party and the Co-Operative
> leadership to meet and prepare plans. Such plans should certainly be
> increased. But that is not enough. Such action of the masses must be
> prepared in every city and town and village if it is to be effective. The
> obligation and duty of every Trades Council and local Labour Party is to
> the take the initiative *now* and not wait patiently to hand over the question
> to the central leadership ...
>
> The Socialist League therefore must do more than express the spirit
> of protest against war and fascism. It should be in the forefront of the
> Trades Councils and local Labour Parties urging these, on the basis of
> their experience in resistance to the war of intervention against Russia in
> 1920 and their experience of the General Strike in 1926, to work out plans
> of working class resistance to fascism and war, to organise local
> conferences to popularise and amplify the plans, to inspire the working
> class and its supporters not merely with the spirit of resistance but the
> spirit of socialism fighting for victory. The fight against fascism and war
> is a fight against capitalism.[9]

Not surprisingly, the Socialist League clashed repeatedly with
the Labour Party leadership on its foreign policy stance, and found
itself fighting a minority position at annual conferences. But significantly, Murphy himself also soon came into conflict with the
League. The growing threat of world war amidst the rise of Nazi
Germany gradually led Murphy to believe that all questions of *home*
policy should become subordinate to questions of *foreign* policy.
Matters came to a head at the League conference in Bristol in June
1935, where a split occurred between a pacifist element who
opposed all wars on principle and those who took the view that
the 'enemy is at home' and that any war waged by the national
government would be a capitalist war for imperialist advantage

which should be opposed. By contrast, Murphy, facing the whole conference from a minority position of one, submitted a memorandum and made a speech arguing it was necessary, despite the fundamental difference between the USSR and the world of capitalism, to recognise the need for a pact of mutual assistance between the national government and Russia against the greater aggressor, Nazi Germany. Despite the enmity towards the Russian government by the national government, Murphy believed it would be forced into an alliance with the USSR to support a war against Nazi Germany. Therefore, it was necessary, he argued, to campaign in support of League of Nations sanctions, including if necessary military sanctions, against German (and Italian) fascist aggression. Murphy's new found faith in the detested League of Nations, despite the fact that it had originally been set up to secure a united bloc of states or *cordon sanitaire* against the USSR, stood in sharp contrast to his earlier assessment in the early 1920s:

> In theory [the League of Nations] proposes to unite the nations of the earth. In practice it attempts to cover the imperialism of the Great Powers as they grab colonies and possessions from defeated enemies. Its existence is a mockery of its public aspirations. But its aspirations are the moral cloak to hide the machinations of the imperialists.
>
> Examine it more closely. Its representatives are representatives of the various governments well selected from the victors and the vanquished in the imperialist war. The governments are similar to the British government. The British government is a capitalist government maintaining the dictatorship of the capitalists. Its state machine, with its army and navy, its schools and churches, its police and its lawyers, is the weapon to prevent the accession of the working class to power.
>
> Its policy is based upon the preservation of a class society of property owners and non-property owners, wherein the non-property owners, or proletariat, must be free to work or starve for the owners of property or the capitalist class. That is the dictatorship of capitalism . . .
>
> Upon such democracy the British government is founded. Upon such democracy, therefore, is based the League of Nations. To support the League of Nations is to support the terrorism and dictatorship of the capitalists. It is an enemy of the working class, aiming at the re-establishment of world-wide capitalism, which means always the subjection and enslavement of the workers.[10]

But he now saw the League of Nations as the main deterrent to fascist aggression. Undoubtedly the key factor influencing Murphy's changed stance was the USSR's entry into the League of Nations in September 1934, which was presented as a diplomatic move aimed at providing some security for the USSR and delaying the outbreak of war. The triumph of Hitler in Germany had convinced Stalin it was necessary to undertake a political somersault by joining the League of Nations, which he had hitherto denounced as an imperialist 'club of thieves', as a means of attempting to coax France and Britain into a common bloc against Hitler. Murphy, accepting that the USSR's entry into the League of Nations meant it could no longer be dismissed as a tool of imperialism, and faced with the looming prospect of world war with its direct threat to 'socialist' Russia, argued it was now necessary for the Socialist League to campaign for sanctions by the western powers.

Ironically, Murphy's policy shift mirrored that adopted by the Communist Party. This was because the USSR's changing foreign policy interests had led the CP to dutifully carry out a 180-degree U-turn by finally abandoning its ultra-left line of castigating the Labour Party as 'social fascist'. It was replaced with a new call for an alliance between the USSR and the western powers through the League of Nations, on the basis that the issue before the world was not socialism *versus* capitalism but the preservation of what was left of political democracy and of 'socialist' Russia *versus* fascism. This was accompanied by attempts to engage in joint activity with Labour Party members against the rise of fascism in Britain, and a renewed campaign for CP affiliation to the Labour Party. Meanwhile, the dispute within the Labour Party over whether support should be given to the League of Nations sanctions against Italy to halt her aggression against Abyssinia culminated in the downfall of its pacifist leader George Lansbury, although the Labour Party remained opposed to the rearmament programme of the 'national' government.

Although the Socialist League was generally very sympathetic towards the USSR, its annual conference unanimously rejected Murphy's proposal to campaign for sanctions by the League of Nations. It feared supporting a non-socialist government with imperialist intentions because of the likelihood of it introducing military and industrial conscription, and the danger that the war would be directed against the USSR by a combination of the capitalist powers. Having lost the conference vote, Murphy abided by the decision, and in September, as general secretary of the League, even helped to organise anti-war conferences and mass meetings for the purpose of popularising the official policy. So long as the League's propaganda was of a general and abstract character dealing with war in general, and not a specific war, it was not too difficult for Murphy to accept. But the sense of urgency created by the changing international situation, notably Italy's invasion of Abyssinia in October 1935, soon led him to renew his opposition to official policy, and to agree with the Communist Party's call for the use of military sanctions by the 'democratic powers' within the League of Nations to stymie Mussolini's plans. He was no doubt influenced by the CP's argument that critics of the League of Nations, such as the Socialist League, ILP and pacifists, were 'playing into the hands of the Tories' and deserting the defence of the USSR. Moreover, the apparently overwhelming popular support for the implementation of a sanctions policy by the national government and League of Nations, as revealed in a national 'peace ballot' conducted at the time, reinforced his stance.[11]

THE POPULAR FRONT

During the next few months of early 1936, Murphy increasingly felt that the growing power of Nazi Germany and fascist Italy was a threat not merely to socialism but to human civilisation. Moreover, following the outbreak of civil war in Spain in July 1936, Murphy, like many others on the left, became convinced that a fascist victory in Spain to overthrow the newly elected Republican government would make a new world war inevitable. The conviction that foreign policy was becoming a subject which transcended normal political behaviour led him to the conclusion that a broad 'People's Front', consisting of a coalition of all British parties and individuals, including Liberals and even 'progressive' Conservatives, on the basis of an agreed programme of immediate demands was necessary to bring about the defeat of the national government and to put in its place a government that would be prepared to base British foreign policy on the restraint of Hitler and Mussolini by an alliance between Britain, France and the USSR. In effect, this meant advocating the working class ally itself with openly capitalist forces. It marked a radical shift from advocating the overthrow of capitalism by the working class as a prerequisite for peace to favouring class collaboration in order to oppose fascism and defend 'democracy'. In effect, the goal of international socialism had now become equated with defence of the USSR. But Murphy justified his abandonment of a revolutionary socialist stance as a necessary tactic in the face of a rapidly changing and dangerous world order.

Murphy's call for a political realignment to co-ordinate the forces of the left and centre against the national government was by no means unique. For example, the Next Five Years Group, set up in early 1935 and composed of renegade Labour supporters and the Conservative MP Harold Macmillan, had already unsuccessfully attempted to encourage an inter-party alliance that advocated a clear policy of 'collective security' through the League of Nations combined with the need for planning in all aspects of domestic economic affairs. But Murphy's specific proposal was undoubtedly influenced by the adoption of the 'Popular Front' policy by the Comintern at its Seventh Congress in July 1935. This had encouraged communist parties to build alliances with all 'democratic' forces, including bourgeois ones, against fascism. Of course, the roots of this Popular Front stance lay in the cynical manipulation of the Comintern in the interests of Soviet foreign policy. Requiring an alliance with France and Britain, Stalin had to demonstrate that the USSR was a 'reliable' ally, that is an ally that did not threaten the rule of bourgeois democracy. In France and Spain the Comintern's decision had led to the establishment of Popular Front governments based on alliances between communist, socialist and radical or liberal parties. Meanwhile, in Britain, the outcome of the October 1935 general election, in which a new national government headed by a Conservative prime minister Neville Chamberlain (who succeeded the retiring Baldwin in 1937) emerged, undoubtedly also underlined for Murphy the apparent remote possibility of the Labour Party ever being returned to power unless it was prepared to collaborate with much broader political forces.

But the Socialist League's annual conference in June 1936 reaffirmed its opposition to the League of Nations and to the policy of a People's or Popular Front. It opposed it on the grounds that it would require the working class to abandon the class struggle as the basis of political action. Instead, the League advocated a 'united front' limited to working-class parties and organisations, which in Britain meant the Independent Labour Party, Communist Party and Labour Party. Meanwhile, Stafford Cripps initiated a series of discussions with representatives of the ILP and CP which eventually led to the launch of a 'Unity Campaign' between these three organisations around a programme of defence of the Spanish Republic, opposition to rearmament by the national government, the return of a Labour government, and for the affiliation of the CP to the Labour Party. Significantly, the CP supported this united front policy, for the moment at least, because the Comintern could not as yet stomach an alliance with Liberal opponents of the national government such as Lloyd George, architect of anti-Russian intervention in 1919.

However, Murphy regarded this proposition as hopeless from the outset and that, if pursued, it would wreck the Socialist League itself. Although he formally accepted the League's policy of support for the affiliation of these bodies to the Labour Party, he was not prepared to make this the principal question of the campaign in which all three organisations would appear on the same platform, thereby openly flouting the decisions of the Labour Party and risking the League's expulsion. As a result, in the summer of 1936, Murphy resigned both his post as general secretary and his membership of the Socialist League. In the engineers' union *AEU Monthly Journal* he explained the nature of his about turn from class politics to an all-class alliance:

> I have not the slightest doubt about the urgency or the need for a People's Front in Britain. So convinced am I of the need for it that I unhesitatingly say that the fate, not only of this country, but that of the whole world, depends upon its formation and its victory in the course of the next few years.
>
> Because I hold this conviction I am devoting all the energy I possess to the purpose of uniting the common people of Britain against Fascist aggression abroad and Fascist encroachments of our liberties at home ... Only the overwhelming concentration of forces of democracy to prevent the unleashing of the Fascist war forces can prevail to maintain peace and the possibility of progressive social and political development.
>
> To concentrate the progressive forces so that the so-called 'National Government' can be replaced by a people's government is as imperative as the mobilisation of international democracy through the League of Nations.[12]

Murphy castigated the failure of the left to recognise the need to subordinate its aspirations for socialism to the defence of parliamentary democracy:

> The political opposition ... is divided against itself in party formations based upon differences which have more significance in relation to the

future of society than to the immediate period before us. Instead of a concentration upon the immediately practical measures upon which they could agree, fears, prejudices, personal interests, institutional conservatism, block the road to unity of progressive democracy. It is an amazing fact that despite the agreement of Liberals, Labour, Communists and many Tories on the need for international democratic unity in defence of peace against Fascist aggression, these forces do not make a common front against that which menaces peace and democracy ...

I am a Socialist. I want Socialism to come as quickly as possible. I believe that the world will never have permanent peace until its economy is transformed and founded on Socialist principles. But Socialism cannot be established in any country until the majority of the people are ready to establish it ...

In this period it is the task of the real Socialist and democratic leaders to marshall the sum total of the social forces available against the dominant reactionary power in order that democracy can defeat it and advance to its next state of social evolution.

That is why I am for the formation of the people's front in Britain.[13]

Murphy now joined forces with a variety of Liberal figures, including Allan Young (who had been involved in Harold Macmillan's attempts to achieve a 'centre' party alliance), Alan Sainsbury (the grocery tycoon) and a few others from the 'New Britain' group, to form a 'People's Front Propaganda Committee'. This new body, which became a rival to the Socialist League's Unity Committee, appointed Murphy as a full-time organiser. He arranged a series of meetings in London and strove to build up support from the widest possible coalition of anti-government organisations. One such meeting in December 1936, attended by more than 2,000 people in the Friends Meeting House, was addressed by Robert Boothby MP (Conservative Party), Richard Acland MP (Liberal Party), G. D. H. Cole and William Dobbie (Labour Party) and John Strachey (Communist Party).[14]

Franco's military assault on the Spanish Popular Front government made the argument for a Popular or People's Front against fascist aggression more urgent, and under the banner of the Spanish Medical Aid Committee, Labour, Liberal, Conservative and Communist Party supporters began to work together to send medical services and supplies to the Republican forces, conducting a campaign against the so-called 'non-interventionist policy' of the British government. In January 1937, Murphy's wife Molly offered her services as a nurse to the Spanish Medical Aid Committee and went to Spain as a member of the British Medical Unit, looking after the wounded on the battlefront around Madrid, returning home exhausted in July 1937.[15] This direct personal link with the battlefront spurred Murphy on to a new bout of intense activity, speaking at a series of meetings and conferences for one of the many organisations interested in the campaigns for aid to Spain, including the Spanish Medical Aid Committee, the People's Front Propaganda Committee, the Left Book Club, local Labour Party branches, Liberal associations, co-operative guilds, trade union branches and other adhoc conferences. He also wrote an extended series of articles on foreign policy in the *AEU Monthly Journal*, outlining the threat to parliamentary democracy and world peace posed by German, Italian and Japanese imperialism.

It is important to emphasise that Murphy's Popular Front differed markedly from the united front which the Comintern had advocated during the early 1920s in a number of crucial ways. First, whereas the united front was to link working-class parties (parties based on the working class) the Popular Front extended to bourgeois parties. It was thus a class collaborationist policy in the fullest sense of the term. Second, whereas the united front constituted a practical agreement to fight for certain specific objectives, nothing more and nothing less, the Popular Front involved common electoral programmes and support for bourgeois governments. Third, whereas the condition of the united front was complete ideological independence and freedom of criticism, the Popular Front involved an abandonment of revolutionary socialist criticism of other parties in the alliance. Fourth, whereas the united front was to be only one aspect of the Communist Party's work, the Popular Front campaign became the entire strategy of Murphy. Moreover, he ignored the fact that the 'anti-government' elements who were supposed to combat fascism included people like Winston Churchill, the arch-reactionary of 1926 and a man who had uttered admiring statements about Mussolini's Italy. Such politicians opposed the national government's appeasement policy not because they stood for the rights of small nations or workers' freedom to organise, but essentially because they were concerned with a militant defence of British imperialism. Yet even the politicians who were prepared to stand by and watch Spanish workers be defeated by Franco were now expected to take the helm in the anti-fascist struggle. In reality, if the working class was to defeat fascism, it had to mobilise its own economic, political and physical might, something which the

Popular Front prevented precisely because the price of an alliance with the 'democratic bourgeoisie' was the undermining of independent working-class struggle.

Although the alternative 'Unity Campaign' launched by the Socialist League received widespread support from Communists and Labour Party members, it soon floundered, partly as a result of internal political differences between the ILP and CP, and partly because the Labour Party consistently opposed any united working-class action which involved co-operation with the CP. Thus, when the Labour Party enforced its discipline against the Socialist League's defiance of a ban on joint work with the CP, the League was obliged to completely dissolve its organisation. It was the failure of this left-wing united front campaign which persuaded the anti-fascist movement to reconsider its strategy in favour of a much broader Popular Front, and from the end of 1937 the CP put its growing weight behind such demands, thereby belatedly aligning themselves with Murphy's own stance. The central strategic preoccupation of the Popular Front campaign, to which Murphy as well as the CP were now both committed, was to engineer a split in the Conservative Party which would enable Labour to enter a new coalition government with anti-appeasement Conservatives and Liberals.

The Hornsey Labour Party branch, to which Murphy had transferred from Islington, was overwhelmingly in favour of the Labour Party taking the lead in the formation of a Popular Front and sent him as its delegate to the Labour Party conference in Southport in June 1939. Speaking to a composite resolution, Murphy argued there was no chance of Labour unseating the national government in a general election given its weak parliamentary standing. Only by uniting with other parties opposed to the government (including the Liberal, Co-operative and Communist Parties) on a short-term agreed programme of international and home policy could things be changed, with the election of a People's government led by Labour. He refuted arguments that this represented an abandonment of socialism, on the basis that the immediate choice was not that of capitalism or socialism but the continued existence of the pro-fascist Chamberlain government and the advance towards socialism through the preservation of democracy, peace and liberty. But the resolution was overwhelmingly defeated,[16] and the People's Front Propaganda Committee, which had failed to build a sizeable base of support, was now submerged into the wider Popular Front campaign supported by the Communist Party.

THE SECOND WORLD WAR

After Austria and Czechoslovakia had been left to fall under Nazi control in 1938, the British Conservative prime minister Neville Chamberlain maintained a policy of appeasement towards Germany.[17] British ruling-class opposition to fascism only hardened when Hitler's expansionist aims were recognised as posing a threat to British imperialism and its interests, and when Germany invaded Poland, an ally of Britain. Taking into consideration its long-term interests, the British ruling class had little option but to declare war against Germany, but even then a negotiated settlement with Hitler was by no means out of the question initially. Thus, when the Labour Party challenged the Chamberlain government over its disastrous conduct of the war early in the summer of 1940, they won sufficient support from the Conservatives to oblige Chamberlain's resignation. When Churchill formed his national coalition government he brought in a number of Labour Party leaders, including Clement Attlee, leader of the Labour Party, and Ernest Bevin, the general secretary of the Tranport and General Workers Union, who became minister of labour and national service.

While a small number of Trotskyists (expelled from the CP) and ILP members characterised the war as an imperialist conflict and championed a revolutionary socialist policy, the Labour left and communists argued that an imperialist outcome could be avoided because the anti-fascist nature of the war would unleash democratic forces in Britain which would transform British society itself. Murphy came to very similar conclusions. Viewing the Second World War as completely different from 1914–1918, essentially because he believed fascism represented a fundamental threat to the very nature of civilisation, Murphy offered his full support to the new coalition government's war effort:

> However true it may be (and I, personally, accept this view) that the war is rooted in capitalist imperialism, it has become, and will increasingly become a war of the people of all lands against the most aggressive and reactionary form of imperialism known to history. Nazi Germany, Italy

and Japan have thrown down the gauntlet of world domination ... Any country which attempts to bargain with them once the guns have been fired across its frontiers, can only do so to negotiate capitulation. Thus, the conflict of imperialism has become the conflict of peoples for self-preservation against the new conquerors. And the alternatives confronting the people of this and all other countries are those of being conquered separately—or of collectively overthrowing the would-be conquerors.[18]

However, Murphy believed the Churchill government could not be trusted to wage the war against fascism effectively, given its overriding concern to retain vested interests and positions of privilege intact:

> It is the 'strangest of all wars', because it is a war which the British ruling class must fight, and whatever its result they as a class cannot win. If Nazi Germany wins they lose their power, their empire, their prestige, their property and become, with the rest of us who are not exterminated, subject to Nazi domination in every phase of their lives. They cannot win the war unless the working class joins forces with them against the common enemy. They cannot secure that co-operation unless they sacrifice their hold on property, vested interests and power.[19]

He placed his faith, once more, in the optimistic belief that the sheer pressure of events would lead to a social crisis, which in turn would inevitably usher in a new socialist political leadership:

> I support this war against Fascist Imperialism not because I am a British Imperialist; I support it because I am confident that in this war Britain has to become Socialist, or perish as an independent community. It is not a question of choice between the rule of one Imperial Power as against another. The technique of British Imperialism is out of date ... I have confidence in the vast majority of the people of this country that will permit neither Nazism to conquer nor those who put the interests of property before the interests of their country indefinitely to lead them.[20]

Following the outbreak of war Murphy took the decision to return to the shopfloor in the engineering industry to earn a living at his old trade as a turner. Despite the fact he was aged 51 and had not worked in a factory for 20 years, he obtained full-time employment in a London railway engineering workshop for nine months, and afterwards transferred to an aircraft factory where he worked as an inspector for eight months. In both factories he was elected an AEU shop steward. During the evenings he volunteered his services as an air-raid warden, lectured on current affairs for the Workers' Educational Association and finished writing his autobiography entitled *New Horizons*. The return to the shopfloor was motivated not merely by financial considerations. Finding himself moving increasingly within a middle-class milieu during the 1930s, Murphy was sensitive to criticism that he had 'lost contact with the workers'.[21] In addition, he believed that by returning to work on the shopfloor he could, instead of merely preaching to the working class from the sidelines, be in a position to directly inspire them to 'victory production'. It reflected his confidence in the working class to see through the ineptness of politicians and to show their 'mettle'. However, this time around it was not based on a belief in workers acting for themselves to fight employers and transform society, but rather to work more efficiently to increase output to win the war. In an account of his shopfloor experiences, which were later published in a book entitled *Victory Production!*, Murphy explained:

> The relationship between management and workers should no longer be that of employers and employees belonging to two separate castes, each struggling for its 'rights' against the other, but a functional relationship in which all elements within the sphere of production combined to produce the maximum for a common purpose. If this great vision of a new type of society being forged by the war were to become the vision of all concerned it would really be true 'that neither property nor vested interest of any kind shall be permitted to obstruct the prosecution of this war to our final victory'.[22]

He postulated that if only management would take workers into their confidence to discuss with them production difficulties, plans and methods, they would respond. In the process, managers would learn to manage and workers would learn of the problems of management. Thus, he called for joint production committees, for increased effort by workers to raise productivity, and for opposition to the use of the strike weapon during the course of the war. At the same time, he argued the central bottleneck to planned 'victory production' was the government, which refused to make the war effort full-scale. He demanded the government declare the war an 'all-in war', with all land, factories, mills, mines, transport and others means of production becoming the property of the state for the duration of the war. He also called for conscription of all persons aged between 16 and 60. This centralised form of state control was defended by contrasting Germany's state regimentation of capital and labour by means of a political dictatorship in the hands of the Nazi Party on the one hand, with the socialist pooling of all the production resources of the country into one great reservoir of power owned and controlled by a socialist state on the other.

He believed centralised authority should be concentrated in the hands of a minister of production, who would have overriding authority over every industry. These industries would in turn be represented by managers and directors drawn from management and trade unions, with all administration decentralised to regional executives who would deal directly with joint production committees in the factories. At the same time he believed there should be the introduction of a three-shift system of seven working days for seven days a week, with holidays staggered throughout industry to create less interruption of production, and absenteesim dealt with by propaganda under the heading 'Every minute lost here is a gift to Hitler', with the naming of the worst offenders where necessary. Murphy acknowledged: 'It may be argued that all this means a great deal of regimentation. Yes it does. War demands regimentation. We are now a nation at war. We are all soldiers ... and must be regimented willingly or perish.'[23] His argument was that with such a socialist plan for 'victory production', management and workers would unite together and 'there would be no further incentive to strive subversively or openly against one another to satisfy private interests that would have been removed'.[24]

Of course, to fully appreciate Murphy's wartime stance it is necessary to keep in mind his enthusiastic and unconditional defence of the USSR from fascist aggression. Despite his expulsion from the Communist Party and the bitter recriminations that followed, Murphy had retained a passionate commitment to the defence of 'socialist' Russia throughout the 1930s as the most reliable ally against any further extension of fascism. Even the Moscow purge trials of leading 'old' Bolsheviks which were held during 1936–1938, unleashed by Stalin as he systematically imposed his dictatorship by exterminating any possible rivals or threats to his rule, had not diminished this deep loyalty. The outbreak of the Second World War merely reinforced his longstanding attachment to the USSR's defence. Thus, Murphy's call for a socialist plan for 'victory production' was probably motivated as much by the need to assist the USSR as by the desire to transform British society in a socialist direction.

However, this did not mean Murphy accepted every single decision and action on the part of Stalin and the Comintern.

Although he had consciously avoided engaging in any public polemic with the Communist Party since his expulsion, after the outbreak of war he felt compelled to criticise its zigzagging political line, which was changed according to the dictates of Russian foreign policy. Thus, from 1934 the CP had argued for 'defence of the democracies' against fascism, subordinating the class struggle to a Popular Front with all democrats regardless of their class or politics, and when war broke out they offered fawning support to the government. However, the Comintern's line changed after the signing of the Hitler–Stalin non-aggression pact in August 1939, and the CP now denounced the war as imperialist and claimed workers' worst enemies were not Hitler and Mussolini but 'Churchill and Attlee, Blum and Daladier'. Thus, early in 1940, amidst government incompetence in Britain and the fall of France, the CP campaigned for friendship with the USSR, for the defence of democratic rights and living standards, improved air raid precautions and facilities in working class areas, against profiteering, and for the creation of a new government 'truly representative' of the people of Britain, which could pave the way for an enduring 'people's peace'. The CP-inspired People's Convention held in London in the autumn of 1940 attracted a good deal of support from pacifists and workers exposed to the blitz and rigours of the war effort.

Murphy vigorously defended the Hitler–Stalin pact on the basis that the apparent reluctance of Britain and France to ally themselves with the USSR against fascism had left Stalin with no choice, and that the pact was merely a tactical move by the USSR designed to give it a breathing space before eventually having to join the war against Hitler. However, he also expressed his opposition to the Russian invasion of Finland as 'a crude example of power politics and political and military aggression as any provided by capitalist powers'.[25] Moreover, he openly criticised the CP for its switch in policy, accusing it of attempting to play on the suffering of workers as a result of the war so as to foment action against the employers. He opposed the People's Convention campaign as a programme of 'bluff and defeatism' and 'a misuse of legitimate demands for the furtherance of a defeatist purpose'.[26]

After Hitler's invasion of the USSR in June 1941, the CP, under the influence of the Comintern, carried out a 180-degree turn to became a full-blooded supporter of the Allied war effort, demanding the invasion of Europe so as to open a second front against Hitler and to relieve Nazi pressure on Russia. By September 1941 the People's Convention had followed suit and urged more production for the war effort to assist the USSR. In the engineering industry, where the party was relatively strong, CP shop stewards became the most enthusiastic supporters of war production and the fiercest opponents of unofficial strikes. Although party membership rocketed to reach a height of over 50,000 in 1942, reflecting the immense popularity of the Russian war effort, Murphy continued to retain his antipathy towards the CP. He maintained that the campaign for a People's Convention was a 'retarding factor' against the efforts to make an all-out war, effectively 'prolonging the life of Hitlerism'.[27]

Arguably, the Second World War was not really a war against fascism at all, which somehow rose above class interests as Murphy assumed. On the contrary, it was essentially a conflict between imperialist ruling classes (on this occasion Britain, Germany, the USSR and Japan), each aiming to increase their power and influence on a global scale. Of course, this did not mean that socialists could afford to be indifferent to fascism's threat to bourgeois democratic freedoms, such as parliament and trade union organisation, which were the fruits of past workers' struggles. However, it should not have meant capitulating to the 'democratic' British government and abandoning the class struggle either. Fascism and the conditions creating it could only be defeated by the working-class fighting to overthrow their rulers. It required socialists attempting to turn workers' genuine anti-fascist feelings away from the imperialist war aims of Britain's rulers and towards independent working-class politics and support for the liberation of the colonies. Indeed, the best example of how to defeat fascism was provided by the liberation of Italy, Greece and Paris, through mass strikes and armed revolutionary uprisings that threatened to transform the nature of society. It was precisely this type of approach which Murphy completely scorned.[28]

Significantly, there was a degree of ambiguity in Murphy's arguments during the war years which stemmed from his genuine desire to defeat fascism. This sometimes led him to suggest ways of waging the war which would only have been possible for a revolutionary workers' government. But his attempt to fit workers' demands within the framework of the national capitalist state continually led him to fall back on talk of cross-class alliances, and therefore into a position where workers were subordinated to the needs of British imperialism. Thus, what characterised his 'socialist plan of production', to be implemented through parliament, was the lack of real democratic control by the producers themselves, apart from some superficial participation in a state-imposed plan from above. On the one hand, Murphy recognised that the very nature of capitalist society makes effective planning impossible, because capitalism rests on a fundamental division between those who control society and those who do the actual production. As long as this division exists, workers will have a different set of interests from those who control and plan. But on the other hand, his detailed blueprint of a centralised state envisaged a benevolent elite planning society on behalf of the working class. In this scenario his long-standing commitment to the notion of planning had become increasingly detached from any form of genuine workers' control or democracy, demands which he had previously championed.

Ironically, Murphy complained that nearly all the workers' representatives to the Joint Production Committees in the two factories he worked in brought to the new job the habits of trade union negotiation for the remedying of grievances rather than proposals for removing certain bottlenecks in the flow of goods and production. 'Old habits continued, old prejudices remained, and the clash of interests was still going on'.[29] He admitted that what stood in the way of a more energetic and determined attempt to step up production was 'the perpetuation of class relationships'.[30] Yet the fact that independent working-class organisation might be weakened by the process of co-option unleashed by the productionist policy was not seriously confronted. Thus, Murphy's critique of 'old customs and habits' effectively represented an attack upon practices won through workers' struggles by past generations of trade unionists against speed-up, wage-cutting and exploitation. Similarly, his opposition to strikes, on the basis that they dislocated the productive process, had the effect of undermining the defence of working conditions and class solidarity.

Not surprisingly, Murphy soon found the whole experience of working back on the shopfloor rather disillusioning. After seventeen months he abandoned the project and gained full-time employment for the government's War Office as an official lecturer to Her

Majesty's Forces on international affairs, with particular reference to Russia and the Far East. He gave over 300 lectures to troops based in and around London, illustrating his talks with the use of maps drawn on the blackboard, concentrating on providing a factual and informative description of the geo-political situation across the world, rather than pressing his own partisan approach. But he subsequently utilised his lecture notes to write three short books, entitled *Russia on the March, Manual of Soviet Enterprise*, and *The Rise and Fall of Italy's Fascist Empire*, in which he developed his central argument about the need to defend 'socialist' Russia and introduce centralised state planning in Britain.[31] Towards the end of the war he was also employed as a research assistant by the writer Eric Estorik for a biographical book on Stafford Cripps.[32]

POST-WAR RE-EVALUATION

After the war, Murphy, by now in his mid-50s, effectively dropped out of political activity, although he retained membership of his AEU branch, reflecting his continuing commitment to the working-class movement. He had two further short books published. One was entitled *Labour's Big Three*, an appreciative study of the most prominent leaders of the Labour government, Clement Attlee, Herbert Morrison, and Ernest Bevin.[33] The other was simply entitled *Stalin*.[34] This was a hagiographical study which marvelled at Stalin's contribution to the Russian revolution, the military defeat of Hitler and the herculean effort to industrialise the USSR at breakneck speed. The ruthlessness of Stalin's mass repression was justified as necessary to protect the revolution from capitalist restoration:

> Whatever criticism may be made of the mode of operations, of the trials, bureaucracy, fanaticism, and injustices of the period, they must be seen against the background of this fact: that all the trials ... and the terror against the NEP men and kulaks, represent in common the struggle between revolution and counter-revolution in a country surrounded by hostile governments and beset by perils which would allow no time for pleasantries or refinement of procedure. To ignore this is to distort everything. Civil war is not pleasant. It is waged by masses who are now always discriminating, either in the means they use or in their choice of victims ...
>
> ... The GPU, let loose by Stalin swept up the kulaks by the hundred thousand, drafted them with their families into the building of new towns

and cities, the digging of great canals, and the development of Siberia with new industrial enterprises. The struggle was elemental, brutal, ruthless, harsh in its discipline, severe in its conditions—and yet constructive. From the vast concourse of forcibly-removed people emerged new men and women—engineers, builders, architects, leaders of industry and administration, convinced Soviet workers who discovered they were the creators of a new civilisation.[35]

Murphy's defence of Stalin's purges was quite remarkable given the many millions of people who were to lose their lives from repression, famine or forced labour in the Gulag Archipelago. No less than two-thirds of the delegates to the Second Congress of the Comintern in 1920 were eventually executed or died in prison, many of whom he had known personally such as Borodin, Piatnitsky and Molotov. But Murphy was prepared to make every allowance for the obvious lack of political democracy in the USSR on the basis that Russian democracy was economic in character, bringing to the workers greater equality and more freedom from economic insecurity than could be found under capitalism.

Of course, this glowing admiration of Stalinist Russia, which Murphy extended to the satellite states established across eastern Europe on the back of Red Army tanks at the end of the war, was shared by many socialists across the world, who felt it was their duty to stand up for the USSR and the 'socialist bloc' against its capitalist detractors. Like Murphy, they accepted the definition of these countries as 'socialist', planned economies with state owner-ship of the means of production. But this definition of socialism did not include its most essential ingredient: democratic workers' control. After all, an economic plan on its own cannot be enough to define a socialist society. The crucial question is: what is the plan for? For example, the Russian Five Year Plans under Stalin (and subsequent leaders) served no other purpose except to build up the USSR economy to compete with other capitalist economies. For this purpose the workers were directly excluded from decisions. It was a command economy and the commanders were appointed from above, not from below. They were the *nomenklatura*, leading party and state officials who were carefully selected and who performed the functions (and accepted the privileges) of a ruling class. They organised production to accumulate the national wealth at the expense of the Russian workers, exactly the function of the ruling class in every other country of the world. They crushed all opposition, destroyed all workers' rights and established a police state based on the ruthless exploitation of workers. In other words, the USSR was not a 'socialist' society at all. It was a 'state-capitalist' society presided over by a tyranny every bit as savage as any stock exchange-based capitalist tyranny elsewhere. The states established across eastern Europe were exactly the same. The tragedy was that these regimes with which Murphy identified were ones in which the soul of socialism, the activity and control of the self-emancipated working class, was replaced by a new class of privileged bureaucrats and industrial managers.

During the 1950s Murphy survived financially partly through an occasional foray into writing; for example, he was employed by Eric Estorick to write a short historical account of the retail company Marks and Spencer,[36] and partly from the assistance he received from some wealthy friends. One extremely rich benefactor was Alan Sainsbury, a director of the retail company Sainsbury's, who had worked together with Murphy in the People's Front Propaganda Committee. Sainsbury had bought expensive textbooks for Murphy's son Gordon when he attended medical school in London during the war.[37] In future years he continued to provide Murphy with some financial support, supplementing the meagre state pension Murphy and his wife Molly received. Likewise, the house in which the Murphys lived throughout the post-war years, an attractive modern semi-detached residence located in Highgate, North London, was provided by another rich friend at a nominal rent.[38]

Meanwhile, he maintained a network of close friends with whom he regularly socialised and engaged in political discussion. These included Eric Estorick (the author and art dealer), Alan Sainsbury (retail grocery company executive), Bill Higgenbottom (ex-Labour councillor and Prudential Insurance executive), Alan Hill (Heinemann publishing executive), J. B. Priestley (essayist, novelist, playwright and broadcaster), George Cadbury (company executive), Frank Horrabin (cartogropher and ex-Socialist League leader), Vincent Brome (author of a book on Aneurin Bevan), Austin Albu (ex-Labour MP), Earl Browder (ex-leader of the American Communist Party), Joe Freeman (ex-American Communist Party member, poet and author), Arnold Polak (film producer), and Steve Hodges (engineer). Most of these people were in professional occupations and were relatively wealthy. Whilst formally they could be regarded as being politically on the 'left' very broadly defined, most of them were essentially liberal or social democratic rather than socialist in outlook in terms of seeking merely to ameliorate capitalism within the framework of western liberal democracy. In addition, Murphy provided some assistance to a number of labour historians interested in his critical reflections on the shop stewards' movement and British communism.[39]

Significantly, during these post-war years Murphy's political outlook became completely transformed, as he eventually lost both his faith in the USSR and his allegiance to Marxism more generally. The onset of the Cold War, with both the USSR and America threatening each other with nuclear annihilation, and the breach with Tito in Yugoslavia with Stalin refusing to accept any independence from the Moscow line, all helped to shake his convictions about Russia's direction:

> From the year 1916 until 1953 I was a convinced Marxist. From 1920 when I met Lenin in Leningrad and attended what was really the foundation Congress of the Communist International, I was a convinced Leninist ... From 1921 to 1932 I was a leading member of the British Communist Party. During those years, several of which I spent in Russia, I was also a leading member of the Communist International and its kindred organisations.
>
> When I resigned from the ranks of Communism at the introduction of 'Stalinist' methods into the leadership of the British Party, it was not because I had ceased to be a Marxist or Leninist in principle. It may have been conceit on my part, but I regarded myself (on the issues upon which I quarrelled with my colleagues in the leadership of the party) as a much more consistent exponent of Marxism than they were. Whether I was so doesn't really matter, except that it meant I became inhibited from questioning the validity of the basic principles of Marxism and Leninism.
>
> Hence my subsequent criticisms of Stalin and the regime he dominated were always tempered with sympathy for the Soviet Union and its problems, a deep appreciation of its mighty achievements, and always from the Marxist or Leninist point of view ... [But] Shortly after the end of the war, I became more and more distressed at what I regarded as violent distortions of Leninism by the Stalinists. But I got no satisfaction when I turned away from them to gaze on the Western scene. It appeared to me ... that both sides of the 'Iron Curtain' were as much alike as peas out of one pod and that the terms 'Democracy' and 'Peace' had entered in the coinage of 'double-talk' of politicians, statesmen and diplomats alike ...
>
> I withdrew from all political activity and identity with any movement, feeling there was something fundamentally wrong somewhere, maybe in my own mode of thinking and understanding of life and the course of

history. I took Voltaire's advice literally and began to 'cultivate my garden' and critically examine and reflect on the way I had come. . .

The outcome of a couple of years or more of intensive study of Marxism, Leninism, the Russian Revolution and world affairs, etc, was that I ceased to be either Marxist or Leninist. I now regarded these respective 'isms' as a mixture of mythology and oversimplified theories of history, harnessed to a militaristic party of social conquest for the establishment of its own militaristic dictatorship. Rejecting them I began to make for myself a re-evaluation of principles and re-orientate my thinking.[40]

Khrushchev's dramatic 'secret speech' to the Twentieth Congress of the Russian Communist Party in 1956, in which he partially admitted the crimes of his predecessor Stalin, merely underlined Murphy's sense of disillusionment and effectively put the seal on his complete political re-evaluation. The Hungarian uprising later in the year, and its bloody suppression by Russian troops, impelled Murphy to attend his AEU trade union branch and move a resolution of protest directed against the USSR government, denouncing the invasion, demanding the withdrawal of the Red Army and supporting Hungary's claim for national independence. In the wake of British and French imperialist intervention in the Suez Canal against Egypt, Murphy argued: 'there is nothing left to distinguish the "Stalinists" of one country from another, no matter which side of the Iron Curtain they were or what their political and social systems'.[41] Significantly, he drew upon ideas first developed by the German sociologist Robert Michels to paint a bleak picture of the future:

It now appeared abundantly clear to me that whatever the political complexion of all these States, they suffered from the power disease inherent in every institution created by man as it grows from small beginnings to ever larger dimensions. With growth comes centralisation of authority, which carries with it the vesting of social power in the hands of an oligarchy demanding obedience to its authority . . . It is an obvious feature in the growth of the State, political parties, Church, trade unions, industrial organisations, Press and publicity institutions, etc . . .

A remarkable and utterly demoralising scene spreads across the world . . . Over the whole earth the Governments of America, Russia and Britain hold aloft the mushroom hydrogen umbrella of universal death, daring each other to be the first to shoot in an international suicide pact while exchanging notes on disarmament . . .

Hence the great, indeed the dominant issue before mankind is no longer (if ever it was the issue) socialism versus capitalism, or any other 'isms', but life versus death, the elimination of the military power disease

from the life of man that the age of reason, common sense and human
fellowship may be born and flourish.

We are moving through a twilight and nobody knows whether it is the
twilight of the dawn of this new age or the approaching darkness of
universal death. I do not know. I know only this: just so long as the
nations permit Governments of men to rule over them whose minds are
obsessed with power, who think only in military strength, balance of
power, defence of power, engage in double-talk, and lie to the people,
mankind is in the hands of the socially diseased paranoiacs heading the
human race to its doom.[42]

At the end of the 1950s Murphy drafted the outline of a book he
was planning to write, but did not complete, on the British, Russian
and American leaders Churchill, Stalin and Roosevelt. The manuscript reveals a further, even more profound, re-evaluation of many
cherished and long-held views. Thus, he now accepted that Stalin
had transformed the Comintern from an instrument of 'world
proletarian revolution' into an adjunct of Soviet foreign policy. As
a leading member of the Comintern from 1920 to the end of 1927,
and participating in the Stalin-Trotsky conflict, he acknowledged
his actions had aided this transition. Moreover, he conceded that
the USSR planned economy between 1927 to 1940 had effectively
subordinated the entire life of the country to the goal of industrial
revolution. This was the basis of all policy and provided the
motivation for Stalin's brutality and terror. He went on to acknowledge the way Stalin had imposed his will on eastern Europe in 1945,
and then later consolidated this colonisation by imposing the
Russian state pattern in the name of the 'proletarian revolution'.
Finally, he viewed the arms race as representing a battle between
two rival imperialisms.[43]

This process of political re-evaluation was extended even
further when Murphy, aged 70, was commissioned to write an
article in the dissident communist journal *New Reasoner*, produced
by E. P. Thompson and John Saville. The article, entitled 'Forty
Years Hard—For What?', dismissed the Communist Party's
attempts to build a revolutionary party over the previous forty
years, and compared allegiance to Marxism as akin to blind
religious faith:

It is now nearly the end of 1958. No one can deny that the members,
leaders and led, have worked and striven with fanatical devotion,
performed feats of endurance and sacrifice, displayed such energy that
membership in any other party appeared dull and pedestrian. Have what

grievances one may against the leaders and damn them for their authoritarianism and all the rest of it, there were no passengers, no parasites among them. Damn it, a spell in Wandsworth was a 'rest cure'. Yet despite all this terrific energy, financial injections, heavy doses of indoctrination from the elect of Moscow, after twenty years the CPGB was no more than a sect and further away from its objective than when it started its travail in 1920 ... Can it be that all of us, right from the outset, not only had an erroneous mode of thinking, but also the premises from which our thinking stemmed were wrong? All thought develops from assumptions which become the substance of faith. The difference between the scientific mode of thinking and all other modes of thinking lies basically in the supremacy of reason over *all* assumptions whether primary or otherwise. The religionist simply refuses to question the foundations of his belief or primary assumptions.

We British Marxists who witnessed the 1917 Russian Revolution had more religion than reason in our mode of thinking. Our knowledge of Marxism had led us to a number of assumptions, which we accepted as articles of faith ... We were disciples, advocates, expounders, missionaries of the 'Cause'. These theories became the substance of our Faith, containing all we hoped for, enabling us to see what we wished to see. We were subordinating our reasoning to *belief* as all religionists do, transforming theories into doctrines, interpreting the social transformation taking place before our eyes as the 'disintegration of capitalism' despite the fact that life was flouting the basic tenets of our doctrines...

Did we stop in our tracks, ask why we had been forestalled by our new god 'history' and query whether the Russian Revolution could be what its leaders claimed it to be? Not at all. We were missionaries of a faith and cared not two hoots whether it was Peter or Paul who led the Proletarian hosts or whether the Revolution began in Jerusalem or Rome ...

[The Communist Party] became a party of ideologues, interpreting the course of history according to doctrine, and concerned more with loyalty to doctrine than to the living realities of social transformation. It is not subservience to Stalin (though that was bad enough) which accounts for the fantastic gyrations of the CPGB, but the fact that it was beating the air with a false interpretation of the social process and turning itself into a little party of romantic ideologues.[44]

Towards the end of his life Murphy became completely disillusioned with and contemptuous of politics.[45] He now replaced his previous allegiance to Marxism with a mainstream functionalist sociological outlook combined with a blind faith in scientific rationalism and the new school of 'cybernetics'.[46] Thus, in an unpublished manuscript written some time in the early 1960s, he outlined the constant learning process that human beings undertake from one generation to another which drives society constantly forward, from what he termed 'the darkest ignorance into the light of knowledge of modern times'. He argued that 'social cooperation is the fundamental law of life and human society', with the violation of this law within any group, whether through ignorance or stupidity, leading to social disintegration. Thus 'unless there is social cooperation of all parts of an organisation, whether it be a family or a community, a factory or an industry, however small or large and complex it may be, the organisation disintegrates and dies'. He concluded:

> The crisis of our times is nothing other than the clash on a world scale between the conservative upholders of outmoded modes of thinking and ways of life which have dominated mankind as we have emerged from the ages of universal ignorance in man's life history, and the impact of the revolutionary discoveries of the pioneers of science who led us into the nuclear and cybernetic age which are incompatible with a world of social conflict and war and individualistic competition. Science has no impassable frontiers nor demarcation lines, nor iron curtains. It is man's reasoning light of life whereby he gives meaning and purpose to his existence.[47]

Of course, Murphy's rejection of Marxism was representative of a layer of erstwhile Communist Party activists or sympathisers during this period in Britain and elsewhere.[48] Many of those who had been originally attracted to communism during the 1930s and 1940s by the spectacular growth of the USSR economy, the fight against Nazi Germany and support for the Republicans in the Spanish Civil War, became quickly disillusioned during the 1950s Cold War years with its revelations about the real nature of Stalinism. Quite a few turned to various forms of right-wing social democracy as an alternative to the Communist Party. But Murphy's complete renunciation of Marxism, a political tradition which had shaped the best part of his life, was a sad ending nonetheless for such a prominent working-class intellectual.

Conclusion

Aged 76, Murphy died on 13 May 1965 of a cerebral haemorrhage.[1] Whilst he had been only one of a generation of autodidact British Marxists of the early years of the twentieth century, J. T. Murphy was a worker-intellectual *par excellence*. Possessing a distinctive political analysis he wrote down his reflections in the most graphic, concise and lucid form, and combined an avid theoretical enquiry with a long-standing commitment to the working-class movement and the struggle against capitalism in which he played such a prominent role. Moving from syndicalism to communism to left reformism to popular frontism to anti-Marxism, Murphy's political trajectory helps to reveal in graphic relief some of the strengths and weaknesses of the British revolutionary left. This chapter draws out some of the main general themes that have emerged in evaluating Murphy's life and politics.

Undoubtedly, Murphy's chief contribution was his development of revolutionary strategy and tactics within the trade unions. Although Marx, Engels and Lenin had made pioneering efforts to understand the nature of trade unions, they lacked practical experience of mass reformist unions and, not surprisingly, left many questions unanswered. By contrast, Murphy, approaching the problem as a shopfloor activist, was able to draw out some essential features of the dynamics of trade unionism within capitalist society. Not only did he theorise the nature of the union bureaucracy and the conflict between the rank-and-file and union officialdom, he also demonstrated in both word and deed a distinctive practical means to overcome the officials' hold. Certainly, the model of independent rank-and-file organisation, which in certain circumstances has the potential to develop into workers' councils or soviets, owes much to Murphy's distinctive contribution. Moreover, in rejecting the reformist politics of the Labour Party and official union kind, he also eventually made the important realisation of the need to link economic and political action, to fuse trade union work with the building of a revolutionary socialist party that can provide political leadership to workers' struggles in conscious distinction from reformism. Many of the subsequent tactical questions which pre-occupied Murphy during the 1920s and 1930s, such as the relative importance of winning left-wing influence inside the official union machine compared with rebuilding shopfloor organisation, remain of enduring contemporary relevance. Similarly, Murphy's attempt to grapple with the question of what attitude revolutionary socialists should take towards the Labour Party, notwithstanding the many changes in his position over the years, retains many useful lessons for today.

As we have seen, whilst the experience of the Russian revolution and the prestige of the Bolsheviks was undoubtedly a decisive factor in the development of Murphy's politics specifically and the British Marxist movement in general during 1917–1920, revolutionary ideas and organisation developed out of the struggles of the indigenous working class. It was the pre-war struggles in the British Socialist Party and Socialist Labour Party, the syndicalist experi-ence of the shop stewards' movement and its limitations, and the struggle against the First World War and a discredited social democracy, that prepared the disparate Marxist groups in Britain for a unified revolutionary organisation. This did not happen in Britain alone. The situation that led Lenin to break with the Second International and to call for a new Third (Communist) Inter-national was reflected to a greater or lesser degree throughout the international movement. Of course, in Britain, as in Germany, France, Italy and elsewhere, the experience of the Russian revolu-tion and the establishment of soviet power clarified the ideas of a whole generation of the most dedicated revolutionaries. But the enthusiasm with which Murphy and others took up and developed the idea of soviet power and the need for a Bolshevik-type party in Britain is to be explained by the fact that it represented the logical development of the theoretical position already reached as a result of their *own* wartime practice of independent rank-and-file organ-isation.

It should be emphasised that, whatever the differences of interpretation of events in Russia after the early 1920s, many writers would agree that, in its early days the Bolshevik revolution ushered in a period of genuine workers' power inside Russia, something which Murphy's personal observation in Moscow during the early 1920s vividly brings to life in his autobiography *New Horizons*. However, the new social order was to be tragically crushed by the combined impact of civil war and the revolution's isolation internationally. Against the backcloth of a fierce battle between Stalin and Trotsky, the gains of the revolution were lost as a bureaucratic ruling class emerged on the back of a decimated and demoralised working class. The common assumption that Stalinism was the logical irresistible outcome of the Bolshevik revolution neglects the crucial transformation that took place with Stalin's ascendancy and the introduction of the First Five Year Plan (1928–1932) with its forced collectivisation and industrialisation of the USSR. These dramatic changes mark the point at which the bureaucracy transformed itself into a ruling class collectively exploiting a vastly enlarged working class and systematically subjected to competitive pressures to accumulate capital. Stalinism represented a *counter*-revolution, in which the remnants of the 'workers' state with bureaucratic distortions' surviving from October 1917 were destroyed and bureaucratic state capitalism was installed in their place.[2] The existence of the Trotskyist tradition, though largely destroyed in the USSR and confined to the margins of the labour movement in the west, is of major importance, since it indicates that commitment to revolutionary socialism is not equivalent to endorsement of Stalinism, something which has become even more significant in the light of the collapse of Stalinism following the revolutions which transformed eastern Europe in the late 1980s and early 1990s.[3]

At the same time, it needs to be stressed that, despite some important mistakes, the Comintern helped to set the CPGB on a fundamentally sound industrial and political strategy during the early 1920s. Certainly, the first four congresses of the Comintern represented a model of democratic debate which thrashed out revolutionary strategy and tactics, and helped transform the CPGB from a propagandist ramshackle organisation into a combat and interventionist revolutionary party. But it was the gradual degeneration of the Russian revolution and the rise of a Stalinist bureaucracy to power which diverted the Comintern from its original purpose of world revolution and which, in turn, eventually led to the subordination of the CPGB's own policies and Murphy's hitherto self-reliant analytical judgement to the USSR's foreign policy interests.

The argument that the 1920s were essentially non-revolutionary and that therefore the CP's attempt to build a mass party was flawed is highly questionable. Of course, it is true that once the revolutionary climax in Britain of 1919–1920 had passed, there was a collapse of shopfloor organisation in the engineering industry and a sharp fall in trade union membership generally, against the background of mass unemployment and an employers' offensive. But there is much evidence to suggest that from 1924 the working class began to rediscover its combativity, with economic recovery giving workers greater confidence to resist the employers. There were significant new opportunities for the growth of communist influence, reflected in the growth of the National Minority Movement in the unions and the mass mobilisation that occurred during the General Strike of 1926. Even if the working class was far from being in an objectively revolutionary situation in which society was in economic, social and political impasse, there was undoubtedly a radicalisation inside the labour movement from which the Communist Party could have potentially sunk much deeper roots than its, by now, flawed political approach of relying on 'left' trade union leaders allowed it to do. Moreover, the party's ultra-left sectarian isolation during the late 1920s had much more to do with the pernicious influence that Moscow came to exercise on the party's strategy and tactics than unfavourable objective circumstances.

It is also necessary to challenge the notion that the whole project of trying to build an independent revolutionary socialist party was mistaken, and that revolutionaries should instead have joined the Labour Party, seeking to transform it from within rather than standing on the outside. To begin with, it was precisely the lack of mass Bolshevik-type parties across western Europe during 1919–1923, able to lead the working class irrespective of the influence of reformist politicians and trade union leaders, which was the decisive factor explaining the failure to turn revolutionary opportunities into victories, thereby leaving Russia isolated. Moreover, the argument that revolutionaries should remain within reformist parties fails to take into account what would happen if, for example in Britain, the left managed to transform the Labour Party, win an election and start to introduce a radical socialist programme. As Murphy and the Socialist League made clear, a left reformist government of this kind would invariably face the powerful extra-parliamentary resistance of the ruling class, which would attempt to sabotage its policies at every turn. Of course, in such circumstances, many Labour supporters might become radicalised. But that is not at all the same thing as the bulk of its supporters, let alone its key figures, moving over automatically to the need for revolutionary measures against capital merely as a mechanical reaction to the failure of reform. In fact, it is quite likely that Labour ministers would attempt to defuse the crisis by collaborating with the ruling class and watering down its radical pledges. This means there has to be a pole of attraction arguing for a quite different sort of revolutionary politics in every workplace. But to be effective such an argument cannot be a purely ideological one. It has to be an argument in *practice* as well as theory, basing itself upon mobilising the working class against the effects of collaboration, showing that in the self-activity of workers there is an alternative to what the left parliamentarians and union officials offer them.

Although some commentators, including Murphy himself in the mid-1930s, claimed it was possible to build that alternative pole of attraction *inside* the reformist party, all experience before and since shows otherwise. The problem is that the left inside a reformist party spends its time arguing with the leaders in the membership meetings and committees, rather than going out to organise workers in the workplace for immediate struggle *against* those leaders. That is why, although there have often been cases where large sections of reformist parties have split off in a revolutionary direction *after* reformist policies have led to defeat (Germany and Italy in 1920–1921), there is *no case* of the left within a reformist party being able to develop an independent revolutionary politics in time to prevent defeat. Things could be no different with the British Labour Party, whose very structure is built upon the separation of 'politics' and 'economics', a separation most obviously reflected by the 'political' Labour Party and the 'economic' trade unions. Instead, what is needed is a revolutionary socialist party that is both *ideologically* and *organisationally* independent from the Labour Party and able to give a lead to workers' struggles against capital and its reformist apologists. Ironically, despite its Stalinism, the CPGB retained for many years an orientation on the struggles of the working class which enabled it to attract some of the most advanced shopfloor militants into its ranks. This enabled the party to have an influence, particularly on the industrial arena, out of proportion to its relatively small numerical size. The tragedy of the CPGB was not its existence as a separate organisation outside and antagonistic to the Labour Party, but the fact that it failed to effectively maintain a principled opposition to Labour's opportunist leaders whilst at the same time drawing rank-and-file Labour supporters into joint activity in ways that could demonstrate in practice the efficacy of revolutionary as opposed to reformist politics in defence of workers' interests.

Throughout his life Murphy's Marxism suffered from a tendency to view social development in a rather mechanical fashion, to see the working class ridding itself of reformist leaders through the sheer pressure of events. It is likely the absence of English-language editions of most of Marx's early works, of his writings on politics, and (until 1929) of Lenin's *What Is To Be Done?*, reinforced this orientation. This did not mean he did not appreciate the importance of subjective factors, the role of conscious human agency in transforming society. His contribution towards the building of a revolutionary socialist party was evidence of a recognition that the outcome of workers' struggles is not inevitable, but depends on the ideas which influence those involved and their level of confidence and degree of organisation. But Murphy was prone to give way at times to the belief that the 'march of events' would allow socialists to gain a mass following. This tendency to put his trust in the inevitable 'laws of history' was to underpin his early denial of the need for centralised leadership within the shop stewards' movement, as well as his subsequent optimistic fatalism that a Labour government would inevitably be pushed to the left by workers' pressure. It also encouraged his blind faith in the inevitable economic advancement of the USSR, irrespective of the purge of Trotskyists and many millions of others.

As we have seen, the overriding thread affecting Murphy's political trajectory from the early 1920s onwards was his loyal commitment to the defence of the USSR and the Stalinist bureaucracy. It was this attachment which was to profoundly affect his independent analytical judgement and distort his revolutionary socialist politics. The baneful influence of Stalinism inside the USSR and the Comintern was directly responsible for encouraging him to abandon his identification with the working class as the only force that could achieve the fundamental change from capitalism to socialism, and increasingly look to alliances with left trade union officials and Labour Party figures as crucial allies in the battle to transform society. It was an uncritical attachment to the USSR which encouraged him to completely dismiss Trotsky's critique of Stalinism and the rising bureaucracy's policy directives in Britain, China and elsewhere, such that he was prepared to go down in history as the person who moved Trotsky's expulsion from the Comintern. It was Stalinism which encouraged him to wrench the CPGB towards the wild excesses of ultra-leftism during the 'Third Period', and which, ironically, also indirectly led to his expulsion from the CPGB. Combined with the threat of fascism, it was also the chief motivating factor which later led him to take a sharp turn rightwards by trying to build alliances with Conservative MPs within an all-class Popular Front.

Clearly, Stalinism distorted the politics of a whole generation of militants inside the working-class movement, including both members of the CPGB and those who remained outside but were influenced by its approach. Nonetheless, Murphy's political odyssey was particularly distinctive. Despite his relatively early and notorious break from the Communist Party, precisely at the time when Stalin was transforming the USSR, his allegiance to Russian state interests remained undiminished for many years. Ultimately, Murphy's Achilles heel was that in rejecting the critique of Stalinism presented by Trotsky and his small band of British supporters who attempted to build an organisation to sustain the classical revolutionary socialist tradition, he had no alternative theoretical and practical basis from which to assess his negative experience within the Communist Party and of the USSR other than through the spectacles of left reformism and then right-wing social democracy.

Notes

Documents in the Russian Centre for the Preservation and Study of Documents of Recent History (RTsKhIDNI) in Moscow are organised into a series of collections and stored in folders, with a three-part numerical citation given to each document. The first part is the number of the collection (*fond* in Russian), the second part provides the number of the subset or description (*opis*) of that collection, and the third part gives the number of the file or folder (*delo*) in which the document is found. Thus, a document cited RTsKhIDNI 495/100/133 refers to *fond* 495 (the Comintern), *opis* 100 (the Communist Party of Great Britain) and *delo* 133.

A similar catalogue system operates in the Communist Party of Great Britain (CPGB) archive located in the National Museum of Labour History in Manchester, where there are minutes of central committee and political bureau sessions and the personal papers of Rajani Palme Dutt and J. T. Murphy, as well as James Klugmann's notes.

Abbreviations

NMLH   National Museum of Labour History, Manchester
PRO   Public Record Office, London
RtsKhIDNI   Russian Centre for the Preservation and Study of Documents of
            Recent History, Moscow
WCML   Working Class Movement Library, Salford

Notes to Preface
(Pages xviii–xxvi)

1 A. Gramsci, *Selections from the Prison Notebooks* (London: Lawrence and Wishart, 1973), pp. 5–23.

2 See S. Macintyre, *A Proletarian Science: Marxism in Britain 1917–1933* (London: Lawrence and Wishart, 1980) and R. Samuel, 'Class Politics: The Lost World of British Communism: Part Three', *New Left Review*, No. 165, September/October 1987, pp. 52–91.

3 J. T. Murphy, *The Workers' Committee: An Outline of its Principles and Structure* (Sheffield Workers' Committee, 1917, republished London: Pluto Press, 1972).

4 J. T. Murphy, *Preparing For Power* (London: Jonathan Cape, 1934, republished Pluto Press, 1972); *New Horizons* (London: John Lane/The Bodley Head, 1941).

5 J. Hinton, *The First Shop Stewards' Movement* (London: Allen and Unwin, 1973); B. Pribicevic, *The Shop Stewards' Movement and Workers' Control* (Oxford: Blackwell, 1959).

6 K. Morgan, *Harry Pollitt* (Manchester: Manchester University Press, 1989); J. Callaghan, *Rajan Palme Dutt: A Study in British Stalinism* (London: Lawrence and Wishart, 1993).

7 For a brief early attempt, see J. Hinton's 'Introduction' to *Preparing for Power* by J. T. Murphy (London: Pluto Press, second edition 1972), pp. 11–16; and his 'Introduction' to Murphy's *The Workers' Committee* (London: Pluto Press, second edition 1972) pp. 3–8. Also see C. E. Hartley, *Jack Murphy: Syndicalist and Socialist: The Early Years* (Northern College Trade Union and Industrial Studies dissertation, no date, but written in the early 1980s).

8 See W. Kendall, *The Revolutionary Movement in Britain 1900–1921* (London: Weidenfield and Nicholson, 1969), pp. 234–56.

9 See J. Hinton and R. Hyman, *Trade Unions and Revolution: The Industrial Politics of the Early British Communist Party* (London: Pluto Press, 1975), pp. 14–22; and W. Thompson, *The Good Old Cause: British Communism 1920–1991* (London: Pluto Press, 1992), pp. 39–40.

10 L. J. Macfarlane, *The British Communist Party: Its Origin and Development Until 1929* (London: Macgibbon and Kee, 1966), pp. 280–81; and Thompson, *The Good Old Cause: British Communism 1920–1991*, p. 15.

11 H. Pelling, *The British Communist Party: A Historical Profile* (London: Adam and Charles Black, 1958).

12 See N. Fishman, *The British Communist Party and the Trade Unions 1935–*

1945 (Aldershot: Scholar Press, 1995); F. Beckett, *The Enemy Within: The Rise and Fall of the British Communist Party* (London: John Murray, 1995); and Callaghan, *Rajan Palme Dutt: A Study in British Stalinism.*

13 M. Murphy, *Nurse Molly: An Autobiography* (unpublished manuscript, no date, but written in the early 1960s), Murphy papers, NMLH. An edited version of this document entitled *Molly Murphy: Suffragette and Socialist* is to be published by the Institute of Social Research, University of Salford.

14 The Communist Party was subject to considerable police harassment during the 1920s and 1930s, with constant raids of party headquarters to remove boxes of key documents by the Special Branch. In addition, the party faced the continuing threat of being declared illegal. For this reason it was customary to destroy minutes and records of leading party committee meetings other than those taken by hand to headquarters of the Comintern in Moscow.

Notes to Chapter One
(Pages 1–29)

1 J. T. Murphy, *New Horizons* (London: John Lane/The Bodley Head, 1941), p. 21.

2 Ibid., p. 22.

3 Ibid., p. 27.

4 Interview with Alison Macleod, 5 August 1994.

5 Murphy, *New Horizons*, p. 28.

6 J. Hinton, *Labour and Socialism: A History of the British Labour Movement 1867–1974* (Brighton: Wheatsheaf, 1983), pp. 40–63.

7 See Hinton, *Labour and Socialism*, pp. 64–82 and H. Pelling, *The Origins of the Labour Party 1800–1900* (Oxford: Clarendon Press, 1965).

8 See B. Holton, *British Syndicalism 1900–1914* (London: Pluto Press, 1976) and J. White, 'Syndicalism in a Mature Industrial Setting: The Case of Britain', in *Revolutionary Syndicalism*, ed. M. Vander der Linden and W. Thorpe (Aldershot: Scholar Press, 1990).

9 *Solidarity*, April 1914.

10 Murphy, *New Horizons*, p. 35.

11 Ibid., p. 40.

12 Ibid., p. 42.

13 Ibid.

14 J. Connolly, *Socialism Made Easy* (Dublin: Plough Books, 1971), p. 36.

15 Ibid., pp. 38 and 40–41.

16 C. L. Goodrich, *The Frontier of Control* (London: Bell, 1920, republished London: Pluto Press, 1975).

17 Ibid., pp. 24 and 27.

18 Ibid., p. 19.

19 K. Allen, *The Politics of James Connolly* (London: Pluto Press, 1990), pp. 71–74.

20 K. Marx, *The Communist Manifesto* (Harmondsworth: Penguin, 1972), p. 105.

21 Ibid., p. 104.

22 Quoted in S. and B. Webb, *The History of Trade Unionism* (London: Longman, 1919), p. 638.

23 B. Pribicevic, *The Shop Stewards' Movement and Workers' Control* (Oxford: Blackwell, 1959), pp. 32–33.

24 J. B. Jefferys, *The Story of the Engineers* (London: Lawrence and Wishart, 1945), pp. 165–66; G.D.H. Cole, *Workshop Organisation* (Oxford: Clarendon

Press, 1923), republished Hutchinson Educational, 1973, pp. 15–16; H. A. Clegg, *A History of British Trade Unions since 1888: Volume 2, 1911–1933* (Oxford: Clarendon Press, 1985), pp. 83–84.

25 W. A. Orton, *Labour in Transition* (London: Philip Allan, 1921), pp. 88–96; G. D. H. Cole, *Trade Unionism and Munitions* (Oxford: Clarenden Press, 1923); E. and R. Frow, *Engineering Struggles: Episodes in the Story of the Shop Stewards' Movement* (Manchester: Working Class Movement Library, 1982), pp. 34–77; P. Maguire, 'Politics and Industrial Conflict: Government, Employers and Trade Union Organisation 1915–1922' (DPhil, University of Sussex, 1983).

26 See W. Gallacher, *Revolt on the Clyde* (London: Lawrence and Wishart, 1978); W. Gallacher, *Last Memoirs* (London: Lawrence and Wishart, 1966), pp. 68–85; T. Bell, *Pioneering Days* (London: Lawrence and Wishart, 1941), pp. 106–18; I. McLean, *The Legend of Red Clydeside* (Edinburgh: John Donald, 1983), pp. 28–85; H. McShane and J. Smith, *No Mean Fighter* (London: Pluto Press, 1978), pp. 72–82; J. Hinton, *The First Shop Stewards' Movement* (London: Allen and Unwin, 1973), pp. 103–61;

27 Clyde Workers' Committee leaflet, Beveridge Collection, British Library of Political and Economic Science, section 3, item 5.

28 Hinton, *The First Shop Stewards' Movement*, p. 172.

29 Ibid., pp. 162–65.

30 S. Pollard, *A History of Labour in Sheffield* (Liverpool: Liverpool University Press, 1959), pp. 247–48; J. W. Mendelson, S. Owen, S. Pollard and V. M. Thornes, *Sheffield Trades and Labour Council 1858–1958* (Sheffield: Sheffield Trades and Labour Council, 1958), p. 65; N. Connole, *Leaven of Life: The Story of George Fletcher* (London: Lawrence and Wishart, 1961), pp. 76–91.

31 Murphy, *New Horizons*, pp. 44–45.

32 W. Moore, 'Verbatim Report of a Discussion Between Veteran Engineers in Sheffield' (Sheffield, 1953), p. 2.

33 J. T. Murphy, *Preparing for Power* (London: Jonathan Cape, 1934, republished London: Pluto Press, 1972), pp. 126–27.

34 J. T. Murphy, 'The Drive into the Factories', *Labour Monthly*, Vol. 7, No. 11, November 1925.

35 *Ministry of Munitions History* (London: HMSO, no date), Vol. 6, Part 1, p. 35.

36 J. T. Murphy, 'Difficulties of Shop Stewards', *The Socialist*, 10 July 1919.

37 *Ministry of Munitions History*, pp. 37–38.

38 Murphy, *Preparing for Power*, p. 132.

39 J. T. Murphy, 'Their Ideas', in A. Gleason, *What the Workers Want: A Study of British Labour* (New York: Harcourt, Brace and Howe, 1920), p. 190.

40 Murphy, *New Horizons*, p. 57.

41 Ibid., p. 57.

42 J. T. Murphy, '1917 Arrives', *Pravda*, 9 March 1927, RTsKhIDNI 495/100/461.

43 J. T. Murphy, 'For London Workers', *Solidarity*, September 1919.

44 J. T. Murphy, 'The Task Before Us', *The Socialist*, September 1917.

45 *Solidarity*, February and May 1918.

46 J. T. Murphy, *The Firth Worker*, No. 14, March 1918.

47 Murphy, *New Horizons*, p. 65.

48 J. T. Murphy, *The Workers' Committee: An Outline of its Principles and Structure* (Sheffield Workers' Committee, 1917, republished London: The Pluto Press, 1972), p. 14.

49 Ibid., p. 15.

50 Ibid., p. 23.

51. Ibid., p. 26.

52 J. T. Murphy, 'The Unit of Organisation: Branch versus Workshop', *The Trade Unions: Organisations and Action* (Oxford: Ruskin College, 1919), pp. 10–11.

Notes to Chapter Two
(Pages 30–53)

1 J. Hinton, *The First Shop Stewards' Movement* (London: Allen and Unwin, 1973), pp. 275–76.

2 J. T. Murphy, 'What is the Future of the Shop Stewards' Movement?', *Solidarity*, September 1918.

3 J. Hinton, 'Introduction' in J. T. Murphy, *The Workers' Committee: An Outline of its Principles and Structure* (Sheffield Workers' Committee, 1917, republished London: Pluto Press, 1972), p. 6; Hinton, *The First Shop Stewards' Movement*, pp. 280–81; B. Pribicevic, *The Shop Stewards' Movement and Workers' Control* (Oxford: Basil Blackwell, 1959), pp. 89–92.

4 *The Progress of Amalgamation*, Report of the Third National Rank and File Conference, Birmingham, 34 March 1917, The Metal, Engineering and Shipbuilding Amalgamation Committee.

5 J. T. Murphy, 'An Open Letter to the Rank and File Conference' *Solidarity*, March 1917.

6 *Fusion of Forces*, Report of 5th National Shop Stewards' Conference, Newcastle upon Tyne, 13–14 October 1917, National Metal, Engineering and Shipbuilding Amalgamation Committee, pp. 19–21.

7 J. T. Murphy, 'Trade Unionism in the Melting Pot', *The Socialist*, 17 April 1919.

8 Murphy, *The Workers' Committee*, p. 18.

9 J. T. Murphy, 'What is the Future of the Shop Stewards' Movement?', *Solidarity*, September 1918.

10 J. T. Murphy, 'Workshop Organisation', *Solidarity*, March 1917.

11 Ibid.

12 J. T. Murphy, 'The World Revolution and the Immediate Tasks before the Industrial Organisations of the British Workers', *The Worker*, 19 March 1921.

13 Murphy, *The Trade Unions: Organisations and Action* (Oxford, Ruskin College, 1919), p. 31.

14 Hinton, *The First Shop Stewards' Movement*, pp. 283–86.

15 J. T. Murphy, 'The Approaching Crisis', *Solidarity*, February 1917.

16 J. T. Murphy, *Preparing for Power* (London, Jonathan Cape, 1934, republished London: Pluto Press, 1972), p. 159.

17 Hinton, *The First Shop Stewards' Movement*, p. 336.

18 *The Miners Next Step* (Unofficial Reform Committee of the South Wales Miners, 1912, republished London: Pluto Press, 1973). The pamphlet called for a fighting miners' trade union in Wales and a programme based upon immediate

improvements in workers' conditions leading ultimately to ownership and control of the coalfield.

19 Murphy, *The Workers' Committee*, p. 13.

20 Ibid., pp. 13–14. It is more than likely that Murphy would have also been aware of the description of the 'shifting of the leadership in the trade union world from the causal enthusiast and irresponsible agitator to a class of permanent salaried officers expressly chosen out of the rank-and-file of trade unionists for their superior business capacity' provided by S. and B. Webb in their first edition of *The History of Trade Unionism* published in 1894 (London: Longmans, second edition 1920), p. 204.

21 Ibid., p. 14.

22 J. T. Murphy, *Compromise or Independence? An Examination of the Whitley Report with a Plea for the Rejection of the Proposals for Joint Standing Industrial Councils* (Sheffield: Sheffield Workers' Committee, 1918), p. 9.

23 Murphy, *The Workers' Committee*, p. 14.

24 J. T. Murphy, 'Open Letter to Rank and File Conference', *Solidarity*, March 1917.

25 J. T. Murphy, *New Horizons* (London, John Lane/The Bodley Head, 1941), pp. 44–45.

26 J. T. Murphy, 'Should We Capture the Trade Unions?', *Solidarity*, June 1918.

27 *The Miners Next Step.*

28 T. Cliff and D. Gluckstein, *Marxism and Trade Union Struggle: The General Strike of 1926* (London: Bookmarks, 1986), p. 70.

29 See Pribicevic, *The Shop Stewards' Movement and Workers' Control 1910–1922*, p. 27.

30 For example, Tom Bell became President of the small craft union, the Scottish Iron Moulders' Union (T. Bell, *Pioneering Days* [London: Lawrence and Wishart, 1941], p. 162).

31 Murphy, *New Horizons*, p. 81.

32 W. Kendall, *The Revolutionary Movement in Britain 1900–1921* (London: Weidenfeld and Nicholson, 1969), p. 167; Pribicevic, *The Shop Stewards' Movement and Workers' Control*, pp. 91–92.

33 Murphy, *Preparing for Power*, p. 97.

34 Murphy, *New Horizons*, p. 81.

35 Hinton, *The First Shop Stewards' Movement*, p. 293.

36 Murphy, *The Workers' Committee*, pp. 8–9.

37 J. T. Murphy, *Solidarity*, September 1918.

38 J. T. Murphy, 'Their Ideas' in A. Gleason, *What the Workers Want: A Study of British Labour* (New York: Harcourt, Brace and Howe, 1920), p. 188.

39 J. T. Murphy, 'Report on the Industrial Aspects of the Working Class Movement in Britain', Communication to Amsterdam Sub-Bureau of the Third International, Amsterdam, March 1920, RTsKhIDNI 495/100/5.

40 D. Gluckstein, *The Western Soviets* (London: Bookmarks, 1985), p. 71.

41 Murphy, *New Horizons*, p. 44.

42 *ASE Monthly Journal and Report*, February 1918.

43 *Ministry of Munitions History*, Vol. 11, p. 44.

44 Hinton, *The First Shop Stewards' Movement*, p. 263.

45 E. Anderson, *Hammer or Anvil: The Study of the German Working Class Movement* (New York: Oriole Editions, 1973), p. 38.

46 J. T. Murphy, *The Workers' Dreadnought*, 20 April 1918.

47 Hinton, *The First Shop Stewards' Movement*, pp. 267–68.

48 Ibid., pp. 287–88.

49 Cliff and Gluckstein, *Marxism and Trade Union Struggle*, p. 67.

50 Murphy, *The Workers' Committee*, p. 17.

51 Murphy, *New Horizons*, p. 57.

52 Murphy, *The Workers' Committee*, pp. 4–5.

53 J. T. Murphy. *Solidarity*, July 1917.

54 Murphy, *The Workers' Committee*, p. 14.

55 Ibid., p. 25.

56 Letter from J. T. Murphy to Walter Kendall, 27 November 1960, Murphy papers, NMLH.

57 Murphy, *Preparing For Power*, pp. 176–77.

58 B. Thompson, *Queer People* (London: Hodder and Stoughton, 1922), p. 271; Webb and Webb, *The History of Trade Unionism*, p. 645.

59 B. Thompson, *The Scene Changes* (London, 1939), pp. 390–92.

60 Between October 1919 and January 1924 a 'Fortnightly Report on Revolutionary Organisations in the United Kingdom and Morale in Foreign Countries' was prepared for the Cabinet by Basil Thompson, head of the Special Branch. In 1921 it was claimed that 'Murphy has never been paid by this Department, though he was reporting for and being paid by an unofficial employers' agency during the war'. PRO CAB 24/125/CP 3100, 30 June 1921.

61 'Powerful People Behind a Plot', *Daily Herald*, 13 August 1919; 'The Plot against Labour', *Daily Herald*, 14 August 1919.

62 In Moscow in 1921, a joint commission of the Comintern and Red International of Labour Unions was set up to investigate French newspaper allegations that Murphy was a 'police spy'. Although the Commission accepted Murphy's innocence, and did not question his integrity, they thought both Murphy and the Sheffield Workers' Committee had acted unwisely in having anything to do with 'Mr Brown' *(New Horizons*, pp. 172–73). His case was not assisted by the manner in which W. F. Watson, leader of the Amalgamation Committee Movement, was forced to admit to taking money from the police for supplying information, although he claimed such information was deliberately misleading. Unlike Murphy, Watson was expelled from all rank-and-file bodies, although his action made Murphy's lack of judgement even more apparent, as he himself later acknowledged. The 'police spy' charges arose again in 1928 after Murphy had returned to Britain after 18 months in Moscow, following renewed fabricated allegations in a Russian White Guardist paper *Poslednia Novesti* which was edited in Paris ('J. T. Murphy's Reply to Gutter Attack', *Workers' Life*, 18 May 1928). Later in the 1930s, after Murphy's expulsion from the Communist Party, there was renewed innuendo about Murphy having been a police agent.

63 J. T. Murphy, 'The Truth about the Strike', *The Firth Worker*, No. 14, March 1918.

64 J. T. Murphy, *The Socialist*, 17 July 1919.

65 J. T. Murphy, *Compromise or Independence? An Examination of the Whitley Report with a Plea for the Rejection of the Proposals for Joint Standing Industrial Councils* (Sheffield: Sheffield Workers' Committee, 1918).

66 Murphy, *New Horizons*, p. 80.

67 J. T. Murphy, 'Notes and Observations on the Working Class Movement in Great Britain', ECCI, 1920, RTsKhIDNI 495/100/9.

Notes to Chapter Three
(Pages 54–86)

1 J. Hinton, *The First Shop Stewards' Movement* (London: Allen and Unwin, 1973), p. 319.

2 Letter from J. T. Murphy to Walter Kendall, 27 November 1960, Murphy papers, NMLH.

3 J. T. Murphy, A. MacManus, T. Bell and W. Paul, 'A Plea for the Reconsideration of Socialist Tactics and Organisation' *The Socialist*, 2 January 1919.

4 Hinton, *The First Shop Stewards' Movement*, p. 301.

5 'A Revolutionary Period', *The Socialist*, 30 January 1919.

6 J. T. Murphy, *New Horizons* (London: John Lane/The Bodley Head, 1941), p. 63.

7 Ibid., p. 68.

8 Letter from J. T. Murphy to Earl Browder, 1 September, 1961, Murphy papers, NMLH.

9 'A Soviet Republic for Britain', *The Socialist*, 12 December 1918.

10 Murphy made a feature of the election campaign demands on behalf of the returning soldiers and their dependants, and wrote a pamphlet on the question entitled *Equality of Sacrifice* (London: Socialist Labour Party, 1918) which contrasted the vast wealth accruing to arms manufacturers and other industrialists as a result of the war with the scant provisions made for the widows of these servicemen and for soldiers permanently disabled.

11 'A Soviet Republic for Britain', *The Socialist*, 12 December 1918.

12 For example, see the 1919 pamphlet written by BSP members W. Gallacher and J. Campbell. *Direct Action: An Outline of Workshop and Social Organisation* (republished London: Pluto Press, 1972).

13 C. Rosenberg, *1919: Britain on the Brink of Revolution* (London: Bookmarks, 1987).

14 C. Smith, 'The Years of Revolt', *International Socialism*, first series, No. 48, June/July 1971, pp. 18–22.

15 Murphy, *New Horizons*, p. 82.

16 Ibid., p. 83.

17 Rosenberg, *1919: Britain on the Brink of Revolution*, pp. 55–69.

18 This section draws extensively on James Hinton's *The First Shop Stewards' Movement*, pp. 308–17.

19 J. T. Murphy, 'Preparing for the Crisis', *The Socialist*, December 1918.

20 J. T. Murphy, 'Manifesto to the Rank and File Movement', *Solidarity*, December 1919.

21 A. Callinicos, 'The Rank and File Movement Today', *International Socialism*, second series, No. 17, 1982, pp. 1–38.

22 Ibid.

23 J. T. Murphy, 'Preparing for the Crisis', *The Socialist*, December 1919; *The Worker*, 20 December 1919.

24 J. T. Murphy, 'Manifesto to the Rank and File Movement', *Solidarity*, December 1919.

25 J. T. Murphy, *The Trade Unions: Organisations and Action* (Oxford: Ruskin College, 1919), p. 19.

26 J. T. Murphy, 'Manifesto to the Rank and File Movement, *Solidarity*, December 1919.

27 Murphy, *The Trade Unions: Organisations and Action*, p. 20.

28 *The Worker*, 14 February 1920.

29 Hinton, *The First Shop Stewards' Movement*, pp. 317–18.

30 T. Bell, *Pioneering Days* (London: Lawrence and Wishart, 1941), p. 176.

31 A. Henderson, *The Aims of Labour* (London, 1918), pp. 61–62.

32 See D. Coates, *The Labour Party and the Struggle for Socialism* (Cambridge: Cambridge University Press, 1975).

33 W. Kendall, *The Revolutionary Movement in Britain 1900–1921* (London: Weidenfeld and Nicholson, 1969), pp. 245–46.

34 J. T. Murphy, 'Appeal for a United Effort: An Open Letter to Socialists', *The Socialist*, 5 June 1919.

35 *The Socialist*, 19 June 1919; *The Call*, 8 April 1920.

36 *The Call*, 12 February 1920.

37 The Amsterdam Bureau conference took place in February 1920. After the fourth day it dispersed because of police surveillance, but not before the police had succeeded in arresting most of the foreign delegates. Murphy, Mikhail Borodin (a Russian Bolshevik emissary), Louis Fraina (an American communist) and a few others managed to hide out and continue the discussions at Rutgers' home. The Bureau itself was only in existence for less than three months. By the time word of the anti-political and anti-trade union resolutions adopted at Amsterdam reached Moscow, the Bureau was promptly shut down.

38 J. W. Hulse, *The Forming of the Communist International* (Stanford: Stanford University Press, 1964), pp. 152–60

39 J. T. Murphy, *The Socialist*, 31 March, 10 April and 6 May 1920.

40 J. T. Murphy, 'The SLP and Unity: An Open Letter to the Party', *The Socialist*, 6 May 1920.

41 Ibid.

42 J. T. Murphy, 'Notes and Observations on the Working Class Movement in Great Britain', 1920, RTsKhIDNI 495/100/9; see also R. Challinor, *The Origins of British Bolshevism* (London: Croom Helm, 1977), pp. 229–32.

43 Letter from J. T. Murphy to S. J. Rutgers, 21 April 1920, RTsKhIDNI 495/100/6.

44 Petrograd was renamed Leningrad in the 1920s and is now known by the pre-1917 name of St Petersburg.

45 Murphy, *New Horizons*, p. 105.

46 Ibid., p. 108.

47 E. H. Carr, *The Bolshevik Revolution 19171923*, Vol. 3 (London: Macmillan, 1953).

48 Murphy, *New Horizons*, p. 135.

49 Ibid., p. 147.

50 A. Rosmer, *Lenin's Moscow* (London: Pluto Press, 1971), pp. 68–71.

51 Ibid., p. 116.

52 J. T. Murphy, 'Forty Years Hard: For What?', *New Reasoner*, Winter 1958/9.

53 V. I. Lenin, 'The State and Revolution'. *Selected Works*, Vol. 2 (Moscow: Progress, 1970), pp. 283–375.

54 Murphy, *New Horizons*, p. 118.

55 J. T. Murphy, *Workers' Life*, 20 January 1928. Whenever a delegate from a foreign party arrived from beyond the frontier of the republic, it was the practice to arrange for a conversation with Lenin. Despite his many responsible duties as chair of the Council of People's Commissars and party leader, Lenin displayed a keen interest in the workers' movement abroad. He arranged similar meetings to Murphy's with Tom Bell (*Pioneering Days*, p. 219), Willie Gallacher (*Last Memoirs* [London: Lawrence and Wishart, 1966], pp. 153–54) and Harry Pollitt (*Serving My Time* [London: Lawrence and Wishart, 1940], p. 139).

56 Murphy, *New Horizons*, p. 129.

57 Ibid., p. 116.

58 Ibid., p. 117.

59 See Chapter Four for further discussion of such issues.

60 *The Second Congress of the Communist International: Minutes and Proceedings*, Vol. 2. (London: New Park, 1977), p. 34.

61 V. I. Lenin, *On Britain* (London, 1959), pp. 460–61.

62 Of the eight members of the National Administrative Council of the SS&WCM who had been elected in August 1917, six—A. MacManus (the chair), G. Peet (the secretary), J. T. Murphy (the assistant secretary), T. Hurst, W. Gallacher and T. Dingley—joined the Communist Party by the time of the Leeds Unity Convention in January 1921.

63 'Letters from Moscow to the Shop Stewards' and Workers' Committees', *Solidarity*, November 1920; 'Report of the Condition and Work in Britain of the Shop Stewards' Movement', *The Communist International*, No. 16–17, 1921; 'Report of the Leeds Unity Conference', *The Communist*, 5 February 1921.

64 Kendall, *The Revolutionary Movement in Britain 1900–1921*, pp. 234–56.

65 Pankhurst alleged that 'Rothstein was subsidising these candidatures with Russian funds'. Sylvia Pankhurst Papers, International Institute of Social History, Amsterdam, quoted in Kendall, *The Revolutionary Movement in Britain*, p. 252.

66 Murphy, *New Horizons*, p. 86. Murphy also received a substantial sum of Russian money to finance the campaign for a British Bureau of the Red International of Labour Unions. See Chapter Four.

67 Ibid., pp. 159–60.

68 T. Cliff, *Lenin: Vol. 4: The Bolsheviks and World Revolution* (London: Pluto Press, 1979), pp. 94–99.

Notes to Chapter Four
(Pages 87–132)

1 M. Murphy, *Nurse Molly: An Autobiography* (unpublished manuscript, no date, but written in the early 1960s, Murphy papers, NMLH), p. 22.

2 Ibid., p. 67.

3 Ibid., p. 86.

4 J. T. Murphy, *New Horizons* (London: John Lane/The Bodley Head, 1941), p. 152; p. 135.

5 The following account is based on C. Smith, 'The Years of Revolt', *International Socialism*, first series, No. 48, June/July 1971, pp. 18–22.

6 J. B. Jefferys, *The Story of the Engineers* (London: Lawrence and Wishart, 1945), pp. 226–27.

7 Speech at the Fourth Congress of the Communist International, 7 November–3 December 1922. Abridged Report (Communist Party of Great Britain, 1923), p. 62.

8 T. Cliff and D. Gluckstein, *Marxism and the Trade Union Struggle: The General Strike of 1926* (London: Bookmarks, 1986). Cliff and Gluckstein suggest that Lenin played no leading role whatsoever in the RILU, being far too burdened with other tasks. In fact, Lenin met with Murphy on two occasions to discuss the practical steps involved in setting up the International and organising its first Congress, and also edited its first manifesto. See Murphy's *New Horizons* pp. 160–61 and Molly Murphy's unpublished autobiography *Nurse Molly*, pp. 77–79.

9 Louis Fraina, the American communist, claimed he received $50,000 from the Comintern in 1920, $20,000 of which he passed on to Murphy to take to Britain (T. Draper, *The Roots of American Communism* [Chicago: Elephant, 1989]). Although Murphy denied this, he agreed that 'the Russian trade unions financed the campaign' for the Red International of Labour Unions in Britain. ('Forty Years Hard—For What?', *New Reasoner*, Winter 1958–59). The Moscow archives reveal that Murphy wrote a lengthy account to the Comintern of how he disposed of £12,600 entrusted to him, which illustrates the way the money was handled. £2,600 went to the National Administrative Council of the Shop Stewards' and Workers' Committee Movement, and £5,600 to the British Bureau of the RILU (see F. Beckett, *Enemy Within: The Rise and Fall of the British Communist Party* [London: John Murray, 1995], pp. 17–18). According to the 'Fortnightly Report on Revolutionary Organisations in the United Kingdom' presented by Special Branch to the Cabinet, 'Murphy appears to be the direct agent of Moscow and is reported to have given money to several of the militant members of the Sheffield

Workers' Committee, each of whom pledged himself to secrecy regarding the transaction'; 3 February 1921 (PRO/CAB 24/119/CP 2541).

10 'Manifesto of the Provisional International Council of Trade and Industrial Unions to the Organised Workers of Great Britain', January 1921, signed by M. Tomsky, A. Rosmer and J. T. Murphy, *Solidarity*, 7 January 1921.

11 J. T. Murphy, *Stop the Retreat! An Appeal to Trade Unionists* (London: Red International of Labour Unions, 1922).

12 'The Red Trade Union International', *The Communist*, 23 July 1921.

13 J. T. Murphy, *The 'Reds' in Congress: Preliminary Report of the First World Congress of of the Red International of Trade and Industrial Unions* (London: British Bureau of RILU, 1921).

14 Murphy, *New Horizons*, p. 172. Cliff and Gluckstein, *Marxism and the Trade Union Struggle*, pp. 50–52.

15 J. T. Murphy, *The 'Reds' in Congress*. Although the South Wales Miners Federation, representing 300,000 workers, toyed with the idea of affiliation, it never actually took the final step.

16 Speech at the Fourth Congress of the Communist International, 7 November–3 December 1922. *Abridged Report* (Communist Party of Great Britain, 1923), p. 227.

17 J. T. Murphy, 'The Fourth Congress: A Special Report on the Recent World Congress of the Comintern', *Communist Review*, Vol. 3, No. 11, March 1923.

18 *International Trade Union Unity* (London, 1925), pp. 17–18.

19 Murphy, *New Horizons*, p. 158.

20 Cliff and Gluckstein, *Marxism and the Trade Union Struggle*, pp. 50–52.

21 CPGB executive committee meetings 13 October and 23 October 1923, CPGB Archive, NMLH, 495/100/58.

22 J. T. Murphy, 'Report of the Red Trade Union Congress', *Communist Review*, Vol. 1, No. 6, October 1921; Organising Bureau meeting, 22 January 1922, CPGB Archive, NMLH, 495/100/59.

23 *Report of the Control Commission to the Sixth CPGB Congress*, 17–19 May 1924.

24 Meanwhile at the international level, despite exaggerated claims of success, the RILU proved to be an embarrassing failure. After the defeat of the German revolution in 1923 the Russian leaders realised that the period of revolutionary offensive across western Europe had come to a temporary end. This encouraged them to look for allies and security from imperialist attack elsewhere. As a result, the RILU made a sharp turn and announced it wanted to join the Amsterdam International with a view to achieving unity between revolutionaries and reformists. But it did not conclude that it had been mistaken in the past in attempting to build a trade union International at an official level (Cliff and Gluckstein, *Marxism and the Trade Union Struggle*, p. 55).

25 J. T. Murphy, 'The Road to Power', *Labour Monthly*, Vol. 2, No. 1, January 1922.

26 J. T. Murphy, 'The World Revolution and The Immediate Tasks Before the Industrial Organisations of the British Workers', *The Worker*, 19 March 1921.

27 Cliff and Gluckstein, *Marxism and the Trade Union Struggle*, p. 96.

28 J. T. Murphy, 'On Leading the Masses', *Communist Review*, Vol. 2, No. 4, February 1922.

29 'Trade Unionists: The Communist Party Calls You to Action', *The Communist*, 10 September 1921.

30 J. T. Murphy, 'The Road to Power', *Labour Monthly*, Vol. 2, No. 1, January 1922.

31 J. T. Murphy, 'Trade Union Blacklegs', *The Communist*, 30 September 1922.

32 Cliff and Gluckstein, *Marxism and the Trade Union Struggle*, p. 99.

33 R. Palme Dutt, *Labour Monthly*, October 1922.

34 J. MacFarlane, *The British Communist Party: Its Origin and Development until 1929* (London: Macgibbon and Kee, 1966), p. 302.

35 J. Klugmann, *History of the Communist Party of Great Britain: Formation and Early Years 1919–1924*, Vol. 1 (London: Lawrence and Wishart, 1968), p. 77.

36 Murphy, *New Horizons*, pp. 181–82.

37 In the early days of the Communist Party, the leading committee was referred to as the executive committee, but was later renamed the central committee.

38 *Report of the Party Commission on Organisation* presented to the Fifth Congress of the CPGB, p. 10.

39 J. T. Murphy, 'The Party Conference', *Communist Review*, Vol. 4, No. 9, January 1924.

40 MacFarlane, *The British Communist Party*, p. 83. Meanwhile, Murphy was also involved in an acrimonious critique of 'extravagant and contradictory statements' that appeared in the party newspaper *Workers' Weekly* edited by Palme Dutt, which was considered by the political bureau in December 1923. Although the political bureau conceded some of his criticisms, Murphy agreed to withdraw his charge of 'political incompetence' which he levelled at Palme Dutt (CPGB political bureau meeting, 28 December 1923, CPGB Archive, NMLH, 495/100/104 and CP/IND/Dutt/26/02).

41 K. Morgan, *Harry Pollitt* (Manchester: Manchester University Press, 1989), p. 32.

42 Cited in F. Claudin, *The Communist Movement: From Comintern to Cominform* (Harmondsworth: Penguin, 1975), p. 63.

43 Speech at the Fourth Congress of the Communist International, 7 November–3 December 1922. *Abridged Report* (Communist Party of Great Britain, 1923), pp. 226–27.

44 CPGB central committee meeting, 13 April 1923, RTsKhIDNI, 495/100/103.

45 *From the Fourth to the Fifth World Congress*, Report of the Executive Committee of the Communist International, London: CPGB 1924).

46 *International Labour Movement 1923–24*, RILU Executive Bureau Report to Delegates to Third RILU Congress. The frank rejection of the policy of splitting and the restriction of the functions of the British Bureau of the RILU to the fostering of minorities in existing unions completed the transition from the initial stage of RILU policy, the building up of rival organisations to the Amsterdam International and the Amsterdam unions, to the second stage of

penetration into the Amsterdam unions through the development within them of revolutionary minorities. E. H. Carr, *Socialism in One Country 1924–1926 Vol. 3, Part 1* (London: Macmillan), pp. 122–23.

47 J. T. Murphy, 'The Party Conference', *Communist Review*, Vol. 4, No. 9, January 1924.

48 *Communist Review*, February and March 1924.

49 *Speeches and Documents of the Sixth Congress of the CPGB*, 17–19 May 1924.

50 *Report of the Control Commission to the Sixth Congress of the CPGB*, 17–19 May 1924.

51 *Workers' Weekly*, 6 June 1924.

52 MacFarlane, *The British Communist Party*, pp. 87–89.

53 Simultaneously with the reorganisation of the CP, there was the establishment of systematic party training groups. Hitherto, the educational side of the movement had been carried out independently of the party by the Plebs League. The Plebs League had emerged from the strike of militant worker-students at Ruskin College, Oxford in 1909, whose members had formed their own Central Labour College, published their own educational journal *Plebs* and co-ordinated a network of local part-time labour colleges which expanded rapidly in the immediate post-war years of industrial and political turmoil. Historical materialism, economics and industrial unionism constituted the main elements of Plebs education. Its stated aim was 'To develop and increase the class consciousness of the workers, by propaganda and education, in order to aid them to destroy wage-slavery and to win power'. But the Marxism of the movement was highly abstract and formal in character, with contemporary political issues shirked, and with no treatment of the role of a revolutionary political party. A breach developed between the CP and the League from 1922 and Murphy wrote an article for *Plebs* criticising the content of Labour College education: 'What "certain fundamental elementary principles" do you propose to get across [he asked, referring to a recent statement of aims], merely the fact of the class struggle and never a single suggestion as to *how* the workers are to wage the struggle? No mention of what are the fundamental and elementary requirements of victory in the struggle? Shall we spend months unravelling the Theory of Value and never mention the elementary fact that the workers must have a revolutionary workers' party—lest we be accused of party politics?' ('Wanted: The Marxism of Marx!', *Plebs*, Vol. 15, No. 4, April 1923). But despite the rift between the two groups, it was only after the inadequacy of Communist education had been underlined at the Fifth Comintern Congress in 1924 that the CP made an effort to develop a systematic alternative to the labour colleges, with a central training school and notes and syllabuses, aimed at making education more directly political and under the leadership of the party itself. See A. Miles, 'Workers' Education: The Communist Party and the Plebs League in the 1920s', *History Workshop Journal*, No. 18, pp. 102–14; C. Tsuzuki, 'Anglo-Marxism and Working Class Education', *The Working Class in Modern British History*, ed. J. Winter, (Cambridge: Cambridge University Press, 1983), pp. 187–99; J. P. M Millar, *The Labour College Movement* (London: National Council of Labour Colleges), no date, but published in the early 1980s).

54 J. T. Murphy, *The Communist*, 9 September 1922.

55 E. H. Carr, *Socialism in One Country 1924–1926*, Vol. 3 (London: Macmillan), pp. 117–18.

56 *International Trade Union Unity* (London, 1925), p. 18.

57 M. Murphy, *Nurse Molly: An Autobiography*, p. 85.

58 See next chapter for details on the rise of Stalin.

59 See J. Hinton and R. Hyman, *Trade Unions and Revolution: The Industrial Politics of the Early British Communist Party* (London: Pluto Press, 1975), pp. 14–22; and W. Thompson, *The Good Old Cause: British Communism 1920–1991* (London: Pluto Press, 1992), pp. 39–40.

60 H. A. Clegg, *A History of British Trade Unions since 1889, Volume 2: 1911–1933* (Oxford: Clarendon Press, 1985), pp. 369–77.

61 At the Trade Union Congress of 1925 Alonzo Swales, the leaders of the engineers' union, stated in his presidential address: 'We are entering upon a new stage of development in the upward struggle of our class. The new phase of development which is world-wide has entered upon the next and probably the last stage of revolt. It is the duty of all members of the working class so to solidify their movements that, come when the time may be for the final last struggle, we shall be wanting neither machinery nor men to move forward to the destruction of wage slavery and the construction of a new order of society based upon co-ordinated effort and work with mutual goodwill and understanding.' Quoted in C. Harman, 'The General Strike', *International Socialism*, first series, No. 48, June/July 1971, pp. 23–28.

62 See M. Woodhouse and B. Pearce, *Essays on the History of Communism in Britain* (London: New Park, 1975), p. 88 and 92; and Hinton and Hyman, *Trade Unions and Revolution*, pp. 33–34.

63 J. T. Murphy, 'The Nine Months Truce', *Communist Review*, Vol. 6, No. 5, September 1925.

64 J. T. Murphy, 'Workshop Committee: The Real Path To Unity', *Sunday Worker*, 20 September 1925; *Workers' Weekly*, 18 September 1925.

65 J. T. Murphy, 'The Drive into the Factories', *Labour Monthly*, Vol. 7, No. 11, November 1925.

66 J. T. Murphy, *Workers' Weekly*, 16 October 1925.

67 *Communist Papers*, Documents Selected From Those Obtained on the Arrest of the Communist Leaders on 14 and 21 October 1925, Cmd. 2682 (London: HMSO, 1926).

68 Murphy, *New Horizons*, p. 212.

69 J. Klugmann, *History of the Communist Party of Great Britain: Vol. 2: The General Strike 1925–1926* (London: Lawrence and Wishart, 1969), pp. 78–79.

70 Letter from J. T. Murphy to Molly, Wandsworth Prison, 5 March 1926, Murphy papers, CPGB Archive, NMLH.

71 '25,000 Workers Greet Released Comrades', *Workers' Weekly*, 16 April 1926.

72 Quoted in C. Harman, 'The General Strike', *International Socialism*, first series, No. 48, June/July 1971, pp. 23–28.

73 J. Symons, *The General Strike* (London: Cresset Library, 1957), p. 46.

74 *British Gazette*, 5 May 1926.

75 *British Worker*, 5 May 1926.

76 A. Bullock, *The Life and Times of Ernest Bevin: Vol. 1: Trade Union Leader 1881–1940* (London: Heinemann, 1967), p. 333.

77 J. T. Murphy, 'Sheffield Council Asks for Help', *Workers' Weekly*, 21 May 1926; B. Moore, *The General Strike in Sheffield* (Sheffield: Sheffield City Libraries, 1981), p. 19.

78 J. T. Murphy, 'Fight for Life: Revolution Not in Sight', *Workers' Weekly*, 30 April 1926.

79 L. Trotsky, *Trotsky's Writings on Britain, Vol. 2* (London: New Park, 1974), pp. 138–39; p. 139.

80 Ibid., p. 119.

81 See Chapter Five for details of Murphy's critique of Trotsky.

82 J. T. Murphy, 'Fight for Life: Revolution not in Sight', *Workers' Weekly*, 30 April 1926.

83 'A Serious Situation', Special Strike Bulletin of the Sheffield District Committee of the Communist Party, No. 7, 12 May 1926, quoted in Moore, *The General Strike in Sheffield*, p. 22.

84 *Essays on a History of Communism in Britain* by Pearce and Woodhouse presents an orthodox Trotskyist analysis which makes the unjustified assumption that revolution was on the agenda and that the CP should be blamed for its failure to overthrow capitalism. In fact this interpretation reveals a disregard for the real balance of class forces and level of consciousness of workers. Despite the fact the General Strike of 1926 involved millions of workers in a real conflict with the government, there was no real turmoil in government ranks at the threat posed to the state, and the strike was characterised by its bureauratic control from above by the TUC and relatively passive nature.

85 Hinton and Hyman, *Trade Unions and Revolution*, pp. 35–37.

86 Letter from Executive Committee of the Communist International to CPGB Central Committee, 17 April 1926, RTsKhIDNI 494/100/304. However, only two months before the General Strike, a meeting of the Sixth Plenum of the ECCI had approved the policies adopted by the CPGB. In his opening speech Zinoviev said that the best results over the past year had been gained in Britain (and China). The policy of the CPGB showed how united front tactics should be used (J. Degras, ed., *The Communist International 1923–1928, Volume 2*, [London: Frank Cass, 1971], p. 262).

87 J. T. Murphy, *Preparing for Power* (London: Jonathan Cape, 1934, republished London: Pluto Press, 1972), p. 168.

88 T. Cliff and D. Gluckstein, *The Labour Party: A Marxist History* (London: Bookmarks, 1988), pp. 107–08.

89 *The Second Congress of the Communist International*, Vol. 2 (London: New Park Publications, 1977), p. 188.

90 Speech to Fourth Congress of the Communist International, 7 November–3 December 1922. *Abridged Report* (Communist Party of Great Britain, 1923), p. 61.

91 Quoted in H. Dewar, *Communist Politics in Britain: The CPGB from its Origins to the Second World War* (London: Pluto Press, 1976), p. 38.

92 CPGB central committee meeting, 6 April 1923, RTsKhIDNI, 495/100/103.

93 *Workers' Weekly*, 8 February 1924.

94 J. T. Murphy, 'The Labour Government: What We Must Do', *Workers' Weekly*, 15 February 1924.

95 'The British Labour Government and the CPGB', *Communist International*, No. 30, January 1924; *Workers' Weekly*, 22 February 1924.

96 J. T. Murphy, 'The Fourth Congress: A Special Report on the Recent World Congress of the Comintern', *Communist Review*, March 1923.

97 J. T. Murphy, 'The Party Conference', *Communist Review*, Vol. 4, No. 9, January 1924.

98 R. Palme Dutt, 'British Working Class after the Elections', *Communist International*, No. 8 (new series), 1924.

99 J. T. Murphy, 'How a Mass Communist Party Will Come to Britain', *Communist International*, No. 9 (new series), 1925.

100 J. T. Murphy, 'The Coming of the Mass Communist Party in Britain', *Communist International*, No. 13 (new series), 1925.

101 R. Palme Dutt, 'The British Working Class Movement, the Left Wing and the Communist Party', *Communist International*, No. 12 (new series), 1925.

102 British Commission, 2 July 1924, RTsKhIDNI 495/100/133.

103 *Abridged Report of the Fifth Congress of the Communist International*, 17 June–8 July 1924.

104 Letter from Executive Committee of the Communist International to CPGB, December 1924, RTsKhIDNI 495/100/135.

105 A statement on the left wing in the Labour Party presented by Murphy was adopted at the CPGB Political Bureau meeting, 6 March 1925, CPGB Archives, NMLH, CP/CENT/PC/01/14.

106 J. T. Murphy, 'How a Mass Communist Party Will Come to Britain', *Communist International*, No. 9 (new series), 1925.

107 Cliff and Gluckstein, *The Labour Party: A Marxist History*, pp. 115–16.

108 CPGB political bureau meetings, 2 January, 6 March 1925 and 31 March 1925, CPGB Archives, NMLH, CP/CENT/PC/01/07, CP/CENT/PC/01/14 and CP/CENT/PC/O1/09.

109 Quoted in R. Miliband, *Parliamentary Socialism* (London: Merlin Press, 1973), p. 153.

110 Cliff and Gluckstein, *Marxism and the Trade Union Struggle*, p. 144.

Notes to Chapter Five
(Pages 133–162)

1 The following account is based on the analysis provided in C. Harman, *How the Revolution was Lost, International Socialism*, first series, No. 30, 1967 and T. Cliff: *Lenin, Vol 3: Revolution Besieged* (London: Pluto Press, 1978); I. Deutscher, *Stalin: A Political Biography* (Harmondsworth: Penguin, 1974); T. Cliff, *Trotsky: Volume 3: Fighting the Rising Stalinist Bureaucracy* (London: Bookmarks, 1991).

2 V.I. Lenin, *Collected Works*, Vol. 32 (Moscow: Progress Publishers, 1974, p. 48.

3 I. Deutscher, *The Prophet Unarmed: Trotsky 1921–1929* (Oxford: Oxford University Press, 1970), p. 268; L. Trotsky, *The Stalin School of Falsification* (New York: Pathfinder Press, 1962), pp. 89–99.

4 See R. Pipes, *Concise History of the Russian Revolution* (London: Harvill, 1990); R. Blackburn, 'Fin de Siècle: Socialism after the Crash', *New Left Review*, No. 185, January/February 1991; P. Hirst, 'The State, Civil Society and the Collapse of Soviet Communism', *Economy and Society*, Vol. 20, No. 2, May 1991.

5 A. Callinicos, *The Revenge of History* (Oxford: Basil Blackwell, 1991).

6 J. T. Murphy, *New Horizons* (london: John Lane/The Bodley Head, 1941), pp. 150–51.

7 L. Trotsky, *The Third International after Lenin* (London: New Park, 1974), p. 61.

8 J. Degras, ed., *The Communist International 1923–1928:* Vol. 2 (London: Frank Cass, 1971), p. 190.

9 K. McDermott and J. Agnew, *The Comintern: A History of International Communism from Lenin to Stalin* (Basingstoke: Macmillan, 1996), p. 45.

10 See E. H. Carr, *Socialism in One Country: 1924–1926* (London: Macmillan, 1959), Vol. 3, p. 124.

11 L. Trotsky, *The Lessons of October* (London: Bookmarks, 1987, first published in Russian in 1924 and translated into English in 1925).

12 See L. Trotsky, *The History of the Russian Revolution* (London: Pluto Press, 1977), pp. 975–1016 and T. Cliff, *Lenin: Vol. 2: All Power to the Soviets* (London: Pluto Press, 1976), pp. 335–78.

13 Trotsky, *The Lessons of October*, pp. 71–72.

14 'The Truth about Trotsky', *Workers' Weekly*, 5 December 1924.

15 S. Bornstein and A. Richardson, *Against the Stream:History of the Trotskyist Movement in Britain 1924–1938* (London: Socialist Platform), pp. 2–5; H. Wicks, *Keeping my Head: The Memoirs of a British Bolshevik* (London: Socialist Platform, 1992), pp. 43–44.

16 'A Splendid Rally of London Members: Keen Discussion on Trotsky', *Workers' Weekly*, 23 January 1925.

17 J. T. Murphy, 'Introduction', *The Errors of Trotskyism: A Symposium* (London: CPGB, 1925), p. 28.

18 Bornstein and Richardson, *Against the Stream*, p. 12.

19 Although it is difficult to believe, new information emerging from the Comintern archives appear to show that Lenin secretly provided at least £55,000, the equivalent of about £1 million today, to help get the CPGB off the ground. A meeting of the ECCI Budget Commission on 3 January 1922 noted that an annual subsidy of £24,000 had been supplied to the CPGB, presumably for 1921. According to party files seized during a police raid, the Comintern allocated £5,000 in 1924 and a year later the figure had risen to £16,000. (See McDermott and Agnew, *The Comintern*, pp. 21–22 and 56.) The budget for 1927 was £21,000 (letter from Albert Inkpin, the secretary of CPGB, to Bennett, Comintern representative in Moscow, 24 February 1927, RTsKhIDNI 495/100/425).

20 Murphy, *New Horizons*, p. 114.

21 See Murphy's letters to Kuusinen at the ECCI on the 9 January and 13 August 1923, RTsKhIDNI 495/100/113 and 495/100/114.

22 L. Trotsky, *Where is Britain Going?* (London: New Park, 1970), pp. 129–30.

23 Trotsky had supported the formation of the Anglo-Russian Committee as a temporary mechanism through which to expose the left bureaucrats' failure to honour their radical policies. It was for this reason that he criticised the Russian leaders for deciding to keep the Committee going even after the betrayal of the General Strike. Later it became clear to Trotsky that the Russian leaders had never intended to use the Committee as a genuine united front to enhance the struggle in Britain: 'The point of departure of the Anglo-Russian Committee, as we have already seen, was the impatient urge to leap over the young and too slowly developing communist party. This invested the entire experience with a false character even prior to the General Strike' (see Trotsky, *The Third International After Lenin*, p. 97).

24 Trotsky, *Where is Britain Going?*

25 ECCI theses 'The Lessons of the General Strike', 8 June 1926, *Communist Review*, July 1926.

26 'Russian Union's Telegram', *Workers' Weekly*, 9 July 1926.

27 National Secretariat for Great Britain, 29 July 1926, RtsKhIDNI 495/72/14.

28 ECCI Presidium, 7 August 1926, RTsKhIDNI 495/2/60a.

29 Stalin's speech was delivered on the 7 August 1926. J. Stalin, *Collected Works: Vol. 8, 1926* (Moscow: Progress, 1954), pp. 205–14; RTsKhIDNI 495/2/60b.

30 Murphy, *New Horizons*, p. 229.

31 *Workers' Weekly*, 13 August 1926.

32 'Thesis on the General Strike', CPGB Eighth Congress, 16–17 October 1926.

33 Ibid.

34 J. T. Murphy, *The Political Meaning of the General Strike* (London: CPGB, 1926).

35 The only real exception to this lack of self-criticism was Palme Dutt's reassessment of the General Strike which emphasised the unconditional nature of the surrender and failure of the left-wing leaders of the TUC, not as an isolated act of cowardice but as the culmination of nine months of acquiescence in the right wing's sabotage, since Red Friday, of preparations for the struggle. However, Palme Dutt made no explicit attempt to critically re-evaluate the Communist Party's role in the strike and its attitude towards the 'left' on the TUC ('Britain's First General Strike', *Communist International*, No. 21, 1926, no date, but probably June).

36 L. J. MacFarlane, *The British Communist Party: Its Origin and Development until 1929* (London: Macgibbon and Kee, 1966), p. 169–73.

37 *Workers' Weekly*, 17 September 1926.

38 *Report of the Eighth Congress of the CPGB* (London: CPGB), 1926.

39 J. T. Murphy and R. P. Arnot, 'The British Trade Union Congress at Bournemouth', *Communist International*, Vol. 3, No. 1, 15 October 1926.

40 J. T. Murphy, 'The English Strike and the Trade Unions: Summary of the Bournemouth Conference', *Bol'shevik*, No. 18, 30 September 1926. As E.H. Carr notes, it was a signal mark of favour for a foreign communist to be invited to write in *Bol'shevik*, the political-economic fortnightly of the central committee of the Russian Communist Party (*Foundations of a Planned Economy 1926–29*, Vol 2 [London, Macmillan, 1971], p. 335).

41 CPGB central committee meeting, 14 October 1926, RTsKhIDNI 495/100/ 347.

42 'Our Party and the TUC', *Communist International*, Vol. 3, No. 2, 30 October 1926. Significantly,the CPGB central committee article was published in the English, but not in the Russian, edition of *Communist International*.

43 Bukharin's speech was delivered on 23 October 1926. See *International Press Correspondence*, Vol. 6, No. 85, 3 December 1926.

44 'The Lessons of the General Strike', *International Press Correspondence*, Vol. 6, No. 91, 30 December 1926; RTsKhIDNI 495/100/337; 495/165/116; 495/ 165/123.

45 *International Press Correspondence* Vol. 7, No. 11, 3 February 1927.

46 Ibid.

47 CPGB central committee meeting, 14 October 1926, RTsKhIDNI 495/100/ 347.

48 Letter from Bob Stewart to Murphy, 1 October 1926, RTsKhIDNI 495/ 100/357.

49 Letter from Murphy to CPGB political bureau and executive committee, 12 November 1926, RTsKhIDNI 495/100/339.

50 Back in Britain two years later, Murphy wrote a letter to Bukharin in which he complained that the ECCI Presidium's resolution endorsing his critique of the CPGB leadership in *Communist International* had never been published. As a result, as far as the mass of British party members were concerned, the party's official reply to Murphy, which had been widely publicised in *Workers' Life*, *The Communist* and *Communist International*, had remained unanswered. As Murphy explained: 'Consequently so far as our party membership is concerned and especially its executive committee, it appears that Arnot and Murphy and the

ECCI were thoroughly trounced and our party EC came out of it triumphant. Whatever the real situation may have been this is undoubtedly the real situation here', RTsKhIDNI 495/100/520.

51 M. Murphy, *Nurse Molly: An Autobiography* (unpublished manuscript, no date, but written in the early 1960s), p. 96.

52 Murphy, *New Horizons*, p. 242.

53 Chapter Six examines the nature of Murphy's relationship with the CPGB whilst he was in Moscow.

54 Murphy, *New Horizons*, p. 248.

55 V. Kahan, 'The Communist International: 1919–1943: The Personnel of Its Highest Bodies', *International Review of Social History*, Vol. 21, 1976, pp. 151–85; G. Nollau, *International Communism and World Revolution: History and Methods* (Connecticut: Greenwood Press, 1961), pp. 157–58.

56 J. T. Murphy, 'The First Year of the Lenin School', *Communist International*, 30 September 1927, Vol. 4, No. 14.

57 Murphy, *New Horizons*, pp. 244–45; M. Murphy, *Nurse Molly: An Autobiography*, pp. 100–01.

58 Murphy's knowledge of Russian appears to have been fairly rudimentary, although it was proficient enough for him to deliver a 20 minute prepared speech in Russian to 5,000 people at the Bolshoi Theatre in Moscow on the occasion of Molly's birthday on International Women's Day, 8 March 1928 (Murphy, *New Horizons*, pp. 245–46).

59 Murphy, *New Horizons*, p. 150.

60 McDermott and Agnew, *The Comintern*, p. 44; A. Kuusinen, *Before and After Stalin* (London: Michael Joseph, 1974), p. 60.

61 The Communist International had a number of different bodies, including the ECCI, the Presidium, the Political Secretariat, and various national secretariats. The world congress of the Comintern elected the Executive Committee, the ECCI, as its governing body. The ECCI could be compared with the central committee of a national communist party. It consisted of people elected by the congresses from the delegates of all the member parties, almost all of whom lived in Moscow. The ECCI was given extensive powers to issue instructions which were binding on all affiliated parties. The Presidium, elected by the ECCI, worked as a standing organ with full powers to act in the name of the ECCI in the intervals between sessions, and corresponded to the political bureau of a national communist party. Meanwhile, the day-to-day activities of the Presidium were handled by an even smaller group known as the Political Secretariat. The frequency of meetings of the Comintern organs roughly indicate the degree of their activity. Thus, after 1922 the world congresses of the Comintern ceased to meet once a year, as laid down in the statutes, but were summoned less seldom; the 4th Congress met in 1922, the 5th in 1925, the 6th in 1928, and the 7th and last in 1935. Between the fifth and sixth congresses, the ECCI met 16 times, the Presidium 118 times (E. H. Carr, *Socialism in One Country 1924–1926*, Vol. 3, Part 2 [London: Macmillan], p. 902).

62 Some commentators (McDermott and Agnew, *The Comintern*; A. Thorpe, 'Moscow's "Control" of the Communist Party 1920–1939' [Paper presented to the Communist Party of Great Britain 1919–1991 Conference, Oxford University

Department of Continuing Education, April 1997]) have emphasised the degree of local party autonomy that was possible within the framework of a centralised world movement. However, this autonomy was strictly circumscribed and limited mainly to day-to-day operational issues. All the major strategic issues were laid down by the Comintern in Moscow and adhered to by the various national sections.

63 Commission on Internal Relations, 17 November 1926, RTsKhIDNI 495/100/337.

64 Political Secretariat meeting, 18 February 1927, RTsKhIDNI 495/3/9.

65 ECCI Plenum, 16 December 1926, RTsKhIDNI 495/165/359; 'Report and Resolution on the Souvarine Case', *International Press Correspondence*, Vol. 7, No. 9, 27 January 1927. Boris Souvarine had already been expelled from the Comintern by the Fifth Congress for Oppositional factional activities in the French Communist Party, although he was informed 'the door remained open for him to return to the Comintern provided he act as a Communist should act'. But since that date, he had become involved with the French Opposition journal titled *Revolution Proletariene* which, it was alleged, conducted 'a definite anti-communist and definite anti-party activity'. The confirmation of his expulsion from the Comintern was supported by the French delegation to the Congress.

66 'Call to the Fighting Chinese Masses', *International Press Correspondence*, Vol. 6, No. 83, 1 December 1926.

67 *Byulleten Oppozitsii*, No. 1–2, July 1929.

68 The ECCI issued a statement, signed by Murphy, Humbert-Droz, Smeral and Kuusinen, arguing that 'Chiang Kai-shek has gone over to the side of the imperialists' (*Pravda*, 15 April 1927, republished in *International Press Correspondence*, No. 41. 16 April, 1927).

69 Murphy's speech to Swedish Communist Party Congress, 4 June 1927, RtsKhIDNI 495/100/133.

70 I. Deutscher, *The Prophet Unarmed: Trotsky 1921–1929* (Oxford: Oxford University Press, 19700), p. 358. Vuyovitch was a Yugoslav delegate and former leading figure in the Communist Youth International, who had supported Trotsky's fierce indictments of Stalin's policy in China at the Eighth ECCI Plenum in May 1927. The specific charges against Trotsky and Vuyovitch were that they had attempted to split the Comintern and Russian Communist Party, slander the Soviet party leadership, and had supported underground oppositional activity in association with 'alien elements'. M. Reiman, *The Birth of Stalinism: The USSR on the Eve of the 'Second Revolution'* (London: I. B. Tauris), p. 31.

71 Murphy, *New Horizons*, pp. 275–77.

72 Ibid., p. 275.

73 Ibid., pp. 274–75.

74 J. T. Murphy, 'The Last Great Split in World Communism' , *Picture Post*, 17 July 1948.

75 Ibid.

76 *International Press Correspondence*, Vol. 7, No. 57, 13 October 1927; also see Bornstein and Richardson, *Against the Stream: A History of the Trotskyist Movement in Britain 1924–38* (London: Socialist Platform, 1986), p. 21.

77 'International Executive: J. T. Murphy's Report of the Year's Work', *Workers' Life*, 14 October 1927.

78 'The Opposition Condemned: Congress Unanimous in Support of the ECCI', *Workers' Life*, No. 38, 14 October 1927.

79 Speech to ECCI Presidium, 22 November 1927, RTsKhIDNI 495/2/90.

80 Murphy, *New Horizons*, p. 255.

81 Ibid., p. 273.

82 Ibid., pp. 255–84.

83 Ibid., pp. 252–53.

84 'Greetings From the Communist International', Murphy's Speech to CPGB Ninth Congress, *Reports, Theses and Resolutions*, October 1927.

Notes to Chapter Six
(Pages 163–200)

1 See M. Reiman, *The Birth of Stalinism: The USSR on the Eve of the 'Second Revolution'* (London: I. B. Tauris, 1987); I. Deutscher, *Stalin: A Political Biography* (Harmondsworth: Penguin, 1974); C. Harman, 'Russia: How the Revolution was Lost', *International Socialism*, first series, No. 30, 1967.

2 S. F. Cohen, *Bukharin and the Bolshevik Revolution: A Political Biography 1888–1938* (Oxford: Oxford University Press, 1980), pp. 160–212.

3 In 1929 Trotsky was deported to the Prinkipo Islands in Turkey where he wrote his *History of the Russian Revolution* and a series of articles urging a workers' united front against fascism in Germany, whilst also organising the International Left Opposition. In 1933, after the victory of Hitler, he began the movement to create a Fourth International which, while basing itself on the Bolshevik tradition and on the first four congresses of the Comintern (1919–1922), sought to build revolutionary parties in place of the bankrupt Stalinist organisations. In 1935 he wrote *The Revolution Betrayed*, his major indictment of Stalinism. In a series of occasional pieces Trotsky also developed revolutionary strategy and tactics towards the major crises of the day, including the Spanish Civil War, the Popular Front in France, and the Second World War. He became the principal defendant *in absentia* at the Moscow Trials where he was accused of being a Hitler agent and anti-USSR terrorist, and was simultaneously subjected to a campaign of vilification throughout the world. In 1937 he was admitted to Mexico where he lived until August 1940 when he was assassinated by a Stalinist agent. Trotsky's key contribution is best understood as an attempt to maintain the classical Marxist tradition with its orientation on working-class self-emancipation from below, in conditions defined by, on the one hand, the success of the advanced capitalist countries in weathering revolutionary pressures, and on the other, the betrayal of hopes raised by the Russian revolution by the rise of Stalinism in the USSR.

4 For further elaboration of such views see T. Cliff, *State Capitalism in Russia*, distributed in duplicated form in June 1948 under the title 'The Nature of Stalinist Russia' (London: Bookmarks, 1988) and P. Binns, T. Cliff and C. Harman, *Russia: From Workers' State to State Capitalism* (London: Bookmarks, 1987). Until his death Trotsky insisted that the USSR was a 'degenerated workers' state', in which the bureaucracy had succeeded in politically expropriating the proletariat but leaving the social and economic foundations of workers' power untouched. The contradictions of that analysis, according to which the workers were still the ruling class of a state which denied them all political power, did not prevent Trotsky's more dogmatic followers extending it to China and eastern Europe, even though

the result was to break any connection between socialism and the self-emancipation of the working class: socialism, it seemed, could be imposed by the Red Army or peasant guerillas. However, the Palestinian Trotskyist Tony Cliff refused to accept this line of reasoning and argued that the USSR and its replicants in China and eastern Europe were bureaucractic state-capitalist societies, in which the bureaucracy collectively fulfilled the role performed under private capitalism by the bourgeoisie of extracting surplus value and directing the accummulation of capital (see A. Callinicos, *Trotskyism* (Minneapolis: University of Minnesota Press, 1990).

5 D. Hallas, *The Comintern* (London: Bookmarks, 1985), pp. 124–25.

6 K. McDermott and J. Agnew, *The Comintern: A History of International Communism from Lenin to Stalin* (Basingstoke: Macmillan, 1966), pp. 98–118.

7 Hallas, *The Comintern*, p. 128.

8 Ibid., p. 126.

9 Letter from Murphy to CPGB political bureau, 29 January 1927, RTsKhIDNI 495/100/412.

10 N. Branson, *History of the Communist Party of Great Britain 19271941* (London: Lawrence and Wishart, 1985), pp. 4–15.

11 L. J. MacFarlane, *The British Communist Party: Its Origin and Development until 1929* (London: Macgibbon and Kee, 1966), p. 302.

12 Ibid., pp. 177–78.

13 Letter from Murphy to Albert Inkpin, 8 April 1927, RTsKhIDNI 495/100/412.

14 J. T. Murphy, 'Anti-Communist Propaganda and the Task of the English Proletariat', *Pravda*, 23 April 1927.

15 *Resolution of the Eighth Plenum of the ECCI.*

16 From its birth in 1893 the Independent Labour Party (ILP), led by Keir Hardie, had attracted people committed to socialist politics as opposed to social democracy, and effectively formed the left wing of the Labour Party during the first 20 years of the century. But the ILP was essentially orientated on parliament as opposed to industrial struggle. As a result of such electoral considerations most of its leaders were generally even more conservative than the union bureaucracy during the Labour Unrest of 1910–1912, and they stood entirely on the sidelines during the militant extra-parliamentary industrial and political struggles of 1919. Nonetheless, by the mid-1920s the organisation had 30,000 members and in the 1924 general election there were 114 ILP members among the 150 Labour MPs (see D. Howell, *British Workers and the Independent Labour Party* [Manchester: Manchester University Press, 1983].

17 *Political Report of the Central Committee to the Tenth Congress of the CPGB*, January 1929.

18 Murphy's Report on the Ninth CPGB Congress to the ECCI Presidium, 28 November 1927, RTsKhIDNI 495/100/411.

19 CPGB Archives, NMLH, CP/IND/KLUG/06/06.

20 CPGB central committee meeting, 17–18 March 1928, CPGB Archives, NMLH, CP/IND/KLUG/06/06.

21 Ibid.

22 Quoted in E. H. Carr, *Foundations of A Planned Economy 1926–1929, Vol. 2* (London: Macmillan, 1971), pp. 359–60.

23 MacFarlane, *The British Communist Party*, pp. 196–99.

24 *Report of the Proceedings of the British Commission at the Ninth Plenum of the Comintern*, open letter to members of the CPGB (London: CPGB, September 1928), pp. 132–52.

25 Ibid., pp. 153–65.

26 Letter from Murphy to ECCI Presidium, 14 January 1928, RTsKhIDNI 495/3/55.

27 Murphy Memorandum on Ninth ECCI Plenum, March 1928, RTsKhIDNI 495/100/494; *Report of the Proceedings of the British Commission at the Ninth Plenum of the Comintern*, pp. 166–74; 'Ourselves and the Labour Party', *The Communist*, March 1928.

28 Murphy's proposal for a new federated party received the support of only one member of the central committee, A. Horner, with sixteen votes against, at a meeting held in July 1928 (CPGB central committee meeting, 30 June–2 July 1928, CPGB Archives, NMLH, CP/IND/KLUG/06/06) and every member of the British delegation to the Sixth Comintern Congress, except B. Brain, also rejected Murphy's proposals at three special meetings held to discuss them (CPGB political bureau meeting, 17–19 September 1928, CPGB Archive CP/IND/KLUG/06/06).

29 *Report of the Proceedings of the British Commission at the Ninth Plenum of the Comintern*, pp. 195–203.

30 History since the First World War was divided into three periods: 1917–1924, the 'first' period of revolutionary upheaval; 1925–1928, the 'second' period of relative capitalist stabilisation; 1928 onwards, the 'third' period of the final crisis of capitalism and renewed revolutionary upsurge. On the basis of this periodisation the communist parties were instructed to abandon united front work, to engage in directly revolutionary propaganda and agitation, to undertake 'independent' leadership of workers' struggles and to concentrate their fire on social democracy (dubbed 'social fascism') as the main enemy. As one commentator has argued: 'Thus, three periods can be clearly distinguished. During the first period the Comintern is mainly an instrument to bring about revolution. During the second period it is mainly an instrument in the Russian factional struggles. During the third period it is mainly an instrument of Russian foreign policy' (F. Borkenau, *The Communist International* [New York: Ann Arbor, 1962], p. 419).

31 Extracts from the 'Thesis of the Sixth Comintern Congress on the International Situation and Tasks of the CI', *The Communist International 1919–1943 Documents*, Vol. 2, pp. 455–64.

32 J. T. Murphy, 'Is There a "Right" Danger in our Party?', *The Communist*, Vol. 3, No. 10, November 1928.

33 'Discussion on the Revolutionary Movement in the Colonies', *International Press Correspondence*, Vol. 8, No. 76, 30 October 1928. Significantly, Murphy had also sat on the Colonial Commission at the Second Comintern Congress in 1920.

34 Quoted in H. Pelling, *The British Communist Party: A Historical Profile* (London: Adam and Charles Black, 1958), p. 49; *Sixth World Congress of the C.I. International Press Correspondence Report*, p. 17–44.

35 CPGB political bureau meeting, 17–19 September 1928, CPGB Archives, NMLH, CP/IND/KLUG/06/06.

36 Letter from Murphy to CPGB political bureau and central committee, 19 September 1928, RTsKhIDNI 495/100/513.

37 Ibid.

38 Letter from Pollitt to CPGB central committee, 25 September 1928, RTsKhIDNI 495/100/513.

39 Letter from Murphy to CPGB political bureau and central committee, 27 September 1928, RTsKhIDNI 495/100/513.

40 MacFarlane, *British Communist Party*, p. 302.

41 CPGB political bureau meeting, 1720 September 1928, CPGB Archives, NMLH, CP/IND/Klug/06/06; J. T. Murphy, 'Strong Attack on Maxton', *Sunday Worker*, 6 January 1929.

42 J. T. Murphy, 'Is there a "Right" Danger in our Party?'. *The Communist*, Vol. 3, No. 10, November 1928.

43 Ibid.

44 Ibid.

45 J. T. Murphy, 'There *Is* a Right Danger', *Communist Review*, vol, 1, No. 1 (second series), January 1929.

46 MacFarlane, *British Communist Party*, pp. 216–17.

47 'Central Committee Party Policy Discussion', *Workers' Life*, 30 November 1928.

48 J. T. Murphy, 'There *Is* a Right Danger', *Communist Review*, Vol. 1, No. 1 (second series), January 1929.

49 In the process, the critics somewhat overstepped the mark and carried the party's policy at the Tenth Congress even further to the left than the Comintern wanted. Indeed in autumn of 1929 the move to the left got out of hand and began to assume the form of a general attack upon the whole leadership. Many of the leaders contributed to the confusion by attacking each other for right-wing deviations, so that even stalwart supporters of the new line, like Murphy, who according to Page Arnot was the epitome of 'ultra-leftism', was accused by the secretariat of 'right-wing deviation' for suggesting that the CP advance concrete demands at a forthcoming Labour Party conference. A Meerut Prisoners' Defence Committee had been set up earlier in the year to campaign for the release of 33 prisoners (including several agents of the CPGB) on trial in Meerut, India, for conspiracy. The trial had dragged on for four years and become a central feature of communist agitation. Murphy proposed that members of the defence committee attending the Labour Party conference should submit an emergency resolution condemning the Labour government and demanding the release of the prisoners, and that a protest demonstration be held if the resolution were not accepted (J. T. Murphy, 'The Fight against the Right Danger', *Communist Review*, vol, 1, No. 11, second series, November 1929). The CP secretariat primly informed Murphy that it was not part of the new line to deceive the workers by asking them to demand anything from the Labour government. 'The old line was to make the Labour Party and the trade unions fight for the "partial demands" of the working class. Our new line is that the Labour Party is a completely social-fascist party, that the reformist unions are strike-breaking instruments and that the party must independently organise and lead the struggle on concrete issues' ('Secretariat's Reply', *Workers' Life*, 29 November 1929). Murphy angrily condemned the secretariat's

statement as 'ultra-leftism' and incompatible with the adopted programme of the Communist International (J. T. Murphy, 'The Fight against the Right Danger', *Communist Review*, vol, 1, No. 11, second series, November 1929). See MacFarlane, *British Communist Party*, pp. 237–38.

50 *'Closed Letter' of the Presidium of the ECCI to the Central Committee of the CPGB*, 27 February 1929.

51 *Class against Class*, Communist Party Election Programme (CPGB, 1929). Murphy also wrote another pamphlet produced by the party for the 1929 general election entitled *Revolutionary Workers' Government* (CPGB, 1929) which reiterated many of the same arguments.

52 Murphy's vote of 331 compared with the Labour's Party's 15,590. Out of the 25 CP parliamentary candidates, only two received worse votes than Murphy ('The Communist Figures', *Workers' Life*, 7 June 1929).

53 J. T. Murphy, 'After the General Election', *Communist International*, Vol. 6, No. 18, August 1929.

54 *Protocol: Tenth Plenum of ECCI*, 1929; *International Press Correspondence*, Vol. 9, No. 51, 17 September 1929.

55 *Theses on the International Situation and the Immediate Tasks of the C.I. Adopted by Tenth Plenum*, CPGB, 1929.

56 'The Tasks of the CPGB: The Tenth Plenum and the International Situation', *Communist Review*, Vol. 1, No. 9 (second series), September 1929.

57 J. T. Murphy, 'Choosing our Leadership: Revolutionary Theory and Clear Political Line', *Workers' Life*, 11 October 1929.

58 'Report of the Communist Party Congress', *Workers' Life*, 25 November 1929; MacFarlane, *British Communist Party*, pp. 231–40.

59 J. T. Murphy, 'Growth of Social Fascism in Britain', *Communist Review*, Vol. 2, No. 1 (second series), January 1930.

60 'Report on Party Organisation' and letter from CPGB organising department to Anglo-American Secretariat, 17 June 1930, RTsKhIDNI 495/38/24.

61 Murphy also argued that the lack of understanding of the new methods of work and the desire to eradicate the 'right danger' had led some comrades into a left sectarianism which isolated the party even more from the workers. He provided a lunatic example of this: 'In the preparations for March 6, the Manchester Working Bureau put forward, among other proposals, that a number of leading comrades should on March 6 lead a march of workers on to Burnley Barracks and call on the soldiers in uniform to demonstrate with the workers in the streets. Now, no member of our party will question the desirability of propaganda amongst the troops. But when it is realised that in Burnley we had not a single party cell in the mills, that the whole party membership in Burnley did not muster a dozen members, that there had not been the slightest preparation for mass action of the workers, no preliminary work amongst the soldiers, indeed, that *there are no Burnley barracks and no soldiers* in Burnley, then the absolutely unreal and romantic line of approach by the Bureau can be seen at a glance ('The Right Danger in New Clothes', *Communist Review*, Vol. 2, No. 6, second series, June 1930).

62 *Communist Review*, August 1932.

63 Branson, *History of the Communist Party of Great Britain 1927–1941*, p. 39.

64 *The New Line Documents of the Tenth Congress of the CPGB*, January 1929, p. 92.

65 S. Lerner, *Breakaway Unions and the Small Trade Union* (London: Allen and Unwin, 1961).

66 J. Higgins, 'Dual Unionism in Britain', *International Socialism*, No. 47. 1971.

67 *Sunday Worker*, 19 May 1929.

68 MacFarlane, *British Communist Party*, pp. 255–60.

69 J. T. Murphy, 'The Outlook', *Communist Review*, Vol. 1, No. 7, July 1929.

70 *Agenda and Report of the Sixth Annual Conference of the National Minority Movement*, 24–25 August 1929.

71 J. T. Murphy, 'The Outlook', *Communist Review*, Vol. 1, No. 7, July 1929.

72 *Workers' Life*, 30 August, 27 September and 4 October 1929.

73 CPGB political bureau meeting, 12 June 1930, CPGB Archives, NMLH, Microfiche Reel 11.

74 Branson, *History of the Communist Party of Great Britain 1927–1941*, p. 55.

75 J. T. Murphy, 'New Unions and their Place in the Revolutionary Struggle', *Communist Review*, Vol. 2, No. 8, August 1930.

76 'Open Letter' quoted in 'The Road to Victory', *Report of CPGB 12th Congress*, November 1932, pp. 9–10.

77 M. Squires, *Saklatvala: A Political Biography* (London: Lawrence and Wishart, 1990), pp. 208–23.

Notes to Chapter Seven
(Pages 201–233)

1 Letter from Murphy to CPGB political bureau and central committee, 19 September 1928, RTsKhIDNI 495/100/513.

2 CPGB political bureau meeting, 20 March 1930, CPGB Archives, NMLH, Microfiche Reel 11.

3 CPGB political bureau meeting, 26 February 1930, CPGB Archives, NMLH, Microfiche Reel 11.

4 'Communist Candidate for Brightside', *Daily Worker*, 30 January 1930.

5 J. T. Murphy, *The Labour Government: An Examination of its Record* (London: CPGB, 1930).

6 Letter from Murphy to CPGB political bureau, December 1930, CPGB Archives, NMLH, Microfiches Reel 11.

7 J. T. Murphy, 'Significance of Llandudno Conference', *Communist Review*, Vol. 2, No. 11, November 1930.

8 'Murphy Winning Mass Support in Brightside', *Daily Worker*, 15 October 1931; 'Votes For Communist Candidates', *Daily Worker*, 29 October 1931.

9 R. P. Dutt, 'The New Phase in Britain and the Communist Party', RTsKhIDNI 495/100/521; 'The Defeat of the Labour Party', *International Press Correspondence*, 3 November 1931.

10 CPGB central committee meeting, 17 January 1932, RTsKhIDNI 495/100/822.

11 J. T. Murphy, 'The Election and our Party', unpublished article submitted to *Daily Worker*, 13 November 1931, RTsKhIDNI 495/100/758.

12 J. T. Murphy, *The Handrags of 'Law and Order': An Exposure* (Sheffield CP, 1932).

13 CPGB central committee meeting, 15 March 1931, RTsKhIDNI 495/100/741; CPGB central committee meeting, 16 January 1932, CPGB Archive, NMLH, Microfiches Reel 3.

14 CPGB central committee meeting, 17 January 1932, RTsKhIDNI 495/100/824.

15 Letter from Murphy to Harry Pollitt, 10 March 1932, RTsKhIDNI 495/100/840.

16 Ibid.

17 'Credits for Russia', *Labour Monthly*, January 1922.

18 'Credits for Russia Means Less Unemployment', *Sunday Worker*, 25 October 1925.

302   The Political Trajectory of J. T. Murphy

19 *The World Situation and Economic Struggle: Theses of the Tenth Plenum* (London: CPGB, no date, but probably late 1929), p. 11.

20 'World Unemployment and the Soviet Five Year Plan', 21 August 1930, *Writings of Leon Trotsky 1930* (New York: Pathfinder, 1975), pp. 353–62.

21 Letter from Harry Pollitt to Murphy, 24 March 1932, RTsKhIDNI 495/100/840.

22 Letter from Murphy to Harry Pollitt, 27 March 1932, RTsKhIDNI 495/100/840.

23 'Editorial', *Communist Review*, Vol. 4, No. 4, April 1932.

24 Letter to Murphy from CPGB secretariat, 13 April 1932, RTsKhIDNI 495/100/840.

25 Letter from Murphy to CPGB secretariat, 21 April 1932, RTsKhIDNI 495/100/840.

26 Ibid.

27 Letter from CPGB secretariat to Murphy, 30 April 1932, RTsKhIDNI 495/100/840; CPGB political bureau meeting, 7–8 May 1932, RTsKhIDNI 495/100/826.

28 Letter from Murphy to CPGB political bureau, 8 May 1932, RTsKhIDNI 495/100/840.

29 Letter from CPGB secretariat to Murphy, 8 May 1932, RTsKhIDNI 495/100/840.

30 Letter from Murphy to CPGB political bureau, 8 May 1932 RTsKhIDNI 495/100/840.

31 'J. T. Murphy Expelled from the Communist Party', *Daily Worker*, 10 May 1932.

32 'Political Bureau Answers False Article in "Communist Review"', *Daily Worker*, 10 May 1932. Reprinted in *Communist Review*, Vol. 4, No. 6, June 1932 and *International Press Correspondence*, Vol. 12, No. 22, 1932.

33 Ibid.

34 Ibid.

35 'The Expulsion of Murphy and the Fight against Opportunism', CPGB Political Bureau Report sent to ECCI Anglo-American Secretariat, June 1932, RTsKhIDNI 495/100/839.

36 Ibid.

37 CPGB political bureau meeting, 8 May 1932, RTsKhIDNI 495/100/826.

38 'Statement of the Political Bureau on J. T. Murphy', *Communist Review*, Vol. 4, No. 6, June 1932.

39 Shortly after Murphy's expulsion, in August 1932, a small handful of British Communist Party members sympathetic to Trotsky ideas, known as the 'Balham Group' because of their south-west London location, were also expelled. They subsequently went on organise themselves as the British section of the new Fourth International (See R. Groves, *The Balham Group: How British Trotskyism Began* [London: Pluto Press, 1974]).

40 'The Expulsion of J. T. Murphy', statement by Comrade Hal Wilde to the CPGB secretariat, 14 June 1932, RTsKhIDNI 495/100/839.

41 'Communist Party Organisations Endorse Expulsion of Murphy', *Daily Worker*, 16 May 1932.

42 CPGB central committee meeting, 4 June 1932, RTsKhIDNI 495/100/822.

43 J. Jacobs, *Out of the Ghetto* (London: Calverts North Star Press, 1978), p. 87.

44 'Manchester Guardian's United Front With Murphy', *Daily Worker*, 12 May 1932.

45 J. T. Murphy, 'Why I Left the Communist Party', *The New Leader*, 20 May 1932.

46 M. Murphy, *Nurse Molly: An Autobiography* (unpublished manuscript, no date, but written in the early 1960s), Murphy papers, NMLH, pp. 108–09.

47 Letter from Harry Pollitt to ECCI Anglo-American Secretariat, 11 May 1932, RtsKhIDNI 495/100/833. Bedales School was a progressive private boarding school influenced by Fabian and left-wing traditions which attracted the children of prominent people like Bertrand Russell. This must have helped Murphy square his conscience about sending Gordon to a private school, despite the fact it was regarded as a completely scandalous thing for a communist to do. He was able to afford to send Gordon there primarily because he obtained scholarships and managed to get some of the fees waived, although he also had to make payments from the money he received for writing articles for *Pravda*. (After his expulsion from the CP, his income from the Socialist League and Molly's as a private nurse also helped to pay the fees.) However, it should be noted that in accepting an income from *Pravda* during this period he had also foregone his salary from the party as a full-time functionary. After his expulsion numerous innuendoes were made about Murphy's financial wherewithal, for example, that he was paid above the average skilled worker's rate; that he failed to place speakers' fees into the party's central pool; and that he lived in middle class surroundings with fitted carpets in his flat. (Such insinuations made by some CP members were reported to me in interviews with Bill Moore, 16 February 1994; Alison Macleod, 5 August 1994; Monty Johnstone, 18 August 1994; and Walter Kendall, 7 July 1995.) These claims seem unlikely, but proved useful in denigrating Murphy's contribution to the party.

48 Such claims made by some CP members were reported to me in interviews with Alison Macleod, 5 August 1994 and Monty Johnstone, 18 August 1994. Also see F. Beckett, *The Enemy Within: The Rise and Fall of the British Communist Party* (London: John Murray, 1995), pp. 63–64.

49 Interview with Monty Johnstone, 18 August, 1994.

50 J. T. Murphy, *New Horizons* (London: John Lane/ The Bodley Head, 1941), pp. 305–06.

51 R. H. Tawney, 'The Choice Before the Labour Party', *Political Quarterly*, Vol. 3, No. 3, 1932, p. 9.

52 During 1929–1931 the ILP had 142 members among Labour's MPs, 37 of whom were financially sponsored by the ILP. Each was asked to accept the 'policy of the ILP as laid down by the decisions of the Annual Conference'. But only 11 ILP-sponsored MPs agreed, along with seven others. When the second Labour government collapsed in 1931 the ILP tore itself apart, with its conference voting to leave Labour in despair, whilst the majority of MPs left the ILP to stay with the Labour Party. From this point on ILP membership plummeted (see R. Miliband, *Parliamentary Socialism* [London: Merlin Press, 1973], p. 195). The tiny group of

British Trotskyists who had been expelled from the CPGB were advised by Trotsky from June 1933 to practise 'entrism' inside the ILP on the basis of a short-term attempt to win over some of its members who were 'centrists' (vacillating between revolution and reform) to the authentic Marxist tradition and opposition to Stalinism.

53 B. Pimlott, *Labour and the Left in the 1930s* (Cambridge: Cambridge University Press, 1977), pp. 48–49.

54 J. T. Murphy, 'The Socialist League Conference', *Adelphi*, July 1933.

55 J. T. Murphy, 'Why I Have Joined the Socialist League', *New Clarion*, 15 April 1933.

56 Pimlott, *Labour and the Left in the 1930s*, p. 52.

57 T. Cliff and D. Gluckstein, *The Labour Party: A Marxist History* (London: Bookmarks, 1988), p. 171.

58 J. T. Murphy, *Fascism: The Socialist Answer* (London: Socialist League, 1935).

59 J. T. Murphy, 'Why I Have Joined the Socialist League', *New Clarion*, 15 April 1933.

60 Murphy, *Fascism: The Socialist Answer*).

61 T. Cliff, *State Capitalism in Russia*, distributed in duplicated form in June 1948 under the title 'The Nature of Stalinist Russia' (London: Bookmarks, 1988).

62 S. Cripps, 'Can Socialism Come through Constitutional Means?' in C. Addison, ed., *Problems of Socialist Government* (London: Gollancz, 1933), p. 66.

63 J. T. Murphy, 'Why I Have Joined the Socialist League', *New Clarion*, 15 April 1933.

64 J. T. Murphy, 'After the Labour Party Conference', *Adelphi*, November 1932.

65 J. T. Murphy, 'The Future of the Labour Party', *Adelphi*, April 1933.

66 J. T. Murphy, *Modern Trade Unions: A Study of the Present Tendencies and The Future of the Trade Unions in Britain* (London: Routledge, 1935), pp. 129–47.

67 Ibid., p. 103.

68 J. T. Murphy, 'The Moral Roots of the Crisis', *New Britain*, 4 April 1934.

69 J. T. Murphy, *Preparing for Power* (London: Jonathan Cape, 1934, republished London: Pluto Press, 1972), p. 202.

70 J. T. Murphy, 'Why I Have Joined the Socialist League', *New Clarion*, 15 April 1933.

71 Of course, apart from the particular circumstances of the early 1920s there *have* been occasions when the extreme weakness of the revolutionary left has necessitated different tactics. Thus, Trotskyists in the 1930s and 1940s, as well as the Socialist Review Group (the precursor of the Socialist Workers Party) used 'entrism' inside the Labour Party. But it was a tactic imposed by great weakness and as soon as it had served the purpose of helping revolutionaries to stand on their own feet was abandoned by some of its participants. Others, who saw it as a long-term policy, inevitably became subject to absorption by the reformist milieu and abandoned workers' struggle outside the confines of Labour Party organisation (see D. Hallas, 'Revolutionaries and the Labour Party', *International Socialism*, second series, No. 16, pp. 1–35).

72 See C. Harman, *The Lost Revolution: Germany 1918 to 1923* (London: Bookmarks, 1982).

73 See R. Croucher, *Engineers at War 1939–1945* (London: Merlin Press, 1982); W. Hannington, *Unemployed Struggles 1919–1936* (London: Lawrence and Wishart, 1977); P. Piratin, *Our Flag Stays Red* (London: Lawrence and Wishart, 1978); B. Alexander, *British Volunteers for Liberty: Spain 1936–1939* (London: Lawrence and Wishart, 1982).

74 N. Branson, *History of the Communist Party of Great Britain 1927–1941* (London: Lawrence and Wishart, 1985), pp. 188 and 55–56.

75 J. T. Murphy, 'Why I Have Joined the Socialist League', *New Clarion*, 15 April 1933.

76 Letter from Mrs Andrews to Mr J. S. Middleton, Secretary of the Labour Party, 31 January 1936, NMLH, LP/SL/35/18.

77 'What is Happening in the British Labour Party and Socialist League', *Communist Review*, Vol. 8, No. 7, July 1935.

78 J. T. Murphy, 'The Year in Review', *Socialist Leaguer*, May 1935.

79 Letter from Murphy to J. S. Middleton, Secretary of the Labour Party, 5 February 1936, NMLH, LP/SL/35/16.

80 J. Molyneux, *Marxisn and the Party* (London: Pluto Press, 1978).

Notes to Chapter Eight
(Pages 234–260)

1 B. Pimlott, *Labour and the Left in the 1930s* (Cambridge: Cambridge University Press, 1977), p. 46.

2 B. Crick, *George Orwell: A Life* (Harmondsworth: Penguin, 1980), p. 205.

3 M. Murphy, *Nurse Molly: An Autobiography* (unpublished manuscript, no date, but written in the early 1960s, Murphy papers, NMLH), p. 68.

4 M. Tyldesley, 'The House of Industry League: Guild Socialism in the 1930s and 40s', *Labour History Review*, Vol. 61, No. 3, winter 1996, pp. 309–21.

5 A. Rigby, *Initiation and Initiative: An Exploration of the Life and Ideas of Dimitrije Mitrinovic* (East European Monographs, Boulder, 1984).

6 During late 1935 Murphy also became, with H. L. Hutchinson, a director of a New School of Political Science. The school provided correspondence courses for students covering a wide range of different economic and political issues, including the history of the working class movement, the British labour party, the history of the Three Internationals, Marxist economics, the state, the Russian Revolution and Fascism. Students were sent a written lesson on a chosen subject, with a list of recommended books and some questions, to which written replies were requested and examined. The School was 'not a school of propaganda for a particular creed. Its method is that of science, objective and deductive, assisting people in the sifting of facts as the means of arriving at their own conclusions' (the New School of Political Science handbill, no date, but probably late 1935).

7 Rigby, *Initiation and Initiative*, p. 130.

8 Ibid., p. 131.

9 J. T. Murphy, 'The Conference of the Socialist League', *Adelphi*, July 1933.

10 J. T. Murphy, 'Who Shall Conquer?', *Solidarity*, 21 January 1921.

11 J. T. Murphy, *New Horizons* (London: John Lane/ The Bodley Head, 1941), pp. 312–19.

12 J. T. Murphy, 'Why I Am For a People's Front', *AEU Monthly Journal*, November 1936.

13 Ibid.

14 'Disunity over the "People's Front"', *Daily Herald*, 15 December 1936.

15 M. Murphy, *Nurse Molly: An Autobiography*, p. 116–43.

16 *Labour Party Report of the 38th Annual Conference*, Southport, 29 May– 2 June 1939.

17 A. Roberts, *Eminent Churchillians* (London: Phoenix, 1995).

18 J. T. Murphy, *Russia On The March: A Study of Soviet Foreign Policy* (London: Bodley Head, 1941).

19 J. T. Murphy, *Preparing for Power* (London: Jonathan Cape, 1934, republished London: Pluto Press, 1972), p. 336.

20 Murphy, *New Horizons*, pp. 345–47.

21 Ibid., p. 237.

22 J. T. Murphy, *Victory Production!* (London: Bodley Head, 1942), p. 73.

23 Murphy, *Victory Production!*, p. 156.

24 Ibid.

25 Murphy, *New Horizons*, p. 335. See also *Russia on the March*, pp. 73–79 and 'A Disservice to the Working Class', *AEU Monthly Journal*, Vol. 7, No. 2, February 1940.

26 Murphy, *Victory Production!*, p. 41.

27 Ibid.

28 For elaboration of such arguments see C. Bambery, 'Not All In It Together', *Socialist Worker Review*, September 1989, pp. 18–21 and 'Was the Second World War a War for Democracy?', *International Socialism*, second series, No. 67, Summer 1995, pp. 37–95. The tiny group of Trotskyists in Britain took a position against the war as an imperialist war. But they recognised that in a situation where the vast majority of workers accepted the idea that the war should be supported as a fight against fascism, it was not possible to mechanically echo the slogans put forward of Lenin in 1914, for the defeat of one's own ruling class and the turning of the war into a civil war. However, this did not mean capitulating to the 'democratic' British government as Murphy did. To fight the Nazis, the Trotskyists argued workers also had to fight their rulers in Britain, such as Chamberlain, Halifax and Butler, who had wanted to appease Hitler. There could be no unity either with war leader Churchill, a vicious class warrior. On the contrary, fascism and the conditions creating it could only be defeated by the working class. This meant the Trotskyists argued workers should not abandon the class struggle at home during the war. They opposed calls for class unity when workers bore the brunt of the war whilst the ruling class still enjoyed lavish lifestyles. They supported workers' strikes made illegal during the war. They attempted to turn workers' genuine anti-fascist feelings away from the imperialist war aims of Britain's rulers and towards independent working-class politics and support for the liberation of the colonies. Above all, the Trotskyists argued that the best way to stop Hitler was workers' revolution. Workers in Paris would have to rise up and seize power from their own collaborationist government if they wanted to defeat the Nazis. They appealed to the workers of Berlin to rise up against Hitler, something Churchill never dared to call because he feared revolution. Finally, they argued that the best example of how to defeat fascism was provided by the liberation of Italy, Greece and Paris through mass strikes and armed revolutionary uprisings that threatened to transform society.

29 Murphy, *Victory Production!*, p. 114.

30 Ibid., p. 116.

31 J. T. Murphy, *Russia On The March: A Study of Soviet Foreign Policy*; *Manual of Soviet Enterprise: Intimate Questions Answered* (Bognor Regis: John Crowther, 1943); *Rise and Fall of Italy's Fascist Empire* (Bournemouth: John Crowther, 1943).

32 Interview with Gordon Murphy, 28 March, 1995; see E. Estorick, *Stafford*

Cripps: Prophetic Rebel (New York: John Day, 1941). For a comparison see E. Estorick, *Stafford Cripps: A Biography*, London: Heinemann, 1949).

33 J. T. Murphy, *Labour's Big Three* (London: Bodley Head, 1948).

34 J. T. Murphy, *Stalin: 1879–1944* (London: Bodley Head, 1945), The book was also translated into French and published in Paris by Les Editions Universelles in 1945.

35 Ibid., pp. 163 and 167.

36 J. T. Murphy, 'A History of Marks and Spencer', Murphy papers, CPGB Archive, NMLH, no date, but written in the late 1940s.

37 Interview with Lord Alan Sainsbury, 1 March 1995.

38 Interview with Gordon Murphy, 28 March, 1995.

39 Murphy's assistance in commenting on drafts of the following books was acknowledged by their authors: J. MacFarlane, *The British Communist Party: Its Origins and Development until 1929* (London: Macgibbon and Kee, 1966); Kendall, W., *The Revolutionary Movement in Britain 1900–1921* (London: Weidenfeld and Nicholson, 1969); and R. Martin, *Communism and the British Trade Unions 1924–1933* (Oxford: Clarendon Press, 1969).

40 J. T. Murphy, 'Twilight or Dawn?', *Peace News*, 7 December 1956.

41 Ibid.

42 Ibid. It is interesting to compare Murphy's arguments at this point with his review of Robert Michels' book *Political Parties* many years earlier (J. T. Murphy, 'The Challenge to Democracy', *The Socialist*, 15 January 1920).

43 J. T. Murphy, 'Working with Destiny', unpublished manuscript, Murphy papers, CPGB Archives, NMLH, no date but probably written in the late 1950s.

44 J. T. Murphy, 'Forty Years Hard—For What?', *New Reasoner*, No. 7, 195859.

45 Interview with John Arnold (Arnold Polak), 13 July 1995.

46 Interview with Monty Johnstone, 18 August 1994.

47 J. T. Murphy, unpublished manuscript, Murphy papers, CPGB Archives, NMLH, no date, but probably early 1960s.

48 A. Koestler, I. Silone, A. Gide, R. Wright, L. Fisher and S. Spender, *The God That Failed: Six Studies in Communism* (London: Hamish Hamilton, 1950); A. Koestler, *The Invisible Writing* (London: Hutchinson, 1969); I. Silone, *Emergency Exit* (London: Victor Gollancz, 1969).

Notes to Conclusion
(Pages 261–267)

1 It should be noted that the actual date of Murphy's death, confirmed by his death certificate and his son Gordon, contrasts with the incorrect dates provided by many other commentators including: J. Hinton, 'Introduction' to J. T. Murphy, *Preparing for Power* (London: Pluto Press; second edition, 1972), p. 15; J. Hinton, 'Introduction' to J. T. Murphy, *The Workers' Committee* (London: Pluto Press; second edition, 1972), p. 9; W. Kendall, *The Revolutionary Movement in Britain 1900–1921* (London: Weidenfeld and Nicholson, 1969), p. 368; E. and R. Frow, *Engineering Struggles: Episodes in the Story of the Shop Stewards' Movement* (Manchester: Working Class Movement Library, 1982), p. 448; Tyldesley, 'The House of Industry League: Guild Socialism in the 1930s and 1940s', *Labour History Review*, Vol. 61, No. 3, Winter 1996, p. 320.

2 T. Cliff, *State Capitalism in Russia*, distributed in duplicated form in June 1948 under the title 'The Nature of Stalinist Russia' (London: Bookmarks, 1988), pp. 164–60.

3 A. Callinicos, *The Revenge of History* (Oxford: Blackwell, 1991), p. 16.

Index

Ackland, Richard 234
Adelphi 234
AEU Monthly Journal 242, 244
Aitkin, George 151
Albu, Austin 255
All Power 88, 93
Amalgamation Committee Movement
    6, 14, 16, 24, 25, 31–35
Amalgamated Engineering Union
    (AEU) 89, 202, 247
Amalgamated Society of Engineers
    (ASE) 4, 13, 16–20, 44, 52
Anglo-American Secretariat 168, 175,
    181
Anglo-Russian Trade Union Commit-
    tee 112–15, 122, 144–51, 161
Aristotle 2
Attlee, Clement 246, 250, 253

Baldwin, S. 119, 147, 158, 169, 206
Bedales School 215
Bell, Tom 15, 55–57, 67–71, 104, 182,
    184
Berkeley, G. 2
Bevan, Aneurin 219
Bevin, Ernest 120, 246, 253
'Black Friday' (1921) 89, 93, 97, 100
Blum, L. 250
British Socialist Party (BSP) 12, 23, 54–
    58, 67–86, 123, 125, 227, 262
British Gazette 119
British Union of Fascists 231
British Worker 119
Brome, Vincent 255
Browder, Earl 151, 255
'Brown, Mr' 49–50, 215
'Bolshevisation' (of communist parties)
    137
Borodin, Mikhail 71, 105, 107, 254

Boothby, Robert 243
Bukharin, N. 76, 113, 136, 151, 153,
    154, 157, 164, 166–67, 175

Cadbury, George 255
Campbell, Johnny 85, 96, 128, 176
*Can Socialism Come by Constitutional
    Means?* (Cripps) 223
Cant, E. W. 109
Castle, Barbara 219
Chamberlain, Neville 241, 246
Churchill, Winston 158, 244, 246–47,
    258
'class against class' 191
'closed letter' (ECCI) 190
Cole, G. D. H. 218, 243
Commission on Internal Relations
    (Comintern) 155
Compromise and Independence
    (Murphy) 52
Communist International 88, 128, 147–
    49, 185, 211
Communist International (Comintern)
    and second congress 65, 73, 76–86,
        92, 136
    and third congress 106, 136
    and fourth congress 90, 94, 106,
        124, 127, 136
    and fifth congress 95, 112, 129, 138,
        155
    and sixth congress 167, 179–80, 181,
        182–85
    and organisation 151–55
    and west-European bureau 71
Communist Party of Great Britain
    (CPGB)
    and 'Bolshevisation' 107–10
    and colonial debate 182–85

311

and congresses 84, 104, 109, 137, 140, 146, 158, 171, 173, 187, 189, 193

and General Strike 111–22, 142–51, 264

and independent trade unions 194–200

and Labour Party left 72–76, 83–84, 122–32, 172–82, 227–30, 264–66

and Murphy's expulsion 205–16

and 'new line' 163200, 201–04

and parliament 82–83

and political bureau 88, 104, 107–09, 130, 139

and Popular Front 231, 239, 246, 250–51

and Russian influence 8586, 111–13, 126, 129–30, 141-42, 151–57, 163–76, 190–94, 200, 263, 266–67

and SS&WCM 8485

and second world war 239–46, 249–51

and trade union work 81, 91–122, 194–200

and Trotskyism 137–42, 157–62, 208, 211, 212, 215, 246

Communist Party of China (CCP) 155–57

The Communist 88, 101, 187

Communist Review 88, 98, 100, 108, 193, 197, 297, 209, 210, 213

Connolly, James 8, 9–12, 35, 42, 56

Cook, A. J. 93, 114, 146–49, 186

Cripps, Sir Stafford 218, 223, 241

Daily Herald 50

Daily Herald League 8

Daily Worker 199, 202, 209, 209, 211, 231

Daladier, E. 250

De Leon, Daniel 9, 56

'direct action' 60–61, 228

Dobbie, William 243

'dual unionism' 6–7, 25, 32–35

Dublin lock-out 8

Duncan, W. 151

Eastern Commission (Comintern) 152

Elsbury, Sam 196

Engels, F. 133, 261

The Errors of Trotskyism (Stalin *et al.*) 140

Estorick, Eric 255

Executive Committee of the Communist International (ECCI) 103, 126, 142–45, 148–51, 153–62, 168–85

and plenums 149, 155, 172, 179–80, 187, 192, 201, 211, 214

Fascism: The Socialist Answer (Murphy) 221

First Five Year Plan 160, 165–68, 200, 222, 254

Firth Worker 26

Franco 243, 244

Fraina, Louis 712

Freeman, J. 151, 255

Gallacher, Willie 15, 53, 65, 69, 96, 107, 174–76, 184, 187, 192

George, Lloyd 13, 59, 242

Goldman, Emma 76

Hands off China committees 168

Hands off Russia movement 59

Hardie, Keir 8

Hardy, George 151

Hargreaves, Leonard 18–20

Haywood, 'Big Bill' 151

Hegel, G. W. F. 2

Henderson, Arthur 131

Hicks, George 112, 142

Higgenbottom, Bill 255

Hill, Alan 255

Hitler, A. 194, 217, 220, 221, 236, 239, 246, 249, 250, 251

Hodges, John 57

Hodges, Steve 255

Horrobin, Frank 255

Hume, D. 2

Hyndman, H. M. 8

industrial unionism 6–7, 25, 32–35

Inkpin, G. 104

International Control Commission (Comintern) 155
International Federation of Trade Unions (IFTU) 91
International Press Correspondence 88, 142
Independent Labour Party (ILP) 3, 23, 56, 67, 173, 217, 232, 241, 245
Irish Transport Workers Union 8

joint production committees 252

Kai-shek, Chiang 155–57, 164, 183
Kamenev, L. 138, 144
Kant, I. 2
Katayama, S. 151
Klime 85
Khrushchev, N. 257
Krupskaya, N. 140
Kuomintang 155–57, 183
Kuusinen, O. 140, 148, 151, 153, 154, 155, 175

Labour Government; An Examination of its Record (Murphy) 202
Labour Monthly 100
Labour Party 4, 23, 67–68, 122–23, 191, 202–04, 220
    and disaffiliation of local parties 131, 170
Labour Representation Committee (LRC) 4
Labour Unrest 4–6, 228
Labour's Big Three (Murphy) 253
Lansbury, George 218, 239
Larkin, Jim 8
Laski, Harold 8
League of Nations 238–40
Left Book Club 244
Left Wing Communism (Lenin) 79
Left Opposition (Russia) 135, 139–41, 142–51, 155–62, 167
Lenin, V. I. 76, 79–86, 95, 103, 111, 113, 123–24, 134, 136, 139, 165, 177, 230, 266
Lenin School 153
The Lessons of October (Trotsky) 138–40

Liebnecht, Karl 229
Lismer, Ted 16, 21–22, 93
Locke, J. 2
Lozovsky, A. 94, 106–07
Lux Hotel 151–52, 160
Luxemburg, Rosa 229

Marshall, Fred 202
MacDonald, Ramsay 74, 112, 114, 131, 191, 202–03, 217
MacManus, Arthur 15, 23, 24, 25, 53, 55–57, 65, 67–71, 104, 112
Macmillan, Harold 241
MacLean, John 15, 16
Manual of Soviet Enterprise (Murphy) 233
Manuilsky, D. 151, 153, 154, 192
Mann, Tom 6, 93, 98, 202
Marx, K. 11, 133, 261
Maxton, James 186
McShane, Harry 15
Melanchansky, G. N. 112
Mellor, William 219
Michels, Robert 257
The Miners' Next Step (Unofficial Reform Committee) 36, 38–39
Miners' Federation 39, 114, 147
Mitrionovic, Dimitrije 234
Modern Trade Unions (Murphy) 225
Molotov, V. M. 140, 151, 254
Mond, Air Alfred 169
Mond-Turner talks 169, 186
Morrison, Herbert 191, 222, 253
Mosley, Oswald 231
Murphy, Gordon 88, 151, 215, 255
Murphy, Molly 87–88, 151–52, 215, 234, 243–44, 255
Murry, John Middleton 234
Mussolini, B. 240, 244

National Administrative Council (NAC) 24–25, 44–49, 51–52, 54, 84–85
National Unemployed Workers' Movement 194, 205, 231
New Britain 234–35
New Britain Movement (NBM) 235–35

New Economic Policy (NEP) 134, 163, 165
New Horizons (Murphy) 247
New Leader 214
New Reasoner 258
National Left Wing Movement (NLWM) 131–32, 176–82, 187–90, 201
National Minority Movement (NMM) 96, 108, 114, 147, 168, 170–72, 194–98, 264
National Union of General and Municipal Workers (NUGMW) 97, 170
National Union of Tailors and Garment Workers (NUTGW) 196
Nietzsche 234

Page Arnot, Robin 147–51, 174, 182, 201
Palme Dutt, R. 88, 102, 104–05, 126, 128–29, 177–80, 201, 203–04
Pankhurst, Sylvia 71, 82
Paul, William 55–57, 67–71
People's Convention 250–51
People's Front Propaganda Committee 243–46, 255
Petrovsky, D. (Bennett) 168, 174, 182
Peet, George 24, 57, 87, 93
Piatnitsky, O. 153, 154, 175, 254
Plea for the Reconsideration of Socialist Tactics and Organisation (SLP) 56
Plebs League 54
Pravda 88, 142, 180, 184, 214, 215
Preparing For Power (Murphy) 216–17, 228, 229
Priestley, J. B. 255
Pritt, D. N. 219
Provisional International Council of Trade and Industrial Unions (PICTU) 92
Polak, A. 255
Political Meaning of the General Strike (Murphy) 146
Pollitt, Harry 53, 88, 96, 104–05, 109, 174, 177–80, 182, 199, 201, 205–26
Purcell, Alfred 95, 112, 119–20, 142
Pythagoras 2

Radek, K. 76, 136
Ramsey, D. 65, 80
'Red Friday' (1925) 115
Red International of Labour Unions (RILU) 87, 91–96, 106–07, 124, 142, 195, 197
Reed, John 76, 81
Rees, Sir Richard 234
Rise and Fall of Italy's Fascist Empire (Murphy) 253
Rosmer, Alfred 92, 94
Rothstein, Theodore 69
Roy, M. N. 151
Roosevelt, F. 258
Rust, William 214
Russia
    and February 1917 revolution 22–23, 67
    and October 1917 revolution 23, 57, 262–63
    and rise of Stalinism 133–37, 163–68, 222–23, 253–55, 258, 263
Russia on the March (Murphy) 253
Rutgers, S. J. 71, 75

Saklatvala, S. 125
Sainsbury, Alan 243, 255
Sankey Commission 59
Saville, J. 258
Sheffield Trades and Labour Council 42, 44, 120
Shop Stewards' and Workers' Committee Movement (SS&WCM) 23–29, 29–53, 54–56, 65–66, 84–85, 93
Snowden, Philip 202
The Socialist (SLP) 25, 26, 56–58, 72
The Socialist (Socialist League) 219
'social fascism' 167, 181, 193–94, 221
Socialist Labour Party (SLP) 6, 12, 16, 23, 25, 31, 42, 54–58, 67–86, 104, 107, 227, 262

Social Democratic Federation (SDF) 4
Social Democratic Party (of Germany)
    229
Socialist League 216–33, 234–46
    and organisation 218–20
    and left reformism 220–33
    and threat of war 234–46
    and 'Unity Committee' 241–45
Sokolnikov, G. Y. 140
Solidarity 26, 41, 47, 51, 78, 93
South Wales Socialist Society 67, 69–70
Souvarine, Boris 155
Spanish Medical Aid Committee 244
Spencer, H. 2
Spinoza, B. 2
Stalin, J. 113, 133–62, 163–68, 173,
    241, 249–50, 253–54, 256–58
Stewart, Bob 112, 150
Strachey, John 243
Suffragette 87
The Sunday Worker 88, 131
Swales, Alonzo 112, 114–15, 120, 142
syndicalism 5–12, 31–53

Tanner, Jack 53, 65, 78–80, 85
Tomsky, Mikhail 92, 112
Thaelman, E. 151
Thales 2
'Third Period' 180–82, 183, 185, 190,
    194, 200, 206, 212, 215
Thomas, J. H. 59, 120
Thompson, E. H. 258
Tito (Broz, J.) 256
trade union officialdom 36–41, 60–63,
    96–102
Transport and General Workers Union
    (TGWU) 97
TUC general council 61, 100–02, 112–
    22, 144–51, 169
Trevelyan, Sir Charles 219
Triple Alliance 58–59, 61, 64, 89, 93
Trotsky, L. 95, 106, 155, 160, 263, 267
    and China 155–57
    and credits to the Soviet Union 208,
        211, 212, 215
    and expulsion from Comintern 157–
        62

and General Strike 120–21, 142–51
    and Russia 134–42
Turner, Ben 169

Ulbricht, W. 192
United Clothing Workers Union
    (UCWU) 195–97
United Left Opposition 164–68
United Mineworkers of Scotland
    (UMS) 195
Unity Committee 67–76
Unofficial Reform Committee (URC)
    35, 38–40

Vickers (Sheffield) 5, 18–20, 50–51
Vulvan (Southport) 50
Vuyovitch, V. 157

Wall Street Crash 202
Walton Newbold, J. 125
Watson, W. F. 32
What is to be Done? (Lenin) 266
Wheatley, J. 186
Where is Britain Going? (Trotsky) 121,
    142
Wilkinson, Ellen 219
Williams, Robert 93, 95
Wise, Frank 219
The Worker 51, 93, 184
The Workers' Committee (Murphy) 26–
    29, 30, 33, 35, 39, 41, 42, 46, 47,
    62
Workers' Life 171, 184, 189, 193
Workers' Weekly 88, 108, 117, 120–21,
    126, 128, 147, 171
Workers' Committees
    across the country 21–25, 30–53,
        54–66
    and the Clyde 14–15, 41, 43–44, 48–
        49, 69
    and first world war 41–49
    and leadership 46–49
    and Sheffield 15–21, 24, 25–27, 30–
        53, 54–66
    and soviets 54–60, 63–66
    and trade union officialdom 36–41

workers' control 35–36
Workers' Educational Association 247
Workers' Political Federation 176–82, 201, 211
Workers' Socialist Federation (WSF) 67, 69–70
Women's' Social and Political Union (WSPU) 87

Yarodsky 112
Young, Allan 243
Young Communist League 193, 195

Zinoviev, G. 76, 91, 95, 112–13, 121, 129–30, 136, 138, 140, 144, 154, 158
'Zinoviev letter' 128